How Clients Make Therapy Work

How Clients Make Therapy Work

The Process of Active Self-Healing

Arthur C. Bohart and Karen Tallman

American Psychological Association
Washington, DC

Published by
American Psychological Association
750 First Street, NE
Washington, DC 20002

Copies may be ordered from
APA Order Department
P.O. Box 92984
Washington, DC 20090-2984

In the U.K., Europe, Africa, and the Middle East, copies may be ordered from
American Psychological Association
3 Henrietta Street
Covent Garden, London
WC2E 8LU England

Typeset in Goudy by EPS Group Inc., Easton, MD

Printer: Braun-Brumfield, Inc., Ann Arbor, MI
Cover designer: Design Concepts, San Diego, CA
Technical/Production Editors: Tanya Y. Alexander and Eleanor Inskip

Library of Congress Cataloging-in-Publication Data
Bohart, Arthur C.
    How clients make therapy work : the process of active self-healing
    Arthur C. Bohart, Karen Tallman.
       p.   cm.
    Includes bibliographical references and index.
    ISBN 1-55798-571-5 (case : alk. paper)
    1. Psychotherapy.   2. Patient participation.   I. Tallman, Karen.
  II. Title.
  RC480.5.B64   1994
  616.89'14—dc21   98-48623
                                          CIP

British Library Cataloguing-in-Publication Data
A CIP record is available from the British Library.

Printed in the United States of America
First Edition

CONTENTS

PREFACE

Interest in psychotherapy integration has become a major movement, stimulated by early works by Goldfried (1982), Wachtel (1977), and Arkowitz and Messer (1984), among others. Many practitioners now consider themselves to be "eclectic" (Norcross, 1986). Others have become interested in identifying common factors that exist across different approaches (Grencavage & Norcross, 1990).

This book focuses on the common factor in psychotherapy that we think is most important: the active, creative involvement of the client. We think the role of the client has been neglected in books on psychotherapy, virtually all of which focus on the therapist and what the therapist does. Yet the research supports the idea that the client's involvement is the single most important factor in whether therapy works or not.

In this book we try to spell out the role of the client in producing change. We also spell out implications of this for therapy practice. We believe that our view can provide an integrative basis for the actual practice of psychotherapy in which contributions from humanistic, psychoanalytic, and cognitive–behavioral perspectives can all be used. Ultimately, if we are right, focusing more on clients' self-healing potential should lead to the development of more effective ways of helping them. Our ideas are in line with, and have been influenced by, those of Jerold Gold (1994) and Barry Duncan and his colleagues (e.g., Duncan, Hubble, & Miller, 1997; S. D. Miller, Duncan, & Hubble, 1997).

Many therapists have said that psychotherapy is a learning process. Yet that has typically meant that they have only incorporated ideas from laboratory studies of learning into their work. By and large they have not used theory and research on learning in education. Although we have not relied extensively on such research (except in chapter 7), we believe an educational metaphor for what happens in therapy is a good one. We have tried to take seriously the idea that therapy is more of a learning and educational situation by using ideas and metaphors from education throughout the book.

Our theoretical backgrounds predispose us to view the client as an active self-healer. We both consider ourselves to be Rogerian at heart. However, we are also integrative and eclectic, believing there are good ideas in many diverse approaches. We have presented at meetings of the Society for the Exploration of Psychotherapy Integration. In his therapy practice, Art regularly uses cognitive–behavioral and family systems ideas, in addition to humanistic–experiential ones. He had extensive psychodynamic training in graduate school, and some psychodynamic ideas, particularly from some of the modern approaches, continue to help him conceptualize clients' problems. Karen has used strategic ideas, and specifically has incorporated an emphasis on goal work into her approach. She also considers herself a bit of a "closet behaviorist," and believes cognitive–behavioral techniques are particularly useful.

Art's background includes work with a wide range of client problems. In recent years, however, he has primarily focused on sex and couples therapy. Thus, a number of examples in the book deal with sex therapy. Still more recently, he has been receiving training in eye movement desensitization and reprocessing. Karen's therapy experience has primarily revolved around working with "difficult" or "severely disturbed" clients, such as those with diagnoses of schizophrenia, borderline personality disorder, and bipolar affective disorder. Several examples of work with these kinds of clients are included.

We have also included examples of individuals who have self-healed mostly on their own, without therapist assistance. All case examples have been disguised and fictionalized to protect the individuals' identities. Some are composites of several individual cases. We believe we have remained faithful to the core processes of "what really happened," however.

If you do not believe it already, we hope that through reading this book you get a sense of and a feel for the power of that ally (or adversary) who shares the therapy situation with you—the client. It is our hope that this book will help you make that person your ally and not your adversary, and that it will help you draw on that ally's incredible healing powers to achieve the goals that have brought the two of you together.

ACKNOWLEDGMENTS

Although books are officially listed as being written by the authors named on the cover, in fact most books have many more authors than that. Many people have usually contributed to the final published version. This book is no exception. The two most important people who helped bring this book into being are Hal Arkowitz, PhD, and Margaret Schlegel, LCSW. Hal first suggested to us the idea that the client could be the "integrative therapist" in 1993. Hal's own subsequent interest in self-help research became a source of support. His initial interest and encouragement to submit a proposal got us started. Then, in many ways he was the "spiritual father" of the book. His comments on an early draft of Part I set the tone for our later revisions. Finally, several extended conversations with him over very strong coffee helped us form our ideas for the book. Hal is a genuine open-minded explorer and a true integrationist. But he comes from an integrative behavioral point of view, whereas we come from an integrative client-centered and humanistic point of view. He kept us "honest" and kept reminding us to keep it balanced.

T. S. Eliot's *The Wasteland* is dedicated to Ezra Pound with the phrase "the master craftsman" in Italian. We don't know Italian, so we can't rewrite the phrase to make a dedication to "the master craftsperson," but if we could, we would give it to Margaret Schlegel. Our book isn't *The Wasteland*, but Margaret voluntarily spent hours of her own time carefully going over it and making major and significant suggestions that led to several hundred excessive pages being cut, and the book taking on a much more workable form. To the extent that this book is organized and readable, she is majorly responsible. To the extent it isn't, we didn't manage to carry forward some of her organizational ideas.

Once our book reached "final rough draft" status, Linda McCarter, development editor for American Psychological Association Books, made many helpful suggestions that improved its readability and organization.

We stress the importance of empathy in our book, and the empathic reading by both Margaret Schlegel and Linda McCarter led to significant improvements in the book.

We also want to thank Larry Leitner, PhD, Jeanne Watson, PhD, and Jerold Gold, PhD, colleagues who graciously contributed time to read early drafts of various chapters and offer helpful feedback for revisions.

In addition, we want to thank the following graduate students in the Marriage, Family and Child Counseling Program at California State University, Dominguez Hills, who read an early draft of the book and provided helpful feedback on the ideas and on how it read: Christina Sullivan, Mary Beth Lydic, Ron Fredette, Alice Haas, Ana Arguello, Lisa Drake, Klara Detrano, Nancy Piper, Maureen Reilly, Dalia Ahronia, Deborah Andorka-Aceves, and Olga Estrada.

We also want to thank Mary Lou Holls, who read a draft of chapter 7 and provided feedback.

Finally, we want to thank the following, with whom we have had intellectually stimulating dialogues that contributed to the development of this book: Barry Duncan, Jerold Gold, Bob Rosenbaum, Al Mahrer, Maureen O'Hara, Del Jenkins, Tom Greening, Larry Leitner, and Bob Neimeyer, among others. Art particularly wants to thank Les Greenberg, who has been a continual source of interesting dialogue and support over the past 10 years, and the Society for the Exploration of Psychotherapy Integration, which has provided a fertile ground for integrative thoughts.

INTRO-INDUCTION[1]

Occasionally one meets a very active client. Lynda was a recently divorced woman who came in to therapy to cope with the separation. She and her ex-husband continued to fight over his unambitious lifestyle. She entered therapy and started talking out the problem. The therapist probably could not add more than 50 words per session. The client was effectively working through problems in the presence of the therapist. She made eye contact only occasionally, as if she were attending to her own thinking process. In six sessions she concluded her ex-husband wasn't going to change and she needed to move on with her life.

What is the nature of the client who is sitting across from you, the therapist? That is the question we address in this book. Following in the footsteps of Carl Rogers, Robert White, Milton Erickson, modern strategic and solution-focused therapists, and others, our view is that the client is a creative, active being, capable of generating his or her own solutions to personal problems if given the proper learning climate. For us, therapy is the process of trying to create a better problem-solving *climate* rather than one of trying to fix the *person*. This is not a subtle theoretical distinction. It has direct implications for the attitude we adopt toward clients and for how we implement what we do.

The premise of our book is that the most important common factor is the client (Tallman & Bohart, 1999). Research evidence converges to suggest that the active efforts of clients are responsible for making psychotherapy work. It is because of this that differences in effectiveness among different approaches have only infrequently been found (Bohart & Tallman, 1996). We argue that clients have a strong, proactive self-healing

---

[1]This title is a bit of a play on words: We hope to "induce" you into finding the ideas of this book interesting and involving.

capacity, no matter how emotionally troubled they may be. They can be used as the therapist's creative collaborator. Therapy is most effective when it provides a context and resources that help clients mobilize and "channel" these already existing self-healing capacities. And it is particularly effective when the therapist and client are both open to the possibility of involving the client as "co-therapist," or equal partner in the process. In this, we hope our book offers a healthy corrective to the pathology orientation of the field, which focuses far more on client disability than on client ability. Overall we see this book as in keeping with Seligman's (1998) recent call for psychology to focus more on positive mental health rather than on pathology.

In medicine, there has been an increasing interest in holistic and mind–body approaches. These ideas all include the idea that the human body has a great deal of self-healing potential, and that medicine, as much as it works on the body, must also rely on and mobilize the person's self-healing capacities. This idea has been less emphasized in recent writing on psychotherapy, in which mainstream opinion has largely focused on healing coming from the application of various technological interventions. This book is in accord with the movement toward mind–body medicine. We believe that persons have a great capacity not only for physicial self-healing but also for psychological self-healing. Therapy needs to mobilize that self-healing potential. The "interventions" that do this are not only the technological ones but also the therapist's ability to listen to and empathically understand the client and respect the client's own agency, creativity, ideas, and expertise. Technology is seen not so much as techniques that operate on clients but rather as tools for clients to use to help them utilize their self-healing capacities. What therapists do only works if it supports, channels, relies on, or mobilizes these capacities.

Each of the major approaches to psychotherapy—psychodynamic, humanistic, cognitive, behavioral, and strategic systems—has its own unique potential to mobilize clients' self-healing capacities. Each can provide a context in which these self-healing capacities become productive again. Different therapy approaches provide different pathways or tools, and different clients may prefer or be better able to use different paths or tools. All approaches can be effective if they take into account the primacy of clients' self-healing capacities. In fact, each approach has its own unique contributions to make.

Throughout this book, we hope to persuade the reader of the following:

1. It is the client's self-healing capacities and resources that are responsible for resolution of problems and for change in everyday life and in any form of psychotherapy.
2. Clients, as do all human beings, have built-in capacities for

learning and creative problem solving. In fact, many problem behaviors represent clients' attempts to solve other problems in their lives and to make creative adjustments to their perceived environments. The capacity for creative problem solving can be enhanced or supported by the person's resources and interpersonal and physical environments, or it can be limited and distorted by these same factors. Clients' capacities for creative problem solving can also be limited by feelings of helplessness, fear, or discouragement.

3. Clients experience "symptoms" or "presenting problems" and come to therapy when these self-healing capacities or resources are inaccessible or blocked.

4. Therapy can be most effective when it makes use of these self-healing capacities and resources.

5. To practice from a self-healing perspective does not mean one cannot use the major theoretical frameworks (e.g., cognitive–behavioral, strategic, humanistic, and psychodynamic). But it does mean that one must be willing to adopt a particular set of assumptions about the nature of people, problems, and change. Some theoretical frameworks seem to naturally adopt these assumptions; for others, some adaptation may be required.

6. If the assumptions underlying the self-healing model are adopted, it will be less critical in most cases in which commonly accepted "interventions" suggested by the different theoretical frameworks are offered to the client. Clients' self-healing capacities are potent enough to make use of whatever (within limits) they are offered in psychotherapy, as long as they are willing to invest themselves in their use.

7. Client involvement in the therapy process is the single most powerful force in investing life in therapy. The most important thing therapists can do to be helpful is to find ways of supporting, stimulating, and energizing client investment and involvement.

8. The second most important thing is to stimulate and support powerful client learning and meaning-making processes.

In addition to making and supporting these arguments, we hope to show how the self-healing model can be integrated with the major theoretical frameworks of psychotherapy practice today. And, although our framework for practicing psychotherapy is implicit in much of what we say about the self-healing model of psychotherapy, we also present our approach to therapy as one example of how the model is put into practice.

What can a practitioner hope to get from reading this book? This is not a "how-to" book. We do not give specific suggestions for "what to do when" or what to do with what disorder. There are plenty of books on that. Instead, what we hope to convey is an *attitude* that will (a) help use the best that the client has to offer, (b) present some general strategies for how to proceed in a given moment, and (c) help allay the therapist's anxiety about needing to come up with "just the right" intervention at the right time. This attitude should allow you, the therapist, to see opportunities that you might otherwise not see and allow you to relax with the client. The attitude helps you be aware of the positive potential in your client so that you can draw on it and creatively incorporate it in whatever you do. It should help you feel you have more options. Will it make you a more effective therapist? We believe so, but, as we discuss in chapter 2, the data show that as long as therapists provide a supportive, positive relationship, and some structure and tools that clients can use to work on their problems, there are a wide range of ways therapists can be effective. Therefore, with most of your clients, you probably are honoring their self-healing potential sufficiently to be fairly effective. We hope this will give you greater flexibility to extend the range of your effectiveness.

What are the principles of client self-healing discussed throughout this book? We briefly list them below.

1. There are proactive elements in the client's behavior, even in dysfunctional behavior and in resistance and defense.

2. Therapists must understand things from the client's perspective to be helpful. This is more than just a superficial understanding to diagnose and ingratiate oneself with the client. It is a subtle, complicated enterprise. Otherwise, therapists may misunderstand the clients' intentions and the world they live in. Furthermore, it must be ongoing. A therapist's initial understanding may no longer be correct.

3. Clients have a lot of built-in intrinsic generativity and creativity. Some probably have more than others, but all have some. This means clients in varying degrees can solve their own problems, come up with their own ideas, and actively contribute to the therapy process by investing their own creative understanding in whatever the therapist is doing. Clients often generate good solutions.

4. Clients know the intimate details and the intimate ecological connections that are created by their problems, and they have a sense of the factors that create the problems. They also have a much more intimate sense of what is possible in their life space than does the therapist. Therefore, they are experts equal to the therapist. A therapist has to be very cautious about applying his or her external knowledge and

"objective" point of view as to what is best, because he or she may not understand the ecological factors involved in the client's problem. The client has to live with the consequences of implementing the therapist's directives.

5. Clients actively translate the lessons and experiences of therapy into their life contexts. What clients do after therapy will never be perfect replicas of what therapists think they are teaching the clients, any more than what students learn in classes are perfect replicas of what the teacher is teaching. Even with something so simple as the teaching of handwriting, individuals end up developing their own idiosyncratic handwriting styles. Clients will develop their own idiosyncratic uses and understandings of whatever they have learned in therapy. Therefore, therapists cannot expect a one-to-one translation of technique into client behavior.

6. Therapist behavior follows from a respectful attitude that supports a belief in the client's sensibility and intelligence and a continual attention to the client's perspective.

Following on these principles, we want to suggest that no matter what else you do as a therapist, your primary goal with any response, any comment, any intervention is to *stimulate and support generative client thinking* and understanding processes—that unless clients are intelligently thinking along with whatever you are doing, they will not learn. We want you to realize that whatever you do must make sense to clients, that the goal is to literally "make sense," ultimately, so that they can intelligently apply and use whatever they are learning. In this regard, even in the most directive therapy, you are a good teacher, someone who facilitates their thinking and understanding.

Margaret, 33, had been diagnosed as paranoid schizophrenic. She found everyday life very difficult, but she found herself a niche in business as a word processor and had worked for a local company for 7 years. At work, however, she struggled painfully with the social elements. She was frequently misunderstood, and she showed anger quickly. In therapy, she focused her concerns mostly on difficult family relationships. One day, she described how she perceived another worker as suffering. Margaret felt the co-worker might be feeling "paranoid" about issues related to the company's announcement of impending layoffs. She decided to comfort the co-worker. She came up with and implemented this idea totally on her own. This event seemed to signal a change in her progress. Over the following weeks, she casually reported increasing social contacts with others. Her perception of her social situation changed a great deal, even though she seemed unaware herself of the change. Yet her descriptions in therapy of events at work over the next several weeks changed considerably in a positive direction. She started getting together with individuals and groups after work. With time she became so skilled and confident that she resolved many of her more troublesome family relationships.

In terms of doing therapy, we want you to be open to the possibility that sometimes "less is more," that is, that you do not always have to intervene. Clients can often come up with creative solutions themselves if given the proper workspace to do so. Sometimes all you have to do is supportively listen, while clients think things out for themselves.

Finally, we want you to be aware that therapy is an intelligent two-person enterprise. This means that you, the therapist, are also an active thinker, creatively generating solutions in collaboration with the client, not passively following a cookbook. In this regard, we also expect you will be an active reader of this book, and we hope it stimulates you to think, no matter how much you ultimately end up agreeing or disagreeing with us.

ORGANIZATION OF THE BOOK

In Part I, we present our model of the client as self-healer. People often grasp new concepts by contrast, so we begin our discussion in chapter 1 by contrasting our view with the medical model of psychotherapy. In chapter 2, we describe support for the client-as-self-healer model. This support includes quantitative and qualitative empirical research, as well as clinical case material. In chapter 3, we describe how clients self-heal in everyday life and give examples.

In Part II, we approach therapy as a resource for clients when self-healing fails in everyday life. In chapter 4, we more fully describe the assumptions about clients, problems and change that underlie the self-healing model, and why clients may need to come to therapy. In chapter 5, we view therapy as a form of education and describe different ways therapy promotes self-healing. We particularly examine how the provision of a basic empathic relationship can be helpful. In chapter 6, we describe how the perspective of the client as active self-healer fits in with the major theoretical approaches.

In Part III, we present a view of therapy as a meeting of minds. Chapter 7 deals with processes that block and interfere with the client's proactive involvement in the therapy process and how to facilitate overcoming those blocks. Once these blocks are overcome, clients can use their intrinsic meaning-making capacities, channeled and supported by therapist activities, to resolve their problems. In chapter 8, we discuss these meaning-making capacities, which include a capacity for productive thinking, a capacity to learn from experience, a capacity to reevaluate old ideas and values, a capacity to change perspectives, and a capacity to generate new behaviors and new possibilities. In chapter 9, we present our own view of therapy. It is written as a "manual" of sorts—not a manual of what to do when, but a guidebook for what it means to adopt a mindset of therapy as a meeting of minds. In chapter 10, we consider issues of practice in relation to our ideas.

In Part IV, which consists of chapter 11, we examine implications of the idea of the client as an active self-healer for various issues related to the profession of clinical psychology. We consider implications for the topic of psychotherapy integration, for the development of new therapeutic strategies, for training, for research, for practice under the medical model, for the use of self-help materials, and for working with involuntary clients.

I

THE NATURE
OF SELF-HEALING

1

WHAT DO WE MEAN BY THE CLIENT AS ACTIVE SELF-HEALER?

Molly was a 10-year-old girl referred for therapy by her mother. Her parents were divorced. She was referred because she was having trouble adjusting to her changed life: new school, new friends, new apartment. In addition, she was sleeping in her mother's bed.

An intake interview was done. Molly's family was labeled as dysfunctional, and Molly was seen as triangulated in a parental conflict situation. She was diagnosed as suffering "separation anxiety disorder" and was referred to a children's social skills group.

Molly then began to experience nightmares and was seen individually by the therapist. The therapist explored Molly's perceptions of her parents' relationship and how these were presumably affecting Molly. After 6 months there was little improvement. Molly was then sent to see another therapist. This therapist suspected that Molly had been sexually abused. At one point Molly asked the therapist if she had ever felt ugly, and based on that, the therapist also concluded that Molly had self-esteem problems.

After no progress was made, she was referred to a psychiatrist, and medication was prescribed. Still no change. Finally she was referred to the group of Barry Duncan, Mark Hubble, and Scott Miller (1997). These therapists hold the view that (a) therapists must work within or from the clients' frame of reference and (b) therapists should rely on clients' creativity and resources.

In the first session, the therapist asked Molly what *she* believed would be helpful for the problem of nightmares and not sleeping in her room. Molly expressed astonishment that someone had asked her opinion, and suggested that she barricade herself in her bed with her stuffed animals and pillows. At the next session she reported that her plan was working, and therapy ended successfully within a session or two after. What is particularly interesting is what Molly had to say about her experience. Below we reproduce some of what she said to the therapist on videotape at her third session:

"Psychiatrists [therapists] just don't understand . . . you [the client] also have solutions, for yourself, but they say, 'Let's try this and let's try that. . . . ' So, *what I'm saying to all psychiatrists is we have the answers, we just need someone to help us bring them to the front of our head. . . .* I feel a lot better now that I came up with the solution to sleep in my own room and I did it and I'm proud of myself. And I couldn't be proud of myself if you told me [to do what I did] . . . *you don't get as much joy out of doing something when somebody told you to do it; you want to be proud of it.*" (Duncan et al., 1997, pp. 25–26, italics in the original)

"My other therapists never asked me what I wanted to work on. . . . I should come in and tell the person, 'This is what's happening with the situation,' and they're [the therapists] saying 'Your mom tells me you're doing such and such a thing.' . . . And you come in there to talk to a person, to get them [problems] out of your system and get them worked on. Instead of she [the therapist] telling or he telling you what [she or] he thinks has happened, 'Your Dad's doing this, your grandfather's doing this,' it's not really helping because you're sitting there going, 'Uh-huh, uh-huh,' and that's why I usually dreaded going to therapy. . . . And it is like they [therapists] think they are some almighty power or something. . . . It's like hang on, *I am also somebody.*" (Duncan et al., 1997, p. 28, italics in the original)

This case example illustrates many of the points we will make throughout this book, but it particularly points out that clients, even children, can provide solutions to their own problems when the therapists assume that the client, not the therapist, is really the expert on the client's problem.

One point of view is often best presented by contrasting it to a different point of view. We contrast our client-as-active-self-healer point of view with that of the currently dominant medical model of psychotherapy. These two points of view are not properly called theories. Rather, they are metatheoretical perspectives that come before and underlie specific approaches to psychotherapy and psychopathology. They represent different images of the person and of the nature of the process of psychotherapy. Different theoretical approaches to psychotherapy (e.g., cognitive–

behavioral, humanistic, psychodynamic) can be practiced under either paradigm. In actual therapeutic practice, the two basic underlying paradigms are frequently mixed, especially at the present time. However, for purposes of clarity and illustration, it is important to conceptually separate them and contrast them.

THE MEDICAL MODEL AND PSYCHOTHERAPY

Psychotherapy originally arose from medicine. Despite efforts to free it from medicine over the years, much of its practice is still heavily influenced by medical-like thinking. This thinking is so ingrained that in many cases therapists are unaware of how heavily they are influenced by it. Yet, as Orlinsky (1989) noted, the dominant model of psychotherapy is still a medical-like "treatment" model. In the medical model, the therapist is analogous to a physician. He or she is the expert on the nature of the client's problems and on how to remediate those problems. He or she forms a diagnosis of the client and then prescribes treatment. Treatment consists of applying interventions appropriate to that diagnosis. These interventions cause change in the client, thereby alleviating the symptom. Orlinsky noted that most therapy models are actually mixes of the medical model and other models. However, the medical treatment model predominates.

The Medical Model

We first consider the medical model in medicine in more detail. Then we consider it as applied to psychotherapy.

Role of the Physician in Medicine

Traditional "allopathic" medicine (Weil, 1995) has a number of characteristics. First, when a person has a physical problem, they go see the doctor. The assumption is that the person does not know what the real problem is, although the person might be able to identify the symptom. Diagnosis of the real problem is up to the doctor. Then he or she decides for the patient what the treatment is and applies the treatment to the problem.

Role of the Patient

The primary job of the patient during the diagnostic phase is to *recount* information to the doctor. The act of talking to the doctor is that of *reporting*. The doctor usually asks questions. Doctors will rarely be interested in the client's theories about what the problem is. Instead they will ask questions to get the information that they want. The client is often encouraged, nonverbally, to remain silent except when answering questions. There is no real dialogue between doctor and patient other than in the form of the physician's asking questions and gaining information. The doctor's reasoning may or may not be shared with the client. In many cases the client will not know why the doctor arrives at his or her diagnosis. The patient's "collaboration" here is to answer the doctor's questions as well as possible.

After the physician has diagnosed the problem and prescribed treatment, the job of the patient is to actively comply with the treatment. Patient collaboration in this context means *active compliance*. That means, for example, doing the back exercises, taking the medication, or otherwise following the physician's regimen.

Furthermore, patients must comply with treatments as prescribed. There is no room for patient creativity. If a patient were to creatively modify treatments prescribed by the physician, this could bring disaster from a medical perspective. For instance, one is to do back exercises as prescribed, or one might actually make one's back worse. Certainly one is not to experiment with doses of medication on one's own.

Nature of the Problem

Medicine basically adopts a materialistic view (Dossey, 1995) of problems. The physical symptom is seen as having a physical cause—a foreign agent in the body, such as a virus or a bacterium, a broken bone or a ruptured organ, a faulty gene, runaway cells, chemical imbalances, and so on. A physical problem is a mechanical problem. For the most part, the problem is viewed as affecting *parts* of the body, for example, specific organs or organ systems. Thus, an illness is the infestation of an organ system with a bacterium or a virus, or it is something wrong in the valves of the heart, or it is runaway cells in a cancer.

Assessment

Medicine relies on the idea of differential diagnosis. Different disease entities have their own nature, and different treatments will be needed to work on them. Accurate diagnosis facilitates treatment: Identifying which particular disorder it is leads to the proper treatment being applied. The ideal is to find specific treatments that will operate on specific disorders. Radiation will be used for cancer, but not for a bacterial infection. Different antibiotics will be used for different bacterial infections. Assessment leads to a diagnosis, which in turn leads to differential treatment.

Treatment

After the physician makes a diagnosis, he or she decides on the treatment. The treatment is something that is applied to the disorder. Material problems will require material resolution. The material resolution, such as medication or surgery, is an external force that is applied to the disorder from without and alters the condition of the disorder. The model of cure is mechanistic: The medication or the surgery is the mechanism that alters the disorder.

Treatments can be applied to disorders independently of the person having the disorder. The person is the "site" of the disorder. Thus, a skin cancer tumor will be treated fairly much the same regardless of whose skin it is on. In this respect, the patient plays a passive role in the treatment. The drug or surgery causes the cure. The treatment is the proximal agent of change. The physician is the distal agent of change. The patient is the site of the operation of the treatment. The *person* does not have to even be there, so to speak, for the treatment to work, and in fact the person is not there frequently, being drugged into unconsciousness.

Relationship Between Physician and Patient

The relationship between physician and patient is of minimal importance in terms of cure, although a good relationship between the physician and the patient may increase the patient's probability of complying with the physician's directives. The idea that the relationship could somehow be curative in and of itself is anathema to medical thinking. To quote the psychiatrist S. Alan Savitz, "Before the advent of antibiotics, doctors could do very little to actually heal people. They just sat by patients' beds, holding their hand and trying to make them feel a little better. Now, they can really do something for people, patient's don't just feel better because of the human touch, they *are* better" (Wylie, 1994, p. 32). The negative attitude toward the relationship as a possible curative factor is clear in this quote. It is as if medicine would be invalidated if it were to be true that the relationship had powerful curative elements. The idea that a good bedside manner does more than just soothe the patient and make the patient more cooperative with the physician is rejected.

Role of Faith and Hope

Traditional Western medicine has little use for faith and hope as mechanisms of cure. Faith and hope are important if they mobilize patients' energies to help fight off disease and comply with treatments, but faith and hope by themselves have minimal curative effect. This follows from the mechanistic, materialistic view of medicine. Because no mechanism is physically operating on the body, faith and hope could not really have any specific curative effects. The physician Dean Ornish, who has written on how relationship and lifestyle can have a profound effect on health and healing, has talked about how his ideas have been greeted with disdain by many of his colleagues. Traditional medicine now admits that attitude can play some role in increasing survival, but it still assumes that the "real" curative agents are the drugs, surgeries, radiation treatments, or whatever other material and mechanical things the physician does. Weil (1995) documented a number of cases of "miracle cures" and noted how uninterested physicians are in such stories. Most physicians even have such stories, but they tend to dismiss them as unexplainable flukes. In a similar manner, it is a real insult to say that a treatment works because it is "just a placebo," as if that means that it is not a *real* treatment.

Summary of the Medical Model

To sum up, the medical model assumes that

- Symptoms represent various disease states or disorders, which are materialistic.
- The physician is the expert who can figure out what the problem is.
- The initial job of the patient is to recount information to the physician, and to comply with and participate in any testing that the physician wishes to have done.
- The physician takes this information and makes a differential diagnosis and prescribes some kind of treatment.
- The treatment is differentially tailored to the disorder, chosen by the physician, based on what works with what disorder.
- The second job of the patient is to comply with the treatment—for example, take the pills, do the back exercises.
- The treatment works materially and mechanistically; that is, it operates on the disorder in some sense and changes it.
- This happens relatively independently of the patient's mental state or the state of the relationship between physician and patient, although the patient's mental state may influence how hard the patient tries to overcome the disorder and comply with treatment.
- The relationship between physician and patient is important only insofar as it increases client compliance and soothes patients when other more effective treatments may not be available.

Application of the Medical Model to Psychotherapy

Medical thinking and language is ingrained in the practice of psychotherapy. The idea that psychotherapists are "treating disorders" is an example of the influence of the medical model. Such language, and such ways of thinking about psychotherapy, have grown more common, rather than less, in recent years, despite earlier behavioral, cognitive, humanistic, and family systems rebellion against medical-model thinking. The medical context in which psychotherapy "lives" in the real world has caused therapists to adopt medical terminology despite the fact that most therapists see what they do as educational. Many of them talk about "treatments." This, despite the fact that Hans Strupp, (Norcross et al., 1993) a prominent thinker and researcher on psychotherapy, has pointed out that psychotherapy really is *not* a treatment.

In recent years, under the pressure of managed care, therapists have returned to the medical model, increasingly viewing therapy as a process of diagnosis by the expert therapist, development of a treatment plan by the expert therapist, and application of that treatment to the client by the expert therapist. Where there was once a trend toward calling the consumers of psychotherapy *clients*, in recent years the field has reverted back toward calling them *patients*. Below we examine the medical model as applied to psychotherapy.

Role of the Therapist

As with the physician, in the medical model of therapy the therapist is the expert on what is wrong with the client. The expert therapist interviews the client and then makes a diagnosis of the client's problem. On the basis of the diagnosis and on the data gathered, the therapist decides what kind of treatment the client needs.

Role of the Client or Patient

The role of the client in the medical model of therapy is analogous to the role of the patient in medicine. The client's role during the assessment phase of therapy is to answer the therapist's questions as fully as possible so that the therapist can make an accurate assessment and diagnosis of the client's problems. Then the client's job is to comply with the treatment. As with the physician, client collaboration really means compliance with the therapist's treatment regimen.

View of Problems

Psychological problems are viewed as pathology or as disorders, analogous to medical conditions. The *Diagnostic and Statistical Manual of Mental Disorders* (4th ed., DSM–IV; American Psychiatric Association, 1994) thus becomes the preferred diagnostic method (e.g., Task Force on Promotion and Dissemination of Psychological Procedures, 1995; Task Force on Psychological Intervention Guidelines, 1995). The pathology is the result of dysfunctional mechanisms within the person. These dysfunctional mechanisms vary from theory to theory but include dysfunctional egos, defenses, and character structures in psychoanalysis; dysfunctional self-regulatory mechanisms and conditioned behaviors and emotional responses in behaviorism; and dysfunctional schemas and automatic thoughts in cognitive theory. Psychological disorders have their own unique structure and etiology, just as physical disorders do. Like physical disorders, they are discrete entities that exist within a person's personality and that disrupt healthy functioning. A significant departure from the medical model is that the disorder is not physical or material. Instead it is psychological. But, analogous to medicine, the disorder still arises from the dysfunctional workings of certain systems within the organism. Therapy operates on dysfunctional parts of people—their habits, their schemas, their ego structures.

The assumption of the medical model that psychological problems are like medical disorders can be illustrated by two articles in the *APA Monitor* on borderline personality disorder (Sleek, 1997a, 1997b, p. 20). These articles were replete with descriptions such as "people *with* borderline personality disorder." There was a reference to a pamphlet by Randi Kreger and Paul Mason called "Walking on eggshells: When someone you care about has borderline personality disorder." Referring to someone as *having* borderline personality disorder, or to people *with* borderline personality disorder, is a clear transference of medical language into the psychological realm. One could easily write analogous books about physical disorders: "Walking on eggshells: When someone you care about has hemophilia." The medical metaphor is clear.

Thus, theoretically at least, the therapist works with parts of persons rather than whole persons (see Millon, Everly, & Davis, 1993). Nor are persons seen as persons-in-contexts, with problems arising from person–context interactions. *Persons* get DSM diagnoses, not person–context interactions (i.e., there is no such diagnosis as a "depressive person–situation interaction"; in the DSM, persons have the problems, even if influenced by context).

Assessment and Diagnosis

As in medicine, the role of the therapist is to conduct an intensive examination of the client, through interviews, behavioral observations, and diagnostic testing. The data gathered are then used to make a diagnosis, preferably using the DSM. Then, on the basis of this diagnostic procedure, differential diagnosis will lead to selection of an appropriate treatment strategy for the client's particular disorder. The therapist, not the client, decides on the appropriate treatment strategy.

Nature of Treatment

The medical model of therapy relies on the drug metaphor (Stiles & Shapiro, 1989). This means psychological problems can be "treated" with the psychological equivalent of appropriate "medications," only in this case the treatments or the medications are psychological techniques. Techniques are described as mechanisms that will produce cure by modifying the underlying dysfunction.

As the physician prescribes specific treatments for specific disorders, so the therapist diagnoses the specific disorder and applies the appropriate treatment. The "force" of healing is seen as coming from the external treatments applied to the client by the therapist. Therefore, it is important that the treatment be "powerful" and be specific to the disorder. To most potently treat anxiety, for instance, the therapist should specifically design treatment to work on anxiety symptoms.

These models are mechanistic, although not material. They are mechanistic in that the assumption is that the problem is a dysfunctional mechanism, that it is relatively isolated and discrete, and that the cure is to fix the dysfunctional mechanism. The therapeutic procedure operates on the dysfunctional mechanism. The client must use his or her mind to comply with the treatment (e.g., explore childhood, listen to and absorb insight-producing interpretations, and challenge dysfunctional cognitions), just as in medicine the patient must use his or her body to comply with treatment (e.g., do the back exercises). But it is the *intervention* that changes things (the interpretation and the process of cognitive restructuring). Curative power is seen as residing in the treatments, not the client.

Because healing power comes primarily from therapists' interventions, the medical framework does not allow the possibility that (a) clients could heal on their own with therapist support or (b) clients could use a wide range of different interventions to right a particular problem (i.e., it is not necessary to tailor specific interventions to a particular problem). However, if psychological problems are not medical-like syndromes or pathologies, there may be many idiosyncratic paths to various "disorders." Therefore, there might be many different interventions that might work for a given disorder. There would be no necessary reason why there would be any a priori superiority to matching different treatments to different disorders. Rather, as we argue in this book, mobilizing the so-called nonspecific factor of the active client's thinking, creativity, and problem solving could (and frequently does) override the distinctiveness of both the disorders and the different treatments, resulting in problem resolution and growth. In other words, if the healing force comes primarily from within the client, and not from the intervention, then the whole medical model of assuming the necessity of different treatments for different disorders falls apart.

Relationship Between Therapist and Client

For those who follow the medical model of therapy, the relationship between therapist and client either is of secondary importance or is an intervention in its own right. Goldfried (1997) noted that for many cognitive–behaviorists the relationship has been analogous to the role of the anesthetic in medicine—something that allows the potent interventions of the therapist to operate. The therapist must establish a good relationship, but the establishment of such a relationship is seen as a strategic intervention in its own right. One even learns the "skills" of doing so in graduate school. The establishment of a good relationship functions by building client trust so that the client will open up, self-disclose, and comply with treatment. Therapist empathy may lead to clients feeling understood, but the function of this is to make clients more amenable to therapist interventions. It would not be entirely out of place to suggest that empathy and a warm, caring attitude are used to "soften up" clients so that they are more open to influence by the therapist.

As with medicine, there is skepticism toward the idea that the relationship could have curative effects. In fact, the idea that the relationship could be powerfully curative is as anathema here as it is in medicine. Therapy is only really legitimate if it can create "powerful interventions" that go beyond the so-called nonspecific helping qualities of the relationship. The thoughts of Foa et al. (1983) on behavior therapy express this attitude toward the relationship: "the personal qualities of the therapist, which appear to be essential to the outcome of psychotherapy, have less impact on the more precisely formulated techniques of behavioral therapy. It is likely that the more powerful the therapeutic procedure employed the less potent will be the effect of the therapist" (p. 15, quoted in Safran & Segal, 1990). If the relationship does prove to have curative effects, then, from the medical point of view, the specific curative ingredients should be identified, so that therapists could deliberately implement them as interventions. In other words, the relationship qua relationship should not really exist in the medical model.

Role of Hope and Faith

In a similar manner, the idea that faith and hope, or other nonspecific effects, could be helpful is treated with disdain. Those who think in medical terms want therapy to go beyond such effects to provide more potent interventions. For instance, Barlow (1994), in arguing that clinical psychology now has such potent interventions, said, "For the majority of psychological disorders, the 'dodo bird hypothesis'—stating that all psychotherapies are of equal effectiveness, *with suggestion or other more general 'placebo' factors as a mechanism of action*—no longer holds true" (p. 118, italics added). In the next chapter, we discuss why we think Barlow's conclusion about the dodo bird verdict is wrong. For now, we would like the reader to note the implied negative view of suggestion and placebo factors.

Terminology

The two currently popular terms *treatment* and *intervention* reflect the medical model. It is common to talk about psychotherapy as the *treatment of conditions* in a manner completely analogous to how physicians talk about treating medical disorders. Szasz (1998) argued that the whole concept of therapy as a medical-like treatment originated with Freud, who tried to have it both ways, at times seeing therapy as a medical-like enterprise, and at other times rejecting the idea that therapy was a medical-like treatment. This basic ambivalence, found in Freud, continues to permeate the field. Compatible with our view, Strupp (Norcross et al., 1993) argued that therapy is not a treatment, as did Fisch (1990) from a strategic point of view.

The term *treatment* implies the existence of an entity (such as a drug) or a procedure (such as surgery) that is being applied to something else from without. In medicine, it further implies that the healing force originates from the entity or procedure. Thus one applies salve to a skin condition, or one treats pneumonia with antibiotics or cancer with chemotherapy or radiation.

The use of this term with psychotherapy, therefore, implies that the therapist applies an external agent, which is the treatment, to the condition. This agent acts on the condition to modify it. The agent that makes therapy work is not primarily the client but the therapist's potent treatments.

The concept of *intervention* implies intrusion or invasion. To intervene in a dispute is to step into it from outside and to alter it. Thus the legal system might intervene in a labor dispute or in a dispute between husband and wife. To intervene in the course of nature is, for instance, to apply external force to alter the path of a river. Medical procedures, such as surgery, certainly can be seen as interventions.

Similar to the term treatment, intervention implies an external force that is going to alter the course of the client's life. It also implies a hierarchical relationship in which the person applying that force is greater, more knowledgeable, and wiser than the one being intervened with. There is even an implication that had the expert not intervened, the people being intervened with would not have had the sense or the intelligence to make any changes themselves. Occasionally, the term intervention is appropriate when applied to therapy, primarily when the therapist is dealing with reluctant clients. However, for the most part, it does not seem to accurately portray a process which in most respects must be collaborative to be effective.

Thus, the two most popular terms currently used to describe psychotherapy—treatment and intervention—portray the process as one in which an outside expert intervenes in a course of events to change it. The force of healing and change comes from an external agent. Neither term is, therefore, compatible with the idea that the healing force primarily comes from the client. However, the terms are so ingrained in the language used to talk about psychotherapy that we have found it impossible to completely eliminate their use.

MODEL OF THE CLIENT AS ACTIVE SELF-HEALER

We believe that the primary healing agent in psychotherapy is the client, and the therapist is an important and valuable addition to the client's active efforts. Therapists assist and promote change by helping clients mobilize, focus, and use their own resources for self-change. Orlinsky, Grawe, and Parks (1994) said, "We view psychotherapy as 'the activation through the process of interpersonal communication of a powerful endogenous therapeutic system that is part of the psychophysiology of all individuals and the sociophysiology of relationships' (Kleinman, 1988, p. 122)" (p. 278). Our model is compatible with others who are stressing the importance of the client as active healer (Duncan, et al., 1997; Gold, 1994; S. D. Miller, Duncan, & Hubble, 1997; F. Shapiro, 1995). Most human beings generally solve problems as a daily part of life, and many overcome significant personal problems on their own. Most people self-right most of the time without therapists' assistance. They do this by using naturally occurring self-righting processes. These naturally occurring self-righting processes are also the processes therapists rely on. What therapists do is help clients use these processes more efficiently, through the provision of support, coaching, or information. Special circumstances, including the nature of the client's problem, the client's history, limited client resources, biological constraints, or constraints in the client's environment, can interfere with and limit the effectiveness of the individual's natural self-righting processes, and that is when the client comes to therapy.

A greater focus on the client's self-change processes helps explain many puzzling things about the nature of therapy, such as why there are so many different "brands" and why they all appear to work about equally well. Focusing more on what clients do with therapist interventions and less on the interventions themselves can facilitate progress in the field and help individual therapists practice more efficiently.

Role of the Client

The basic tenets of our model of the client as active self-healer are as follows. First, the client is the primary change agent in therapy, not the therapist or the therapist's techniques. Second (and this is why different therapies seem to work about the same; see chapter 2), the active self-healing efforts of the client frequently overwhelm differences in technique or strategy or philosophical approach. Third, clients are generative. They are not merely the passive recipients of interventions that "operate on" them. Rather they are the ones who invest interventions with life, create the effects interventions are supposed to produce, and actively use these interventions in their own unique, creative ways. They heal by blending interventions with their own views of what their problems are, their own ideas on how to solve them, and the contexts of their lives. To use the analogy of analysis of variance, there is no pure "effect" of a psychotherapeutic intervention independent of interaction with the client.

Fourth, as clients talk with their therapists, they are active participants in therapy. They are *thinking about* themselves, themselves in relation to us, what they are saying, their experience, what we, the therapists, are saying in relation to them, what we are doing, whether what we are doing fits with their goals or not, whether what we are doing is plausible and makes sense, whether they can do what we think they can do, and so on. They are *experiencing* themselves in relation to us, they are experiencing themselves in relation to themselves, they are reexperiencing old events, and they are experiencing us. They are *matching* their experiences with us to prior experiences with significant others, with schoolteachers, bosses, and other healers they have visited, and evaluating these matchups. And finally, they are *acting*. They are talking, trying to give us what they think we need to help them solve their problems, they are testing us out, and they are testing themselves out. In sum, they are as active and generative in therapy as therapists are.

Some clients seem passive and dependent in therapy, apparently swallowing everything the therapist says, and looking to the therapist as the expert. However, even they are actively synthesizing. There is an active inner life going on, usually not shared with the therapist, in which clients are thinking about what the therapist is doing, covertly agreeing or disagreeing, and planning how they can get what they think they need (Rennie, 1990, 1994a, 1994b).

The client is the intelligence that ultimately makes the therapy process run. In some sense, clients are themselves the therapists. Clients can be creative, going well beyond the input that therapists give them to develop what they need. Therapy is primarily made by clients, not by therapists.

Role of the Therapist

However, therapists can be enormously valuable to clients. They are resource providers, information providers, idea providers, strategy providers, supporters, mentors, and coaches. Therapists help by discussing with clients, listening to them, helping them clarify their thoughts and strategies, giving them feedback and information, and suggesting procedures that clients creatively institute. The therapist helps clients focus their creative energy in productive directions. The therapist is also a supplier of materials that the client can use. And, finally, the therapist is a teacher of skills, who helps the client forge new life solutions. But, as with the teaching of any advanced, complex skills, "students" only really master the skill when they are able to "make it on their own."

The role of the therapist in our model is to be a kind of participant consultant (M. R. Goldfried, personal communication, April 28, 1996), who both participates in a co-constructive dialogue with the client and consults, offering advice and suggestions. Although the therapist has expertise, the therapist is not an expert on the client, or even necessarily on the client's problem or even on what the solution will be, as in the medical model. Instead, the only expert on the client is the client himself or herself. The therapist is primarily a process expert whose expertise consists of (a) helping clients clarify their problems, (b) helping them develop and define potential solution pathways, and (c) once a solution pathway has been defined, helping the client find ways of attaining that solution. The therapist is more like a home-decorating consultant who helps clients clarify what they want and then helps them get it. As with clients seeking the help of a home-decorating consultant, some clients will require relatively minimal consultation and guidance, whereas others will require a great deal more.

The issue of whether the therapist is directive or nondirective is reframed in our model. The therapist can adopt either stance and still support the active client's self-healing efforts. What is more important is the manner of how the therapist is directive or nondirective. The therapist can certainly take the lead, but there should be a continual, active collaboration. The directive therapist should be like a good dissertation mentor, guiding and supporting, but not directing, ordering, or unilaterally deciding for the student. As a good mentor gives students a good deal of room for their contributions and initiative, so should therapists. Therapists can be highly active and suggestive, and still fundamentally respect client initiative, intelligence, and generativity. The issue is the attitudes the therapist holds: Does the therapist genuinely respect the client as an equal contributor to the process? Does the therapist genuinely trust the client and have faith in the client's ultimate internal wisdom and self-healing capacities? Does the therapist really want to hear the client's perspective and treat it as another perspective, not as a manifestation of psychopathology? And is the therapist genuinely interested in the client's point of view? Therapists who have this general set of attitudes will be helpfully supportive of the client's therapeutic efforts.

Therapists, therefore, are not doctors, who operate on clients with potent interventions that make change happen in clients. Rather therapists are resources used by clients in their self-healing, self-righting efforts. Power is ultimately in the client's hands, even when therapists think they are physicians "treating" the client. Within this framework, any and all ideas and tools from all approaches to therapy may be valuable.

Assessment and Diagnosis

Because the therapist is not the expert on the client, problem definition should be a collaborative enterprise, in contrast to medicine. We borrow a metaphor from the community psychology movement in the 1970s. The role of the community psychologist was not to be the expert who goes into the community, diagnoses what is wrong, and then unilaterally prescribes for the community what is to be done. Instead, the community psychologist's role was to carry on a dialogue with the community. Definitions and potential solutions were jointly developed as the community psychologist's expertise blended with the community's expertise. The community psychologist was a resource for the community to use. The process was one of mutual give-and-take with the community, of the psychologist "thinking along" with the community in dialogue.

Viewing the helping process this way, something like a *DSM* diagnostic system, which simply classifies problems in a context-independent way, would not be ideal, although it could be used. Rather, much more usable framings of the community's problem, contextually sensitive to the dynamics of community and its unique parameters, would be more useful. Diagnostic labels might not even be used in developing workable conceptions of problem, solution, and strategies for resolution.

The role of the community psychologist was construed this way because the power for change was seen as ultimately residing in the community, and because it was assumed that the community knew itself and its problems better than did the outside expert. At the same time, we want to emphasize that the professional is an important resource: mobilizing, contributing to, and bringing together potential healing forces in the community. Even if ultimately the wisdom and the healing force reside in the community, the professional is often needed to mobilize and channel them. We believe therapy is similar.

Nature of Problems

It is assumed that psychological problems arise from an interaction of systems—the living system, which is the individual, interacting with the various systems in which he or she is embedded. Problems emerge from the limitations or constraints of each system intersecting with other systems. The constraints that produce problems are a function of the individual's nature (life history, biology, current social roles and statuses) intersecting with constraints in the environment (job constraints, relational constraints, constraints owing to poverty and racism, cultural constraints). Problems exist contextually. Problems are not a property of the individual in isolation. Problems are a part of life and continually arise. Individuals continually need to resolve problems, and most of the time they do it successfully enough to keep life moving along. They come to therapy when constraints involved in the interaction of themselves with their environments block or disrupt naturally occurring problem-solving efforts sufficiently that the individual gets stuck and is unable to make progress on his or her own. Something is getting in the way of their own natural self-healing efforts. We elaborate further on this in subsequent chapters.

Nature of Therapy

Therapy is a whole-person enterprise. Most theories reduce clients to part persons and part processes: egos, schemas, defense mechanisms, conditioned responses, lack of differentiation, emotionally unprocessed material, and so on. However, therapy is two whole persons in dialogue with one another, not one wielding an axe to cut out dysfunctional cognitions, or a trowel and cement to strengthen ego structure, or a scalpel to deepen differentiation. Therapists do not really treat specific mechanisms in clients. What they do is talk to whole persons, listen to them, respond, suggest, and teach. This is also one reason differential treatment may often not be necessary, because the whole person who is the client can take and use whatever he or she is given to solve his or her problems.

Therapy is most basically the provision of a supportive context wherein individuals' naturally occurring self-righting and self-healing capacities can once again operate. Therapists first provide an empathically supportive *working space* in which clients can use their own active intelligence to engage in the generative thinking processes that they have been too stressed and overwhelmed to engage in everyday life. Clients can relax, take a deep breath, and step back and begin to look at their life's problems from a new, fresh perspective. Therapists empathically listen, are nonjudgmental, and allow clients a place to tell their stories.

Second, therapists can engage in a co-constructive dialogue with clients, a "meeting of minds," in which it could be said that "two heads are better than one." Clients have the opportunity to externalize their thoughts, run them by another person, and examine them from a different perspective. They gain some objectivity and use the therapist's response to more accurately gauge their way of dealing with the world. Therapists and clients think together, explore together, and even experience together, in ways that facilitate the client's problem-solving creativity. In this context, therapists may offer ideas, advice, interpretations, and empathic reflections or ask questions to stimulate thought.

Third, therapists provide their own interpersonal interactivity. Clients learn through the direct experience of being treated differently by the therapist, and through themselves behaving differently with the therapist.

Fourth, therapists provide techniques and procedures that help clients focus and use their naturally occurring self-healing processes. These include the whole armamentarium of therapist techniques: role playing, challenging dysfunctional cognitions, paradox, and so on. Techniques do not "operate on" clients, but rather are tools that clients use to explore, think, have new experiences, and generate change.

Fifth, therapists function as coaches and teachers. They help the client acquire new skills. However, even here clients only learn through their own active synthetic efforts.

Sixth, therapy happens outside the therapist's office. Clients creatively incorporate the material from therapy into their lives. This is a dialogic process whereby they try out what they have learned, modify it, try it out again, and so on, until they have creatively synthesized it with their lives.

Overall, our model holds that because clients are the major force that makes therapy work, therapy is most effective when therapists are respectful of clients and of their capacity for change. They are respectful of their views, leaving them a wide berth to change, not always in ways the therapist had in mind. Therapists should incorporate clients' frame of reference and try to use it whenever possible, rely on clients' own problem-solving capabilities, and be open to their generating novel solutions. Self-healing happens in all clients, but that does not mean all clients can heal totally on their own. Therapists are often needed.

Function of the Relationship

The most important thing the therapist generally has to offer the client is a relationship. However, this is not because the relationship is curative (although it can be). Instead, the relationship is helpful for two reasons. First, a good relationship involves the client in the process, and client involvement is what energizes whatever goes on in therapy. Second, the relationship provides a context or workspace where clients can generatively work on their problems through mobilization of their own initiative and of their own problem-solving capacities. Most fundamentally, the therapist provides an opportunity for dialogue with another intelligent being. Through dialogue, clients are able to think out their problems more productively, experience aspects of their problems they need to experience to learn from and about them, and explore neglected aspects of their experience that might provide solutions. It may particularly help by focusing attention on a problem and clarifying it.

The relationship is probably most important because it promotes a climate within which clients can feel safe and prized, and begin to trust and use their self-healing capacities. For some clients, a good dialogical relationship will be all they need. Others will want and require techniques. Techniques need to be thought of as themselves part of the dialogue.

Summary of the Client-as-Active-Self-Healer Model

1. Clients can and do heal themselves.
2. They can do this in many cases using any of the diverse materials provided by therapists of differing orientations.
3. However, on occasion, some specific approach might match up better with a given problem or at least turn out to work more efficiently.
4. The client is an active, creative agent and is the source of the energy that drives therapy—power resides in the client's hands to make change happen.
5. Therapy is not like medicine; exercises and procedures are not surgical techniques that "operate on" clients.
6. Rather, the exercises and procedures facilitate clients to focus their own active self-healing energies.
7. Clients make creative discoveries in applying what therapists offer them to their lives.
8. The ultimate healing takes place at home and not in the therapy office, for the most part, as clients integrate their therapy experiences into their lives.
9. The role of the therapist is (a) to provide a safe place; (b) to provide an opportunity for creative, exploratory dialogue; (c) to provide materials and resources that help clients fashion solutions; and (d) to train specific skills when needed.
10. Whether the therapist should be active or nondirective is not an issue. Far more important are the attitudes that the therapist holds toward the client and the kind of climate the therapist creates.

Relation of the Medical Model to the Client-as-Self-Healer Model

Although we do not believe the medical model is a good model for therapy, there is nothing inherently contradictory about using a model of therapy that is based on the idea of the client as an active self-healer in a medical-model context. We can distinguish between the medical model of *therapy* and the medical model of *psychopathology*. The medical model of psychopathology depicts psychological problems as discrete disorders in a manner analogous to physical disorders. One can believe that psychological problems are disorders and believe in the DSM but still realize that psychotherapy is not a medical-like activity in which treatments are applied to disorders. Instead, it is a relationship where one person provides a rich learning context and another mobilizes his or her resources.

From the standpoint of the client as active self-healer, therapy is not something that is applied to a client but rather as something done with a client, no matter what the origin of a problem. The process of therapy, as opposed to a medical-like process, is that of two intelligences working together to help the client learn, master, understand, and cope with life's difficulties. The difficulties may be environmental, psychological, a mix of psychological and physical, or purely physical. Thus, a psychologist could help a client mobilize his or her self-healing potential to deal with a natural disaster (environmental), a conflict over what the client wants and what the client thinks he or she should want (psychological), problems stemming from schizophrenia (a mix of biological and psychological), or cancer (biological). Therefore, a psychologist can work in medical contexts, use medical-model diagnoses, and still operate from a client-as-active-self-healer perspective. Even if the problem fits the medical model, therapy is better conceived of as helping clients mobilize self-healing potential to deal with it. As seen in the next chapter, we believe that the data are more compatible with the model of the client as active self-healer than they are with the medical model of psychotherapy.

Nonetheless, we share the concerns of many others about how the medical model is currently influencing the field of psychotherapy. The eminent psychologist Rogers Wright, director of the Association for the Advancement of Psychology, said "psychotherapy should be separated from the medical model entirely" (quoted in Wylie, 1994, p. 30). Similar to our view, Wright said, "the first thing I say to a client is, 'I am not the expert, I have no magic, no pills; all I know about is the learning process, and you are the only expert on you, you have to make the decisions about what happens to you.' . . . But the medical model is the converse of that" (quoted in Wylie, 1994, p. 31). Yet the medical model is currently dominant in the field today and is even legitimized in major documents from the American Psychological Association, such as the Template (Task Force on Psychological Intervention Guidelines, 1995) and the Division 12 "empirically validated treatments" guidelines (Task Force on Promotion and Dissemination of Psychological Procedures, 1995). The chances of psychotherapy separating itself from the medical model, even if that were desirable, are not strong at the present time.

How did this situation come about? Although psychotherapy originally arose from medicine, its essential nonmedical nature was acknowledged as early as Freud (Szasz, 1998). As alternative approaches to therapy developed, many departed more and more from the medical model. During the 1960s, behavioral, humanistic, and family systems approaches were all severely critical of the medical model and of the *DSM* diagnosis. Why did this trend not continue?

The major reason for the current dominance of the medical model appears to be financial. The force driving the reversion to the medical model is the recent emergence of managed care. Third-party payers think in medical-model terms, as does the federal government. Therefore, to get reimbursement for the provision of psychotherapy, practitioners must use the medical model. Federal sponsorship of research has also recently come to require the medical model (Goldfried & Wolfe, 1996). This means that therapists must diagnose with medical tools (e.g., *DSM*), make treatment plans based on diagnosis of disorders, and use treatments that have been empirically shown to work with those specific disorders using research strategies compatible with the medical model. A related change has been the bias toward the use of short-term therapies. Ironically, some of the most effective short-term therapies (e.g., strategic and solution-focused therapies) are based on assumptions that are antithetical to the medical model (see chapter 9).

Yet many therapists work within the framework of the medical model and do it effectively. Strategic therapists are a good example, with some of the more well-known ones (e.g., Rosenbaum, Hoyt, & Talmon, 1990) working in managed-care contexts. Many therapists at the present time must work within two systems: the client–problem system and the payment system. To work most effectively with the client–problem system, we believe that the model of the client as self-healer is best, but to work with the payment system, therapists must also be fluent in the medical model and use it so that their clients can get financial support for therapy. They can resolve the inherent stress in this either by adopting the medical model too much or by understanding that they are working with two systems that can be reconciled when thinking in terms of the final outcome—relief of client suffering. In chapter 11, we discuss how to work with the client-as-self-healer model when dealing with managed-care health care entities and the medical model.

CONCLUSION

The medical model, when applied to psychotherapy, dictates a hierarchical relationship in which

- The more-knowing expert (the "therapist-physician") assesses and then diagnoses what "disorder" the less knowing patient has.
- The therapist then chooses treatment and applies it. Treatments are described along the lines of the drug metaphor, that is, as things that operate on clients to change them. The force of healing is described as primarily coming from outside.
- Healing will be most potent when specific techniques or treatments are tailored to specific patient disorders. The re-

lationship itself is not primarily a healing agent but rather the "anesthetic" that makes patients more amenable to therapists' interventions. In the medical model of therapy, nonspecific factors such as hope and faith are viewed as less potent than specific therapist interventions.

In contrast, the view that the client is the primary healing force in therapy dictates a more potentially egalitarian relationship in which

- Both the therapist and the client have their own areas of expertise.
- Definitions of client problems should be a joint enterprise. Only clients know the particulars of their lives and therefore how, ultimately, problems emerge from their lives and how they feed back to influence their lives.
- The healing force in therapy primarily comes from clients. Therapeutic techniques are not analogous to drugs. They do not operate on clients. Rather they are tools clients use to self-heal. Techniques have no life to them if clients do not invest them with life. Clients can use many different tools to heal their problems. Therefore, differential treatment may only occasionally be required.
- Client faith, hope, and involvement in the therapy are key to its success. The relationship between therapist and client is more than a soothing balm that makes clients amenable to treatment. It is an important platform that supports clients' self-healing efforts.

In the next chapter, we review evidence that is compatible with the idea of the client as an active self-healer but that conflicts with the medical-model view of psychotherapy.

2

RESEARCH RESULTS THAT MAY SURPRISE YOU—HOW DO WE KNOW THE CLIENT IS AN ACTIVE SELF-HEALER?

In this chapter, we consider the empirical evidence for the view that the client is an active self-healer. For purposes of understanding, we contrast it to the medical model of therapy. We review research and clinical examples relevant to each of the following positions.

If the medical model of therapy is correct, then we would expect evidence that

1. Differential treatment effects would be the norm; it should be easy to demonstrate that specific approaches are differentially effective for specific disorders or problems.
2. Techniques are powerful, are potent, and have specific effects.
3. The relationship between therapist and client is secondary to techniques in terms of potency.
4. The expertise, training, and experience of the therapist are crucial.
5. The client's ability to self-heal on his or her own is the exception rather than the rule.

On the other hand, if the client-as-self-healer model is correct, then we would expect evidence that

1. Differential treatment effects might not be easy to demonstrate; clients' abilities to self-heal could tend to overwhelm differences between the effects of different therapeutic approaches for different disorders.
2. Techniques will neither be the primary causes of therapeutic change nor be seen by clients as that important.
3. The therapist–client relationship, which provides clients with dialogue, healthy challenges, and a supportive workspace for their self-healing efforts, will be more important than techniques and will be seen by clients as more important.
4. The expertise of the therapist, as defined in terms of professional training or experience, may make less of a difference in effectiveness than one might believe if the medical model were true.
5. Differences between the effectiveness of professionally provided therapy and self-help procedures should be small or nonexistent; clients may often be able to use self-help materials to achieve as much positive benefit as they would from professionally provided therapy.
6. If differential treatment effects are found, they will be more likely to be found as a function of a match between which therapeutic "tool" is most helpful for which *client* (aptitude-by-treatment interaction), rather than which therapeutic approach works best with which *disorder* (medical-model thinking).
7. Clients may recover using placebos, because of clients' active self-healing potential.
8. Many clients may spontaneously recover or grow without therapy.
9. Clients are the major force that makes therapy work.
10. Clients are active agents in and out of therapy.

EVIDENCE AGAINST THE MEDICAL MODEL BUT COMPATIBLE WITH THE CLIENT-AS-SELF-HEALER MODEL

We begin by considering the famous (or infamous, depending on one's allegiances) "dodo bird verdict" that all psychotherapies work about equally well for different disorders. This is a finding that is compatible with our client-as-self-healer model but incompatible with the medical model

(Orlinsky, 1989). If, as in the medical model, psychotherapeutic techniques are powerful and primary, then it should be easy to demonstrate that different techniques (i.e., different approaches to therapy) are differentially effective for different disorders. However, this has not proved to be the case.

The Dodo Bird Verdict

In *Alice in Wonderland*, the dodo bird is the judge of a race and announces that "everyone has won, and all must have prizes." Luborsky, Singer, and Luborsky (1975), after reviewing research on the effectiveness of psychotherapy to date, announced that the dodo bird verdict held true for psychotherapy: There was no evidence for the superiority of any therapy over any other.

Since Luborsky and his colleagues announced the dodo bird verdict, other comprehensive research reviews have repeatedly drawn the same conclusion (e.g., Lambert & Bergin, 1994; Smith, Glass, & Miller, 1980; Stubbs & Bozarth, 1994). Studies that have specifically included comparisons between different approaches to psychotherapy frequently have found no difference (Elkin, 1994; Grawe, Caspar, & Ambuhl, 1990; Project MATCH Research Group, 1997; Sloan, Staples, Cristol, Yorkston, & Whipple, 1975). For instance, Greenberg and Watson (1998) found equivalence between client-centered therapy and process-experiential therapy for the alleviation of depression, and their results were equivalent to those obtained by cognitive therapy. The Project MATCH study found equivalence among three different treatments for alcoholism (Project MATCH Research Group, 1997). The 1995 *Consumer Reports* survey (see Seligman, 1995) also found no evidence for differential effectiveness of different therapies for any disorder. Meta-analyses comparing different approaches have also often found no differences (R. Elliott, 1996; Robinson, Berman, & Neimeyer, 1990). The most recent meta-analysis of over 100 studies, including many on cognitive–behavioral approaches for different disorders, once again confirmed the dodo bird conclusion (Wampold, Mondin, Moody, Stich, Benson, & Ahn, 1997).

There are three implications of the dodo bird verdict. First, it implies that there is no evidence that any one specific therapy is more effective on an overall basis than any other. Considering that the wars in the field of psychology in the 1950s through the 1970s over which therapy was better were turf wars over who had the best theories of psychopathology and psychotherapy, this suggests that no particular theory had a corner on "the truth" about human beings or about change.

The second implication is that the idea that different approaches might work best for different disorders also is not, for the most part, true. To quote Bergin and Garfield (1994), "with some exceptions, . . . there is massive evidence that psychotherapeutic techniques do not have specific effects"[1] (p. 822). They noted two types of possible exceptions: First, in some cases with some more severe disorders, cognitive and behavioral approaches may be superior; and second, certain client personality traits may make some clients better able to use some approaches than others (p. 824). Nonetheless, on an overall basis, the dodo bird verdict holds far more often than it does not hold. This means that, on the average, for most clients who come to therapy, it does not matter which therapy approach is used, as long as it is one for which there is some research evidence of effectiveness (which is true of all the major approaches).

The third implication of the dodo bird verdict is that techniques may not have that much to do with the effectiveness of therapy. Instead, "common factors" across different therapy approaches, such as the therapeutic relationship, may be more important. In fact, Lambert (1992) estimated that techniques account for only about 15% of the variance in therapeutic outcome, common factors account for 30%, placebo effects for 15%, and naturally occurring healing aspects of the clients' lives for 40%.

The number of findings supporting the dodo bird verdict is substantial, so substantial that if it were a finding that fit with everyone's biases, the field would long ago have proudly accepted it as one of its well-established "facts" and would have moved on to deal with its implications. Instead, it continues to be debated, and attempts are constantly being made to discount it (Barlow, 1994; Beutler, 1995; Fisher, 1995; Norcross, 1995). We consider objections to it next.

Objections to the Dodo Bird Verdict

A number of objections to the dodo bird verdict have been raised. One has been that even though there is no overall statistically significant difference among major approaches, cognitive–behavioral approaches consistently show the largest mean changes, albeit nonsignificantly. However, as Smith et al. (1980) noted, this may be an artifact. The types of changes produced by cognitive–behavioral therapies are very specific and more easily measured than the kinds of changes brought about by psychodynamic therapies. Therefore, the apparent superiority of these approaches may be a function of the kinds of measures used in studies of them.

In addition, even if the small differences in favor of the cognitive–behavioral therapies proved to be real, the more important fact is that there is still substantial overlap in effectiveness, and such small differences are probably not clinically significant (Wampold, 1997). In the meta-analysis by Wampold et al. (1997), the most optimistic estimate of difference between different therapies, an effect size based on using the absolute

[1]From "Overview, Trends, and Future Issues," by A. E. Bergin and S. L. Garfield, 1994, in A. E. Bergin and S. L. Garfield (Eds.), *Handbook of Psychotherapy and Behavior Change* (4th ed.), New York: Wiley. Copyright 1994 by Wiley. Reprinted with permission.

value of differences between different therapies, ignoring the sign of the differences, was .21. In comparison, the average effect size for psychotherapy versus no treatment in previous studies was .82, for psychotherapy versus placebo was .48, and for placebo versus no treatment was .42 (Wampold et al., 1997).

A related objection has been that many of the studies done did not have a large enough sample size to obtain significant differences. However, some studies did have large enough sample sizes, yet the dodo bird verdict still was found (e.g., some of the recent studies in Wampold et al., 1997). Furthermore, as Cohen (1994) pointed out, with a large enough sample size, one can probably find a significant difference between any two groups being compared on any dimension. Certainly, if we increase the sample size sufficiently, any difference will eventually become significant, but once again we must wonder if that is important compared with the substantial overlap in effectiveness between the different therapies being compared.

A third objection is that there are now a number of studies demonstrating differences in effectiveness between different approaches, and therefore the dodo bird verdict can now be dismissed (Barlow, 1994; Task Force on the Promotion and Dissemination of Psychological Procedures, 1995). For instance, the Empirically Validated Treatments document from Division 12 of the American Psychological Association (Task Force on Promotion and Dissemination of Psychological Procedures, 1995) cited a number of cases in which one therapy has been shown to be superior to some other therapy for a specific disorder. However, Wampold (1997; Wampold et al., 1997) concluded that the number of such studies does not exceed what one might expect to find by chance. Wampold et al. pointed out that individual studies that find differences cannot be used as counterexamples, because a few studies will be significant by chance. Instead one must look at the entire corpus of results. When one looks at these studies in toto with other studies, they do not exceed the number one would expect by chance. Furthermore, in many cases where one therapy has been shown to be superior to another, differences tend to wash out when the allegiance of the investigator is controlled (R. Elliott, 1996; Robinson et al., 1990).

A fourth objection is that most of the studies have been done on depression, and the dodo bird verdict has not been reliably demonstrated for other disorders. However, Wampold et al.'s (1997) meta-analysis includes studies on a wide range of disorders other than depression, with almost half of them on anxiety. Many individual studies (e.g., Meyer, 1981; Sloane et al., 1975) were done on client groups that included a range of neurotic and personality disorders. Greenberg, Elliott, and Lietaer (1994) concluded, based on their meta-analysis comparing experiential therapies to other therapies, that the performance of experiential therapies is equivalent to other therapies for any disorder studied. Thus it is plausible that the dodo bird verdict exists for disorders other than depression.

A fifth objection is that while there may be little evidence that different therapeutic treatments are differentially effective for different disorders, there is some evidence that different clients do better with different therapies (Beutler, 1995; Norcross, 1995). For instance, Beutler et al. (1991) found that dependent individuals seem to do better with therapy instead of self-help, whereas reactant (i.e., highly independent) individuals do better with self-help. Furthermore, Pinsof, Wynne, and Hambright (1996) concluded that there are problems for which family therapy has been demonstrated to be more effective than individual therapy.

However, these findings do not support the medical model, which is that different approaches or techniques should be differentially effective for different *disorders*. Instead, these findings are ones we would expect from our perspective of the client as self-healer. Clients differ in their personalities, and if they are the primary "healing forces" in therapy, it would be expected that they might find some approaches more compatible with their way of doing things than other approaches, just as different individuals take to different forms of exercise. Similarly, if the problem involves the whole family, it makes sense that having the whole family involved in the problem-solving process will be more effective. At the same time, the idea that different treatments may be differentially effective with different client personalities needs further empirical corroboration (Garfield, 1994).

Overall, we believe the evidence for the dodo bird verdict is substantial, and the objections do not warrant its being overturned. The situation is analogous to a criminal trial, such as in the O. J. Simpson case, versus a civil trial. In the criminal trial, many observers believed there was a "mountain of evidence" against the defendant. Yet, guilt had to be established beyond a reasonable doubt, and defense lawyers focused on raising doubts about each bit of evidence: the bloody glove, the DNA testing, the socks on the floor in the defendant's bedroom, and so on. By focusing on and criticizing each bit of evidence, they were able to raise sufficient doubts so that the jury did not convict beyond a reasonable doubt. In the civil trial, however, where the criterion was different—proof needed only to be established by a "preponderance of evidence"—the jury convicted.

We believe the dodo bird verdict is analogous. "Defense lawyers" (Barlow, Beutler, Norcross, and others) who want to dismiss the dodo bird verdict can, piece by piece, raise objections to this or that individual study that found no difference, or to this or that meta-analysis. They can argue that maybe the sample size was not large enough, or raise the specter of the few studies that found differences between therapies. If a trial before a jury of 12 objective observers were held and the criterion was that the dodo bird verdict must be proven beyond any reasonable doubt, the anti–dodo bird defense team might prevail. On the other hand, if the case were heard in a civil court, where the criterion was a preponderance of evidence, we believe the jury would find in favor of the dodo bird verdict.

Considering that hundreds of studies have been done on psychotherapy, and that researchers have been highly motivated to discount the dodo bird verdict and prove the superiority of their favorite approaches, and yet the evidence still is in favor of it, the dodo bird verdict deserves to be taken far more seriously than it is. Why does it continue to be debated? The reasons for this are not surprising. Bergin and Garfield (1994), commenting on this, said the following:

> With some exceptions . . . there is massive evidence that psychotherapeutic techniques do not have specific effects; yet there is tremendous resistance to accepting this finding as a legitimate one. Numerous interpretations of the data have been given in order to preserve the idea that technical factors have substantial, unique, and specific effects. The reasons for this are not difficult to surmise. Such pronouncements essentially appear to be rationalizations that attempt to preserve the role of special theories, the status of leaders of such approaches, the technical training programs for therapists, the professional legitimacy of psychotherapy, and the rewards that come to those having supposedly curative powers.[2] (p. 822)

We do not believe that the dodo bird verdict must inevitably hold true in all cases. It will not be surprising if cases are found in which it does not hold. Some may already exist, such as the use of eye movement desensitization for trauma (F. Shapiro, 1995), but more research is needed. As a concrete example, one of us (Bohart) does sex therapy and would never consider suggesting years of psychoanalysis to a client with premature ejaculation problems instead of the stop–start technique. In addition, we believe that by enhancing the understanding of how clients self-heal, the development of more powerful procedures may become possible and the dodo bird verdict ultimately may be superseded.

However, at the present time, the dodo bird verdict mostly seems to hold. What is important about this is that if the medical model were true, the dodo bird verdict should be the exception to the rule. Instead, it appears to be the rule, and cases that contradict it seem to be the exception. This suggests that therapy is not medical like.

---

[2]From "Overview, Trends, and Future Issues," by A. E. Bergin and S. L. Garfield, 1994, in A. E. Bergin and S. L. Garfield (Eds.), *Handbook of Psychotherapy and Behavior Change* (4th ed.), New York: Wiley. Copyright 1994 by Wiley. Reprinted with permission.

Reconciling the Quandary

There are undoubtedly many factors involved in the finding that different therapies work about equally well. One of the solutions to the problem has been to look for common factors across different approaches to therapy. A "common" common factor has been the therapist–client relationship. We shall see that the relationship is important. But we do not consider it to be a sufficient explanation for the dodo bird verdict. Instead we suggest that one solution to the problem of the dodo bird verdict is to focus on the client as the primary common factor or source of change in psychotherapy. Our explanation for the dodo bird verdict is that it occurs because the clients' ability to use whatever therapists offer them overwhelms any differences that might exist between techniques or approaches.

The reason there are 400 or more differing approaches to psychotherapy and the reason that they all may work approximately equally well[3] is that they each allow clients the opportunity to work through and resolve their own problems. Even if different techniques have different specific effects, it is clients who take these effects and actively use them to modify their own lives. Thus a client could use cognitive restructuring (Beck, Rush, Shaw, & Emery, 1979), emotional exploration (e.g., Greenberg & Watson, 1998), empathic reflections (e.g., client-centered therapy; Greenberg & Watson, 1998), or interpersonal techniques (Klerman, Weissmann, Rounsaville, & Chevron, 1984) to alleviate their depression. Similarly, clients could work through posttraumatic stress disorder using Foa and Rothbaum's (1997) cognitive–behavioral techniques or the process-experiential techniques of Greenberg, Rice, and Elliott (1993; see also Paivio & Nieuwenhuis, 1998). Clients translate the learning in therapy into meaningful information for their own lives, even if different therapies provide different learnings.

Exercise is an analogy. It is as if we gave clients a wide range of exercise options with the goal of building up their cardiovascular fitness. Despite different methods and approaches, and despite possible theoretical reasons for expecting that some might work better than others, we discover that the active efforts of clients in using the devices lead to functional equivalence of outcomes. What is most important is how much each client invests in the use of the device or method, more so than the device or method itself.

If we are right, then the dodo bird verdict should appear in other places besides the comparisons of different therapies to one another. If the client's "magic" is the most powerful force in therapy, then a host of therapeutic variables may prove to be less important than we have thought.

---

[3]This is a bit of overstatement because not all of the 400 have been researched.

As we shall see, the dodo bird verdict does show up in other types of comparisons.

Is Professionally Provided Therapy Needed?

If the medical model is correct, we would expect professional, well-trained therapists to be considerably more effective than less trained or experienced therapists, and professionally provided therapy considerably more useful than self-help procedures. On the other hand, if the client as active self-healer is the major force making therapy work, then such differences might turn out to be less important. We would once again find the dodo bird verdict of no significant difference.

Therapist Experience and Training

If the therapist is the primary agent of change in therapy, then the therapist's experience and training should make a substantial difference in effectiveness, as with electricians and brain surgeons (Christensen, 1992). However, overall differences in therapist experience have not been found to produce significant differences in outcome. Christensen and Jacobson (1994) cited a number of research reviews that found no evidence of significant differences between professionals and paraprofessionals in terms of effectiveness. Evidence also has not generally found support for the idea that more experienced therapists are more effective (Christensen & Jacobson, 1994; Lambert & Bergin, 1994). One example of the findings that experience and training do not make large differences in outcome is a study by Strupp and Hadley (1979), who found that experienced therapists were no more helpful than a group of untrained college professors selected for their relationship skills. Similarly, Jacobson (1995) found that novice graduate students were more effective at doing couples therapy than trained professionals, and Svartberg and Stiles (1991) found in a meta-analysis of studies on short-term psychodynamic therapy that inexperienced therapists were more effective than more experienced therapists. On the other hand, a meta-analysis by Stein and Lambert (1995) did find evidence of small differences in effectiveness in favor of more well-trained and experienced therapists. Beutler (1995) argued that experience alone does not necessarily make one a better therapist, but specific structured training and practice in a specific approach does. Nevertheless, what we find impressive is that trying to find evidence of differences in effectiveness as a function of training and experience is similar to trying to find evidence of differences among therapies. It is so hard to find evidence of anything more than small differences.

This does not mean that all therapists are created equal. There is evidence that some therapists are more helpful than others (Luborsky, Mc-

Clellan, Woody, O'Brien, & Auerbach, 1985; Orlinsky & Howard, 1980). However, this appears to be due to differences in personal qualities. We might expect personal qualities to be important in providing the kind of supportive climate clients need to work out their problems (see our model in chapter 8).

We do not know if this set of findings on therapist experience and training is due to the active efforts of the client. There are undoubtedly many variables involved. Yet these findings are compatible with our idea and incompatible with the medical model.

Professional Psychotherapy Versus Professionally Provided Self-Help Materials

In studies that have compared self-help with professionally provided therapy, the dodo bird verdict again proves to be the norm. Meta-analyses by Scogin, Bynum, Stephens, and Calhoon (1990) and Gould and Clum (1993), each of 40 studies, found that self-help treatments, such as self-help books, were as effective as treatments by therapists for a wide range of problems. For instance, Gould and Clum found that self-help was effective for such problems as depression, fears, headache, and sleep problems. Self-help was less effective for habit problems such as smoking, drinking, and overeating. Other studies have produced other dodo bird findings, such as that there appears to be no difference in effectiveness between different self-help books or between conditions in which the self-help book is combined with a class or with brief telephone contacts (Arkowitz, 1997a, 1997b). In a study in which cognitive self-help procedures were taught to depressive students in a class, the results were comparable with those obtained from the classic study of depression, the National Institute of Mental Health (NIMH) collaborative (Arkowitz, 1997a, 1997b).

Computer-provided therapy has also proved to be as effective as professionally provided therapy. Selmi, Klein, Greist, Sorrell, and Erdman (1990) found that computer-administered cognitive–behavioral therapy worked as well as therapist-administered therapy for depression. A study at a major southern California health maintenance organization also found that computer-assisted therapy worked as well as therapist-provided therapy (Jacobs, 1995). The computer-assisted therapy was the therapeutic learning program (Gould, 1989), based on Gould's (1978) theory of adult development. Key assumptions, compatible with our view presented in chapter 3, were (a) psychological growth continues throughout life; (b) growth involves a dialectic between two opposing forces—a need to grow and adapt and a need for safety; and (c) psychological problems result from the growth process getting stuck when the person encounters a problem he or she cannot adapt to. The program consisted of a segment in which clients identified their problems and what possible actions they could take to remedy the problem, a segment in which they evaluated these actions, and finally a segment in which they identified the fears getting in their way of acting. Their evaluations were entirely their own, and no specific behaviors or solutions were suggested by the program. Thus the program could be seen as a specific structure designed to promote client-directed self-healing. In a controlled trial, 10 sessions of computer-provided therapy were compared with 10 sessions by therapists who were rated highly by supervisors for being effective. There were no significant differences in effectiveness between the two groups.

The self-help books and computer-assisted therapy programs used in these studies were written by professionals. However, these studies suggest that the expert therapist's application of techniques is not always necessary. If the professional were the primary agent of change, it would be unlikely that a self-help book or a computer program would turn out to be equally effective. Certainly no surgeon could write a self-help book that would be as effective as a patient seeing a professional surgeon. Thus, once again, these data are an example of the dodo bird verdict.

The Therapeutic Relationship

If the medical model is correct, then the relationship between the therapist and the client should not be a powerful determinant of outcome. Instead, power for change should primarily reside in the "potent techniques" used by therapists. We have already noted Lambert's (1992) estimate that techniques account for about 15% of variance in outcome, whereas therapeutic common factors, such as the relationship, account for about 30%. Other research has found that the therapeutic alliance is the strongest predictor of outcome in therapy across widely differing approaches (Horvath, 1995) and even seems to be a major factor in the effectiveness of drug interventions for depression (Krupnick et al., 1996).

Evidence that the relationship may be more potent than specific interventions contradicts the medical model. However, does it not suggest that the therapist is still the major potent force for precipitating change in therapy, only now through the therapist–client relationship instead of through techniques? In other words, do these findings not contradict our thesis that the primary healing force comes from the client? The evidence on self-help materials implies that the therapist–client relationship is not necessary. Although the relationship may be the most potent factor provided by the therapist, clients can get better without it.

The therapist–client relationship, as with self-help books and computer programs, is simply one tool clients use to grow. What the therapeutic relationship and self-help books all have in common may be that they provide clients the opportunity to have a "healthy dialogical relationship" with another person or self-help material. Good therapists, as well as good self-help materials, provide healthy challenges to clients, and some kind of opportunity for a structured systematic interaction may be particularly helpful in promoting productive client thinking and problem solving. However, as we see later with studies of journaling, the structured interactions need not be the products of professional therapists.

Summary

The dodo bird verdict holds, or mostly holds, in that different treatments do not as a rule seem to be differentially effective for different disorders; there is little difference between therapists based on their training or experience; self-help approaches seem to be about as effective as professionally provided therapy; and there seem to be no differences between different modalities of providing self-help. When one considers all these data together, it is hard to ignore their implications. If the therapist were that potent, then we would not expect such consistently negative results across different approaches to therapy, different techniques, differences in training and experience, differences between professionally provided therapy and self-help, and differences in different modalities of providing self-help. This all converges on the conclusion that the medical model is not an adequate model of how therapy works and implies that the primary source of change, the "force" of change, comes from the client.

Next we consider direct evidence for the thesis that it is the client who is the primary agent of change.

DIRECT EVIDENCE FOR CLIENT SELF-HEALING OUTSIDE OF PSYCHOTHERAPY

Direct evidence for self-healing comes from demonstrations that individuals can overcome their problems without either professionally provided therapy or professionally guided self-help. These findings illustrate the considerable self-healing capacities that (at least many) individuals possess.

Spontaneous Recovery

Many individuals seem to overcome their problems without psychotherapy. This has been called *spontaneous recovery*. The rate of spontaneous recovery has been debated (Bergin & Lambert, 1978). Furthermore, it has varied from study to study, and probably varies depending on the type of problem as well. However, Lambert (1992) estimated it to be generally around 40%.

Other research has shown that substantial numbers, if not the majority, of alcoholics and smokers overcome their problems without professional assistance (Calahan, 1987; W. R. Miller & Rollnick, 1991; Prochaska, DiClemente, & Norcross, 1992; Robbins, 1979). Many "borderlines" gradually mature out of their symptoms as they get older (Kroll, 1988), as do many individuals who have engaged in antisocial behavior (Tedeschi & Felson, 1994). Even some individuals' symptoms of obsessive–compulsive disorder may recover without therapy (Yaryura-Tobias & Neziroglu, 1997). Major longitudinal studies (Chess & Thomas, 1984; Vaillant, 1993) have found that individuals often change for the better without professional assistance. For instance, Chess and Thomas presented the case of Stuart, who was both an academic underachiever during his elementary school years and behaved socially in ways that eventually alienated his classmates. He and his parents had some therapy, but it did not appear to be successful in changing his underachieving style, although by early adolescence Stuart had righted his social life. However, he seemed to be heading for a life "as a playboy who would utilize his social talents and charm to exploit his parents, friends, and especially women" (Chess & Thomas, 1984, p. 240). In late adolescence and early adulthood, without the aid of therapy, Stuart made "a truly remarkable turnaround" (p. 240). He became serious about his studies and eventually graduated with honors from college. By age 22, he had a steady girlfriend and was contemplating marriage, had a definite career commitment, and was scheduled to start graduate work at a leading university.

Spontaneous recovery may even be occurring for those in therapy. Clients do a good deal of work on their own. For instance, it has been found that when clients return to therapy after a week, 70% of them report changes that have occurred to them outside of therapy during that week (Reuterlove, Lofgren, Nordstrom, & Ternstrom, in press, cited in S. D. Miller, Duncan, & Hubble, 1997). In addition, there is evidence that 60% or more of clients improve from the time they make an appointment with the therapist to the time they come in for their first appointment (S. D. Miller et al., 1997). Both of these findings suggest highly active clients who are thinking about their problems before and between sessions. We have noted in our own therapeutic experience how much we actively think through our problems *on the way to the therapist's office*.

There are many factors involved in whether individuals are able to self-right without the aid of professional therapists. Prochaska and his colleagues have documented a number of strategies that individuals use. We consider these later. Beyond these factors, some others include the availability of social support in the person's network of relationships, context, maturation, resilience, placebo effects, and nonprofessional help.

Social Support

A good deal of research has suggested that a person's social support networks play a role in whether or not the person breaks down and needs to seek professional assistance (Bankoff & Howard, 1992). Data show that many individuals who do not seek out professional therapy often turn to friends, ministers, and the like. Having a supportive marriage can also be a major turnaround factor for individuals whose lives previously had been dysfunctional (Vaillant, 1993).

It is interesting to note that those in therapy increase their utilization of nonprofessional social support resources (Cross, Sheehan, & Kahn, 1980), suggesting that therapy may help partially by supporting clients' own active utilization of naturally occurring resources already potentially available to them. Those who have sought out help from both nonprofessional sources and professional sources have sometimes reported greater satisfaction with the help provided by their nonprofessional sources (Gurin, Veroff, & Feld, 1960).

As an example of the helpfulness of supportive listening, Burton, Parker, and Wollner (1991) found that breast cancer patients about to undergo surgery who received a single 45-minute preoperative interview from their surgeons, dealing with a variety of concerns and issues related to the surgery, had less distress about body image, less anxiety, less depression, and were coping with the results of surgery better at a 1-year follow-up than control participants who did not have the interview. The surgeons were trained in empathic listening and were encouraged to allow the patient to express feelings, but not to use any active attempts to intervene therapeutically. Furthermore, those patients who had an additional psychotherapeutic intervention showed only a few small additional gains over and above the effects of the preoperative interview. This study suggests, as we discuss in chapter 5, that giving clients a chance to articulate and express their concerns helps them think about them, and perhaps reframe the problem situation and put it in perspective.

Context

Contextual changes often seem to be a precipitator of personal growth. For instance, Elder (1986) found that entering the army provided the opportunity for a process of personality development in a group of young men who previously had below-average grades in high school and were low in assertiveness and self-confidence. By age 40, these men had shown dramatic gains in psychological competence.

Vaillant (1993) noted a number of cases in which the death of a parent seemed to precipitate a spurt in psychological development. He also gave the example of Eugene O'Neill's mother, Ella, who was able to give up a lifelong addiction to morphine by entering a convent. In particular, Vaillant discussed the importance of what he called *sacred places* in personal transformation, places that allow people to wonder, imagine, and play with new ideas and possibilities.

Maturation

Maturation is a nebulous variable. It is unlikely that maturation all by itself magically guarantees psychological growth, and there are certainly cases in which aging and maturation do not equate to personal development. Undoubtedly, other factors interact. Nonetheless, both Chess and Thomas (1984) and Vaillant (1993) reported cases in which no one clear event seemed to precipitate personal change but in which individuals over time simply seemed to change for the better. McAdams and de St. Aubin (1998) and others have emphasized the phenomenon of generativity, based on Eric Erickson's developmental theory. Generativity, as defined in Erickson's theory, has to do with becoming concerned with promoting the welfare of future generations. A number of individuals do seem to "mature into" becoming more concerned about promoting the welfare of other human beings as they age into their 30s and 40s (McAdams & de St. Aubin, 1998).

Resilience

There is now considerable support for the idea of the human as an active, resilient, self-righting agent. Orlinsky et al. (1994) noted that therapy draws on a powerful endogenous self-healing process that is a part of all human beings. Masten, Best, and Garmazy (1990), researchers on human resilience, concluded that "studies of psychosocial resilience support the view that human psychological development is highly buffered and self-righting" (p. 438). In Vaillant's (1993) longitudinal study, 11 men were identified at age 25 as "broken beyond repair." Yet at age 60, 8 of them were in the top 25% in terms of mental health. Oliver Sacks (see Schleier, 1998), a neurologist, commented on the resilience he had observed among those with various neurological disorders, with many of them able to create reasonable accommodations to life. In a different area, Jenkins (1995) pointed out how creative and resilient African Americans have been in coping with and surviving slavery and racism.

Not every individual is equally resilient. Studies of resilience have found that about 10% of children who grow up in high-risk circumstances are highly resilient (Werner & Smith, 1982). The majority of the rest are resilient in varying degrees. The degree of resilience seems to be a function of a variety of factors, and some individuals have more strikes against them than others. Biology seems to play a role, with those with difficult tem-

peraments having a harder time unless they happen to run into a facilitative psychosocial environment. Others may not be lucky enough to run
into someone who provides support that is lacking in the individual's immediate family. Optimism also seems to be an important protective factor
(Seligman, 1990). Nonetheless, we agree with Masten et al. (1990), about
the self-righting potential of all humans, believing that, moderated by the
constraints of environment and biology, all individuals are inherently self-
righting.

Prochaska and Colleagues

Prochaska (1995) and his colleagues have been on the forefront of
studying persons' ability to self-change and overcome a variety of problems,
such as the cessation of smoking, on their own. Prochaska, Norcross, and
DiClemente (1994), in keeping with our perspective, said that "in fact, it
can be argued that all change is self-change, and that therapy is simply
professionally coached self-change" (p. 17). Prochaska and his colleagues
have discovered that individuals who self-heal generate most of the same
strategies professional therapists use. These change strategies include the
following:

- consciousness-raising (insight, challenging dysfunctional cognitions, etc.)
- dramatic relief (earlier termed *catharsis*; including emotional
  activation and expression)
- self-reevaluation (including reevaluating one's values in relation to one's behaviors)
- environmental reevaluation (evaluating how one's behaviors
  are affecting one's environment, for instance, how one's alcoholism may be leading to neglect one's physical environment and one's family relationships)
- self-liberation (having a sense that one can make needed
  changes in one's life, similar to Bandura's (1997) concept of
  self-efficacy)
- contingency management (arranging the reinforcers and
  stimulus conditions in one's environment in such a way that
  one supports more healthy behavior)
- stimulus control (removing cues from one's environment that
  precipitate dysfunctional behavior, or building in cues that
  trigger more functional behavior)
- counterconditioning (learning to replace more dysfunctional
  habits with more functional habits)
- social liberation (advocating for the rights of the oppressed
  as a way of changing and empowering the self)

Studies by Prochaska et al., (1994) have shown that successful self-changers in the natural environment use a variety of the different change strategies, whereas most therapies tend to emphasize only a few. Moreover, Norcross and Aboyoun (1994) found that therapists in their own self-change efforts tend to act like persons in the street, using a wide range of the change strategies, whereas they only use the few compatible with their theory when they work with their clients! Prochaska and colleagues have also shown that success in therapy depends on a match between the client's stage of change and the kinds of therapeutic strategies being used by the therapist (Prochaska, 1995).

Placebo Effects

Placebo effects are often treated by medical and psychotherapy researchers alike as if they were somehow "dirty." It is almost an insult to say that something is merely a "placebo" effect. Yet as Weil (1995) pointed out, placebo effects should be of great interest. Some of the placebo findings in medicine are truly amazing, with patients showing cure rates higher than untreated controls (although not as high as for whatever drug is being tested). Evans (1985; cited in Rossi, 1993), for instance, estimated that placebos have about 55% of the curative power of active medications. It has also been suggested that if physician and patient both believe in the treatment, the placebo effect may account for as much as 70% of the effectiveness of medical treatments (Roberts, Kewman, Mercier, & Hovell, 1993).

Reports of placebo effects on specific cases, such as Klopfer's (1957) account of the effects of a placebo on alleviating the symptoms of terminal cancer, are little short of astounding. In this case, a patient, Mr. Wright, with lymphosarcoma had huge tumor masses the size of oranges in various parts of his body, and various other signs which led the physicians to believe he was terminal. Mr. Wright was given a new drug, Krebiozen, which was being tested for its effectiveness in alleviating cancer. There was initially much optimism about this drug, and Mr. Wright's hopes were raised considerably. Within a few days of his first injection, he showed major improvement: Tumors had melted away, and he was out of bed and moving around. Within 10 days he was discharged from the hospital.

However, within a few months reports began to surface that Krebiozen might be ineffective, and Mr. Wright relapsed. At this point, Klopfer tried an experiment. He told Mr. Wright that he had just gotten a new, super, double-strength version of Krebiozen. However, what he actually injected into Mr. Wright was just water. Nevertheless, Mr. Wright once again showed a near miraculous recovery. He remained symptom free for another 2 months until newspapers reported the final American Medical Association announcement that Krebiozen was worthless. Within a few days, Mr. Wright relapsed significantly and died.

The power of placebos has repeatedly been found in psychotherapy research also. While, on the whole, studies have shown that "real" psychotherapy works better than placebo therapies (one case in which the Dodo bird verdict does not hold), substantial change has been shown to occur from placebos. For instance, in the NIMH collaborative study (Elkin, 1994), there were actually no significant differences between the placebo treatment and cognitive therapy for the alleviation of depression, and Robinson et al. (1990) found that when researcher allegiance effects were controlled, placebo treatments for depression turned out to be about as effective as professionally provided therapy.

Because placebos are not presumed to be "active," the implication is that clients, believing they are being treated with something helpful, mobilize their own resources to self-right and self-heal. It is even possible that psychotherapy in general is nothing more than an "active placebo" (Weil, 1995). Weil argued that a lot of medications actually function as active placebos. That means that although they have active effects on the body, these effects do not actually do the healing. Instead, the healing occurs through the clients' self-healing.

In a similar manner, most therapy techniques could be active placebos. For instance, relaxation procedures may have an active effect, but it may not specifically be relaxation that helps clients change. Perhaps, rather, the more specific and active the procedure, the more plausible it becomes to clients and mobilizes their hope, energy, creativity, and self-healing. This might even explain why techniques that evoke strong emotion may be particularly helpful. They mobilize clients' involvement, commitment, and persistence. In many therapy research studies, specific techniques are presented with highly plausible rationales that link them with problem resolution. Placebo or other "nonspecific" control treatments may also be presented with a plausible rationale. However, if the specific techniques are specifically active in a plausible fashion, while effects of placebo treatments are less clear and less specifically and plausibly linked to outcome, clients may conclude they are being helped more by the specific treatments. This may mobilize their active efforts and hope more so than in the placebo control group, thus leading to better outcome, but not because the specific technique is really causing the outcome.

In any case, the placebo effect should not be disparaged. It is not an anomaly. Rather it provides the natural baseline for client self-healing.

Nonprofessionally Coached Self-Help

Additional evidence on self-help procedures further strengthens the thesis that clients are powerful and active change agents. The self-help procedures previously considered were designed by professionals. However, there are self-help procedures in which virtually no professional guidance is given, and positive effects still are produced. We consider these next.

Self-Help Groups

As many, if not more, individuals receive personal guidance and assistance through self-help, or mutual support, groups as they do through professionally provided therapy (Goodman & Jacobs, 1994; Jacobs & Goodman, 1989). There is not a great deal of data on the effectiveness of mutual-support groups, but what there is suggests that they can be as helpful as professionally provided therapy (Goodman & Jacobs, 1994; Jacobs & Goodman, 1989). Nonprofessional mutual-support groups for depression were found to be as effective as professionally provided therapy (Bright, Baker, & Neimeyer, 1997).

Journaling and Other Forms of Self-Disclosure

Pennebaker (1990, 1997) showed that expression and self-disclosure appear to be both psychologically and physically beneficial. In one study, college students wrote about a traumatic experience for 15 minutes a day for 4 consecutive days. At a 6-month follow-up, these students, compared with a control group, showed a 50% drop in visits to the student health center. Harvey and his colleagues (Harvey, Orbuch, Chwalisz, & Garwood, 1991) found that giving traumatized individuals a chance to "tell their story" and engage in "account making" is healing. In a related finding, Segal and Murray (1994) found that talking into a tape recorder worked about as well as cognitive therapy in helping individuals resolve feelings about traumatic experiences. Compatible with the findings of Pennebaker (1990, 1997) and Segal and Murray (1994), an early study by Schwitzgabel (1961) found that paying juvenile delinquents to talk into a tape recorder about their experiences led to substantial improvements in their behavior, including fewer arrests.

In sum, clients can self-help without professional assistance, through self-help groups and self-help activities such as self-disclosure and journaling.

DIRECT SUPPORT FOR THE CLIENT AS SELF-HEALER INSIDE PSYCHOTHERAPY

Client Involvement

Evidence for the importance of the client as active self-healer in therapy comes from studies that have found that degree of client participation in therapy is the most important variable in outcome along with the therapeutic alliance. Orlinsky et al. (1994) found that 69% of the studies done show that client cooperation versus their being resistant is associated with positive outcome. Similarly, the client's role investment in the therapy has also been found to be associated with positive outcome in nearly 70% of the studies. Client openness versus defensiveness has also been found to be associated with outcome in 80% of the studies. Finally, clients' collaborative style, versus their being more controlling or dependent, is associated with positive outcome in 64% of studies. Orlinsky et al. (1994) noted that "patients who are cooperative and open . . . are more willing to participate, can more readily absorb the experiences generated by effective therapeutic operations, [are] thus . . . more likely to benefit from therapy" (p. 363). They also noted that "the quality of the patient's participation in therapy stands out as the most important determinant of outcome" (p. 361).

Client Motivation and Goals

Given that the client's participation is so important, one might expect that clients' motivation for therapy would play an important role in outcome. However, results on this are conflicting. Garfield (1994) concluded that there is no strong evidence that client motivation is associated with outcome of therapy, although it may play a role in whether a person enters therapy or not. On the other hand, Orlinsky et al. (1994) reported that 50% of 28 studies found that client motivation is associated with outcome. This is beyond the number one would expect to be significant by chance. Orlinksy et al. noted that this is especially true if motivation is assessed from the client's perspective, and 80% of the studies found a positive relationship with outcome.

It should be noted that motivation may not be exactly the same as involvement. Some definitions of motivation focus on what individuals want. Thus, some clients might say that they are motivated for therapy when they mean that they want to overcome their problems. But that is not the same as motivation meaning "involved, motivated, active, goal-directed behavior." Thus, although it seems odd, a person might become involved in an open, participative way in therapy even though he or she was not initially motivated to start it. Conversely, we have had a few clients who were motivated to start therapy, but for whatever reasons were unable to become involved in it (Bohart, 1995a). It therefore makes sense that involvement is more important than motivation. The greater importance of involvement also fits with our perspective, in that if it is the client who ultimately provides the "healing magic," then it would follow that it is his or her involvement and willingness to actively listen, think, try out interventions, absorb whatever experiences and information are being provided, and work with these things in a productive, generative way that ultimately makes change happen in therapy.

Associated with motivation is the client's expectancy that therapy will be of help. Following from Jerome Frank's (1974) work, many have assumed that client expectations for success should predict therapeutic outcome. This also fits with research in other areas in which it has been found that optimism, for instance, is associated with a variety of positive outcomes in life (Seligman, 1990). Garfield (1994) reported that studies have found conflicting results with regard to expectation and noted methodological problems with the research. Nonetheless, Garfield's review, which focused primarily on studies of pretreatment expectancies, cited more positive than negative studies, suggesting some role for the effects of expectancy.

In modern psychological personality research, the concept of *goals* is often treated as the equivalent of the concept of motivation (see Cantor & Zirkel, 1990). Goals can be viewed as a motivational construct, and it is assumed by many therapists (e.g., De Shazer, 1985; Zilbergeld & Lazarus, 1987) that having clear, concrete, and specific goals is motivating. Defined this way, there is evidence that motivation does matter. Garfield (1994) cited studies suggesting that those who actually come to therapy have a more specific formulation of their problems than do those who may call for an appointment but who do not show up. Similarly, Orlinsky et al. (1994) reported that clarity of goals and consensus on goals between therapist and client are associated with positive outcome.

Summary

Although the evidence is not uniform, it generally favors the hypothesis that clients who are motivated in therapy, who have expectations that therapy will help, and who have a clear sense of their goals and what they hope to achieve will be more likely to achieve something in therapy. Going beyond this, their level of involvement and openness to the process appears to be the single most important factor in whether therapy helps or not.

Orlinsky et al. (1994), drawing conclusions from their review of research on process and outcome in psychotherapy, concluded that ". . . strong links [have been] observed between outcome and patient's positive cooperation and inner openness [and] . . . less consistent links observed between outcome and therapist interventions" (p. 363). Bergin and Garfield (1994), in their summary overview to their volume on psychotherapy research, concluded the following:

> Another important observation regarding the client variable is that it is the client more than the therapist who implements the change process. If the client does not absorb, utilize, and follow through on the

facilitative efforts of the therapist, then nothing happens. Rather than argue over whether or not "therapy works," we could address ourselves to the question of whether or not "the client works"! In this regard, there needs to be a reform in our thinking about the efficacy of psychotherapy. Clients are not inert objects upon whom techniques are administered. They are not dependent variables upon whom independent variables operate. . . . It is important to rethink the terminology that assumes that "effects" are like Aristotelian impetus causality. As therapists have depended more upon the client's resources, more change seems to occur.[4] (pp. 825–826)

EVIDENCE ON CLIENT AGENCY

There is some research beginning to show how clients actively and agentically shape therapy to their own ends.

David Rennie

In an intriguing series of studies, Rennie (1990, 1994a, 1994b) conducted qualitative analyses on interpersonal process recall data (R. Elliott, 1986) on 14 therapy sessions from 12 different therapist–client pairs. The clients were diverse and were in therapy for different problems. The therapists represented a spectrum of theoretical points of view, including humanistic, cognitive–behavioral, and behavioral, although no psychodynamic therapists were included. Soon after the session, which was taped, clients met with Rennie and listened to the tape, stopping it whenever they wanted to comment on what was going on in the session or what they were thinking at the time.

Rennie's work vividly illustrates the active, agentic quality of clients as they undergo the experience of psychotherapy. Rennie found that the central, core category describing the clients' experience was that of client reflexivity. "Reflexivity thus refers to clients' monitoring and evaluation of thinking and feeling, to their enactment of thinking and behavior in response to that monitoring, and to their construction of personal narratives" (Rennie, 1990, p. 159). Some of the processes Rennie described included the following: Clients scan their feelings, locate dimly perceived areas of tension, focus on a particular area, and come to feel they are on a path of discovery of new meaning. When clients are deeply engaged in exploring personal meaning, the therapist becomes a shadowy figure in the background.

---

[4]From "Overview, Trends, and Future Issues," by A. E. Bergin and S. L. Garfield, 1994, in A. E. Bergin and S. L. Garfield (Eds.), *Handbook of Psychotherapy and Behavior Change* (4th ed.), New York: Wiley. Copyright 1994 by Wiley. Reprinted with permission.

Some of Rennie's most important findings concern the fact that clients do a lot of work covertly. That is, they do not report to therapists all that they are thinking. Clients report being busier in their own minds than in what they actually say to their therapists, even if they have a good relationship with their therapist. One of the reasons for this is that clients can think faster than they can talk. Another is that if they do not have to put their thoughts into words, they are able to think in terms of images, and that facilitates rapid thinking. Third, they are able to play with ideas in their private thoughts. "Clients do not have to suffer the reification of ideas that sometimes comes about through verbalization" (Rennie, 1990, p. 162).

In a study on clients' deference to the therapist, Rennie (1994a) noted the following. First, clients actively appraise their therapists' plans and strategies and contrast them with their own preferences on what should be going on. Second, they actively appraise the therapist and their experience in therapy, and sometimes feel critical. They deal with this by deciding if, in context, the therapist's criticisms are important or valid given the broader context of how therapy is going, and may attenuate or stifle the criticism. This may also be done out of gratitude for the therapist's efforts and out of a desire not to hurt the therapist's feelings. Third, they try to understand the therapist's frame of reference. This may be done to try to understand the purpose underlying the therapist's communications or actions, or to try to understand confusing aspects of therapy. Fourth, clients struggle to accept therapists' limitations. Clients may be willing to tolerate negative aspects of therapy if therapy is generally going well, or if the negative aspect seems to fit into an overall therapeutic plan that they accept. Clients may realize that the therapist, too, is human, and therefore forgive mistakes. The client may realize that some mistakes occur because the client has not shared all the things going on inside his or her own head. Finally, clients try to metacommunicate to therapists their wishes and intentions. This is often done indirectly, through nonverbal cues.

Rennie (1994a) reported the case of a client who wanted to understand her own self-pity. However, the Gestalt therapist was not sympathetic to *why* questions and instead encouraged the client to simply accept her self-pity and to work from there.

> The client revealed during the inquiry that she had since heeded her therapist's wishes in terms of what she verbally focused on . . . but that, inwardly, she was still preoccupied with the question of "Why." . . . While the client was talking about her difficulties in competing at university, she was inwardly linking the difficulties to her ongoing preoccupation. (p. 432)

Thus, inwardly, the client continued to try to figure out why while overtly complying with the therapist's agenda.

In sum, Rennie's research demonstrates the highly active, agentic nature of the client. Clients get what they want and "work on" the therapist as much as the therapist works on them.

Tallman, Robinson, Kay, Harvey, and Bohart

Compatible with Rennie's (1990, 1994a, 1994b) work, in a therapy analogue study, Tallman, Robinson, Kay, Harvey, and Bohart (1994) deliberately gave some clients "nonexperiential" empathy responses—responses designed to be generally and loosely semantically accurate but lacking the rich experiential quality of truly good empathy responses. Other clients received good experiential empathy responses. It was predicted that the clients would find the nonexperiential responses less immediately empathic and so have to think about them before responding, leading to a longer reaction time in responding. This was confirmed. In addition, an interpersonal process recall procedure was used with clients (R. Elliott, 1986). Clients listened to the tapes of their sessions and evaluated the therapists' responses. It was predicted that clients would report nonexperiential responses as less helpful than more experiential empathy responses. This was also confirmed.

However, of more interest, the therapists' responses the researchers saw as the most helpful were not necessarily the responses seen as most helpful by the clients. Furthermore, the researchers were often surprised by the reasons that clients thought some responses were helpful and others were not helpful. Yet most clients felt the sessions were useful, and therapists and clients were more likely to agree on the overall usefulness of the session. Even though participants saw the specific nonexperiential responses as less useful, there was little significant difference in overall usefulness between experiential and nonexperiential sessions as rated by the participants.

Finally, of even more interest was how some participants handled some of the vapid, nonexperiential empathy responses. We have evidence that these responses were as vapid as we thought, given that they often stopped the interaction cold for several seconds. Nonetheless, there were a number of cases in which the participants actively worked with these vapid responses therapeutically to "make lemonade out of these lemons." This happened in several ways. First, some participants would agree with the therapist's response, as if they were trying to protect the therapist's feelings, and then they would "creatively" interpret the response so they could use it to stay on their own track. This often involved focusing on a part of the vapid response and finding a way of integrating its meaning into the track the client was following. Second, clients would sometimes creatively alter the whole meaning of the response to use it to further their self-exploration process. Third, they might acknowledge the response and then simply go off in their own direction. This is compatible with R. El-liott's (1984) finding of a lot of sloppiness and slippage in insight events: Therapists make mistakes, but clients ignore the mistake part and use the rest.

An example follows below.

> Client: Right during the busiest part of the year for us, my part-ner goes on vacation! I couldn't believe it. I get dumped with super-vising all our employees and making sure our products are all shipped out by myself. When he got back and I talked to him about it, he said he was sorry, but I didn't get a sense of any genuine concern.
>
> Therapist (vapid response): You're angry with him.
>
> Client (after a pause): Well, yes . . . that's exactly right—I *was* angry . . . and you know, the interesting thing about my anger was that after I expressed it to him I realized that what I was more upset about was his lack of concern that he had done this. That makes me realize that what I really need to figure out is how much I can trust him. We've only been in business together for a couple of years. He's never done anything this irresponsible before, but there were smaller things I remember worrying about now as I talk to you. I have a chance to buy him out. I don't know if I can afford it, but as I talk to you I am wondering if I would be better off without him.

Newfield, Kuehl, Joanning, and Quinn

Newfield, Kuehl, Joanning, and Quinn (1991) interviewed family members who were in family therapy because of adolescents with drug abuse problems. What these authors discovered is the highly active nature of the adolescents in getting what they wanted in therapy. Those who have worked with adolescents in family therapy know that it is not unusual for the adolescent to sit silently. This behavior has often been interpreted as "resistant"; presumably, the adolescent feels threatened and under attack and so clams up as a kind of defensive maneuver. In actuality, Newfield et al. found that this silent state is a highly proactive one. Adolescents are quiet at the start of therapy because they are trying to figure out how much their parents and therapist know. This is to use what information they gather to mislead their parents and therapist later on. They also report saying what their parents want to hear, and trying to talk their parents out of the therapist's interventions during the week. While this behavior is certainly not productive from the therapist's point of view, the point is that what looks like resistance is actually a highly proactive strategy. The teenagers may not be pursuing the same ends as the therapist, but their behavior is every bit as agentic and proactive.

Compatible with what we will say about dealing with resistant clients later in this book, this study found that teens wanted therapists who would interact with them in a collaborative fashion and not with unilateral directives. If they thought the therapist did not understand them, they were less likely to cooperate. This was also true when they perceived the counselor as acting like an authority figure and telling them what to do.

Jerold Gold

Gold (1994) described a subgroup of clients who, on their own, discovered ways of integrating different approaches to psychotherapy together. Over a 17-year period, Gold identified 26 such clients. In one case, a client initially sought treatment for bulimia. After seeing a cognitive–behavioral therapist and having made considerable progress, this client was left with vague feelings of tension and anxiety that cognitive–behavioral therapy had been unable to help. The client then thoroughly investigated a variety of psychotherapies, arranged consultations with practitioners of different schools, and finally chose Gestalt therapy for a second round of therapy. Her experience in this therapy helped her to resolve much of her feelings of tension and anxiety. At this point, she then returned to cognitive–behavioral therapy to consolidate gains made from her earlier experience.

In another case, a 50-year-old man began to experience panic attacks in his cognitive–behavioral therapy when certain dysfunctional cognitions or behavioral symptoms were being discussed. Spontaneously he began to engage in a kind of psychodynamic therapy. He accessed memories of his father and searched for unconscious meanings. He realized that his panic attacks were triggered by a feeling that, through therapy, he was separating from his father. As he became aware of this, he became free to resume the cognitive–behavioral therapy.

EMPIRICAL SUPPORT THROUGH RESEARCH INVOLVING
CLIENTS OF PSYCHOTHERAPY

Research generally finds that what clients find helpful in therapy has little to do with the specialized techniques and procedures that therapists find so important. Phillips (1984) interviewed clients who were in a variety of different therapy approaches, including cognitive–behavioral therapy, and found that clients uniformly reported that the most helpful factor was having a time and a place where they could focus on themselves and talk. Other studies typically find clients emphasizing the relationship (having someone listen, someone care, and someone understand), as well as getting advice. For instance, in a review of the literature, R. Elliott and James (1989) found that clients reported the following as the most helpful factors in therapy: the presence of facilitative therapist characteristics, unburdening of distress, self-understanding, and encouragement for gradual practice. Llewelyn, Elliott, Shapiro, and Hardy (1988) found that depressed and anxious clients who received eight sessions of both cognitive–behavioral and psychodynamic–interpersonal therapy rated the following experiences as most helpful: increased awareness, obtaining problem solutions, reassurance, and personal contact. Gold (1980) found that clients in behavior therapy rated the relationship with the therapist as equal to or more important than the specific behavior-therapy techniques used. Burns and Nolan-Hoeksema (1991) found that client-rated empathy of therapists was the highest correlate of outcome in cognitive–behavioral therapy. In a study of behavior therapy by Ryan and Gizynski (1971), clients said that the most helpful components were the therapists' faith, calm sympathetic listening, and the giving of support, approval, and advice. In the study by Sloane et al. (1975), in which psychoanalysis was compared with behavior therapy, the items considered most important by the clients regardless of what therapy they were in were the following:

- The personality of the therapist.
- The therapist's guidance in helping clients to understand their problems.
- The encouragement clients receive to gradually practice facing the things that bother them.
- Being able to talk to an understanding person.
- Helping clients understand themselves. (p. 206)

Lucius, Emley, Lee, and Bohart (1997) interviewed 33 individuals about their experience in therapy. These individuals had been in therapy for a variety of reasons, from relatively specific problems to problems of substance abuse. They found that most of the clients reported that they saw themselves as the change agents in therapy, not the therapist. Furthermore, a surprisingly high number reported negative experiences in therapy (22), but many (18) reported having been able to take these negative experiences and "turn lemons into lemonade."

In sum, from a client perspective, the most important aspects of therapy typically are the "nontechnological" factors: having a time and place to talk; having someone care, listen, and understand; having someone provide encouragement and reassurance; and having someone offer an external perspective and advice. Furthermore, clients see themselves as active agents who are primarily responsible for the changes that occur in therapy.

The *Consumer Reports* study (Seligman, 1995) was a survey of consumers' perceptions of psychotherapy and other forms of mental health services. Surveys were sent out to the readers of *Consumer Reports* magazine, asking if they ever had any therapy experience and, if they did, how helpful it had been. Over 4,000 readers had seen some combination of a professional therapist, self-help group, or family doctor. Basically, the large majority of respondents found their therapy experience to be helpful.

Consumers' perceptions of mental health services generally fit with the conclusions we have reached earlier. First, concerning the Dodo bird verdict, consumers reported no differences in effectiveness among different brands of therapy for any disorder. Second, helpfulness ratings for five different types of mental health professionals—psychologists; psychiatrists; social workers; marriage, family, and child counselors; and general physicians—were calculated on a 0–300-point scale. Only small differences were found among them. There were no significant differences among psychologists, psychiatrists, and social workers. For those who received 6 months or less of treatment, there were no significant differences among mental health professionals and family physicians. Significant differences were found among psychiatrists, psychologists, and social workers on the one hand (average score 223) and marriage counselors on the other (208). For those who received more than 6 months of treatment, mental health professionals were also rated significantly more highly than family physicians (232 vs. 212, respectively). However, even where significant differences were found, the scores were all in the same general range, and differences were not large, as Sechrest (1996) noted in regard to some of the other findings in this study. With the large sample sizes in this study, it would not be surprising that small differences might be statistically significant. Yet on a 300-point scale, for instance, a difference between 208 and 223 in comparing marriage counselors with other mental health professionals does not seem huge. Thus, we conclude that these results support our earlier conclusions that, at best, only small differences have been found among different types of people providing mental health services. Even family physicians did relatively well in this survey.

Relatively small differences were also discovered between clients' ratings of professionally provided mental health services and self-help groups. In fact, the largest helpfulness rating of all was given to Alcoholics Anonymous groups (251). Other self-help groups had an average rating of 215, again not hugely different from the rating given psychologists, psychiatrists, and social workers (223). A final conclusion from the study compatible with our thesis is that Seligman (1995) noted that clients who reported more of an active role in their treatment received more benefits.

The *Consumer Reports* study has been severely criticized (see Vanden-Bos, 1996). However, it is a measure of clients' perceptions of psychotherapy, and its conclusions are in accord with other findings we have summarized.

MOVEMENT TOWARD HUMAN ACTIVITY AND AGENCY IN OTHER DISCIPLINES

Other disciplines are increasingly taking the idea of the human as an active, creative agent seriously. We briefly review examples in education, business, and cognitive psychology.

Education

In education, the idea of the human as an active, constructive learner is one of the two major current points of view (Sfard, 1998). One movement in education is the *active learning* movement (Cooper, 1995). The goal is to "transform the classroom from being an essentially passive environment for information transmission into an interactive forum where the teacher and the student work cooperatively to construct knowledge and make content meaningful and relevant" (Cooper, 1995, p. 1). The following is a list of characteristics (summarized from Matthews, Cooper, Davidson, & Hawkes, 1995):

- Learning in an active mode is more effective than passively receiving information.
- The teacher is a facilitator, coach, or midwife rather than a "sage on the stage."
- Teaching and learning are shared experiences between teacher and students.
- Articulating one's ideas in a small-group setting enhances a student's ability to reflect on his or her own assumptions and thought processes. (p. 3)

Research on active learning approaches now amounts to over 800 studies (Cooper, 1996). These studies generally find either equivalence or superiority to traditional methods.

Business

In business, some are beginning to question traditional top-down models of training. Some surveys have found that such training is experienced by employees as useless. Instead, it has been found that employees informally "train" one another. In this regard, Stamps (1997) noted that "learning and innovation happen on the job every day" (p. 37). With that in mind, Stamps suggested that a *generativity* model of training, relying on the inventiveness and resourcefulness of the learners, may be more useful than the traditional top-down approach.

Cognitive Psychology

Finally, there is evidence to show that humans are active, creative transformers of information. Frick (1987) noted that his structured growth experience procedures demonstrate that people go beyond events to create meaning. He gave an example of the writer Colaizzi learning that history was not linear from reading the historian Oswald Spengler, even though this is not mentioned anywhere in Spengler's writing. Rychlak (1994) showed that when individuals learn a particular "if-then" relationship, they also figure out the opposite possibilities of the if-then relationship. In other words, they *think*. This point is also made by S. C. Hayes and Gifford (1997) from a radical-behavioral perspective. They noted that "humans have a remarkable ability to derive relations among events" (p. 171).

Closely associated with the human as active thinker and learner is the human's capacity for creativity. Ward, Finke, and Smith (1995) pointed out the countless ways humans are continually creative in everyday life. These authors noted, as had Barsalou (1985) and others, that the idea that humans have a set of concepts or schemas in the brain that they then invariably apply to incoming information is simply wrong. Instead, humans are continually modifying concepts to fit new information, to the point at which it might be more accurate to say that they continually invent new concepts, rather than mechanistically use old ones (Glucksberg & Keysar, 1990; Ward et al., 1995).

CONCLUSION

Research evidence is compatible with the idea that the client is the major healing force in therapy but is not compatible with the medical model. In particular,

- Different therapies, using widely different methods and theories, all seem to be about equally effective for most problems.
- Differential treatment of different disorders does, for the most part, seem to be important.
- Training and experience seem to make at best only a small difference in the effectiveness of therapists.
- Self-help procedures and groups, whether designed by therapists or not, seem to be about as effective as professionally provided therapy.
- Many individuals naturally self-heal outside of therapy.
- Client involvement is the single most important factor in successful therapy.
- Clients, and human beings in general, are active and inventive both inside and outside of therapy.

In sum, the evidence is in accord with our view of the human as a creative, active, self-righting agent. Therapy does not really operate in a medical-like fashion, but more likely works by providing a context that supports and mobilizes clients' self-healing potential. Client effort and involvement seems to be the single most important factor in making psychotherapy work. In the next chapter, we present a view of humans as active problem solvers who frequently solve problems in everyday life, and who are often capable of self-healing and self-righting when major problems appear.

3

SELF-HEALING WITHOUT
A THERAPIST

Personal problem solving is a part of life. Dweck and Leggett (1988) observed that everything of value in life involves struggling with challenges: success in career, relationships, raising children, and so on. Personal problems are ubiquitous, from small ones ("My husband and I had a big argument last night") to big ones ("My life seems so empty and meaningless; I don't know why I should go on").

Yet most individuals do not see professional therapists. They cope, survive, and even prevail and grow without professional assistance. Most of the time they come to some kind of satisfactory resolution, sufficient for them to get on with their lives. Life does not follow a neat, linear course; people "make it up" as they go along. Solutions are frequently not pretty or perfect, but they work. Like Humphrey Bogart's character Charlie Allnut in *The African Queen*, people improvise solutions and keep the boat steaming down the river, continually tinkering as they go. It would not be amiss to say that life is continual tinkering. Sometimes it is not even clear how a problem gets solved; *living* solves it. People go to therapy when a problem has been intractable to tinkering, that is, to their own self-help efforts (Norcross & Aboyoun, 1994). In this chapter, we propose a general view of how people live, learn, solve problems, develop, get stuck, and self-heal.

SELF-HEALING AND SELF-RIGHTING

Self-healing and *self-righting* are two related terms that we use to define our approach.

Self-Righting

Researchers who have studied children growing up in high-risk situations have concluded that humans have a built-in self-righting tendency (Masten et al., 1990; Werner & Smith, 1982). We take self-righting to be the tendency of human beings to bounce back from adversity, to take proactive action, and to carve out some kind of reasonably functional accommodation to life within the constraints imposed by the world. The author–neurologist Oliver Sacks noted, referring to people with neurological diseases, how self-righting individuals can be:

> I've learned how resilient and tough human beings can be and what capacities for survival they have, often in the face of what would seem to be impossible circumstances . . . when you go to a hospital like Beth Abraham, which is a hospital for chronic disease . . . the first sight is often very depressing. . . . Then you find people who've adapted in all sorts of ways, stoically or creatively, and can still lead pretty good lives. (Schleier, 1998, p. 82)

Self-Healing

In a medical metaphor, self-healing refers to the human capacity to repair dysfunctional life pathways, to recover from emotionally injurious experiences, and to change ways of being, behaving, and experiencing so that one moves toward greater coherence and functionality. People are capable of self-generated learning to solve personal problems. They are capable of transcending even highly adverse environments to live productive lives (Werner & Smith, 1982) or of surviving in meaningful ways in horrific situations (Frankl, 1963). And, even if they were abused as children, they do not usually grow up to abuse their own children (Widom, 1989). Self-healing comes from a developmental tendency to integrate information and to develop more complex and differentiated knowledge structures for dealing with reality (Kegan, 1982). Self-righting and self-healing go hand in hand. For the rest of the book, we use the two terms interchangeably.

Nature of the Human Being as a Self-Righting Organism

Modern developmental psychologists view the newborn infant as an active, exploring creature, "born to learn." Many theorists, such as Piaget (Cowan, 1978), Mahoney (1991), and Guidano (1987), have proposed that humans have a tendency to seek order and accommodation that allows more coordinated functioning both within the self and with the world. Just like a child struggling to master the Piagetian conservation problem, individuals will work and experiment to develop their understanding of the world and their capacity for dealing with it. White (1959) argued that humans are born with an intrinsic motivation to learn to be effective and competent in dealing with the world.

A key part of the motivation and capacity to develop more workable adaptations is that humans are continually creative (Ward et al., 1995). Humans do not mechanistically apply old concepts to new information. Rather, they creatively generate new concepts, or new variations on old concepts, all the time (Glucksberg & Keysar, 1990). Creativity is a constant and ongoing part of everyday life. As Epstein (1991), a radical behaviorist observed, "The behavior of organisms has many firsts, so many, in fact, that it's not clear that there are any seconds. We continually do new things. . . . When you look closely enough, behavior that appears to have been repeated proves to be novel in some fashion" (p. 362). Humans continuously vary their behavior (if only in small ways) so that they can fine-tune their adjustments to the endless variations presented by reality.

Overall, the human capacity for self-righting consists of the following: a desire to be effective in coping with the world, a capacity for initiative, a desire to pursue and achieve goals, a desire to solve problems and create livable accommodations with life's contingencies and constraints, the ability to bounce back from adversity and to continue to struggle to achieve workable accommodations, a capacity to integrate new information into old learning when needed, a capacity for understanding, a capacity for change when needed for developing new ways of being and behaving, a capacity for exploration when necessary, a capacity for productive thinking and the generation of new hypotheses, and a capacity for creativity. We assume as a basic postulate that all humans have these desires and capacities at least to some degree.

We define a *problem* as something that is disruptive of the person's goals or agenda. People particularly struggle to learn when they encounter problems. When individuals are having problems, by definition, they are feeling unintegrated: There is an incongruity between their goals and their behaviors, their goals and their life situation, different goals, or their behaviors and society. This motivates them to seek ways of resolving the problem.

Two Different Kinds of Learning and Change

There are two different kinds of learning and change that can occur when individuals encounter problems. These are analogous to Kuhn's (1970) concept of *puzzle solving* versus *paradigm change* and the family systems concept of *first-order* versus *second-order change*.

People develop general modalities or blueprints for dealing with life. These general blueprints include their personality traits, their beliefs, their values, their sense of identity (e.g., what is or is not "them"), and their strategies in various areas of functioning. For instance, they may have blueprints about what a happy marriage looks like, how one is to function in the marriage, and strategies for dealing with problems in the marriage. Being married may be part of their identity. Some of these generalized blueprints have their basis in biology: People are born with different built-in propensities for experiencing and coping with situations in certain kinds of ways, that is, with different temperaments and personality predispositions. But personality is more than just biologically based personality traits. It is the organization of these traits along with the person's beliefs, values, and coping strategies. A shy person may organize his or her overall personality so that his or her fundamental propensities toward shyness are harmless rather than incapacitating. To do that, for instance, he or she may come to value a relatively private life. Or, if he or she needs to be out in public, he or she may develop a receptive, empathic, and listening interactive style rather than an aggressive, highly self-expressive style.

Once people have general models for coping in a certain area, that is, once they have made a commitment to certain beliefs and values and have developed a sense of identity and a life structure, they then proceed to try to live their lives within that life structure. People continue to problem solve, learn, and grow, but they do it by fine-tuning their already existing strategies and ways of being. A cognitive–behavioral therapist, for instance, may remain committed to his or her basic belief system, but develops and elaborates his or her skills and perspectives within that belief system. A Democrat or a Republican does not abandon his or her basic belief system, but evolves and expands it as he or she is challenged to apply it to new and different problems. Kuhn (1970), in discussing the process of science, called this the period of "normal science," during which scientists have adopted a paradigm or way of viewing reality. What they then do within that paradigm is "puzzle solve." In a similar manner, individuals in everyday life spend most of their time puzzle solving without attempting to alter their basic personality, strategies for living, fundamental values and beliefs, or ways of being in the world. For instance, a person who believes in remaining married struggles to solve problems in the marriage. A parent who believes in dialogue as a disciplinary method struggles to productively dialogue with his or her child who is being tempted by neighborhood gangs. An alcoholic tries to cope by finding ways of cutting down on his or her drinking, mollifying his or her spouse, or covering up but does not consider fundamentally altering his or her lifestyle by giving up drinking.

Family systems theorists have called this type of problem solving *first-order change*. First-order changes can often be quite productive and creative.

Freud's refinements of his ideas consisted of a series of first-order changes within his fundamental psychoanalytic framework. Puzzle solving in everyday life can lead to a gradual evolution in the way the person deals with the world. In many cases people get more and more adept at "being who they already are."

Puzzle solving works in the following way. When first confronted with a new situation, individuals generalize old learnings to try to understand the new situation. However, new situations are rarely identical to old ones. Individuals must actively explore to use the old learning to understand and cope with the new situation. Applying old learning to a new situation is a creative process (see Ward et al., 1995). Because new situations are never entirely like old ones, often the person will have to tinker to adjust old learning to fit. When an old learning does not immediately and obviously fit, individuals explore to see where it fits and where it does not fit. They vary their behavior (even if in only slight ways), they search to see what is unexpected or different, they try new things out, they get feedback, and gradually they fine-tune a workable solution. This is not necessarily a conscious, deliberate enterprise. Much of this can be done implicitly, experientially, behaviorally, and perceptually, without conscious calculation. The fine-tuning of the old learning is then stored for future use.

In essence, humans are continually "practicing" what they already know. Through that practice, they develop more differentiated and fine-tuned knowledge, just like athletes or musicians who continually practice. In other words, knowledge does not stay static. Even though basic strategies and perspectives may not change in their overall outlines, they are continually being tinkered with and fine-tuned. A good example is a classical pianist who plays the same piece over and over but continues to discover new ways to play it. The store of knowledge of the piece, of the potentialities in the piece, continuously expands. With each new playing, new insights may appear.

It is through this gradual, small, slow accretion process that most people mature and change. Like snapshots from day to day, changes are not necessarily even noticeable over small periods of time. The analogy of the coastline has previously been used (Bohart, 1995b). From far away it looks like it does not change. Yet from close up, it is in continual transition. Only over long periods of time, say from the time a person is in his or her 20s to the time he or she is in his or her 50s, might there be noticeable change in personality.

The second way individuals learn is through a major paradigm shift in the way the person deals with the world. A paradigm shift (Kuhn, 1970), or *second-order change*, occurs when the process of trying to solve a problem precipitates a fundamental shift in perspective, or a whole new way of framing the problem. In terms of personal revolutions (Bohart, 1978; Mahoney, 1980), this includes shifts in personality organization, fundamental shifts in beliefs, adoption of new strategies for living, or alteration of other basic ways of being in the world. An alcoholic "hits bottom" and realizes that his "tinkering" (e.g., trying to cut down) was not working and he must fundamentally change his life.

Realizing that personal growth and evolution can occur at two levels clarifies a commonly debated issue, that of how much people really change. On the one hand, some argue that change is difficult and that humans rarely change (e.g., classical Freudian theory). On the other hand, some believe that change is constant (e.g., Carl Rogers, strategic therapists such as De Shazer (1985)). If we look at the endless variation and puzzle solving of everyday life, then change, growth, and variation are continuous and constant. If we are looking for major alterations in personal ways of being in the world, then these may be less common, at least over short periods of time. Thus, although individuals may continually learn within their general way of doing things, they may not necessarily learn in such a way that they fundamentally alter or revise these ways of doing things. This explains why it often appears that people are not learning and that they are just doing "more of the same."

At one level, a couple may appear to be having "the same" fight over and over again. The general content may be the same, and the manner of the fight may be the same—mutual attack and self-defense. Yet each fight is a little different. Even though they argue about "the same" thing over and over, it is never quite the same. Each attempt, in each fight, is a fresh start, and each partner endlessly tinkers to try to make it go better each time. Each time each person tries to invent new and different ways to persuade the other, or to explain the self to the other. Each person's point of view, and the structure of the fight itself, may therefore subtly change over time. In some cases, although the argument may never get resolved, the couple may gradually evolve a way to live with their differences.

First-order problem solving and fine-tuning may be entirely adequate most of the time, and may lead to a finer and finer tuned ability to cope. It is likely that second-order problem solving only becomes necessary when first-order problem solving persistently fails, creating the need for more fundamental change and a revolution in core ways of being. For instance, a male alcoholic may be continuously tinkering at the first-order level. He becomes more and more adept at hiding his drinking from boss, spouse, and children. He becomes more and more adept at thinking of excuses. He continually tries various strategies to control his drinking. But what does not change, until he bottoms out, or perhaps enters a treatment program, is his basic belief that he *can* drink normally. On the other hand, people may also slowly evolve over time, without major personal paradigm revolutions. For instance, fundamental shifts in goals and motivations are not uncommon as people approach midlife (Helson, 1993; McAdams & de St. Aubin, 1998).

The Dialectics of Problem Solving and the Creation of More Differentiated and Integrated Levels of Functioning

People create solutions through a back-and-forth dialogical process of thinking about or behaviorally trying out new solutions, experiencing the consequences, changing and fine-tuning solutions, again trying them out, again experiencing the consequences, again fine-tuning, and so on. Various writers have identified two components in the process of new meaning making (e.g., Mahoney, 1991; Wexler, 1974): differentiation and integration. *Differentiation*—developing more subtle and differentiated responses or developing more subtle distinctions of meaning—occurs through the process we have been calling fine-tuning. For instance, an athlete might develop more subtle and differentiated moves. A therapist, with practice, develops more differentiated ways of challenging dysfunctional cognitions.

Integration, in a dialectical process, involves resolving contradictions by creating higher order structures that incorporate the two sides of the contradiction or conflict. Such a process is a common part of adolescent self-concept formation (Harter, 1990). An adolescent struggles with the perception that "sometimes I am friendly and sometimes I am irritable." This may lead to the emergence of the higher order concept that "I am moody." In Piagetian conservation tasks, 6-year-olds struggle with the apparent contradiction that when water is poured from a short wide glass into a tall thin glass, it appears either that the tall glass has more or that the wide glass has more. When they coordinate the two dimensions and are able to conserve area, they realize that the total amount has not changed.

The reconciliation of opposites can lead to the emergence of totally new constructs and solutions (Guidano, 1987; Kampis, 1991; Mahoney, 1991). For instance, Marsha was a junior high school teacher in an overcrowded school in a gang-ridden area. It seemed she spent most of her time disciplining rather than teaching. She felt frustrated and was thinking of giving up teaching. The contradiction she was experiencing was, "I came into this area to help children, and yet I spend all my time disciplining. But if I don't discipline I can't teach." As she went back and forth, a whole different way of looking at the problem emerged. Instead of teach versus discipline, she began to think in terms of contact and engagement. Her focus became contacting and engaging students. She began to find ways to creatively mobilize students' interest in such a way that they began to misbehave less and learn more. She did not reach every child, but her "connection" rate went up considerably, and she began to feel better about her job. A dialectical process of struggling with contradictions and conflicts is at the core of self-healing.

Is Self-Righting Always Positive?

We believe that there is a tendency to self-heal. This does not mean it will always work. Some people face problems that persistently defy resolution and may discourage them, leading to a deterioration in their mood and in their functioning. They may become so helpless and demoralized that they begin to behave in ways that are self-destructive rather than productive. Even those who go to therapy will not always make progress. We may not be able to help them mobilize their self-healing capacities sufficiently to overcome their problems. We may not be able to make enough of a connection to get them involved. Or our methods and tools may not be the ones they need.

In addition, saying that there is a tendency to self-heal does not mean that people will all automatically move toward more and more mature, actualized, and prosocial ways of being. To the contrary, if their lives are reasonably functional from their point of view, they may use the self-righting tendency to solve small immediate problems, but they will not make any major changes in who they are, or how they live and cope with life. Unfortunately, this can mean that some individuals will simply become more and more clever and adept at behaving in harmful ways to others. Even those ostensibly acting in the name of good can end up using their inventiveness to become more and more cleverly oppressive. In other cases, individuals may change little, except in small ways, because the environment does not challenge them to really grow and change. Major self-healing and self-righting typically take place only when environmental or developmental challenges create a need for individuals to reorganize their lives.

We believe that most clients will be motivated to find solutions that fit the constraints of (a) preserving their dignity, (b) actualizing their personal goals, and (c) preserving their own sense of identity, while (d) fitting in with others and with society. Many modern developmental psychologists believe that humans (a) are built with intrinsic tendency toward morality and (b) are biologically "prepared" to be socialized, that is, to become functional members of their particular society (Eisenberg, 1998). Therefore, more often than not, most individuals should self-right and self-heal in ways that enhance their social relations with other human beings. However, this will not necessarily be the case, any more than it is the case that all people automatically develop into loving, caring individuals. A male sexual abuser might be referred to counseling against his will and have no intrinsic desire to overcome his patterns of abuse. In fact, he may even adhere to the philosophy that children are sexual beings and should be allowed to enjoy sexual pleasure; therefore he believes he has done nothing wrong. It is conceivable that, left to this own devices, self-righting here may be his finding ways to (a) present himself effectively to the court system so that he is released from it and (b) be more clever in not getting caught. Thus solutions that optimize outcomes for the individual will not magically guarantee optimized outcomes for others and for society.

This does not contradict the fact that ultimately it is the client's power for self-righting that leads to change. However, it does suggest that, as therapists, we function not only as agents of the individual client but also as agents of society. In the case of the individual versus society, our goal is to find a win–win higher order integrative solution for both.

HOW PSYCHOLOGICAL PROBLEMS ARISE

If individuals are continually trying to solve problems, then how do they get stuck and develop psychological problems? We concur with a number of theorists (e.g., Gendlin, 1967; Linehan, 1997; Watzlawick, Weakland, & Fisch, 1974) that psychological problems result in part from a proactive attempt by the person to cope or to restore function. In other words, problems themselves are in part an attempt at self-righting. To understand this, we must understand how problems arise from the forces in a person's life space. We first turn to a consideration of the life space.

The Life Space

The concept of life space was originally introduced by Kurt Lewin in the 1940s. The life space consists of all the forces influencing a person's life. This includes facilitating and restraining forces in relationships, in the job, and in the physical environment. It also includes the person's desires, goals, values, and beliefs, as well as his or her biological constraints and potentialities. The life space is a system, and all these elements influence one another. Some of the interconnections create constraints, and others create possibilities. Constraints are the limits within which an individual must operate to pursue his or her goals. Possibilities are the interconnections that make available various avenues of pursuit for goal attainment.

People have an implicit awareness of the network of constraints and possibilities in their life space. This awareness is not directly focused on and cognized, but nonetheless sensed and felt. People "know more than they can say" (Bohart & Associates, 1996; Polyani, 1967). What they sense are relationships between variables in their life space. In any dense net of interconnected meanings and assumptions, there are always implications that may not have been overtly drawn. As an example, "My dad doesn't like me" may not have been explicitly drawn out and symbolized by a person, but that implication may be sensed or felt from the innumerable small acts of neglect the person has experienced. The person may "know" it even if she or he has never symbolized it to him- or herself. Implications may never have been articulated because (a) the person may have never dwelt on them, (b) they may have been too implicit, or (c) it is too threatening to the individual's life adjustment to draw them.

Ecological Wisdom

People act on what they sense to be "ecologically wise" in terms of their current life space, systemic entanglements, constraints, and so on. People are always trying to find "paths" through these constraints—solutions that satisfy them. What they see as the "path out" from their point of view may make sense given how they experience the world but may be dysfunctional from an outside perspective. Defensive solutions, discussed later in this chapter, are often ecologically wise given the constraints the person is facing. We consider ecological wisdom in greater detail in chapter 8.

Coping

Coping depends on how a person's agendas and resources match up with personal and environmental constraints (Albee, 1982). Occasionally there is a perfect fit, but more often than not the match is only more or less close. This results in the need for continuous dialogue with the environment. As Kelly (1969) said, behavior is "asking a question." One behaves, asks a question, gets information, behaves again, and so on. In many cases, as individuals struggle to solve problems, all they achieve are partial solutions, which then become part of an ongoing solution process, like tacking in sailing. Once one has achieved a "solution," it does not mean the process is finished. One does not solve one's problems by communicating with one's spouse all at once and then be done with it.

The reason that solutions are often partial or difficult to come by is that in real life, solutions have to fit multiple constraints in the person's life space. A woman has the choice of staying with an abusive husband or taking her child and moving out to a life of almost complete poverty. A partial solution may be to move into a shelter, but that may create as many problems as it solves. A man may be depressed because while he has risen to the top of his profession, he is not happy in his community. He has struggled with his sexual identity for years and finally admitted to himself that he is gay. But his clients are all conservative religious businesspeople in a small town. He is married, has three children who go to the local school, two of whom are on the Little League team, and if he comes out he is afraid the whole structure of his life will be destroyed. Thus he is depressed and feels lonely and isolated.

In many cases, individuals are able to find solutions to their problems. A good solution is one that satisfies the constraints and allows them to move forward, creating new possibilities, that feed back and shift the constraints. A bad solution is one that keeps them stuck. We are tempted to suggest that clients who come to therapy are frequently those for whom the multiple conflicting life constraints have made problem solving difficult and complex.

Creation of Psychological Problems

Psychological problems arise when the person encounters a perceived obstacle in his or her life space, and when his or her own attempts to cope with the problem make the problem worse (Watzlawick et al., 1974). Psychological problems are paradoxically often the result of the individual's attempts to cope with a disruptive life event. Many psychological problems result from attempts to restore or preserve functioning, or at least to maintain some kind of status quo. A person experiences hyperventilation and dizziness in public and fears she is having a heart attack. To safeguard herself, she begins to watch her body very closely, and panics at the first sign of new symptoms, thereby creating a panic disorder. Then, to avoid having panic attacks in public, she stays at home. Phobias, panic disorders, and obsessive–compulsive disorders all have at their core some desire to cope with or avoid danger or threat (even if they are partially fueled by a biochemical imbalance). In fact, the very behaviors labeled as pathological in these cases are adaptive in other cases. These coping devices are attempts at restoration or preservation of functioning, only carried to an extreme. In this sense they are not unlike a high fever, which up to a point is restorative.

Dysfunctional behavior is thus an emergent from a whole life situation, including the person's biology, life history, and current circumstances. It involves an attempt to maintain or restore function, to live in an unlivable or unmanageable situation.

As such, clients' problems take considerable creativity. Clients with panic disorder creatively find ways of avoiding going out, and if they must go out, find ways of protecting themselves (such as by taking along a cellular phone, walking near railings, and so on). Alcoholic clients use considerable ingenuity to hide their drinking, explain it away, and mobilize significant others to take care of them. Clients with depression become very adept at inventively self-criticizing and at answering the arguments of those who try to convince them that everything is okay. Clients do a lot of inventive thinking. They are actually trying to invent their way out of problems, but paradoxically they dig themselves in deeper. It is precisely this capacity for creative thinking that therapy can mobilize and rechannel.

Within this context, therapy is itself a constraint changer. The very act of going to therapy changes a person's life space, independent of what the therapist does or does not do. Going to therapy, the person may begin to look at his or her life differently, for instance, even before he or she sees the therapist the first time.

Avoidance and Defense

The term *self-healing* implies that when there is some disruption in the integrity of the life process, individuals are built to begin the process of restoring that integrity, just as they try to self-heal when they are physically wounded. Individuals are active seekers who work to restore balances in their life space, repair pathways and trajectories, and find new pathways if old ones are blocked. This contrasts to views in which a motive to avoid is seen as fundamental and personality is largely viewed as a matter of defensive adjustment.

We are aware of the social psychological literature purporting to demonstrate that people have self-serving biases so that they distort evidence to protect their self-esteem or preserve consistency. However, we are also aware of the controversies over what the data mean (Feshbach, Weiner, & Bohart, 1996). People certainly do avoid painful truths in some circumstances. However, this does not mean they routinely or ubiquitously do this. Contrary to the argument that people live in a world of illusions built around the avoidance of painful truths, humans would not survive if they distorted reality that extensively. Reality is sufficiently malleable, and there are sufficiently many alternative ways of construing reality so that people can create many different ways of living life. But this is not the same as saying that they distort reality in any persistent fashion. Reality is certainly bent to meet their needs, but that is because reality is ambiguous. For the most part, it is not bent past the breaking point. People generally avoid painful truths only when it preserves some ecological balance in their life structure, allows them to fit their perceived constraints, and allows them to keep on functioning. For instance, a woman in a traditional marriage in a traditional culture may "deny" that her husband is cruel, but only because to acknowledge it given the constraints of her life structure would do her no good (she cannot leave anyway, so why focus on it?). To think that her husband is cruel when nothing can be done about it might be disruptive of her ability to live in the "unlivable" situation she is in. She might even be able to construe him as "good and kind" by focusing on the home he is giving her and her children. However, she could not deny, for instance, that he is her husband, without bringing grave consequences on her head. She cannot "distort" her beliefs that much. A basic postulate of ours is that people distort and avoid only insofar as it leads to a workable or viable accommodation with the perceived reality they live in. When it does not, they struggle to change. Sometimes this occurs because problems are created when there is a clash between entrenched avoidances and new life circumstances.

We are more impressed by people's tendency to confront and master problems, even when they involve pain. People only avoid pain when they feel inefficacious to deal with it (Bandura, 1997) or when they see no gain in confronting it. In fact, past hurts are held onto, not because the person has been avoiding confronting these past hurts and working them through, but because the person does not want to get hurt in a similar fashion in the future. The person is continuing to stay on guard for new dangers (Linehan, 1997).

NATURAL HEALING PROCESSES

When individuals confront major personal problems, what are some of the processes they engage in to resolve them? Prochaska and his colleagues (e.g., see Prochaska et al., 1994) have given one schematic of different strategies used by individuals to solve problems. We give our own, based on what we have observed in ourselves, friends, relatives, colleagues, and our clients. The various strategies we give overlap with one another and with the Prochaska list. They probably could be reduced to broader categories. But we did not want to do this because we believe their very specificity gives a better "feel for" how individuals actually solve problems. The following processes seem to be involved in self-healing and self-righting, no matter whether they are done on one's own or with the aid of a therapist: acceptance; attention shift; cessation of self-blame; patience; tolerating uncertainty and ambiguity; creative perseverance; not trying too hard; looking for other paths; goal evaluation; seeking for new perspectives; talking with others; building up one's skills; seeking out models; exposure; doing something different; adopting a metacognitive perspective; creativity; reframing; getting "outside" of oneself, getting a higher purpose, living for others, immersing oneself in a project one finds interesting and important; taking advantage of a change in circumstances; and trusting intuition. We briefly consider each of these below.

Acceptance

Acceptance can be broken into two subcategories: self-acceptance and acceptance of events (including people) in the world. Self-acceptance has been an aim of many psychotherapies, having been emphasized by psychodynamic, humanistic, and cognitive therapies. Those all assume that lack of acceptance of parts of oneself (in psychodynamic theories, lack of acceptance of certain wishes and motives; in humanistic theories lack of acceptance of the feeling side of the self) or of one's whole self (excessive self-blame, particularly emphasized by humanistic and cognitive therapies) blocks more effective proactive functioning.

Accepting events in the world also is a part of self-healing. This can include accepting the end of a relationship, accepting the presence of an illness (but continuing to cope nevertheless), accepting a death, or accepting inevitable imperfections in one's life. The "serenity prayer" used by Alcoholics Anonymous stresses the ability to accept what cannot be changed.

Acceptance is a goal of therapy, but acceptance is also a naturally occurring healing factor in everyday life. Couples often naturally learn to accept one another, people naturally learn to accept deaths and chronic illnesses, and many people even learn to accept themselves over time.

Acceptance is both a product and a process of self-healing, as are many of the other strategies we consider. One cannot just "decide" to accept. One can work at it, but it only comes with time. As it comes, the person's attention is freed up to turn to more productive pursuits. Conversely, as people get involved in more productive pursuits, acceptance often naturally comes.

Attention Shift

It has been argued by many (e.g., Todd & Bohart, 1994) that attentional shifts are a core component of therapeutic healing. People heal by shifting their attention from unproductive pursuits to more productive pursuits. Anything that leads the person to become "unstuck" from overfocusing on a problem may be therapeutic. As the person's attention is freed up to scan the problem situation more broadly, new solutions often present themselves. All therapies attempt to divert attention into productive pursuits, such as effective problem solving (see chapter 7). They also use a variety of techniques to "unfreeze" attention from an unproductive overfocus on the problem so that the client can begin the search for new, corrective information. Free association in classical psychoanalysis is a good example. In cognitive therapy, clients are instructed to pay attention to ignored corrective data. Behavior therapists encourage clients to keep daily records of the behavior to be changed. There is some reason to believe that shifting attention away from what one is accustomed to focusing on facilitates creativity (Ward et al., 1995) and insight (i.e., the attaining of new perspectives). The whole idea of the "incubation" effect in creativity is based on this: Stop thinking about the problem for a while and shift attention to other things, and you may suddenly or spontaneously notice something that gives you a new insight. Strategic therapists have built on this insight, and one of the goals of strategic procedures such as paradox and reframing is precisely to get the person outside or her old frame of reference so that he or she can now notice new ways of viewing problems.

Cessation of Self-Blame

The idea that self-blame is dysfunctional is found in most therapies. Outside of the field of psychotherapy, certain kinds of self-blame have been found to be associated with less effective functioning. Attributions of failure to stable internal characteristics such as a lack of ability have been found to paralyze achievement efforts (Weiner, 1986) and to be associated with pessimism and its negative correlates (Seligman, 1990). The problem with self-blame is that it (a) can be self-paralyzing and (b) distracts attention from work on problems and tasks.

On the other hand, some have argued that some types of self-blame may be less dysfunctional. For instance, Weiner (see Weiner, 1986) and his colleagues found that high achievers sometimes attribute failure to their own internal lack of effort, leading to a productive increase in effort. In a similar fashion, Janoff-Bulman (1989) argued that behavioral self-blame after a rape can help victims cope with the rape, whereas characterological self-blame is harmful (however, this has been disputed; see Frazier 1991). This is the same distinction that Weiner and his colleagues are making. Blaming oneself in a way that highlights aspects of the self that are controllable and changeable may be functional, whereas blaming aspects of the self that are seen as fixed and unchangeable may be paralyzing (Tallman, 1996). Similarly, Tangney (in press) found that guilt (i.e., feeling that one has behaved badly) is not nearly so paralyzing as shame (believing that one is a bad person because one has behaved badly). In sum, ceasing to blame oneself, at least in the characterological sense, seems to be an important positive problem-solving strategy.

Patience

Patience goes along with acceptance. Sometimes persons must patiently accept and live with a bad state of affairs until they are able to change it, or until it changes. Patience is essentially taught by a variety of therapies. Patience is directly encouraged in cognitive therapy, in which, for instance, clients are taught to accept feelings of anxiety while they are learning how to deal with them. Patience is modeled in client-centered and psychodynamic therapies, in that solutions are not immediately presented but instead clients are encouraged to keep on living while they work on their problems.

Tolerating Uncertainty and Ambiguity

Closely associated with patience is tolerating uncertainty and ambiguity until problems work themselves out. Premature jumping to solutions and premature closure often do not solve the problem and can create new problems. It is said that those diagnosed with borderline personality disorder are often "impulsive." In our experience this impulsiveness is often the result of an inability to tolerate uncertainty. The person prematurely leaps to solutions out of feelings of desperation and anxiety, and often these "solutions" create new problems.

Creative Perseverance

Perseverance is closely related to patience but includes the idea of continued active effort to overcome problems. Perseverance is "staying with it" even though it may not initially look promising. There is a difference between functional and dysfunctional perseverance. Functional perseverance involves creative persistence at a task. This means that one thoughtfully varies one's strategies and tries to learn from failure. One does not get too discouraged when it does not too quickly yield to solution. One stays with the problem until one finds some way of mastering it. Mastery may mean actually solving the problem, or it may mean that one learns that one can live with it or successfully live "around it" (i.e., that it won't "kill you"). Dysfunctional perseverance is characteristic of those who feel helpless (see chapter 7) and is characterized by rigid perseveration—doing the same thing over and over even though it is not working.

Not Trying Too Hard

Not trying too hard is a strategy defined negatively. People often create problems by trying too hard. Sexual dysfunctions are an example of this, but so is trying too hard to please a spouse, trying too hard to do everything perfectly, and so on. The old idea that thinking too much about what one is doing can sabotage oneself is an example of this. Not trying too hard is not the opposite of perseverance. One can persevere in a steadily working way, whereas trying too hard has a kind of frantic, rushed quality to it, an almost desperate quality. Trying too hard is often a product of overfocusing on the outcome of problem resolution, rather than on the process (see chapter 7).

Looking for Other Paths

Looking for other paths means standing back and looking for alternative ways of solving a problem. Nickerson (1994) called this the *means–end analysis*. It is the essence of creative problem solving in which one steps back and does not persist in the same old strategy but searches for new or alternative strategies.

Goal Evaluation

One may also stand back and reevaluate one's goals. One may decide that the path one has been traveling on, even if it is going in the direction one has chosen in a fairly smooth way, is not where one wants to end up.

Seeking New Perspectives

Overall, this means seeking to find new and more fruitful ways of construing one's problems. It can include an active search, or it can consist of keeping one's attention open for new information. It goes hand in hand with attention shifts. In solution-focused therapy, for instance, clients are encouraged to remember past successes as a way of getting them unstuck from their current overly negative perspective.

This strategy also goes along with patience and creative perseverance in that one must be continually open to information that may make a difference. Serendipity was not something that just happened to the person who discovered penicillin. Serendipity is a common aspect of problem solving. If one is open, one may just happen to see the job advertised or hear someone express an idea that fits with the problem one is trying to solve, or notice something different in one's environment that precipitates change. Getting clients to openly pay attention is a key part of solution-focused therapy (De Shazer, 1985) in that people often overlook exceptions to the rule when they are stuck in a problem, when noticing the exceptions might help them find a way out. Often one may be able to do nothing at the present time but openly pay attention, being alert for opportunities for change.

Talking With Others

One of the major ways people self-heal is through talking with others, including therapists. With good listeners, people get a chance to think their problems through. Furthermore, there is something relieving about the simple act of sharing problems with another. For one thing, one often learns one is not alone. People can sometimes get helpful advice from others, or a new perspective as well. Often they get support to persist and carry on. We discuss how self-disclosing to another mobilizes self-healing processes in detail in chapter 5.

Building Up One's Skills

People may decide that they need skills in an area and set out to get them. To improve their social life, they may develop their skills for enhancing their appearance and for conversation. They may learn how to dance. They may talk to friends to get ideas about what to try to enhance their love life, and they may then practice and refine these skills on their own. They may also develop their skills with the aid of self-help books.

Modeling

When a person is struggling with a problem, they may seek out models. They may copy how their friends cope with problems. They may use models from television or literature. Talking with friends is often a key source of information for modeling.

Exposure

Exposure is confronting and directly experiencing one's problem and, through a direct experiential confrontation, learning how to master it. Exposure, in everyday life and in psychotherapy, appears to be one of the most important ways people have of mastering fears. It did not take behavior therapists to think of this; as Efran and Blumberg (1994) noted, people have been counseling others who have been thrown off horses to "get right back up" for centuries. The Cowardly Lion in *The Wizard of Oz* is the prototypical individual who learns through exposure and mastery. Because he must for the sake of his friend Dorothy, he faces up to his fears.

Under the generic concept of exposure, we include putting one's attention into the event of strong emotion. Putting oneself in the event of strong emotion is a common therapeutic process, occurring in Mahrer's (1996) experiential therapy, Rice and Saperia's (1984) "problematic reaction point" procedure, Freud's original work with Breuer (Breuer & Freud, 1895/1955), and F. Shapiro's eye movement desensitization (1995). These different processes may all work differently, but what they all have in common is putting oneself in a scene with strong emotion, and then tracking and following that scene until one makes discoveries. It is likely that people do this spontaneously in everyday life if they are lucky enough to talk over a problem with an empathic friend while the feelings are "fresh" and "hot" and the friend does not give too much advice that might shut down the tracking process.

Doing Something Different

Ultimately, with De Shazer (1985), we believe that this is the core of all change activity. It is through doing something differently that one's attention shifts, one is able to gain new perspectives, one is able to have a mastery experience, and so on. Doing something different is also liable to lead to new information that can lead to a shift in strategy. This is often used in everyday life— the person may try to "get away from it all" for a while or try out a new hobby. It is often prescribed by sex therapists, who may encourage clients to try a romantic evening or to go away on a vacation. The insight here is that clients are often stuck in dysfunctional repetitive problem-solving cycles.

Adopting a Metacognitive Perspective

One way to handle problems is to adopt a metacognitive perspective on them. There are various metacognitive perspectives that one might adopt that might be helpful. One may realize that one's problems are not *oneself* (Duncan et al., 1997; Gendlin, 1981). Or one may realize that having problems is normal and problems can actually be used to strengthen one's life (e.g., Wile, 1981). Psychoanalysis encourages the metacognitive perspective that it is normal to have an infantile side of oneself. Christians adopt the metacognitive perspective that they are imperfect creatures, although they are "forgiven."

The key insight is that people often turn "problems" into "Problems" by catastrophizing about them, by negatively judging themselves *because* they have problems (i.e., are not perfect), and by otherwise overreacting to the existence of problems, which are a normal part of life. This gets in the way of proactively focusing on what can be done to promote problem solving and creative coping.

Most approaches to therapy encourage the client to adopt the metacognitive perspective of the impartial observer, or in other words, to dis-identify with the problem. Cognitive–behavioral therapists encourage clients to simply observe their anxiety, let it be, and shift their attention to more life-enhancing behaviors (e.g., Beck, Emery, & Greenberg, 1985; Schwartz, 1997); psychoanalysts encourage free association; and humanistic therapists encourage allowing and accepting of feelings. The meditational stance of the mindful observer may be a therapeutic common factor, encouraged by many different approaches (Martin, 1997).

Creativity

Some personal problems are literally solved, or the process of resolution is started, by creatively coming up with new solutions or new ways of being and behaving. The case we cited in our introduction of the paranoid woman spontaneously deciding to help someone else whom she perceived as feeling paranoid, thus starting a process of active involvement and engagement with others, is an example. The case of Molly (Duncan et al., 1997, cited at the beginning of chapter 1) is another example of someone coming up with her own creative solution.

Reframing

Closely allied to creativity is the strategy of reframing. Reframing involves finding something positive in the problem. The bumper sticker that says "Anything that doesn't kill you makes you stronger" is an example. Many people with life-threatening illnesses have found that they have a new appreciation for life, and come to live it more on a moment-by-moment basis.

Getting "Outside" of Oneself

This includes getting a higher purpose, living for others, and immersing oneself in a project one finds interesting and important. This is also associated with creativity and reframing. For example, sometimes individuals self-heal by helping others. They may volunteer at a hospital, or to help the homeless, or at the local school. One older woman we know helped herself overcome depression by volunteering to be a playground monitor at the local school.

Taking Advantage of a Change in Circumstances

While not a magical panacea, sometimes changes in circumstances can promote positive change. For people with alcoholism, finding new ways home, not stopping at the local bar, and investing in other activities may promote positive coping. This is what Prochaska et al. (1994) called *contingency management*. We have already seen that for some, entering the armed services was beneficial (Elder, 1986). Sometimes it is not so much that one changes one's circumstances as that they are changed. Then it is taking advantage of the change to make personal changes. In one case we know of, an older man took the opportunity of moving to another state to live with his adult daughter to quit drinking.

Trusting Intuition

People often "know more than they can say" about their problems. Learning how to use intuition is increasingly becoming a major problem-solving strategy in business (Agor, 1989). In psychology the idea is reflected in the idea of "trusted feelings," more typically advocated by humanistic therapists. Trusting feelings does not mean trusting *emotions*, but rather feelings that have to do with sensing patterns or relationships, such as "feeling something is wrong in the relationship," "having a feeling that something is going on," and so on (Bohart, 1993). Being aware of this kind of feeling is a common experience (Browner, Muscatine, & Bohart, 1993). Trusting feelings or intuitions means taking seriously the "funny feelings" that one might have about what is going on, or the feeling of a new direction to go in that may not on the surface seem logical or promising.

For instance, Gayle (see Bohart, 1995b) had an uneasy feeling that something was wrong in her relationship. However, both her husband and her psychiatrist discounted this uneasy feeling, the husband asserting that he loved her, and the psychiatrist asserting that this feeling was a residual from her unloving relationship with her father. In fact, months later, the husband admitted that he had been having an affair for a long time, and that he wanted a divorce so that he could move in with his mistress. Gayle's inability to trust her feelings, buttressed by the psychiatrist's dismissal of them, led to months of depression because she concluded that there must be something wrong with her to have this feeling in the first place. Interestingly, when her husband finally admitted he was having an affair, her depression vanished.

Trusting intuitions, however, does not mean mechanistically following them. Intuitions can be wrong, and one can misinterpret them. Effective problem solving involves both thoughtful, logical analysis and intuition, in both business and clinical psychology (e.g., Caspar, 1997).

Conclusion

The foregoing provisional list of problem-solving strategies is derived from both our experiences in therapy and our everyday life experiences. It is not exhaustive (there may be almost as many strategies as there are psychotherapies!) but includes a variety of strategies that we believe are used in everyday life as well as in therapy. These strategies feed into one another, and they are both *processes* and *outcomes* of the struggle to self-right and self-heal. Thus one cannot just choose to come up with a creative solution. One may have to be patient and persevere until a creative solution presents itself. A creative solution itself may then feed into further problem-solving efforts.

Next we consider several cases of persons self-healing and self-righting without (or mostly without) the aid of mental health professionals. We use these cases to illustrate some of the principles we have considered previously.

CASES OF SELF-HEALING

The cases presented next are fictionalized accounts of people we have known in various walks of life. We present the cases, and then discuss how they illustrate some of the ideas presented in this chapter.

Depression: Sarah

Sarah became depressed when her marriage ended. She had been a traditional housewife when her physician husband left her for a younger woman. Sarah got a reasonable settlement after a bitter court battle, though her standard of living did fall. She had to move out of the fancy house in the exclusive neighborhood and move to a condominium in a decent but less exclusive neighborhood. Her friends had mostly been through her husband and his connections, so she found that she lost most of her network of friends as well. The children were grown and, while supportive, were angry with both her and their father for getting divorced. Furthermore, they had their own lives and so were unable to provide extensive or sustained support for her.

Sarah felt abandoned and cast upon the scrap heap, as if she no longer had any value. She felt as if her identity had been completely stripped away. She felt like her whole life was a waste—she had bet it on an illusion.

Sarah went through a period of major depression. She was not completely immobilized, but she cried a lot, often for no reason, she overate, and she had trouble sleeping. She felt suicidal, but she said her religious beliefs kept her from doing anything. Sarah's initial solution was to go back to school and to some kind of career. The trouble was that she felt old, overweight, unattractive, and stupid. She had not been in school for 30 years and had never finished college. Now she had to go back and practically start over. She felt out of place and different compared with the other students.

Initially Sarah was defeated by every little thing. If her car broke down, she broke down. When she misplaced a textbook, she went into a major panic. She got through by calling friends and, for a while, taking medication. Medication seemed to help for a while, but Sarah didn't like the effect it created and so she gave it up. She still retained a few women friends from the old days, and she turned repeatedly to them and to her own mother. For a while she had quite a telephone bill. At first the talking had to do with her marriage—what had she done wrong? Why had this happened? As she talked it out with her friends, her perspective gradually shifted from a focus on her ("I'm no good") to "He's a cad." As her rage consolidated toward her ex-husband, she felt a temporary lifting of her spirits. This did not last long, however, as thinking negatively of him ultimately made her feel helpless.

In the meantime she found herself to be doing well in school. The university she attended had a night program and a considerable number of older students. She met, and bonded with, some older women who were returning to school either because their children had grown up and they wanted something to do or because they, like her, had been unceremoniously abandoned by their husbands. The support she got from them made her feel better. She realized she wasn't alone, and by observing others, she realized that life was not hopeless and over. Whereas she had felt fat and unattractive, around all the older students she realized that many didn't have the "ideal young body" and that she wasn't all that bad! As she began to worry less about this, she eventually got involved in an exercise program with some of her friends and began to lose some of the weight. Eventually she also became involved in campus activities and became the head of the undergraduate association. Through all this, her depression gradually lifted.

How did Sarah overcome her depression? It lifted as she continued to explore to find some meaning in her life. She did not intellectually figure out a new identity, but gradually, by immersing herself in a new life, she acquired a new sense of place and purpose in the world. We briefly categorize the natural self-healing strategies she used:

Acceptance: Sarah gradually came to accept both herself and the loss of her old life.

Attention shift: Sarah gradually shifted her attention from the loss of her old life to her new activities. Instead of concentrating on her loss, she gradually found her attention more and more consumed by school and her new life.

Cessation of self-blame: Sarah moved from blaming herself for the breakup of her marriage to blaming her husband and then to forgetting blame and focusing her efforts on building her life. She also stopped picking on her appearance.

Finding other paths: This was her major strategy. By choosing to go back to school, Sarah embedded herself in a potential "healing context"— a context that provided many opportunities for self-healing.

Patience: Despite many moments of despair and self-doubt, by being patient, Sarah eventually "came out the other end" of her depression and found a new, positive life structure.

Searching for new perspectives: Sarah kept her eyes and ears open and thus gradually found opportunities to move in more proactive directions. She also learned that she was not unique in feeling that she was over-weight, and through a process of social comparison began to feel better about herself. By talking with her friends, Sarah explored new perspectives on the loss of her marriage.

Perseverance: Sarah persevered. Despite her depression she stayed in life and continued to work and to function. She kept her eyes on the tasks—doing well in school and meeting her obligations.

Talking with others: A major self-healing strategy for Sarah was talking with her friends. This facilitated the development of new perspectives, attention shifts, and cessation of self-blame. In addition, her friends gave her support that helped her stay with her new path.

Building up skills: In school, Sarah developed a host of new skills that made her feel more competent, efficacious, and useful.

Exposure: Through talking to her friends, Sarah repeatedly exposed herself to the trauma of the loss. This, in conjunction with taking other proactive steps, helped her finally let go of her old life and develop a new one.

Choosing to help others: Sarah ultimately invested herself in helping others. This went a long way to helping her establish a new identity and finally let go of the old one.

In sum, Sarah used a variety of strategies, many of which fed into one another, ultimately leading to her overcoming her depression and creating a new life for herself.

Alcoholism: Jim

Jim was a 40-year-old college professor. He had been a heavy drinker for years. His wife had periodically complained, but she came out of a subculture where drinking was a part of life, so she did not really feel she had a right to complain. Jim, while having doubts himself, would argue that after all he only drank at night after work. He would go to the local pub and have several beers with friends and talk. Then he would come home and have several scotches until it was time to go to bed. He rarely got "falling-down drunk" and was not abusive when he was drinking. Most of the time his drinking presented no major problem for anyone. However, once he did get so drunk he passed out when his wife was away and he was supposed to be babysitting their 5-year-old son. She had come home and found him on the couch. Fortunately, the son was blissfully asleep, but nonetheless the situation was dangerous.

Jim defended his drinking but nevertheless tried cutting down. He tried limiting himself to only two drinks a night. The he tried switching to wine or beer. In all cases, this would work for a short while, but eventually he would be back to his old ways. Several times, over a 5-year period, he tried quitting altogether. Once he quit for 9 months. Then, at a party where everyone was drinking, he decided it would be safe to have a drink or two. He was soon back to his old ways.

Finally, when he was 40, he went to get a physical examination. He was told that his blood sugar was dangerously high. There were cases of diabetes in his family. This scared him. He realized that he really wanted to live to see his son grow up. He also realized that he had been letting his career slip over the last several years. He realized that there were books he wanted to write. He made an appointment at a local alcoholism treatment center and went to their orientation meeting. He did not like the psychiatrist he met with that night, but the psychiatrist gave him Antabuse. He tried Antabuse for a few days but decided he wanted to quit on his own. He stopped the Antabuse and stopped drinking, without further professional assistance. He has stayed sober for over 14 years.

How did he do it? Most basically, Jim had a perspective shift. While before he had been thinking that he *should* stop, he discovered that he *wanted* to stop because of his child. Jim discovered this through repeated efforts at changing, until he ran into a reason that he felt was personally compelling. Then he began to actively work at changing: avoiding the pub after work, spending more time with his wife and child, and immersing himself in writing his new book. His attention gradually shifted away from his old ways of being and he was able to "let go" of his old life style.

Posttraumatic Stress: Lucy

Lucy was in an automobile accident in which a big-rig truck lost control and smashed into her vehicle. Because she had her seatbelt on, she was not severely injured. However, for months afterward she had flashbacks of the accident and was terrified of driving. Lucy overcame this on her own by forcing herself to drive. Initially she avoided the freeway and got comfortable on surface streets. Then she braved the freeway. At first, she stayed far away from trucks but eventually forced herself to confront driving near them as well. Over a period of months, she overcame her fears, although she still occasionally feels anxious when she sees a truck. The primary methods Lucy used to self-heal were patience, persistence, and exposure.

Anxiety: Don

Don was a graduate student in biochemistry. He was close to starting his dissertation. He had passed all but one of the necessary qualifying exams with flying colors. However, now, as he faced preparing for the last qualifying exam, he began to experience severe anxiety. At first he could not identify the reason. As he frantically thought about it and talked to friends, the source of his conflict began to become clear. Don's family had always wanted him to get a PhD and become a scientist, and Don, without thinking, had adopted that as a career path. However, Don was beginning to have a funny feeling that he did not want to be a scientist. This funny feeling made no sense to him. He had always thought he had wanted to get his PhD in biochemistry and become a famous research scientist. As it came down to the end, though, he suddenly began to experience resistance to finishing. He began to go through an extreme period of self-evaluation and self-doubt, accompanied by chronic, intense, and overwhelming anxiety.

Don coped with this dilemma by talking it over and over with his friends. He was stuck in a kind of endless either or cycle. On the one hand he thought, why not finish the degree? It would be easy for him—he was an excellent student and had already done significant research. Then he could do anything he wanted. On the other hand he thought, I don't want the PhD. Around and around he would go, feeling anxious, and then eventually, depressed and suicidal as well.

Finally, Don decided he was going to commit to graduate school. But that lasted only a few days. Instead, Don then decided to go in the opposite direction and take an "existential leap." He dropped out of school and accepted a job teaching high school. The school was desperate for teachers, and because of his background was willing to hire him on a temporary basis. Within a month the anxiety and depression had vanished. Don decided to continue on his new path and returned to school, only now to get a teaching credential. When one of us last talked with him, a year or so later, he was happy and contented.

What did Don do to self-heal and self-right? First of all, he continued to struggle. Second, he extensively used talking to friends to help him think through the two sides of the dilemma. For a while this was apparently unproductive as it seemed as if all he did was go around in circles. But even this ultimately was productive because at some point Don had an insight: Talking was ultimately not getting him anywhere. He was going to have to make a choice. When he really seriously contemplated committing to graduate school, he became more experientially and vividly aware that that simply did not *feel right* to him—it did not fit. He had to expose himself to the choice, almost make it, and then vicariously experience it, to discover that that did not feel right. Then, despite its being frightening, he decided to drop out of school. As he began to be more proactive, to face up to his parents, and to actually enact his choice by seeking a job teaching, his anxiety and depression vanished. Don had to accept who he was, accept that he was not going to please his parents, and accept that he might be making an irrevokable change in his life path.

Don is a case in which "trusting his feelings" or his intuitions as to what was right for him was part of the ultimate solution to his problem.

Psychosis: Walt

Walt was an artist who had grown up in the 1960s. He had always been a seeker of personal transformation. During the 1960s, he was an LSD user. Through this, Walt became a spiritual person and continued his seeking through an interest in transpersonal philosophies and experiences. He gave up the use of LSD but for many years continued to meditate, to read and study, and to go to various retreats and workshops. Meanwhile he made a living as a potter.

When Walt was 35 he attended a particularly intense weekend workshop, where the leader used meditation and a variety of other activities to help individuals attain higher planes of consciousness. As Walt left the workshop on Sunday he felt lightheaded and a bit strange. The next day he began to have intense psychoticlike experiences. Colors and sound seemed unusually intense. Walt felt strange and cut off from others, and felt that he was indeed living on a higher plane of consciousness. He also heard voices, mostly low mumbles and rumbles, but some of the comments seemed vaguely persecutory. He also had vague visual hallucinations, seemingly flashbacks to his LSD experiences of long ago.

Walt knew that he was having a psychoticlike experience, and this frightened him. However, he did not want to go to a psychiatrist, possibly be hospitalized, or be given drugs he did not approve of. Rather, he preferred the idea of getting some spiritual counseling. While his subjective life felt bizarre and strange, Walt was able to carry out his work as a potter. So, although he was frightened, he saw no reason to panic. However, he was not sure which spiritual teacher to approach. The one who had run the workshop he had attended was in another state. In the meantime, he was talking to his friends. One of them suggested that Walt turn his experience into art. Walt began to do a series of sculptures that expressed his feelings and experiences. Through this series of sculptures, he began to deal with the themes that had been driving his whole life—finding himself, making peace with who he was, and so on. His psychoticlike symptoms gradually abated and disappeared, and Walt ultimately felt more creative and more at peace with himself than he ever had before. Also, his sculptures sold—he felt more fulfilled as an artist than ever.

What helped Walt was first his metacognitive awareness that his problem was manageable. Walt did not panic. Instead, he spontaneously used a strategy advocated by therapists of all persuasions: allow strange experiences to be *as* you carry on with your life. In essence, it is a kind of exposure in which you learn that you can live and manage even in the face of highly discomforting experiences. It even could have been a kind of spontaneous use of the kind of exposure process used in cognitive–behavioral therapy to overcome traumatic experiences that may lead to flashbacks.

In addition, Walt used a kind of spontaneous reframing of the incident. By viewing the experience as something out of which to make art, he focused on it as something useful and informative rather than something awful or wrong. He was able to thus use the experience to gain insight and come to peace with various aspects of his life he had never come to peace with before. He realized, not unlike Washburn's (1988) views of attaining transcendence, that one sometimes had to experience a "dark night of the soul" to move upward. Thus Walt also sought for and experienced a perspective shift.

CONCLUSION

In this chapter, we have considered how people can self-right and self-heal in everyday life. In our view,

- People continually change throughout life, if only in small ways. Most of the time people only make small changes in their ways of being in the world, fine-tuning their personalities, values, and strategies for coping. But sometimes, especially under prolonged stress, they may make major second-order changes.

- People use ideas and concepts as tools. Concepts are not fixed but are continuously and inventively being modified to help individuals cope. People are continuously creative in small ways in everyday life.
- Psychological problems arise when people's coping skills and abilities are unable to handle problems and obstacles that confront them in their life space. Psychological problems are in part a creative, proactive effort to restore or preserve some degree of functional adaptation to the world.
- People continually cope with problems. Many problems and threats to the integrity of the person's ability to cope are solved by individuals themselves, using natural self-healing processes.
- These processes include acceptance; attention shift; cessation of self-blame; patience; creative perseverance; not trying too hard; looking for other paths; goal evaluation; seeking new perspectives; discussing with others; building up one's skills; seeking out models; exposure; doing something different; adopting a metacognitive perspective; creativity; reframing; getting "outside" of oneself, getting a higher purpose, living for others, immersing oneself in a project one finds interesting and important; taking advantage of a change in circumstances; and trusting intuition.

However, people do not always manage to self-heal on their own. In the next chapter, we begin our examination of psychotherapy and consider the obstacles to self-healing that may lead individuals to seek psychotherapeutic help.

II

WHEN SELF-HEALING FAILS

4

SELF-HEALING WITH A THERAPIST

We have three goals in this chapter. Our first is to examine why clients may need the assistance of therapy. Our second goal is to describe what therapeutic change means from the standpoint of the client as active self-healer. Our third goal is to elaborate on what *we* mean by the client as an active self-healer, in contrast to other possible interpretations.

OBSTACLES TO SELF-HEALING: WHY DO CLIENTS COME TO THERAPY?

If clients have so much self-healing potential, why do they need therapy? The answer is twofold: Either their natural environment does not provide sufficient support or resources for self-healing or their ways of coping and self-healing are insufficient to deal with the problems they are trying to overcome. Outside help becomes necessary when individuals have exhausted their own self-healing capacities or resources or when they are not working (Norcross & Aboyoun, 1994). Why might this be so?

First, on the basis of the research on resilience, some individuals may have more obstacles to overcome. Some may have biologically based problems or impediments that place great demands on their self-healing capacities. Others may have had childhoods in which they learned coping strategies that are highly dysfunctional, strategies that not only create problems for them but also get in the way of self-healing. Severe self-criticism is a good example. Similarly, others have had childhoods in which they failed to learn skills, learned to feel helpless, and failed to develop feeling of self-efficacy. They too may be defeated before they start when confronted with a problem that persistently defies resolution.

None of these factors, however, mean that these individuals are incapable of self-healing. To the contrary, as Rosenbaum (1996) pointed out, even clients with severely disabling problems have usually managed to live a life more successful than not. Within the limitations of their life histories, their biologies, and their environments, they have managed to make enough adjustments in life to reach adulthood and to make it to the therapist's office. Even individuals with severe panic disorder who do not leave the house have managed to find a way of living a somewhat livable life while living with their fear—by staying at home. Thus, when these individuals come to therapy, they must also be seen as capable of self-healing and of having succeeded at least to some degree in so doing. Within their strategies and views of the world, they have self-righted as best they could.

Second, there may be a host of specific obstacles to self-healing that clients confront. Next, we catalog some of them.

Helpless Mind-Set or Low Self-Efficacy

As we discuss more fully in chapter 7, some self-defeating behaviors are the result of a self-defeating mind-set, called variously pessimism (Seligman, 1990), low self-efficacy (Bandura, 1997), or an outcome-focused state of mind (Tallman, 1996). If the problem is difficult, and the individuals have repeatedly failed in attempts to resolve it, they may believe they are unable to solve it and begin to experience helplessness (Dweck & Leggett, 1988; Tallman, 1996). Their sense of self-efficacy (Bandura, 1997) erodes. They may use a pessimistic explanatory style to deal with their failures, attributing their failures to global, stable aspects of themselves (Seligman, 1990). They then may prematurely give up. Or they begin to perseverate in their solutions even if they are not working. Or they try new solutions, but in a haphazard, random, or desperate fashion. They begin to defensively avoid the problem. They may blame themselves and feel helpless, or they blame others and feel helpless. This will be especially likely to happen if the problem is occurring in an area in which they have not previously felt efficacious or in which they are afraid to appear incompetent. When individuals feel helpless, threatened, frightened, or on the defensive, they may also rush into short-term, premature, and ineffective solutions, which then create further problems. Thus a young woman growing up in an emotionally abusive home may rush into a premature, ill-conceived marriage to escape. This perpetuates her feeling helpless and trapped, and she may need to come to therapy to attain a sense of hope and confidence that she can make proactive changes in her life.

Ruminative Thinking

Individuals under stress can get trapped in unproductive ruminative thinking (Pennebaker, 1995). High stress can narrow focus so that individuals are unable to "step back" and gain the distance and perspective that might lead to productive insights or perspective shifts. Instead they go over and over the same territory from the same vantage point.

Crisis

Individuals will also be less likely to be able to self-heal on their own if they are so overwhelmed by stress that they enter into a crisis state. In a crisis state, they may not be able to calm themselves sufficiently to be able to engage in the stepwise process of problem solving and mastery. This, again, will be particularly likely if the individual has not had a great deal of luck in solving problems in the particular area in which the problem is occurring, that is, in which they are likely to feel helpless, inefficacious, or low in feelings of mastery.

Failure to Think Creatively

Humans tend to use old knowledge to solve new problems (Ward et al., 1995). This may be dysfunctional when creativity is needed. As Ward et al. noted, creativity is needed precisely when the problem is ambiguous, as are most problems that individuals bring to therapy. Yet, under high enough stress, it is just then that individuals often come more rigid and conservative in holding on to their old ways of ing things.

Lack of Resources

All of these ineffectual ways of problem solving are exacerbated by a lack of resources in the individual's environment (Hobfall, 1989), such as social support networks, time and space for problem solving, and information. We consider each of these in turn.

Social Support Networks

A particularly important resource is a good social support network. Good social support networks provide many functions, such as babysitting so someone can go to work, getting a ride when one's car breaks down, or financial aid in a crisis. Of particular importance is the presence of people who will listen and provide emotional support. Individuals who have good support systems experience lower levels of stress, and thus are more likely to be able to engage in their own self-healing. Yet even when people have someone they can talk to, few have people who are willing to really listen in a way that facilitates self-healing (Carkhuff & Berenson, 1967; Stiles, 1995) when different personal issues present themselves.

Social support is one important resource that can help reduce clients' need for therapy. On the other hand, it has been argued that clients who come to therapy are those who cannot avail themselves of their support networks, because they fear intimacy, or because of early childhood damage in attachment relationships that leads them to misperceive the availability of support. In other words, it is because of the client's *deficits* (which presumably they need the therapist to fix) that they cannot avail themselves of natural support.

We do not preclude the possibility that some clients are less adept at availing themselves of support than others. However, those who blame clients for this may be overestimating availability of support. Stiles (1995) argued that few people in the natural environment will empathically listen for more than 20 minutes. When this was mentioned to one of our clients, that client exclaimed, "Hah! Five minutes is more like it." Yet that client reported that she had people to "talk to." Carkhuff and Berenson (1967) found that the average level of facilitative conditions provided by the person on the street was less than that needed to be even minimally helpful. We have observed beginning counselors (undergraduates in a human service program or beginning graduate students) in role-playing exercises often barrage clients with advice, rather than carefully, empathically listen. If this is what people typically get in their everyday life (and we believe it is), it is not surprising that some have trouble availing themselves of what may appear to be available support, especially with complex and difficult personal issues.

It may be that those who feel a sense of self-efficacy or who adopt a mastery approach to their problem (chapter 7) are able to use barrages of advice or even criticism productively, because they will focus on the information value of what they are being told. Individuals who feel vulnerable, helpless, low in self-efficacy, or are focused on their lack of self-worth may take barrages of advice and criticism in a more personal fashion and thus not be able to use the information in a task-oriented fashion. Thus they may be less willing to approach their networks because they sense that what they need is not there. They quite sanely may be aware that what they need to help themselves self-heal is not available in their personal networks. It is not merely a matter of misperceiving support that is available. Often genuine support at a sufficient level of complexity really is not available.

Time, Space, and Permission

Another major resource that may not be available is the presence of time, space, and permission for productive problem solving. To break out of a ruminative cycle, people may find it helpful to gain some distance and perspective on the problem. However, they are not always able to do this in everyday life. At home or at work, the problem stares them in the face. Their life consumes them, and they simply do not have the mental or emotional time or "space" to truly stand back. Talking to friends, colleagues, lovers, or relatives might not help because they may themselves be too close to the problem. It may help to talk to someone completely outside of the loop, as long as that person provides the time, space, and permission for the client to work on themselves.

Information

Information is another resource that may not be available to individuals in their natural environments. Information can include knowledge of and access to self-help books. It can also include simple social comparison information. A client comes into sex therapy because he believes there is something wrong with him (or his wife, or their relationship). His wife does not have orgasms through intercourse, no matter how hard they have tried. Learning that this is normal can be therapeutic.

Therapists may sometimes provide information to clients that other people have been lucky enough to acquire from significant others in their natural environments. A young man in his first sexual encounter may experience problems with premature ejaculation. If his partner is experienced and patient, she may provide not only the support necessary for spontaneous recovery, but also information and guidance sufficient for the problem to be cured naturally.

Similarly, a person may need to come to a therapist if they have never observed a good problem-solving model, such as a parent or a spouse or a friend who has coped with a problem similar to the one the individual is coping with. The presence of such a model can facilitate self-healing. For instance, a parent who struggled during her first semester in college may be able to provide support and model ideas and strategies for a child who is struggling during her first semester. Absence of a good model, combined with criticism or lack of support, may make the problem worse, leading the individual to seek out therapy.

Wanting Expert Validation

Some people probably do better solving their problems in an interpersonal context, rather than through the use of self-help techniques. If this is their preferred problem-solving style, through interpersonal dialogue, then they may naturally perfer turning to another person, and they may have been unable to turn to people in their own environment. Some problems particularly demand feedback from other people. This may be the case if the person is having trouble knowing the reality of their own feelings and perceptions, or want feedback on the appropriateness and usefulness of their behavioral strategies. It may also be that there are occasions when they want expert feedback, such as about divorce, relationships, or sex. This may occur because they are having difficulty trusting their own decision-making processes.

Inhibiting Environments

As many writers have pointed out (Landrine, 1992; O'Hara, 1997), Western culture is highly individualistic. This leads us to minimize environmental obstacles. Although the *Diagnostic and Statistical Manual of Mental Disorders* (4th ed., *DSM–IV*; American Psychiatric Association, 1994) has an axis that is supposed to take psychosocial factors into account, the fundamental philosophy of the *DSM* is individualistic: The *individual* has the disorder. In contrast, systemic views would suggest that it is *person– environment interactions* that have problems, not persons. We believe this is often the case. Often the problem is that the environment is (a) actively supporting dysfunctional behavior and not promoting self-healing behavior or (b) actively interfering with self-healing. It will be harder for an alcoholic to stop drinking, for instance, if (a) it is an integral part of his work life (as it often is for salespeople, sports writers, athletes, and so on) or (b) it is an integral part of his relaxation patterns (friends, after-hours bars, etc.). Agoraphobic individuals may be supported by their "accomplices" (to use Wachtel's (1993) term), who may inadvertently reinforce dysfunctional patterns.

Interfering Beliefs

There are a number of beliefs that can interfere with self-healing. We review them next.

Believing There Is Something Wrong With Oneself

A major obstacle to generation of productive solutions is a belief that there is something fundamentally wrong with oneself (e.g., Seligman, 1990). Those who believe this either do not search for solutions or do not stick with solutions that might work because they feel doomed and helpless. The individual may try a solution once, and when it does not work the first or the second time, give it up. For instance, to get over premature ejaculation, one must systematically engage in something like the stop–

start technique, deliberately slowing down and stopping. An individual might spontaneously try this, but when it does not work after one trial he will not persistently stay with it. He may conclude there is nothing he can do about the problem because there is something wrong with him and that he must see a specialist. Similarly, a person with poor social skills could possibly learn them on his or her own. However, such learning requires a good deal of practice. A person who thinks his or her social failures mean there is something wrong with him- or herself will get discouraged by initial failures and give up prematurely.

Believing That the Force of Hard Work Will Fix Everything

Another belief that may sometimes block finding a problem's solution is the belief that hard work and trying is all that is required to fix a problem. Such a belief can preclude an open, exploratory attitude that might lead to the discovery of new, healing experiences. This belief functions in a manner reminiscent of ruminative thinking, in that the individual blindly persists in trying, believing that sheer force of will will fix the problem. A man with an erection problem may try to fix it by doing the very opposite of what will help: try harder, rush to penetrate when he gets a partial erection, focus on getting erections instead of focusing on enjoying the interaction. When this does not work, he, too, many conclude there is something wrong with him, that his problem demands expert intervention.

Rigidly Believing That One Is Right

Instead of believing that one is dysfunctional and wrong, one may not self-heal because one believes one is right. Particularly if one is defensive and under attack, one may defend one's way of being or thinking, and therefore preclude exploration and creative problem solving. One spends all one's efforts defending instead of trying to learn.

Believing That the Royal Road to Problem Solving Is Through Intellectual Analysis

People may also get in their own way by overanalysis. This culture teaches logical, rational thinking as the major tool of problem solving. While logical, rational thinking certainly is an important tool, by itself, without experiencing and behavioral experimentation (see chapter 8), it will not necessarily lead to productive problem resolution. Furthermore, it can be misused. When individuals have a problem, there is pressure to analyze what is wrong. Yet sometimes overanalysis can actually exacerbate the problem, by overfocusing attention on the problem and magnifying it. For instance, overanalysis about anxiety may actually magnify the anxiety, when part of the solution proposed by cognitive–behavioral and humanistic therapists alike is to "let the anxiety be" and get on with life (e.g., Beck et al., 1985).

Summary

There are a variety of reasons why individuals might seek out psychotherapy rather than self-heal on their own. Many of the factors involved boil down to contextual factors in the clients' lives. Their natural environment does not provide sufficient support or resources for self-healing and self-righting. Other factors have to do with ways of coping and self-healing that are insufficient to deal with the problems they are trying to overcome. We next turn to a consideration of what clients are looking for in the nature of change from their point of view.

THE NATURE OF CHANGE IN PSYCHOTHERAPY FROM THE CLIENT'S POINT OF VIEW

Psychotherapy is supposed to help people "change." But what is change? Therapists define change in a wide array of ways. Many of their ideas about change are quite abstract and complex. They talk about restructuring personality, strengthening egos, helping clients to live more authentically, helping people become more differentiated, helping people let go of the past, and so on. Behavior therapists talk of changes in behavior. Others talk about first-order changes and second-order changes. There are many different concepts of what change is, from the highly abstract (changes in differentiation, changes in ego functioning) to the very specific and concrete (client is now attaining erections). There are also many different measures of change that have been used in psychotherapy research, from behavioral observation to clients' self-reports, to the use of personality tests, to the use of "objective" indexes such as arrest records or health records or number of hospitalizations, to the observations of third parties such as friends or relatives. What change is is a complex issue.

Yet clients rarely define change in the terms used by therapists. Few clients are concerned about being "more differentiated." Similarly, few define change in terms of change in behavior either. In terms of everyday life, change usually means that whatever one is complaining about has been at least partially resolved. This may mean: "My spouse and I are getting along better now," "I don't get so anxious when I have to go out anymore," "I feel more on track with my career," "I've decided to leave my relationship," "I'm now getting dates," "I feel clearer about what I want," "I'm not so depressed," "I feel less guilty," "Our sex life is better," "I got my mother-in-law off my back," "My daughter seems more comfortable with our divorce," "I don't get so anxious all the time anymore," "I seem to have found myself one more," "I've stopped using drugs," "I've learned how to control my anger so I don't get in trouble so much anymore," "I'm coping better with being alone," "I know I should leave this stupid relationship," I'm finding better ways of managing my daughter," "I'm being more productive," "I don't get so bent out of shape by little things," and "I seem to be better able to say what I think around others." In other words, change can be a change in behavior, a change in feeling, an internal change in self-awareness, a change in knowledge, or a change in attitude.

From the point of view of the client as active self-healer, we consider change to be when whatever an individual is complaining about is resolved, at least partially, in some form or the other. There may be many different signs of change. We know things are changed when things come easier, we just are in a better mood, we no longer feel so anxious, or if we feel anxious it does not seem to be as severe and paralyzing. We are able to "stay with" a problem better, we do not get "thrown" so easily. We feel "back to our old selves," or we seem to now be clearer on what to do. When our spouse says something that used to bother us it now does not get to us, we find ourselves spontaneously reacting more affectionately. We are having sex more often and it is going better. We have made an important decision. Or it is easier to get to work, or we feel more comfortable in a previously uncomfortable interpersonal relationship. We do not seem so plagued by worries. And so on. In many ways, with our clients, our friends, as well as with ourselves, we will not know for sure what caused the change to occur. We will just know that now we are a little bit more where we want to be in life.

In this book, we shall assume that a person has changed when the "problem" they have been struggling with has been dealt with in some form or another so that they are better able to get on with their lives. Frequently, this is not an all-or-none affair. Thus change and problem resolution are often partial, incomplete, and ongoing processes.

OUR VIEW OF THE CLIENT AS ACTIVE SELF-HEALER IN CONTRAST TO OTHER VIEWS

Before we describe in detail our view of the client in therapy as an active self-healer, we want to say what we mean by this idea in contrast to what some others might mean. Some therapists, when they initially hear our claim that clients are the ultimate self-healers, say something like "But don't many therapists already believe that?" There is some truth in this. Prochaska and Norcross (1982) found in a poll of therapists that they attributed two thirds of the variance in therapeutic outcome to the client.

Yet we have encountered many therapists who say they believe that it is clients who are the ultimate self-changers, but whose actions suggest they mean something different by this than what we mean. Most theories of psychotherapy (see chapter 6) acknowledge the importance of the client as an active agent at one level while contradicting it at other levels. In this section we contrast what we mean by the term to what some other therapists might mean by the term.

Consider three stories. First, Bohart attended a continuing education workshop. The workshop was attended by over 50 professionals. At one point the speaker, a distinguished psychotherapy researcher, presented the case of a young man who was experiencing anxiety symptoms and asked how the audience would deal with it. The audience was asked to break up into small groups of three and discuss the case. Bohart was sitting near two professionals, neither of whom he knew, and he formed a group with them. These two professionals immediately set out to decide for the client what was to be done. They debated back and forth over whether the client should be put on medication or not, and over whether it would be best to use a behavioral or a cognitive treatment for him, or perhaps family therapy. At no time was there the slightest mention of consulting the client, to explore the client's experience with him, to find out what kind of treatment the client might have wanted, to find out what the client's theory of change was, or to actively involve the client in treatment planning at all. After talking for about 10 minutes, during which Bohart had remained silent, they asked him what he would do. He reported that his approach would be to engage the client in the very dialogue they were engaging in. At that, they turned back to one another, continued their discussion as to what they thought was the right thing to do, and completely ignored Bohart thereafter. When the presenter subsequently asked for reports from the audience what they would do, every person who spoke prescribed some kind of treatment plan for the client. No one mentioned the possibility that the client could perhaps play an active role in treatment planning. Yet presumably "everyone" believes in the client as active self-healer. The interesting ironic twist to this story is that after everyone had presented their views, the speaker said that it did not really matter what was chosen because the evidence supported the idea that all interventions worked about equally well for this problem.

A second story comes from Kathy Moon (personal communication, August 16, 1997), a client-centered therapist. Client-centered therapists radically believe in the client's self-healing potential, so much so that they believe that the therapist should do nothing more than empathically follow the client. All generation of change comes from the client. Therapists are not supposed to be directive. Moon described one setting where several therapists believed they had to "knock sense" into their clients (a view in which it is the therapist who heals the client by setting the client straight). When Moon mentioned that her approach was different, that she was client centered, she was told that all the therapists at that setting were client centered. Moon suggested that many clinicians believe that they "follow the client," even when they do not.

Finally, at a recent meeting of the Society for the Exploration of Psychotherapy Integration, Jerry Gold (1996b) presented his work on the client as integrative therapist. Gold gave numerous examples of clients actively taking the lead in creatively planning their own treatment. Yet this was met by resistance from some professionals in the audience, who believed that the therapist could not trust the client to make the right decisions. After all, it was the therapist who was the expert. Would these same professionals, at the same time, say on a questionnaire that they believed that therapy is a process of helping clients make their own decisions about their own lives, and that clients are the active change agents in therapy? We would not be surprised if they did, given what we perceive as modal beliefs in the field.

What is going on? It is clear that different people mean quite different things by a belief in the client as active self-healer. Many therapists seem to see clients as fundamentally *incapable* when they enter therapy. It is as if, as soon as clients step through the therapist's door, they lose their ability to think intelligently. They are seen, through the eyes of various theories, as deficient and disordered. They are described in such dysfunctional terms it is a wonder they have survived at all (Rosenbaum, 1996). Much of this we lay at the feet of the medical model, which leads us to focus on disorder more than on health (Seligman, 1998).

These therapists may believe that ultimately the process of therapy is one of client self-healing, but they believe that clients are incapable of doing this without therapists providing direction and the techniques and inputs that create change. There are two subviews. One is that clients are so self-deceptive, psychologically undeveloped, and immature that their judgment cannot be trusted. The therapist must provide external correction until the clients come to face up to themselves and develop more mature ways of being. Then they can make mature choices for themselves. The second view is that clients have learned dysfunctional ways of thinking and being. These interfere with their taking proactive care of themselves. They are, however, incapable of modifying these themselves, thus modification must come from outside.

Therapists who see clients as self-deceptive and immature and yet who still claim therapy is a process whereby clients are ultimately responsible for change primarily seem to be focusing on clients' capacity for *agency*. Their view is that clients, being the ultimate change agents, are agents, but agents who have gone astray. Clients' behavior is intentional in an immature, self-deceptive way. Some therapists adopt a moralistic and paternalistic stance, in which they believe they must "correct" the wayward client who is incapable of correcting him- or herself because he or she is too self-deluded or too immature and selfish. Many of those who believe that clients need to be reined in, criticized, confronted, called to task, and so on, act as if they have a fundamentally negative view of human beings. This attitude is reinforced by the fundamentally negative ways most therapists are trained to view clients (Wile, 1981).

Wile (1981) noted that there is a strong moralistic quality to many of the judgments therapists pass on to clients. Therapists tend to pass on moralistic judgments of clients as objective and scientific. But there is nothing objective and scientific about labeling someone as narcissistic, manipulative, colluding, feeling entitled, and so on. These judgments are clearly moralistic and reflect a negative judgmental attitude toward the client no matter how much the professional claims to be on the client's side. We would not even mind so much if professionals would acknowledge they are being moralistic. But they often do not. After all, narcissistic personality disorder is an objectively defined entity in *DSM-IV*, is it not? How can they be accused of being moralistic? We further believe that many of the judgments therapists pass on clients "objectively" are really judgments based on their experience of certain client ways of being as "annoying." Stolorow, Brandchaft, and Atwood (1987) noted that the category of borderline personality disorder is essentially a category for clients whom therapists find to be "pains in the neck."

We would not object to categorizing a client's *behavior* as "acting manipulatively." What we object to is the simplistic extension from the client's behavior to an attribution to his or her character or to his or her intentions as "being manipulative" or as "being a manipulative person." In doing this, the field is making the very same kinds of global attributions to the client's character that cognitive therapists (e.g., Seligman, 1990) argue create dysfunction when clients make such attributions to themselves! In addition, the field is using a simple person-on-the street heuristic to explain clients' behavior: assuming that their overt behavior reflects in a fairly direct fashion their underlying intentions. This is not imaginative. The client-as-self-healer perspective asks therapists to look more imaginatively at the clients' motives and intentions and to assume that even though the behavior looks manipulative, and may even be manipulative, that does not mean clients are self-centered manipulative people who only want to get their way in the simplest way possible. Rather, we prefer to imagine that their manipulative behavior is a behavior that they use because it is the best they can do given their reinforcement history and their personal perspective.

The belief that dysfunctional (or bad) behavior is intentional and agentic has a long tradition in Western Judeo-Christian history. People who behaved badly were seen as too agentic and willful, not bending their wills to the will of God. Christian views vary on this, but some of the more puritan variety adopt a harsh view: Because humans are all sinners based on the Fall, we are fundamentally evil unless we are disciplined into being good and God fearing. In a secular way, many therapists have adopted a similar philosophy. Clients are too willful. They have not tamed their desires, learned to face up to the truth, or learned to take responsibility for themselves. Or they are too demanding. Thus the therapist's job is to correct client agency, to get it to adopt a more proactive path.

The second subview is that clients are capable of being effective agents, but only after they have been taught how to do so from outside. Both Bakan (1996) and Gendlin (1990) pointed out how Western culture minimizes the ability of people to creatively generate anything from within. Instead, learning must be "implanted" in them. They must "internalize" the therapist or the therapist's positive regard for them or what the therapist is teaching them.

We, too, believe that clients are agentic. However, we draw a distinction between agency and internally generated proactive potential for self-healing. We not only believe that clients are agentic but also that they are proactive. They are trying to move their lives forward and to solve problems as best they can. They are capable of making active, creative contributions to their growth process. They may need help and assistance, but they need it in the form of creative constructive feedback and collaboration rather than distrust and external correction. Believing in client-generated self-healing potential means believing that there will be a spontaneous "move" in the direction of self-healing on the part of the client. The therapist's job is to amplify that and help clients clear away obstacles. Although this may at times include helping them evaluate how they think, and teaching them new behaviors, it also means believing that clients are motivated to intelligently self-correct given the proper facilitative context. They can take creative leaps beyond what therapists have to offer to generate their own solutions. Furthermore, they are capable of having valuable ideas about whether the therapist's treatment regimen is right for them or not.

In addition, there is a proactive "thrust" underlying even the most apparently willful negative behavior (see chapter 9). Although clients do occasionally act in self-protecting, avoidant ways, we believe it is less common than some therapists believe, and often is precipitated by therapist behavior. Furthermore, when clients act this way, it is usually because they feel trapped, see themselves as having no other options, or feel inefficacious to do otherwise.

CASE EXAMPLE

The case of a young woman, Sandi (Bohart, 1990), who met the criteria for borderline personality disorder, illustrates several of the ideas reviewed previously including some of the obstacles to self-healing, the nature of change, and our view of self-healing in contrast to what others may mean by that.

Sandi entered therapy at the age of 19 exhibiting unstable mood, suicidality, a recent history of intense and unstable relationships, and substance abuse. She also had had a brief psychotic episode for which she had been hospitalized. Sandi also had been a problem to previous therapists, one of whom had ordered her out of his office because he had become so frustrated with her. This last therapist, a Gestalt therapist, viewed her as not taking responsibility for herself, that is, as being willfully agentic in a negative way. He certainly did believe she could change herself, but saw her as willfully choosing dysfunctional ways of being over taking responsibility and standing on her own two feet. He believed that what she needed was to be confronted with her manipulativeness. However, Sandi experienced his confrontations as punitive and critical, and because she already felt bad and vulnerable about herself, felt misunderstood by the therapist instead of helped.

From our point of view, Sandi's problems made perfect sense given her circumstances. Her problem behaviors arose from her struggle to make a livable life in an unlivable environment. Sandi had a chronic life-threatening physical condition. Her parents were divorced, and far from being supportive, she had a highly self-absorbed mother who ignored Sandi, except when she was criticizing her. In fact, her mother had partially abandoned her, and Sandi had had to go live with her grandmother. Partly due to her physical condition, she was overweight. This had led her to be the target of vicious teasing and rejection in junior high school. Whenever she tried to lose weight, her grandmother would go on a shopping spree and fill the house with goodies (and then later criticize Sandi for being overweight). Despite all this Sandi managed to graduate from high school. Yet when she started college, her grandmother and mother continually denigrated any of her accomplishments, and Sandi had dropped out. In the meantime, believing herself to be unattractive to boys, and yet wanting the same kind of human companionship everybody else wants, Sandi became an easy target for sexual exploitation. This made her feel even worse about herself. In addition, to have some kind of social identity, she hung around with a group that used drugs, and, to fit in, she did also. The previous therapists who had confronted her and told her that she was not taking responsibility for herself had mobilized her rebellion (leading to the incident of being ordered out of the one therapist's office), but also contributed to her own self-criticism and belief that there was something fundamentally wrong with her.

When Sandi came to therapy she was very depressed, had just gotten a divorce after a very brief marriage, and was barely functioning well enough to hang onto a menial job. She did not have much money and was living at home with her critical mother. Nevertheless, it was obvious there there was a strong, struggling person trying to grow and develop and make a livable life despite all her obstacles. She did not want to have a negative self-concept or to be incompetent, overweight, or depressed. She wanted to feel good about herself, develop a sense of competency, live on her own, and develop a sense of greater behavioral freedom. So she had consulted a therapist, despite her bad experiences with previous therapists. The therapist, through empathic listening, provided Sandi with time and permission to think about herself and her life. This was something she did not have in her everyday life. Gradually, over the period of about a year, she spontaneously began to develop more positive social relationships. She joined a church group and made some friends. She learned how to mentally fend off her mother's and grandmother's criticism, and she got and held a decent job. While her self-healing continued for years thereafter, aided by sporadic visits to a therapist, much of it was done by herself. Change for Sandi was an ongoing process.

Sandi's case illustrates a number of obstacles to self-healing. First, she did not have a good social support network. Second, she did not have time, space, and permission to think about herself and her problems. Instead, she was chronically under stress and attack. Third, her environment was actively inhibiting. Not only were her mother and grandmother critical, but they also actively did things to undermine any proactive behaviors Sandi took. Fourth, Sandi had learned to view herself as "bad," and this actively interfered with more proactive problem solving. For instance, viewing herself as bad and unattractive, she did not even try to form more supportive relationships.

In therapy, Sandi also exhibited a number of positive qualities, which we believe are characteristics of clients as proactive self-healers. She had a great deal of intuitive wisdom about her life space, which helped her clarify her problems and eventually find solutions, as long as the therapist was willing to help her mobilize that wisdom. She was motivated to create a better life for herself. She was willing to approach pain and to explore in order to do that. And, over a period of time, she gradually and creatively pieced together more and more solutions to life problems. In the next section, we consider some basic postulates we hold about the client as an active self-healer, and in chapter 9 we discuss how they influence therapeutic practice.

POSTULATES ABOUT THE CLIENT AS AN ACTIVE SELF-HEALER

Clients enter therapy as proactive self-healing beings who are struggling to make their lives better. They have taken a very active, deliberate step to seek therapy. They believe their lives can be better and they can accomplish this by changing themselves in therapy. This suggests a positive attitude. The therapist should support this belief with faith in the client's desire to move forward. We hold the following postulates to be true:

- *Clients are agentic.* Clients are capable of planning and initiating action, and of choosing their own goals. They can take an active role in their own therapy. Even "resistant" client behavior is agentic and proactive.
- *Clients are wise.* They are inventive, creative, and often have many good ideas about their problems and possible solutions. At a tacit, intuitive level, they often understand what is going wrong and have a sense of a healing direction to take. Their behavior, from their point of view, makes sense as a proactive attempt to find a livable life in the world as they know and understand it. From within their frame of reference, they are actively trying to adjust as best they can to their circumstances, to preserve their autonomy, their connectedness, their goals, their power, their pride, and their maneuverability.
- *Clients are generative.* They are capable of reviewing and evaluating their problems, thinking them through, trying out alternatives, and generating new variations on old solutions or generating new solutions. They do not always need to be given a solution by the therapist. Sometimes they can even "make therapy" out of a therapist's chance remark. (See the case of Corsini at the start of chapter 8.)
- *Clients are capable of learning.* Clients are capable of changing their ideas, beliefs, emotional reactions, and behaviors based on encountering new input or on thinking through old experience or through ideas.
- *Clients are continually thinking.* Clients think in the same productive, generative way that therapists do. They evaluate the therapist's ideas, evaluate the therapist, try out new behaviors, and think about what those new behaviors mean in terms of their life experience. What clients "store and process" is a creative product of what the therapist said or did and what the client added to it through his or her own thinking process. When a client engages in a new behavior, her or she does not merely mechanistically build up a new habit. Instead, he or she observes the experience and thinks about implications. Consequences are evaluated, and alternative possibilities are generated. Then all of that is stored, not just the input from the therapist.
- *Clients are continually exploring.* Humans are not unlike many

other animals in that they continually explore their worlds. The world of the human includes both their external environment and their own internal environments. Clients explore from the moment they enter therapy. They will try things out to see what they get back. They will look and listen. They may look depressed, passive, or resistant, but they are still exploring the environment of therapy. They were exploring in their minds as they came to therapy, and when they leave they will explore both cognitively and behaviorally as they reenter their lived-in worlds.

- *Clients are motivated to restore their functioning to as high a level as they can, given their circumstances.* Clients prefer to fit their behavior into the world as they see it as best they can. Most wish for accommodations that get their needs met and coordinate with society. If some have goals or wishes discrepant with society, then they may believe they have to lie, cheat, and manipulate. Nonetheless, they are doing the same thing we all do when we pursue our goals within the constraints imposed by the world—trying to find the best workable accommodations.

- *Other things being equal, clients prefer to approach positive, proactive solutions rather than rely on defensive, avoidant solutions.* Most human beings prefer the behavioral freedom associated with proactively approaching life. They choose defensive solutions when (a) they feel themselves under attack, (b) they believe that to acknowledge something they are disowning would bring about the collapse of the delicate balance of their life structure (this includes feeling overwhelmed), (c) they feel helpless to do anything about something, and (d) they believe nothing can be done or do not know what to do. Clients are more fundamentally proactive than they are defensive.

- *Clients do not always need the therapist's guidance.* Sometimes, some clients only need an attentive listener so they can think things out for themselves. Therapists should not underestimate the service they give in providing this.

- *Different clients have widely different world views, ways of being, ways of healing, ways of living.* Clients come out of widely different cultures and experiential backgrounds. They have different ideas about how the world works, what a good life is, and what is good and bad behavior. A "one-size-fits-all" therapy for anything but the most circumscribed problem is likely to do harm to some clients who are not able to accommodate themselves to what therapists are offering. Some want a lot of emotion; others want a businesslike atmosphere. Some want exploration and discovery; others want techniques.

CONCLUSION

The following are the points we made in this chapter:

- There are a number of obstacles to client self-healing. These include various mental states such as a helpless mind-set or ruminative thinking, lack of resources, inhibiting environments, and inhibiting beliefs.
- Clients rarely define change in terms used by therapists. There are many different possible ways clients may decide that change has happened. Change is often partial, incomplete, and an ongoing process.
- Many therapists claim to believe that clients are the ultimate self-healers. However, they mean something different by this than we do. Often they mean that they see clients as agentic but as willfully and agentically acting dysfunctionally. They see their role as correcting client agency. Our view of client self-healing includes more than just a view of clients' agency. We also believe in a positive proactive self-healing potential.
- Our view of the client as an active self-healer includes a number of basic principles, such as that clients are agentic, wise, and generative; capable of learning, thinking, and exploring; and motivated to approach positive and proactive solutions, among others.

In the next chapter, we examine how psychotherapy helps promote client active self-healing.

5

THE "SCHOOL" OF PSYCHOTHERAPY

We define psychotherapy as a process of helping clients use their inherent capacities for change. The process is akin to that of education. In education, students' built-in capacities for learning are used, mobilized, and supported so that students develop new perspectives, new skills, or their own creative capacity for invention.

We take the idea that therapy is an educational process seriously. Learning may be primarily self-discovered—facilitated by a context that encourages client exploration and creativity. Or the client may be tutored in skills and self-management strategies. Throughout the next few chapters, we portray therapist techniques and procedures not as things that operate on clients to fix them, but rather as things that provide opportunities for self-discovered learning and problem solving.

DISCOVERY-ORIENTED VERSUS PRESCRIPTIVE OR TUTORIAL APPROACHES TO THERAPY

In both therapy and education, there has been a dichotomy between *discovery-oriented* approaches and *didactic, directive,* or *teaching-oriented* approaches. In education, Piagetian approaches (Cowan, 1978) are on the discovery-oriented side. Piagetians do not really believe children can be taught concepts like conservation. Instead, children have to discover them for themselves, in their own time. Adults can facilitate by providing the proper learning materials and experiences, but they cannot show or impart the concept to the child. In contrast, those who follow Vygotsky (Rieber & Carton, 1987) believe that most important knowledge is passed on socially. Children need to be tutored. However, even for Vygotsky, children must be highly active in the learning process. Knowledge is co-constructed. Students are not passive beings being "operated on" by teacher interventions.

Therapy can facilitate learning in these same two basic ways: through emphasizing self-discovery and self-generated creativity or through providing learning experiences that teach the client new skills or new ways of reacting emotionally. Psychotherapies can be arranged along a continuum from those that are primarily discovery oriented to those that are primarily prescriptive or tutorial. The goal of discovery-oriented therapies is facilitating client self-discovery. In contrast, prescriptive or tutorial therapies operate by assuming that the therapist has the answer for the client. The therapist "prescribes" the answer and tutors the client in acquiring that answer. Client-centered therapy is the purest form of a discovery-oriented psychotherapy; a traditional conditioning view of behavior therapy is the purest form of a prescriptive therapy. Other therapies arrange themselves along the continuum, combining elements of both, with some being relatively more discovery oriented (Gestalt, existential, psychodynamic) and others being relatively more prescriptive (cognitive therapy, rational–emotive therapy, modern behavioral approaches; see Figure 5.1).

Client-centered therapy is the purest example of a discovery-oriented therapy. The therapist has no other goals than to facilitate the client's own exploration and discovery process. Psychodynamic therapies are further in on the discovery-oriented side. The therapist has more of an agenda, based on psychodynamic theory. The therapist believes that discoveries involving early childhood experience and transference relationships are the ones that will bear the most fruit. The therapist therefore functions more as a guide to the client's self-discovery process. All of these approaches are generally compatible with Piagetian views of learning, in that the therapist may contribute the materials and experiences that provide a platform for client self-discovery, but it is clients who make the discoveries.

On the other end of the continuum, therapy lies almost completely

Figure 5.1. The continuum of therapies from discovery oriented to prescriptive.

in the therapist's hands in traditional conditioning views of behavior therapy. Not only does the therapist choose the treatment, but the treatment works by automatic conditioning processes that operate on the client mechanistically. There is nothing in the treatment model that relies on anything more than the most minimal active collaboration by the client, and there is certainly nothing that smacks of self-healing. Exposure, for instance, is presumed to automatically "decondition" fear responses.

A little farther in on the continuum lie some of the modern behavioral and cognitive–behavioral approaches. These rely more on an active client. Clients are seen as agentic, and healing occurs primarily through development of coping skills. For instance, exposure works not only by extinction of fears but also by developing feelings of active mastery (Goldfried, 1995). Furthermore, the development of skills is not seen as the attainment of mechanistic responses but of skills that can be flexibly applied (Bandura, 1997). The development of a sense of self-efficacy is also important (Bandura, 1997).

Further in toward the center of the continuum, cognitive approaches combine prescriptive elements with discovery and are very much in keeping with Vygotskian models of learning. Discovery is a structured part of the therapy, but within limits guided by the therapist. This is particularly true of Aaron Beck, who is more discovery oriented than Albert Ellis. However, both Beck and Ellis largely teach through getting clients to think things through for themselves.

We have put strategic and solution-focused therapies right in the middle of the continuum to capture their paradoxical quality. As befits approaches that often uses paradox, games, metaphors, humor, and the like, these approaches are a bit unclassifiable. On the one hand they are highly prescriptive; on the other they are almost completely discovery oriented. They are highly prescriptive in that the therapist is usually directive. At the same time, the philosophy of most such approaches is almost completely discovery oriented. Milton Erickson, the founder of the approach, believed that specific interventions did not change clients in specific directions at all. All they did was "free up" the client's creativity so that clients could creatively solve problems themselves.

Most approaches combine elements of both prescriptive–tutorial and discovery. Modern cognitive–behavioral approaches are highly prescriptive in that the therapist believes he or she has the answers for the client and tutors the client in the answers (i.e, cognitive restructuring, skills training, exposure). However, if one reads transcripts of experts applying these approaches (e.g., Beck et al., 1979; Craske & Barlow, 1993), one observes how much therapists are good tutors, emphasizing a learning climate that relies heavily on clients' active involvement and self-discovery of the meanings, implications, and use of what they are being taught. We give some examples of this in chapters 6 and 9.

MODELS OF THE THERAPIST

From the standpoint of therapy as an educational context, there are several different roles therapists can take. On the discovery-oriented side of the continuum, the client-centered therapist is a companion in dialogue on a journey of discovery. The role of the companion is to accompany the client and to respond empathically in a way that helps the client creatively explore and find new ways of being. The process in psychoanalysis is one of guided self-discovery. The client must make the discoveries, but the therapist knows where it is most likely to be profitable to look. Not unlike Virgil with Dante, the therapist accompanies the client on the journey of self-discovery, but also anticipates what will be found and helps the client interpret it.

On the prescriptive–tutorial side of the continuum, the therapist is a teacher or tutor who imparts knowledge to the client. Good teachers or mentors, even when taking the lead, do it in a collaborative fashion. They help the student think it out for themselves and respect the student's initiative and contributions. Good mentors in graduate school prize their students' creativity, listen and learn from the students, and work collaboratively to co-develop research plans. A good dissertation mentor not only guides but also allows the student to disagree and to find his or her own path, even if it deviates in some respects from what the mentor thinks. Good cognitive–behavioral therapists, such as Beck (Shostrom, 1986) and Meichenbaum (Shostrom, 1986), operate in this way. In contrast, bad mentors have very specific ideas about how things should be done, give their students little leeway, and "train" them in the worst sense of this word— make them over to be exactly like they think they should be and make them conform to a narrowly conceived way of doing things.

We emphasize that a therapist can promote client self-healing by following any of the previously mentioned three roles: companion, expert guide, or tutor. If one is going to be a teacher, for instance, it is *how* one teaches that is important.

THE TWO MOST IMPORTANT PROCESSES IN HELPFUL PSYCHOTHERAPY

From the standpoint of promoting client active self-healing, there are two basic questions to be asked about any therapeutic intervention, response, or relationship: (a) Is it involving to the client? and (b) Is it stimulating the client to think? If these two conditions are met, then therapy is on the right track. Some clients will become involved in almost any kind of therapy and be stimulated to think by it, whereas others will be differentially involved or stimulated to think by different kinds of therapy and therapy relationships. For instance, some clients will be more stimulated to think and will become more involved in a relatively more permissive, nondirective atmosphere in which they are "given their head." Others may be able to get more involved if therapy is highly structured and the therapist has an agenda the client can follow.

Client Involvement

The single most important thing in successful therapy is clients' involvement and investment in the process. Involved clients will frequently be able to use whatever approach to therapy is being offered them. It follows that the most important thing for the therapist to do is to facilitate, support, and help develop client involvement. Helping clients get involved in the process is as important as it is for school teachers to motivate students.

Many factors can play a role in whether clients get involved. Whether they are there voluntarily or not of course is crucial. In addition, some clients find some procedures more plausible than others and thus will be more able to get invested in them. Some procedures will match up better with what clients already believe about their problems, and that will support client involvement more efficiently. Some clients are motivated to change but have trouble involving and investing themselves in the therapy procedures because they feel helpless, overwhelmed, frightened, or discouraged (see chapter 7). Helping clients stay involved when things are going badly is equally important. Therefore, how therapists deal with discouragement and failure is crucial.

The therapist facilitates involvement by creating a good working climate with good conditions for learning. These include some degree of structure, some degree of healthy challenge, some opportunity for self-directed exploration and discovery, and support for clients' own ideas and thinking processes. Because research shows that having an audience can inhibit new learning of complex tasks (Zajonc, 1965), it is particularly important in therapy that an understanding atmosphere be provided in which clients feel safe to experiment and explore and to make mistakes. Mistakes, resistances, reluctances, steps backward, failures, and so on all are natural parts of the learning process.

Getting resistant or defiant clients involved is particularly challenging. How Monty Roberts (1997) works with wild horses provides a metaphor for therapy in such cases. In the past it was thought that wild horses had to be "broken." It was assumed that their fear and "resistance" would have to be overcome by force. The process of breaking a horse so that it could be ridden would often take weeks. However, Roberts found that by carefully listening to horses he was able to provide a context in which the horses became involved in the process on their own. Roberts first demonstrates that he respects the horse's fear and desire to escape the situation. He carefully paces his own behavior to the horse, communicating to the horse that he can be trusted. For instance, he will turn his back on the horse, demonstrating that he trusts the horse. Eventually the horse becomes curious and approaches. When the horse discovers the situation is safe, it "voluntarily" allows itself to be ridden. This process works much more quickly than the breaking approach.

There are important lessons for therapists in this. Some clients will be involved in therapy from the start. Others, because they are frightened or defiant, may resist and stay away, even escape if they could. Some therapists believe, akin to breaking horses, that the answer to this is to confront their resistance and denial. Sometimes the tactics used are not much different from those used to force confessions out of political dissidents in totalitarian countries.

In contrast, we believe that showing clients respect, demonstrating that we as therapists appreciate and understand clients' fear or defiance, and showing clients that we want to communicate with them are better ways to enlist clients' engagement and cooperation. The therapist's attempt to really try to understand and appreciate the client's point of view will help create an atmosphere in which the client is more likely to be willing to open up and involve him- or herself. This will also make it more likely that the client will listen to and try to learn from the therapist's point of view. Clients will become involved to the extent that they can trust the therapist to be on their side as much as the therapist may also represent the interests of their parents, or the court, or society.

Careful empathic listening and responding is one important thing the therapist can do to facilitate involvement with all clients. The procedure of empathic reflecting may help clients overcome feelings of helplessness and become more involved. Careful empathic listening also helps therapists tune into clients' theories of their problems and of change. This helps the therapist explain strategies and procedures in a way that might engage the client's interest. Or it could facilitate a co-constructive dialogue process (see chapter 9) in which the client is actively involved in the choice of procedures. We discuss empathic reflecting later in this chapter.

Stimulating Client Thinking

As in any good educational situation beyond the learning of simple rote memory material, stimulating and supporting the student's thinking and understanding is vital. Accordingly, the most important thing after facilitating client involvement is to stimulate and support client thinking along with whatever else is going on in therapy. In one study (Humphreys & Bohart, 1998), over 100 undergraduates rated films of five famous therapists: Carl Rogers, Hans Strupp, Fritz Perls, Donald Meichenbaum, and

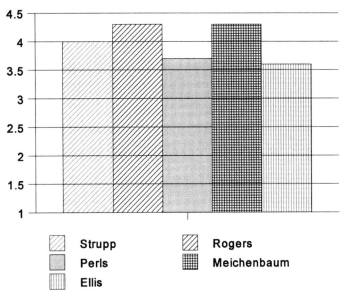

Figure 5.2. Students' ratings of how much therapists stimulated client thinking. 1 = *not all*, 3 = *a moderate amount*, and 5 = *a great deal*.

Albert Ellis. All five were seen as actively facilitating client thinking to at least a moderate degree (see Figure 5.2). Interestingly, the two therapists rated highest at stimulating client thinking were one humanistic therapist (Carl Rogers) and one cognitive–behavioral therapist (Donald Meichenbaum), whereas the two rated the lowest were one humanistic therapist (Fritz Perls) and one cognitive therapist (Albert Ellis).

Techniques, procedures, and therapist responses all can be used in a manner that stimulates clients' thinking and promotes their active understanding. As we explore what therapists do in the following sections, we highlight how this happens. We also discuss the nature of productive client thinking in greater detail in chapter 8. For now, we suggest that whatever the therapist is doing, he or she should be trying to stimulate clients' thinking. Next we turn to the kinds of learning opportunities that therapy provides.

FIVE KINDS OF LEARNING OPPORTUNITIES PROVIDED BY THERAPY

Therapy provides five basic types of learning opportunities. In the next few sections, we review the first and most primary of them, the provision of a good workspace, in detail. Then we briefly review the other four: provision of a context for interpersonal exploration and learning, provision of an opportunity for co-constructive dialogue, provision of structured exercises for exploration, and provision of specific learning experiences and teaching clients specific skills.

PROVISION OF A SAFE WORKSPACE

It has often been suggested that one reason for why all therapies may work about the same is because of the therapist–client relationship. We have previously reviewed evidence (see chapter 2) suggesting that the therapist–client relationship is indeed important. Most traditional views of therapy suggest that the relationship is important because, in one way or another, it is an intervention. Looking at the relationship from the standpoint of an active self-healing client, however, the relationship is most basically helpful because it provides a good workspace. It provides a safe, sheltered "space" within which clients can take a deep breath, step back, consider their problems in context, brainstorm with another human being, gain perspective, feel free to take a look at all sides, make mistakes, generate new alternatives, reexperience old wounds and problematic issues, and find the strength to reconfront life and to try new things out.

From the standpoint of the client as active self-healer, the "healing force" of the therapist–client relationship comes from the client's utilization of the relationship, more so than from what the therapist specifically provides. There is a small amount of evidence compatible with this thesis. First, clients' perceptions of the relationship with the therapist correlate more highly with therapeutic outcome than therapists' perceptions (Horvath, 1995). If the therapist's expertise were the primary determinant of change, it should be the therapist's perceptions of the strength of the alliance that correlates with change. However, to the contrary, it is the client's. Second, in a qualitative study of three sessions of therapy (Bohart & Boyd, 1997), some evidence suggested that to self-heal, some clients may "create" the therapists they need. Clients appeared to have attended to, remembered, and interpreted therapist actions that accorded with their aims. Clients who were struggling to accept something would notice, remember, and interpret their therapists as conveying acceptance. Clients who wanted or needed support to make a decision would notice, remember, and interpret therapist actions as encouraging, supporting, and validating.

Functions of a Safe Workspace

The concept of a good workspace is meant to be metaphorically like a good workbench in a garage. The garage provides the person with a sheltered space away from friends, neighbors, and children, where the person can concentrate and get absorbed in the work. The person can spread out all the elements of the problem on the bench, examine each piece in turn, and stand back, look for patterns, and decide how best to proceed.

With psychological problems, people rarely have the opportunity in everyday life to do this. Instead they have no "space" because of pressing life demands. And instead of having quiet time to spread the problem out and think, they have noisy friends and relatives criticizing them and giving them advice. Yet a personal problem is complex by definition and demands time and room so the person can "free up" his or her intelligence.

A good therapeutic relationship provides such workspace. Therapists are "significant others" who say, in essence, it is okay to devote this time to oneself. Furthermore, good therapists listen empathically, help the client clarify, do not give premature advice or interpretations, and are not critical. In addition, they provide a calming influence that reduces the client's stress level. This frees up the client's ability to stand back and examine his or her problems.

Why a Good Workspace Is Helpful

There are many who are skeptical that simply providing an empathic relationship can really help. In their eyes, it is either mere hand-holding, or too nonspecific to be very potent. Yet consider a client who sees a therapist like Carl Rogers. The client self-discloses and the therapist does "nothing" but empathically listen and respond. How can such a situation be helpful? We consider this most basic of helping situations from two perspectives: the standpoint of those who believe healing flows primarily from the therapist's interventions and the standpoint of the client as active self-healer. The study of this helping situation illuminates the highly active nature of the client. We will see that far more is going on than the provision of nonspecific effects or simply of support or hope.

The Standpoint of the Therapist as Healer

For many, the idea that simple empathic listening to clients' self disclosures can be helpful is upsetting. After all, the therapist isn't *doing* anything. Three classes of objections have been raised. We consider each in turn.

Relationship as hand-holding. First, some argue that the therapeutic relationship does nothing more than provide emotional soothing and support, perhaps instilling hope, but not really changing anything. The psychiatrist S. Alan Savitz compared the therapeutic relationship to the situation in medicine a hundred years ago. To quote him,

> Before the advent of antibiotics, doctors could do very little to actually heal people. They just sat by patients' beds, holding their hand and trying to make them feel a little better. Now, they can really do some-

thing for people, patients don't just feel better because of the human touch, they *are* better. But I'll bet people like their doctors personally a lot less now than they did then. Mental health care is in something of the same position as medical care in those days. . . . Patients may think they prefer "liking" their therapists to actually getting better. Basically, they may be lonely and looking for a friend, rather than trying to change the way they live in a reasonable amount of time. (Wylie, 1994, p. 32)

The idea that the provision of an empathic context provides nothing but the equivalent of hand-holding is not uncommon. Going back to Freud, there has been a suspicion that healing from the relationship is simply a kind of placebo, or transference cure. Skepticism of this sort is captured in a quote from Burns (1980), a cognitive therapist who, in commenting on empathically based, nondirective therapy, said "when you do feel better as a result of achieving emotional release with an empathic and caring therapist, the sense of improvement is likely to be short lived if you haven't significantly transformed the way you evaluate yourself and your life" (p. 60).

Catharsis as harmful. A second objection is that client self-expression, without external corrective feedback or intervention from the therapist, is not only not helpful but also can be harmful. While feeling understood and getting emotions out could make clients temporarily feel better, nothing has really changed, and clients might even change for the worse in the long run. For instance, Burns (1980) noted "if the therapist does not provide objective feedback about the validity of your self-evaluation, you may conclude that [he or she] agrees with you. . . . As a result you probably will feel even more inadequate" (p. 60). Hammond, Hepworth, and Smith (1980, p. 155) said, "With emotionally overexpressive individuals . . . empathic responsiveness, especially that which focuses on the feelings presented, may indeed foster cathartic and temporary symptomatic relief, but it may also defeat the aims of therapy by permitting, reinforcing and perpetuating the client's dysfunctional mode of coping. Such clients need more to encourage their rational processes than to express their emotions freely." Elsewhere, Wachtel (1993) expressed concerns that the therapist's empathic immersion in the experience of the client may preclude the therapist from offering an alternative, objective perspective and from challenging the client to overcome resistances when needed.

Of particular concern is the idea of emotional catharsis. Controversy has raged over the catharsis idea for years. Some have argued that expressing negative emotion is therapeutic and beneficial because it leads to the draining off and release of negative feelings. Others, primarily from the behavioral perspective, have argued that all the expression of negative emotion does is reinforce and strengthen dysfunctional emotion, behavior, and attitudes. Therefore, simply allowing clients to express in therapy without the therapist trying to intervene will only lead to clients becoming more mired in their problems.

Need for specific interventions. A third objection is raised by those who hold that therapy should consist of specific interventions tailored to specific client problems (e.g., Marten & Barlow, 1993). From their point of view, the factors that make the relationship helpful are "nonspecific." Nonspecific factors, by definition, cannot be as potent as interventions specifically tailored to the problem at hand. The only way to make the relationship potent would be to identify the specific factors involved, study how they differentially affect different problems, and then provide them as every other intervention is provided.

Following on this, experiential therapists, who do believe the relationship is a potent source of help, have tried to provide theories of how simple empathic listening can function as an intervention. Some of the alternatives include the possibility that the therapist is modeling self-acceptance (Bohart, 1991), facilitating the client's depth of processing (Sachse, 1992), raising the level of the client's experiencing (Gendlin, 1968), promoting emotional reprocessing (Greenberg et al., 1993), functioning as a surrogate information processor (Wexler, 1974) or surrogate experiencer (Vanaerschot, 1997), or challenging the client's dysfunctional cognitions through empathic reflections (Bohart, 1982; Safran & Segal, 1990). Or perhaps the therapist is reinforcing client statements (Truax, 1966). From a psychodynamic perspective, the empathic therapist helps by replacing the client's negative introjects with positive ones or by facilitating self-structuralization (MacIsaac, 1997).

All of these are predicated on the idea that if the *therapist* is not doing something actively therapeutic by providing an empathic relationship, then no therapy can be taking place. It is as if it is impossible to believe that *clients* can do anything without specific, active, structured intervention by the therapist.

The Standpoint of the Client as Active Self-Healer

There is considerable evidence that "expression" and self-disclosure can be therapeutic in and of themselves. We have already cited studies on the helpfulness of journaling (Pennebaker, 1990; Segal & Murray, 1994), talking into a tape recorder (Segal & Murray, 1994; Schwitzgebel, 1961), the power of a "chat" (Burton et al., 1991), and account-making with trauma (Harvey et al., 1991). Pennebaker (1995), for instance, argued for the therapeutic benefits of self-disclosure. According to him, studies have shown that writing about traumatic experiences "produces improvement in immune function, drops in physician visits for illness, and better performance at school and work, . . . [while] failure to talk or acknowledge significant experiences is associated with increased health problems, autonomic activity, and ruminations" (Pennebaker, 1995, p. 4). Clark (1993) reviewed a number of research studies that have found that (a) individuals in distress feel a need to disclose and (b) such disclosure is beneficial in reducing distress, increasing feelings of self-efficacy, and improving health.

Studies of client-centered therapy (R. Elliott, 1996) provide evidence that expression to a listening other who does nothing but empathically respond can be helpful. In one study, a traditional empathic-listening, non-directive client-centered approach did as well at alleviating depression as did a more active, directive process-experiential approach that consisted of "potent" structured interventions. Both were as effective as cognitive therapy (Greenberg & Watson, 1998).

How can this be? If therapists believe that sitting across from them is a thinking, exploring being and not merely a mindless expressor, then a very different view emerges of the phenomenon of the client expressing to an empathic listener. The client is not merely a passive receptacle having his or her experience level raised, his or her information processing deepened, his or her dysfunctional cognitions challenged, his or her negative introjects replaced, or his or her emotions reprocessed. Rather, sitting across from the empathically listening and reflecting therapist is an actively working, thinking, intelligent, problem-solving client. Clients do not merely respond in lockstep fashion to therapist interventions, but respond *actively*. They do not merely have their depth of information processing deepened by a therapist intervention, but go deeper *because they sense that the therapist is with them and is willing to go deeper*.

We present two cases of client self-healing through dialogue with an empathic listening therapist who does little else. Then we follow those cases with an in-depth discussion of the processes involved.

Case 1: Joe. The client, Joe, was referred by a friend of the therapist's colleague. Joe was very depressed because he and his girlfriend had broken up a couple of months before, and he had not been able to shake the severe depression that followed. He met the criteria for major depressive disorder. His depression was clearly well beyond normal grief. When he came in he looked like he had not slept, and he reported sleep disturbance. He reported despairing mood and suicidal thoughts. He reported a loss of energy and trouble concentrating. He said he could not get his girlfriend out of his mind, and he was doing things like following her and hanging around outside her apartment at night. He had tried other things; friends had taken him out to bars to drink. He had picked up a few girls, but nothing had helped. Joe and the therapist talked for about 1½ hours. The therapist followed a traditional client-centered modality of responding with empathic reflections. He carefully followed and empathized with the despair Joe felt at being trapped in his own feelings—knowing he would like to let go of the relationship and move on but feeling he could not.

The therapist empathized with the humiliation of being dumped; he empathized with the rage and impotence of not being able to do anything when someone else simply is no longer interested in you; he empathized with the aching loneliness and how awful it feels to see couples that are happy together; and he empathized with how, at that moment, that one person seemed to be the only one in the whole world who would do. He allowed and empathized with Joe's feelings that, at that moment, going out with others simply seemed like filling space. No advice was given, no interpretations were presented, and no dysfunctional cognitions were challenged. Yet by the end of 1½ hours, Joe was looking up, looking the therapist in the eye, instead of staring down, and reported feeling much better.

Joe was seen only once. Although no depression scales were administered, it was reported by the friend of the colleague several weeks later that Joe was continuing to do much better. Joe had said he wasn't sure what exactly had happened in the interaction, but he had felt better ever since.

Case 2: Ruth. Ruth, age 20, came in to therapy feeling severely depressed. Once again, assessment revealed that she would meet criteria for major depressive disorder. Ruth was a first-year college student, away from home for the first time in her life. In addition, her parents had just divorced, and the home where she had grown up had been sold. Over the last several months, she had gradually gotten more and more depressed, and her grades had begun to slip.

Ruth reported that she felt she had "lost herself." The old bright, shiny, fun Ruth, who had goals and ambitions, was gone. At this, Ruth began to cry. She proceeded to describe her first year in college. She felt alone and alienated in the huge classes and did not feel she fit in with dormitory life. She was a serious student, and she felt strange and different from the other students, especially her roommate, who seemed mainly motivated to party. Now she did not even have a home to go back to.

Once again the therapist responded primarily with empathic reflections. Through this, Ruth began to step back and explore her experience. She started by reporting that she had lost a sense of purpose and direction. She was not sure why. Somehow the alienation of being at a large campus coupled with the divorce of her parents, which surprised her although she had known there were tensions, left her feeling rudderless. She had always thought her parents were very close and would be able to work through any tensions. She knew that they still cared about her, but that did not seem to help. Also she hated the fact that she did not fit in at school. This was a big conflict for her. Was there anything wrong with her that she did not like the party atmosphere? Was she too serious (her roommate accused her of this)? Had she been too sheltered? Was she too dependent? All these thoughts began to flood through her mind. And she was alone and had no one to confide in.

As Ruth talked about these, she emotionally reexperienced some of the aspects of her problems, including the pain over her parents' divorce and the loss of her old home. In trying to articulate her experience and convey it to the therapist, she also began to sort out its meaning. She realized that she deeply cared about home and family, and that her sense of meaning and purpose was all bound up with that. She further realized that even though she had lost a physical home, that she still felt a deep sense of caring for both parents. She said they were both really nice people and it was so sad that they had not been able to work out their problems. Somehow, realizing how strongly she cared about her parents seemed to anchor her, and Ruth began to resurrect a sense of her own purpose and goals. She began to talk about how she had always had this goal of becoming a research scientist, and her parents had always supported that. It felt so sad to think of her achieving this goal and not having them as a team to share it with. When she had gone home on Christmas, it had felt sad and hollow to tell each parent separately about how well her grades had been that first semester. But Ruth realized that, even though it was sad, she still wanted to pursue her dream of being a research scientist.

By the end of the first session, Ruth seemed considerably better. She had laid out her problem and made several realizations. She had achieved a context on her parents' divorce and on its relationship to her loss of initiative. In so doing she had regained a sense of initiative.

At the second session, Ruth focused on her relationships with other students. She laid out on the table all her feelings of alienation, recounted and reexperienced specific instances of feeling out of tune, and realized that she would have been able to keep in touch with her own compass if she had not suddenly felt totally without a home because of her parents' divorce. She spontaneously realized that she was not out of tune with everyone. There were other serious students. They were just not as "noisy" and visible as the party types. She spontaneously evaluated her worries that she was too dependent and too serious and decided that she was not dependent just because she had a deep connection to her family, and that she was not too serious because she did not like getting falling-down drunk. She started considering the possibility of asking for a change in roommates.

A third session with Ruth was scheduled, but she called in to say she was feeling much better, and thought she did not need to come in. A session for the next week was scheduled just in case, but by then she reported over the telephone feeling fine. She had not asked for a new roommate because there were only a few weeks left in the semester, but she had pursued a friendship with a student in one of her science classes whom she had already known casually. They seemed to hit it off, and she was considering suggesting they room together the next year, but she wanted to wait a little longer to see how the friendship progressed. In any case, Ruth reported that she felt that her "old self" was back.

These two cases are examples in which simple empathic listening provided a very helpful and supportive context for client self-healing. We realize that in many cases therapy will take considerably longer with depressed people, but we also know that successful single-session or very brief therapy is not uncommon (Rosenbaum, 1994). We hope these examples illustrate that far more is going on, at least on the client's side, than mere "hand-holding." We next examine in more detail the active client self-healing processes that are operating when clients are expressing and disclosing to an empathically listening and responding therapist.

Active Client Change Processes Facilitated by an Empathic Listening Context

To see client expression as simply some kind of mechanistic emotional venting is a reductive and simplistic image of what clients are actually doing. When clients express themselves in therapy, they are engaging in a variety of activities. They are struggling to articulate their feelings and experiences, and they are thinking, analyzing, and reflecting upon themselves and their problems. Clients who benefit from expression engage in an active, exploring problem-solving process. At least seven components seem to be involved. These include acknowledging of experience and overcoming shame and secrecy, enhancement of memory, experiential and emotional reprocessing, representation and thinking, role-taking, narrative reworking, and creativity.

Acknowledging of Experience and Overcoming Shame and Secrecy

The first way self-disclosure to an empathic listener can help is that, in order to disclose one's experience, one must acknowledge it and accept it oneself. Acknowledging and accepting one's own experience, as well as disclosing it to another, can help overcome shame and secrecy. This alone can make clients feel better. Feeling better, they then are freer to think about their problems in a more intelligently productive fashion. Wegner and Lane (1995) described how the opposite of self-disclosure—secrecy and thought suppression—leads to intrusive and ruminative thinking. Both Stiles (1995) and Wickramasekera (1998) noted that inhibiting feelings can have a negative physiological impact and that acknowledging, recognizing, and expressing feelings can be therapeutic. Disclosing, if the person feels comfortable doing it (e.g., with an empathic listener), leads to reductions in physiological (e.g., blood pressure, muscle tension, skin conductance) levels when dealing with emotional topics. Stiles (1995) noted, "Undisclosed distressing experiences may be felt as internal pressure [,] . . . may divert attention into superficial, automatic thoughts, and worries . . . and . . . may have negative consequences for health" (p. 83). Talking about an upsetting event can reduce anxiety and promote assimilation of it.

From a feminist self-in-relation perspective, Jordan (1997) suggested that an empathic atmosphere provides a place where clients can bring troublesome feelings into relationship, and where therapists and clients can bear troublesome feelings together. In addition, clients have a chance to "say their truth." In other words, without doing anything else, an empathic atmosphere is therapeutic because the client has a chance to get in touch with themselves, acknowledge their own personal truths and feelings, and then own and assert them to another.

Enhancement of Memory

We know of no evidence for this, but from our own personal experience we know that when we are being empathically listened to we seem to have greater access to our memory. We are more likely to remember useful and relevant bits of information. These become useful in construction of our own solutions to problems.

Experiencing and Emotional Reprocessing

Through disclosure, clients can actively experience problematic issues and emotions. There are two basic processes involved. The first is exposure. Exposure to troubling experience seems to be important in helping clients learn to master and cope, assimilate the problematic experience, let go of it, and move on to more productive ways of being. Direct encounter or exposure to experience is a key component of experiential therapies (Greenberg et al., 1993; Mahrer, 1996) and cognitive–behavioral therapies (Barlow, 1988; Foa & Rothbaum, 1997).

The second process is one of articulating their experience in words (Gendlin, 1968; J. C. Watson & Greenberg, 1996). This has been stressed by Pennebaker (1995) as one of the key components of journaling. Others have argued that forming a link between nonverbal and verbal aspects of experience is necessary for personal reorganization to take place (e.g., Bucci, 1995). Articulating experience in words also helps one think and reflect upon it in productive ways (J. C. Watson & Greenberg, 1996).

There is a good deal of evidence that thinking and verbalizing without experiencing is not as likely to be helpful as thinking and verbalizing with experiencing (Mathieu-Coughlan & Klein, 1984; Rice & Kerr, 1986). For instance, Pennebaker (1990) found that journaling was more likely to be helpful if journalers expressed both thoughts and feelings. Bohart (1980) reviewed a number of studies that found that insight alone, without emotional experiencing, did not seem to be helpful.

However, emotional expression and experiencing is not helpful for mechanistic reasons. One mechanistic explanation is catharsis, which assumes that emotions are like fluids that are drained away through expression. This is essentially a "mindless" view of how expression works, granting no role to the person as an active, thinking being. Other mechanistic explanations are cognitive–behavioral ones that stress extinction and emotional reprocessing. In these explanations, it is assumed that sheer exposure to the emotionally troubling situation somehow automatically leads to emotional reprocessing. Even though this reprocessing includes the correction of dysfunctional cognitions, there is no conceptualization of the client as an active, thoughtful generator of such changes. As an example, Foa and Rothbaum's (1997) treatment for posttraumatic stress involves clients telling the story of their traumatic experience over and over until their "fear structure" is revised. The retelling in a safe situation is portrayed as "correcting" dysfunctional beliefs, but no mention of the client playing an active role is given.

Yet when clients express emotions and tell emotionally traumatic stories, they are doing far more than merely discharging or merely exposing themselves to the emotion so that their fear structures can be revised. They are thinking, articulating experience, struggling to understand it, mulling it over, evaluating it, and narratively restorying it. Emotional discharge and catharsis do not work without an accompanying cognitive, thinking process (Bohart, 1980; Greenberg & Safran, 1987), and even in exposure treatment narrative restorying is going on (Foa, Molnar, & Cashman, 1995).

Representation and Thinking

When clients self-disclose to an empathic listening therapist, many of them spontaneously begin to engage in an active thinking process on their own. They represent their experience in words, spread it out before them, search for patterns in it, make discoveries and insights, develop alternative formulations, and develop new ideas. Some clients do not seem to do this; they seem to stop after answering a therapist's question. However, actively thinking clients continue on their own, often thinking out loud. Through this process, they generate their own solutions.

Some writers have begun to suggest that therapy works by facilitating active client thinking processes. Van Balen (1990) argued that the function of client-centered therapy is to enhance, preserve, or restore what he called the *critical function*. In essence, Van Balen saw client-centered therapy as working by enhancing effective metacognitive functioning. In a similar manner, Zimring (1990) noted that what many therapeutic practices have in common is that they give the client the experience of (a) generating something internally, (b) organizing and comparing the elements that are internally generated, (c) forming a hypothesis, and (d) checking the hypothesis against relevant data. The processes of generating and comparing internal material and then forming and checking hypotheses involving this material may start processes of self-generation, which then continue: "The person changes from reacting to considering" (Zimring, 1990, p. 377).

Zimring mentioned the results of several empirical studies which found that clients thought more clearly after successful client-centered therapy. Humphreys and Bohart (1998) found that Carl Rogers was seen by student raters as stimulating and facilitating client thinking at a high level.

Several writers have identified specific cognitive processes that occur in the self-disclosure process and that account for how clients can change without therapists' interventions (e.g., Clark, 1993). Clark relied on research and theory on dialogue and conversation to outline the potential benefits of a client's disclosing to a therapist, pointing out that people use conversation to solve problems and for creative purposes. Some of the processes noted by Clark are the following.

First, to put something into words, the individual must interpret events as particular instances of more general categories. For instance, to even say "My husband and I had a fight" is to interpret the particular event in terms of the category "fight." Therefore, even in reporting things, the speaker is actively organizing experience by using a variety of knowledge structures to put it into words. Pennebaker (1995) noted that an important benefit of self-disclosure is that it allows clients to translate their experience into words.

Second, the speaker can then react to what he or she has said. The speaker is aware of the evolution of the conversation and may react to this with insights and emotional reactions. Clark (1993) noted "the ability to hear one's explanation spoken aloud may enable the individual to achieve insights . . . the speaker has inference processes that are active during conversation . . . in remembering an event to describe, the speaker has the incident before him/her in its totality" (p. 38). Similarly, J. C. Watson and Rennie (1994) found from a qualitative analysis of therapy that once clients put their experience into words, they then reflect on it.

Third, in explaining things to a listener, the speaker must supply background information. In addition, he or she must work to explain, giving clarifications, elaborations, and proposing reasons and causes for whatever experience he or she is describing. In so doing, the individual is analyzing his or her experience and bringing some coherence into it. For instance, the person may spontaneously notice a connection between two aspects of experience and generate a link between them, thus increasing coherence. Clark (1993) noted, "The processes involved in creating a coherent communication help to organize and clarify the speaker's thoughts and understanding of his/her experience" (p. 35).

Along these same lines, Pennebaker (1995) noted that people have a need to complete unfinished business and to understand the world. Talking (or journaling) helps achieve these aims. In Pennebaker's writing experiments, over 70% of participants said that writing helped them understand both events and themselves better.

In sum, as clients express, they put their experience into words, elaborate on it and clarify it, listen to themselves, gain insights, and reflect on their experience and organize it.

Role-Taking

One of the main objections to simply listening empathically without intervening is that clients need the therapist to offer an outside or alternative perspective. Without it, they will remain trapped in their dysfunctional perspective. However, according to Clark (1993), one of the benefits of self-disclosure is that it forces the discloser to take an outside perspective on experience. Under stress, individuals often experience narrowed attention. To disclose to another person, though, the individual must automatically begin to "stand back," see things in a broader perspective, and let new information in. This is in part due to the basic conversational need to build a common ground (Clark, 1991; Schegloff, 1991) between the speaker and the listener. To create a common ground between two different subjective worlds, the speaker must try to explain things to a listener who was not there, does not know the details of the speaker's life, and may be seeing the world from a different experiential vantage point. Thus, the speaker must actively work to guess at and try to understand the listener's point of view and to communicate his or her experience in terms that will be comprehensible from that point of view. As Clark (1993) said, "while individuals under stress may often experience a loss in perspective . . . conversations require that the individual use more than one perspective. Put very simply, if conversation necessitates the use of multiple perspectives, the individual under stress may benefit from talking about the problem" (p. 37).

Therefore, the very act of trying to communicate to another person can force the individual to take multiple perspectives into account. This is why outside objective feedback from the therapist is not always needed. Clients are capable of reflecting on themselves, when disclosing to a listening other, and creating their own "outside perspectives."

Narrative Restorying of Experience

Another way self-disclosure is beneficial is that it can lead to a productive narrative restorying of experience. In Pennebaker's (1990, 1997) writing experiments, it was found that accounts of events changed subtly over time. Experiences became more storylike, with a beginning, a middle, and an end. Narratives also became shorter and more concise, and irrelevant and tangential issues were weeded out. Central issues and features were highlighted and analyzed. The activity of providing a mental summary of a trauma tended to make it psychologically less daunting and better able to be dealt with. We have already noted that Harvey et al. (1991) found that account-making by clients who had suffered traumatic experiences and who were encouraged to tell their stories helped them overcome these experiences. Similarly, Foa and Rothbaum's (1997) cognitive–behavioral procedure in which clients tell their stories over and over not only leads to emotional reprocessing but also changes in narrative over time, and these are associated with positive outcome (Foa et al., 1995).

Creativity

We have more to say about creativity in chapter 8, so for now we simply note that creativity is enhanced by a nonjudgmental atmosphere in which individuals feel free to suspend old ways of looking at things to scan the whole problem space, looking for new insights or combinations of things. Clients will also feel free to imaginatively play with ideas. Self-disclosure in a safe, nonjudgmental situation may therefore foster clients' creativity independent of anything else the therapist does.

How an Empathic Listening and Responding Therapist Facilitates Active Client Self-Healing Processes

Therapists, by being "conversationally responsive" (Clark, 1993), can facilitate and support the clients' self-healing processes we have reviewed. We first consider how empathic reflecting can do this. We then look at conversational responsiveness in a broader sense.

Empathic Reflecting

Empathic reflecting can be particularly useful for the therapist to adopt with some clients. For some clients, all that is needed is to have the emotional support that comes with feeling that someone is on their side. They then are able to think through their problems themselves. However, empathic responding is more than just the provision of emotional support. Used to its maximum advantage, empathic reflection can more fully engage clients' productive thinking processes. When clients hear their own argument mirrored back to them, for instance, they often spontaneously gain insight into it and revise it. Jackie, a client with bipolar disorder and a history of sexual abuse, was explaining why she argued with her mother-in-law and how she handled her. The therapist paraphrased the client's strategy back to her. Jackie said, "When I hear it said by you, I disagree. I don't like being that way. I have to think about this." In the dialogical process, she understood through another person what she was doing and wanted to change it. This required no value judgment or active intervention by the therapist, just an accurate understanding of the client's argument and a summary reflection.

Empathic reflections can be important in facilitating client involvement in therapy. Clients come into therapy defensively oriented outward toward the therapist, feeling fragile, unintelligent, and damaged. Or they are defensively oriented inwardly, afraid of themselves, and self-critical. Empathic reflections may help them feel really listened to and heard, and they begin to feel safe. They become curious about whatever thoughts and feelings inside had previously scared them, and they turn their attention inward in a proactive way.

Empathic reflections are actually a form of therapist "co-thinking." Rogers's (1986) view of empathic reflections was that they were attempts to test out the therapist's understanding of the client. They were not primarily responses to emotion. Typical empathic reflections might be, "You just don't know what to do" or "You really think if you told him about your background he wouldn't accept you." Such empathic reflections, if skillfully done, seem to fit almost seamlessly into the client's self-examination process. It is as if therapist and client have joined together to reflect on and examine the client's experience. Having someone "think along" with the clients, on their track, helps them get to know themselves better and helps them clarify their thoughts. A major component of good empathic reflections is that they try to capture the unspoken or implicit logic in what the person is saying. Such responses are often in the form of, "If I hear you correctly, you are implying. . . ." Thus, the therapist is helping the client articulate what the client knows implicitly; this helps clients bring their own logic before their eyes so they can evaluate it.

Empathic reflections thus can help clients articulate and acknowledges experience, put it into words, think and reflect on it, and narratively restory it. They also can help clients take a new perspective on their own logic. Finally, when directed at emotion, empathic reflections can facilitate clients' emotional experiencing.

Good empathic reflections are far more than simple acknowledgments of clients' emotions (e.g., "You're feeling overwhelmed" or "You're feeling angry"). Learning to use good empathic reflections is not easy. Gendlin (1984) said that it takes several weeks of continual practice just to become good at the most basic step of empathic reflecting—that of simply saying back to the client what the client has already said. But there is much more to good empathic reflections than this. Good empathic reflections catch the complex cognitive–affective meaning connections implicit in client communications. And that is an understanding that, inevitably, one has to work at. The "landscape" of another person is something one has to journey in for a while to get to know. One cannot assume one knows the other person through a few statements made by the client, any more than one knows a landscape through a few photos.

Empathic reflections can be helpful to any client regardless of level of pathology. In our experience, clients with serious problems often like being listened to just as much as clients with less serious problems. Furthermore, empathic reflections can involve them just as well, and they begin to think more proactively and to spontaneously carry forward their thinking in a productive and problem-solving way.

Conversational Responsiveness

Clark (1993) discussed how a good, responsive listener in general may help when clients are self-disclosing. First, simply interacting with another person who listens and tries to understand may help enhance self-esteem. Second, a good listener may help individuals manage their emotions and defensiveness so that they can effectively problem solve. Third, a supportive relationship may encourage clients to explore the meaning of their problematic experiences and provide a context in which they can discuss new plans and decisions. Fourth, good listeners contribute through various conversational implementations such as providing a useful vocabulary and pointing out terms that need to be clarified. Fifth, paraphrasing and interpreting may help the listener elaborate and clarify experience. Sixth, reflecting may help. Clark (1993) noted that, compatible with what we said earlier, "reflecting back the explanation provided by the distressed individual might provide that individual with the opportunity to correct or elaborate on aspects of the explanation" (p. 44).

What the person most primarily needs when self-disclosing is *conversational responsiveness*. This is responding in a way that "a) addresses the context of the preceding communication, b) provides an appropriate amount of elaboration, and c) is timely with respect to the flow of the interaction (Berg, 1987)" (Clark, 1993, p. 43). Listeners can hurt by not being conversationally responsive, that is, by giving advice when the speaker wants to gripe or when the speaker is exploring and elaborating, or by failing to provide support.

In this regard, White (1965) observed that it is highly therapeutic for clients to discover that their desires and intentions are being heard and responded to by the therapist. White noted that "getting others to understand you carries with it a definite feeling of interpersonal efficacy" (p. 209).

Comparing Disclosure in Medicine With Disclosure in Psychotherapy

Stiles (1995) observed that despite differences in what therapist do, clients disclose a great deal more in psychotherapy than in medicine or in normal social conversation. It is instructive to think about why self-disclosure to a therapist might be helpful, while disclosing to a physician would not be expected to have similar benefits. When one describes physical problems to a physician, one is engaging in the same active, constructive conversational processes one is in psychotherapy. However, it is not generally believed that such active constructive processes of formulating experience into words will have any material effect on physical symptoms (though this belief may be incorrect). In contrast, psychological problems are, in one form or the other, precisely the kind of information-processing or learning problems that ought to be affected by these active constructive processes. Therefore, when a client describes his or her problems to a therapist, there is a potentiality for a therapeutic process to occur, even if the therapist "does nothing." But this is not the same as with a physician. A physician's empathic listening to a patient's description of his or her physical pain may amount to nothing more than "mere hand-holding," with no "real" medical benefit, but the same process with a client dealing with a psychological problem is much more truly active and helpful.

Not all clients, of course, self-heal simply through expression to a receptive, empathic therapist. Nonetheless, we have intensively examined the possibility that such a situation can be highly therapeutic because most theories simply have no way of dealing with it, and thus tend to dismiss it. What we hope to have shown is that a highly active, constructive, cognitive–affective process is occurring when clients are disclosing to a therapist. We have considered earlier in this book why clients may have to come to therapy to get such a platform for their efforts, and why it is so often difficult to engage in such a process in everyday life.

We believe that the processes we have described above form the core of how clients change in therapy. However, not all clients are able to do this through their own verbal self-exploration and expression. First, some may be so demoralized that they are unable to muster the kind of active energetic involvement in the self-exploration process that is required (see chapter 7 for more on this). They may be so stuck in self-recrimination and rumination that simple listening may not provide the kind of interactive experience needed to promote getting unstuck. They may feel so vulnerable and defensive that they do not feel enough safety and emotional freedom to open up. They may need more active strategies to "scaffold" the processes described above. In other words, they may need to reflect in action. Finally, some may get mired in highly abstract intellectual analysis that is not connected to their actual experience. In sum, some clients may require other resources to use. In the next section, we consider the other resources that therapy provides.

OTHER LEARNING OPPORTUNITIES

Four other basic kinds of learning opportunities are provided by therapy. We provide a general look at these four opportunities rather than go into the details of how they are implemented in therapy, because those details are available in many other books. In chapter 9, we provide Figure

9.2, which shows how the five basic learning opportunities go together in how we practice.

Provision of a Context for Interpersonal Exploration and Learning

Many theories hold that clients' difficulties originate in dysfunctional early relationships that have led to internalized self-distrust, negative self-concepts, disowning of experience, problems in trusting others, difficulties in being independent and autonomous, difficulties knowing where oneself leaves off and others begin, difficulties in being close and intimate, and dysfunctional interpersonal strategies for getting needs met. Learning new ways of being and behaving with others may be difficult in the natural environment because people with problematic interpersonal behaviors often chase others away, or bring out the worst in others, before they are able to explore and learn. Also, when a person believes that his or her important needs are not being met, he or she may react with desperation and use whatever is available, rather than take the time to experiment and explore new behaviors. What is available are old behaviors that are often problematic.

The therapy context can provide a good interpersonal learning space. This is emphasized by existential therapists, psychodynamic therapists, some modern radical behavioral therapists (e.g., Kohlenberg & Tsai, 1987), some cognitive therapists (e.g., Safran & Segal, 1990), and feminist therapists (e.g., Jordan, 1997). Therapy offers an environment in which the client can safely test out beliefs about the nature of people and of relationships and experiment with new ways of being. This may occur whether it is part of the explicit agenda of the therapist or not. The therapist creates this environment by being different from people in the everyday lived-in environment. The therapist patiently "stays with" the client through crises, does not overreact to them, helps the client bear feelings (Jordan, 1997), and maintains an optimal therapeutic distance (Leitner, 1995) in which he or she is warm, empathic, and supporting but not overly involved, enmeshed, or intrusive. Furthermore, the therapist helps the client keep "the eye on the prize"—on proactive problem solving and growth. The client may learn that he or she is acceptable, that he or she is worthy of being listened to, and that his or her experience is not so awful that it cannot be acknowledged and borne. The client may also learn that he or she does not have to be sneaky and manipulative to get needs met. The client may also learn that another person (the therapist) is trustworthy and dependable, will be "there," but will not be manipulated or pushed around. Therefore, the client may expand his or her sense of possibility about himself or herself, about other people, and about relationships.

Provision of an Opportunity for Co-Constructive Dialogue

There are a number of dialogical processes that occur between therapist and client that facilitate client thinking, learning, and problem solving. Some clients want more than empathic listening from their therapists. They want feedback—ideas, information, alternative points of view, and insights. As in any good conversation, they may enjoy being stimulated to think by pithy questions. They may particularly find a mutual, co-constructive dialogue in which ideas are traded back and forth to be rewarding and useful.

From the standpoint of the client as an active self-healer, the therapist should see what he or she is doing as dialoging and not as intervening. A good model would be a mentor or teacher. The idea that the therapist is intervening when he or she asks a question, gives an interpretation, or makes a suggestion implies a mechanistic one-way relationship in which the therapist is operating on the client and the client is merely "responding" (Angus, 1992). This can create an implicit bias in the therapist's mind. It implies that the therapist is somehow doing something to the client rather than dialoging. It puts the client in the "one-down" position of someone who is being "done to" or operated on. In other areas of life, one does not see teachers who offer an interpretation of a historical event to their students or an interpretation of a piece of literature as "intervening." Rather, they are sharing information and new perspectives. They are trying to stimulate thinking and understanding. What the teachers are doing is offering students a new vantage point from which to see the work or the event, and that is what the therapist does. Similarly, asking questions to get clients to think, as in cognitive therapy, is no more an intervention than it was for Socrates, who asked questions to get fellow philosophers to think. The mechanistic language of intervention is misleading and can obscure and distort the potential for a useful dialogue in which both parties play an active role.

If the therapist suspects that his or her vantage point on the problem will help the client see new aspects and thereby move toward resolution, the therapist should offer it. However, what is crucial is that it is not offered as the truth but as something for the client to consider. We take it as an article of faith that clients need to see the truth for themselves in anything the therapists offer. Questions, interpretations, and so on should be offered by therapists in ways that *stimulate* clients' own thinking process, rather than in ways that *replace* it.

We therefore believe these therapist activities are best thought of as part of a co-constructive dialogue with the client. Co-constructive dialogue means there is a back and forth, where a therapist's thoughtful response is evaluated and responded to by the client in an equally thoughtful and intelligent manner.

Teaching a Philosophy of Life

Viewing what therapists do as intervention also can obscure another important educational fact about therapy: that therapists often are teaching a philosophy of life, as do religious leaders, political philosophers, and other nonclinicians. This is most explicit with Albert Ellis, whose framework is really a whole philosophical system for dealing with life. It includes, for instance, the belief that thinking in terms of "musts" and "shoulds" is irrational. This philosophy is taught through logical disputation, modeling, and explanation. As does any good philosopher, Ellis teaches by getting his "students" (clients) to think things out for themselves. Other therapies also teach a philosophy of life, but more indirectly. Freudians view humans as having a dark side and emphasize the value of facing up to this dark side and "owning" it. Client-centered therapists model a process philosophy: Life is better lived by holding constructs tentatively and by adopting an open-ended exploratory attitude. Existential therapists encourage a kind of "tragic" view: There is no certainty or ultimate meaning in life; people must choose in the face of nothingness and create meaning out of this nothing.

Provision of Structured Exercises for Exploration

Many of the exercises used by therapists are akin to structured exercises used by educators to promote students' exploration and development of their own ideas. Once again, viewing them as interventions may obscure this fact. For instance, it is said that the gestalt two-chair technique leads to deeper levels of experiencing, the daily record of dysfunctional thoughts and other cognitive exercises "restructure" clients' cognitions, exposure techniques "extinguish" fears, and so on. This language makes it sound like it is the technique that is making these things happen. However, from the standpoint of the client as an active self-healer, these techniques really are *structured exercises* that clients use to explore and learn. They are more like the structured learning activities used by teachers of art, music, drama and literature.

In a drama class, students are often given exercises in which they have to practice improvising a part. This is an activity that allows the student to develop his or her talents. Similarly, in a writing class, a student may be given the exercise of finishing a Hemingway short story. Even more specific structured activities like being assigned to write a particular kind of poem are meant to develop the student's capacities. These exercises do not mechanistically intervene, but rather promote students' self-development.

Many assignments in school can be seen in this light. Students may be given the assignment of researching the literature on a particular topic and coming up with their own research idea. Or they may be given the topic of writing an essay comparing two or more theoretical points of view. By giving structured assignments, teachers are trying to help stimulate students' thinking. In a similar manner, many psychotherapy exercises should be thought of as structured opportunities for learning. Clients have the opportunity to creatively and imaginatively explore and discover new and better ways of being and behaving.

Let us examine some representative exercises. First we look at the gestalt two-chair procedure as used by Greenberg et al. (1993). This procedure is used when a person is experiencing a split in experience, between a "want" side and a "should" side. An example might be a person debating between "I want to be an artist" versus "I should become a lawyer." The person role plays the want side in one chair, and then switches chairs to role play the should side. With appropriate coaching from the therapist, the client goes back and forth, making up a dialogue between the two sides. This leads to successful resolution when the should side, also known as the critic side, begins to soften and to express what it, too, wants or fears (from "You should be a lawyer" to "I'm afraid that if you don't pursue law you'll never make it in life"). The process becomes more deeply experiential also. As these two changes happen, the two sides begin to talk together more collaboratively, and an integration or a consensus is often reached (e.g., "Maybe I'll pursue art for a few years and see how it goes, but I'll be ready to go back to law school if it is not working out").

This technique can be described mechanistically as "deepening" clients' experience, resulting in the softening of the critic side and eventual integration, as if the technique were making these things happen in a billard-ball-like fashion. However, from the standpoint of the client, a different process is occurring. Clients at first often feel awkward and stupid talking to an empty chair. As a result, they may initially just "mouth" the lines. However, the procedure is essentially an acting exercise, and eventually clients begin to "inhabit" the two parts. This is facilitated by the therapist, who constantly urges clients to enter into the roles emotionally by focusing them on what they are feeling. As clients enter into the roles, they begin to speak from them and to imaginatively create the roles and carry them forward. Essentially, this is an exercise in creativity. The client is playing with multiple perspectives on a deeply important personal issue. Furthermore, the client is getting to speak from both sides, and thus to enact and carry forward the implicit logic in both sides. As the client in each role creatively spells out the implicit logic in each position, each position becomes more differentiated. Eventually the dialogue becomes very personal. The client begins to say what is so important and vital about wanting to be an artist, and what is so important and vital about not throwing one's life away on trivial artistic pursuits. As clients begin to articulate important personal meanings from each side, they also begin to feel more deeply, because affect and emotion are closely tied to important personal issues. To say, "I really *want* to be an artist!" is to say it with deeply felt emotion. To say "I'm afraid you're throwing your life away on something trivial and frivolous!" is to say it with deeply felt fear or dismay. Thus the process becomes more deeply experiential.

The client, however, is continually active in this process and is shaping it as much as the process and the therapist are shaping the client. The process does not make people get more experiential. Rather, it provides a platform for this to happen. The exercise is an exercise that clients can use to achieve these ends if they so choose, and if they willingly enter into the imaginative role play. If they do not, even if they go through the motions, the process will not make anything happen. There are clients who go through the motions mechanically and do not benefit from the procedure. Thus this process is not a "therapeutic operation."

In sum, the two-chair technique is an imaginative structured exercise that allows clients to turn over their problem from multiple angles and take multiple looks at it, imaginatively simulate different sides of it, emotionally enter into different aspects of the problem, role play and express the inner aspects of each side of the conflict and thereby illuminate the issues involved, and finally, creatively and actively synthesize a solution.

Consider also systematic desensitization. Suppose a client has a fear of public speaking. We construct a hierarchy and teach the client how to relax. Then we have the client imagine various scenes while relaxed. Traditional conditioning explanations of this process were mechanistic. First, practicing the relaxation behaviors was supposed to mechanistically "make" the client relaxed. Then the pairing of relaxation and scene was supposed to condition a relaxation response to the scene, thereby interfering with the anxiety response already paired with the scene.

However, from the standpoint of the client as an active self-healer, this is not how this procedure operates. First, even learning how to relax is a highly active process by the client. We have used relaxation with a number of clients, and while most take to it, not all do. Some are willing to go through the procedure but do not get relaxed. They do the steps, they breathe deeply, tense and untense their muscles, and so on, but they do not really enter into the process and so it does not work. Two cases illustrate this. One was of a young woman who came in because she was experiencing generalized anxiety. Despite repeated efforts to teach her relaxation, she never seemed to achieve more than a minimal level. It was as if *she* believed the conditioning explanation: If she mechanistically followed the steps of the procedure, it should "operate on" her to relax her. Thus, all the while she was doing the exercises she seemed to be standing outside her experience and observing it, to see if the technique would work. In fact it did not.

Another case was of a Vietnam War veteran who did all the steps but found the procedure did not work because he was unable to enter into it. This was because, as he eventually said after trying it several times, he was unable to let his guard down. (This was not a bad therapeutic outcome because we then gave up working on relaxation and worked on his fear of letting his guard down.) It is clear that it is not the *procedure* that causes relaxation. Instead, it is the person using the procedure who relaxes himself or herself. Relaxation works when the client is willing and receptive. One must enter into it.

After becoming relaxed, the client is asked to imagine anxiety-arousing scenes, which then supposedly get paired by conditioning with the relaxation. The traditional view of desensitization is that the client is merely the "site" for a response to be conditioned to a stimulus (Bandura, 1997). But the client is anything but a mindless, passive participant who is having his or her emotional experience conditioned. Clients are actively thinking and exploring as they imagine the various scenes. Much more learning is going on than that. This exercise too is an imaginative role-playing exercise. The client is imagining himself or herself confronting the feared situation. He or she actively explores the situation in imagination. The scene is never imagined exactly the same way twice. Thus, it is being scanned from different angles as it is imaginatively rotated and varied. Clients are imaginatively simulating variations in effective coping. They learn, among other things, that they can cope with the feared situation (Goldfried, 1995). They are developing a sense of self-efficacy with regard to the situation (Bandura, 1997). In summary, systematic desensitization is not a procedure that "operates on" the client, but rather is a structured exercise that provides an opportunity for the client to imaginatively explore a feared situation.

Parenthetically, clients can work their own creative variations on these exercises to their benefit if the therapist is willing to go along with them. For instance, one client was very tense about an interpersonal problem and wanted to do something rather than just talk. The therapist suggested the variation on the gestalt two-chair technique in which the client imaginatively role plays a dialogue with another person, switching chairs and playing both sides (Greenberg et al., 1993). However the client did not want to do the "jumping back and forth" part. So the therapist let her stay in one chair. She turned away from the therapist and engaged in a very lively conversation. She felt considerably relieved after that. The point is that clients can make variations on these procedures and not only still learn, but in some cases learn better. This is not usually the case with exercises prescribed by physicians, such as back exercises, which must be performed as prescribed in order to have their beneficial effects.

Provision of Specific Learning Experiences and Teaching of Specific Skills

There are cases in which clients lack basic skills or may need to learn new emotional or behavioral reactions. Without certain basic communication and self-management skills, self-healing becomes much more of a hit-or-miss affair. Having these basic skills empowers the individual to creatively problem solve more effectively. Handing the individual some basic skills is like handing the individual some good, effective tools for coping with life. In addition, clients may need the opportunity to learn how to specifically handle certain fears and anxieties, for instance, as with posttraumatic stress or panic attacks.

In these cases, therapy becomes a kind of learning laboratory with a specific curriculum. In this environment clients have the opportunity, through structured exercises specifically targeted to promote certain learnings, to modify reactions and develop skills. In these cases, therapy is more like traditional teaching, in that the teacher is teaching "how to." There is, in this sense, less room for client discovery. Clients learn models for communicating, asserting, managing their emotions (e.g., Linehan, 1993), and so on.

Nonetheless, these basic skills too are not mechanistic scripts that clients simply learn and then run off. In fact, the search to specify the components of basic skills so that they can be taught in such a rote fashion has proved to be disappointing (S. C. Hayes, Follette, & Follette, 1995). What clients are really learning are *templates* for flexible operation. Assertion, for instance, is really practicing a set of ways of being assertive, not so that one can continue to "ape" what one has learned, but so that one can flexibly decide in any given moment how to be assertive. Clients who mechanistically ape their therapists, who just "say lines," will not be as successful as clients who imaginatively enter into the role-play of the exercises, get a feel for the sense in being assertive, and develop their own unique sense of what assertiveness will mean to them. These individuals will be able to spontaneously generate their own unique ways of being assertive to match the contingencies in various situations. We know that a client has "really understood" what it means to be assertive when they can flexibly and creatively adapt assertiveness to different life dilemmas. It is very similar to how we know someone has really understood something in education, such as in calculus—when they can creatively apply it to new problems. In sum, although at times therapy is a matter of teaching skills, it is the clients' active ability to take what they have learned and creatively apply it in their own lives that is the healing element.

HOW CLIENTS CHANGE IN THERAPY

We conclude this chapter with an overview of how clients change in therapy. The idea that all therapies work about equally well has led to many attempts to find common factors among different approaches to therapy. A number of different lists of common factors have been proposed

(Grencavage & Norcross, 1990). Rarely, if ever, is the client seen as a common factor. Grencavage and Norcross found that the vast majority of common factors identified had to do with the therapist and therapy process. The only client factors mentioned were the client's positive hope and expectancies for treatment, the client's being distressed or in a state of incongruence, and the client's actively seeking help. Thus, from the standpoint of various writers on psychotherapy, clients only contribute to the therapy process by (a) hoping it will help, (b) being distressed, and (c) coming to seek help.

Yet an inspection of the other common factors, attributed to the therapist or to the therapeutic process, reveals that most of them are actually client processes in disguise. In other words, the factors that can be found across therapies that make therapy work are *client change processes*. Furthermore, they are client processes that could just as easily operate outside therapy as inside. For instance, included in the category of therapeutic processes are (a) acquisition and practice of new behaviors (something done by clients both inside and outside of therapy), (b) fostering insight and awareness (while therapists may "foster" it, it is the clients who actually achieve it, and they can achieve it on their own outside of therapy), and (c) emotional and interpersonal learning (same as (b)).

The idea that the key change processes are naturally occurring client change processes, which are then fostered or facilitated by the therapist, accords with the contention made by Efran and Blumberg (1994) that many of the things therapists do are simply the things people do in everyday life to change, only couched in professional jargon:

> [A] client's "just plain stupid" ideas become, in the hands of the cognitive–behavioral therapist, a set of "maladaptive cognitions." A young man's uncle advises him to just face his fear but the therapist instead prescribes a regimen of "in vivo exposure." The commonsense admonition is to "take things one step at a time," but the professional proposes "graded exposure" or "systematic desensitization." . . . A coworker might advise an angry colleague to think twice before telling the boss off. The psychoanalyst makes much the same point by interpreting hostility toward an employer as a derivative of prior *authority issues*. (pp. 174–175, italics in original)

Prochaska et al.'s, (1994) findings also support the idea that the same change strategies used by therapists in therapy are the ones used by individuals who self-heal and self-right on their own.

To identify what these core change processes are, we rely on the common-factors approaches of Goldfried and Padawer (1982) and Grawe (1997). Goldfried and Padawer listed the following as common factors in psychotherapy: expectation that therapy will help, therapeutic relationship, obtaining an external perspective on oneself and the world, continued reality testing, and corrective experiences. Similarly, Grawe argued for a common-factors approach to therapy based on research. He identified the following: clarification of meanings, provision of opportunities for mastery and coping experiences, problem actuation (activating the problem in therapy to be worked on "in vivo"), and utilization of client resources (i.e., our client-as-active-self-healer concept). In essence, these change processes consist of individuals learning and developing new ways of being and behaving in therapy by

- overcoming demoralization
- trying to understand their problems when their problems are emotionally alive to them
- thinking about their problems and reflecting on them and clarifying their meaning
- trying things out, practicing, and learning
- having mastery experiences as they directly experience their problems and their efforts to cope with them
- getting an external perspective on their problems, either through their own behavioral and cognitive exploration or through feedback from others

This is often facilitated by the context of a supportive relationship.

These factors boil down to, first, the therapist helping the client overcome feelings of helplessness and demoralization, and, second, a process of learning through thinking, experiencing, and behaving. As we have noted, the single most important thing for therapy to succeed is that the client become proactively involved in the process. This means that a "gatekeeper" to success in therapy is the degree to which the client is paralyzed by feelings of helplessness and the concomittent self-criticism that usually accompanies such feelings. Helping clients who are paralyzed by helplessness or self-doubt become remoralized and enter a proactive coping state of mind so that they can use their self-healing capacities is therefore an "entry-level" skill in successful therapy. After the client is able to become proactively involved, it is the client's use of his or her capacities for learning that leads to self-healing. We describe the first process, that of coping with helplessness and demoralization, in chapter 7, and the second, that of promoting learning, in chapter 8.

CONCLUSION

In this chapter, we examined the five basic ways the "school" of psychotherapy can promote clients' new learning and creativity. These include

- Provision of a safe, supportive workspace in which clients can explore and think through problems
- An interpersonal learning environment in which clients can

learn new ways of being and behaving directly as a function of interaction with the therapist

- A context for co-constructive dialogue
- Provision of guided activities for self-exploration that promote clients attaining creative insights and discovering and developing solutions to their own problems
- Provision of structured learning experiences for modifying affect and behavior and for developing new skills

6

HOW THE ACTIVE CLIENT FITS IN
WITH OTHER APPROACHES

In this chapter, we examine different approaches to therapy and how they fit with the idea of the client as an active self-healer. We first examine what it means to say that a therapeutic relationship is *collaborative*.

TYPES OF COLLABORATION WITH CLIENTS

As we have struggled to articulate our vision of the client as active self-healer, we have come to realize that the idea of collaboration needs to be clarified. There are different types of collaboration. Below we present a taxonomy of them. In Type 1, the collaboration on the part of the client is minimal. In Type 5, it is maximal. Types 3 through 5 constitute what we mean by collaborating with an active self-healing client.

Type 1: Minimal client collaboration; maximal therapist control of change process. At this level, the therapist believes that it is his or her interventions or procedures that precipitate change. Client collaboration is minimal. The client must collaborate in the sense of submitting to the procedure, but all the activity and potency reside in the procedures themselves. The procedure can literally be said to be "operating on" clients without their active participation in implementing them.

This is most characteristic of traditional mechanistic conditioning views of therapy. For instance, the idea behind extinction is that the client is merely exposed to the threatening stimulus over and over until the fear response "extinguishes." There is no active client trying to learn or master anything. Rather, it is a procedure that works on the client. The client need not even do anything, except be present in the face of the feared stimulus.

Type 2: Active client collaboration in the form of compliance; therapist's technique is primarily responsible for change. Here the client must be more active than in Type 1, for instance, by practicing and learning skills. However, a mechanistic explanation is still preferred and responses are still seen as being "stamped in" or conditioned into the organism. Once again, there is no theoretical view of the client as an active intelligence learning as he or she participates in the exercise. The medical analogy here would be to back exercises. The person must actively do the exercises, but the exercises do their work without any active thinking or learning on the part of the client. In therapy, this is again characteristic of traditional behavioral views.

Another version of this is to be found in confrontive alcoholism treatments. The client is viewed as so defended and locked into denial that he or she is incapable of honest, proactive self-change. The client must actively participate in the treatment, but defenses are broken down from without by the therapist.

Type 3: Active client collaboration in the form of compliance and participation; therapist's techniques provide the context for learning but the client is an active agent in the learning. This is characteristic of most modern behavioral and cognitive–behavioral approaches, including the work of Goldfried, Bandura, Meichenbaum, and a host of others. It is also characteristic of most cognitive approaches. At this level, even techniques such as exposure are viewed in a much more active way. It is assumed that exposure works by providing the client with an experience of active mastery (Bandura, 1997; Goldfried, 1995). Skills training is learning the ability to generate responses (Bandura, 1997), not mechanistically learning specific response sequences. As people develop skills, they become more able to be effectively agentic (Bandura, 1997). In cognitive therapy, the therapist is a tutor who identifies clients' dysfunctional thoughts and then tutors them in how to correct them. Clients must be active collaborators in the process and are learning how to think more clearly for themselves. In these models, the therapist is still the expert who knows what specifically the client needs to learn. However, clients are active agentic participants and can ultimately take over their own self-control and self-direction to become their own problem solvers and self-healers (Goldfried, 1995).

Metaphors for the therapist at this level of collaboration would be expert tutor, coach, or mentor. The therapist is expert in certain skills and in the training procedures to help the client acquire these skills and skillfully provides a learning environment in which clients can master these skills.

Type 4: Active client collaboration in the form of compliance, and participation and techniques as liberating client creativity and generativity. This is most characteristic of approaches like experiential therapy and strategic therapy. In these models, the therapist assumes a kind of expert role in that the therapist prescribes techniques or gives directives. However, the goal is to provide a structured activity that allows client self-discovery and creative emergence of new solutions. The exercises are designed to promote client thinking and self-discovery rather than to teach skills. A metaphor for the therapist with this type of activity might be that of drama coach or creative writing teacher, guiding the client through structured exercises to develop his or her own insights and creative solutions.

Most psychodynamic therapies also fall in this category because interpretation can be thought of as a therapeutic technique or procedure designed to further insightful exploration on the part of the client. Good interpretations do not give clients the answer so much as contribute to the self-exploration process. A metaphor for the psychoanalytic therapist might be that of the expert guide, such as Virgil, who guides Dante through the Inferno. The guide knows what the dangers and pitfalls of the journey are and what, in a general sense, Dante must learn. The guide helps Dante see, but cannot tell Dante what Dante must learn. Learning only takes place when Dante himself encounters what he must learn directly.

Type 5: The client as active self-healer, co-director, and collaborator in therapy; client as primary generator of change. At this level, clients are granted an even more active role in therapy. It is assumed that they have the capability to generate answers and solution for themselves. Therapists are liberators, so to speak, but clients already know much of what they need to know to solve their own problems. This is most characteristic of client-centered, constructivistic, narrative, and solution-focused therapies. At this level, the client is treated as a fully equal collaborator. Collaboration is more than client participation and compliance. Clients are full participants in the generative, creative, planning activity of the therapy.

A metaphor for the therapist here would be something like a member of a creative team, such as John Lennon to the client's Paul McCartney, or Richard Rodgers to the client's Oscar Hammerstein. The therapist accompanies the client on the journey of discovery and helps the client when the client encounters obstacles, but the helping is in the form of mutual creative collaboration rather than in the form of either expert guiding (Type 4) or expert tutoring (Type 3).

Each of the collaboration in Types 3 through 5 honor the client as an active self-healer. In our view of therapy (see chapter 8), we nest all the other levels under Type 5. That is, while we might take an active tutorial stance with some clients, as in Type 3, and use a cognitive—

behavioral technique, it would be done in the context of a Type 5 relationship. Other therapists might use other levels as their "base pads"—Type 4 for experiential therapists, Type 3 for cognitive–behaviorists. Practically speaking, different levels may match up better with the preferences of different clients. Some clients will want to be given direction and tutored (Type 3); others will want guided self-discovery (Type 4); and still others will want a fully collaborative dialogical relationship (Type 5) in which therapist and client operate more like colleagues. We use the metaphor of the home decorator: Some clients will want the decorator to coach and educate them; others will want full, equal collaboration.

With this taxonomy in mind, we now examine different approaches to therapy and their compatibility with the client as active self-healer. Some are entirely compatible; some are partially compatible.

SPECIFIC APPROACHES AND CLIENT SELF-HEALING

Approaches That Are Compatible

Client-Centered Therapy

The idea of the client as an active self-healer is not new. Carl Rogers (1957, 1961) postulated a self-actualization motive and argued that clients would heal themselves if given the proper therapeutic conditions. Therapists did not have to operate on clients with interventions. Clients were experts on themselves and implicitly had knowledge of how to escape the binds and traps they were in.

In client-centered therapy, clients spontaneously become their own cognitive, psychodynamic, existential, or behavioral therapists if needed. For instance, as the client talks to an empathically listening therapist, the client refers inward, listens to feelings, and begins to think things through and try things out. The client may begin to carefully compare and contrast her or his personal beliefs to her or his own experience, and begin to modify them (Bohart, 1982). This could look very much like cognitive therapy with the single significant difference being that the process is client generated.

What therapists do is empathically listen, respond from their hearts and souls, and care. It is a mistake to see Rogers as "intervening." Thinking that Rogers is intervening is to apply medical-model thinking to a non-medical-model therapy. From within a client-centered paradigm, it is not the specific effects of particular kinds of therapist responses that are important, but rather the kind of facilitative climate jointly created by therapist and client together.

In Rogers's theory, as in existential therapy, there is no need for the construct of differential treatment, because nothing is being treated. The therapeutic process is a holistic one of listening to another whole person, opening up to that other whole person, and dialoguing with that person. Problems are symptoms of how the person is stuck at the interface between self and world. Getting clients unstuck causes many problems to spontaneously resolve themselves. They do not have to be solved or removed. As a depressed client begins to have faith in him- or herself, begins to once again "get back in the ball game" of life and take steps toward goals, his or her depression melts away. As clients choose life and living, as they affirm their own selves and their own self-worth, and as they trust in their own capacities and life directions, psychological dysfunctions resolve themselves. They do not have to be differentially treated.

Rogers's approach falls into Type 5 of client collaboration. The client is the active director and investigator and has as much power (if not more) in the therapy relationship as does the therapist. The therapist is a research assistant (O'Hara, 1986) or a companion on the client's journey. Therapy is completely discovery oriented, and the approach is completely opposite to the medical model.

A problem with traditional Rogerian therapy, as well as with some psychodynamic approaches (and the direct converse of a problem with cognitive–behavior therapies), is that it restricts itself to Type 5 collaboration. There are times, however, when Types 3 (tutoring in skills) and 4 (providing structured discovery exercises) might be helpful to clients.

Experiential Therapies

Experiential therapies, such as those of Gendlin (1996), Greenberg et al., (1993), and Mahrer (1996), are compatible with the idea of the client as active self-healer in that change is ultimately client discovered and client generated. Therapy is guided self-discovery, but therapists are experts in the use of procedures and techniques that facilitate this process. Client collaboration is primarily of Type 4. Therapists suggest specific activities at specific points to further the process of self-exploration and discovery. For instance, if the client is struggling with an issue concerning his or her father, the therapist may choose to have the client role play a dialogue between him- or herself and the father (Greenberg et al., 1993). Through this dialogue, clients spontaneously generate their own novel solutions.

Duncan, Hubble, and Miller

Duncan, Hubble, and Miller (1997; S. D. Miller et al., 1997) come from the family systems, solution-focused tradition of De Shazer and Berg

(I. K. Berg & Miller, 1992; De Shazer, 1985). They, too, place great emphasis on the client as active self-healer.

Duncan et al. (1997) deliberately set out to study psychotherapy with "impossible cases." These clients were individuals who had repeatedly been failures in prior therapy. Duncan et al. argued that prior therapy attempts failed because therapists did not honor clients' frames of reference and self-healing potential.

Duncan et al. (1997) broke therapy down into three components: exploring, discovering possibilities, and validation. The goals of the *exploring* component are to enlist client participation, to facilitate clients' experiencing the relationship in a positive fashion, and to learn about clients' theories of the problem and of change. These goals are accomplished by viewing the client as healthy, capable, and competent. In addition, the therapist depends on clients' resources and ideas and treats clients' input as central. The therapist strives to promote a good therapeutic relationship by being friendly and responsive, by understanding the client, and by being flexible. Duncan et al. recommended that the therapist think of him- or herself as an alien visiting the client's world, trying to find a completely fresh understanding of it. In this regard, it is recommended that the therapist adopt a "not-knowing" posture. Finally, the therapist should commit to the client's desires for treatment.

The second component of therapy is *discovering possibilities*. The goal of this phase is to look for possibilities for change. One way of doing this is by identifying exceptions to the existence of the problem. Such exceptions can often give suggstions about a course of action. Another way is to identify solutions the client has used in the past that might have previously worked. These can offer leads to the development of new solutions. Still another way is to identify conclusions or new ways of seeing things that may render the problem no longer a problem. These goals are accomplished in several ways. First, the therapist must be change focused. This means the therapist must be looking for change, be sensitive to change, and be aware of small changes and exceptions to the "rule" of the problem. The therapist also helps by amplifying what works. In addition, the therapist must believe in the client's capacity for change. Finally, the therapist must accommodate the client's theory of change.

The third component of therapy is *validation*. The goal of this component is to overcome the invalidation experiences that most therapy clients have suffered. These are the experiences of being labeled as intractable, resistant, and the like. This is accomplished by, first, legitimizing the client's concerns and, second, by validating the sense in the client's point of view. By this, we mean that there is some reasonableness in the client's point, no matter how objectively distorted it looks. For instance, in a case by Duncan et al. (1997), summarized in chapter 9, a woman with multiple personalities resisted integration. The therapist sought for and found the sense in that—in her view, nonintegration gave her greater flexibility and strength. The therapist also believes in the client and in his or her abilities. The therapist tries to accept the client at face value and avoids the role of reality police officer.

The principles elucidated by Duncan and his colleagues are based on the idea that the client has the creative potential to make his or her own changes. By respecting the client's frame of reference, by taking it seriously, by trusting the client, and by facilitating the client's already incipient positive efforts at change as well as prior successful change attempts, the therapist works with client's change potential.

Other Strategic, Solution-Focused Approaches

Most other strategic and solution-focused approaches also are compatible with the idea of the client as active self-healer. Paradoxically, these approaches are the darlings of managed care because they are prescriptive and brief. Strategic therapists can even "talk the talk" of managed care well (Hoyt, 1994). Yet, in fact, strategic therapy is highly nonmedical (e.g., I. K. Berg & Miller, 1992; De Shazer, 1985; O'Hanlon & Weiner-Davis, 1989). Many strategic and solution-focused approaches share the following assumptions. First, change is the norm in human affairs. Psychological problems are not disorders or syndromes but rather "stuck points." Stuck points occur when the client, in trying to solve a life problem, inadvertently picks a solution that exacerbates the problem. For instance, a woman suffers a defeat in life and criticizes herself in an effort to self-right. However, she may not recognize that self-criticism is not working. Yet she continues because she believes that it is right and proper to "be honest with herself." So she escalates her self-criticism, but nothing changes. She feels more and more helpless and depressed, and so criticizes herself more and more.

The goal of many strategic therapies is nothing more than to get the client unstuck, assuming that the client's intrinsic self-healing, self-change capacities will take over from there. Milton Erickson, the "father" of strategic therapies, believed that his interventions were freeing up the individual's unconscious wisdom. The client is the expert on him- or herself, and it is the client who creates the solution and who can properly take credit for the solution. Therefore, the therapist does not "treat" depression. The therapist probably would not even focus on the depression, but rather focus on where the person wants to go in life. When the focus is on goals and helping clients move forward, the depression resolves itself. A problem is solved by not focusing on the problem! The therapist does not really prescribe treatment based on a *DSM* diagnosis. Rather, the therapist's interventions are individualized in terms of the concrete particulars of the client's life and circumstances.

Strategic therapists also emphasize the positive. They focus on health. Clients with problems are routinely asked to review memories in which the problem was absent or in which everything was going well. The idea is that they already know how to make things go well, and all they need to do is be reminded of it. Or clients are asked to imagine the future when the problem has already been solved. This often by itself is enough to help clients find their own proactive ways of moving forward.

Strategic therapies are highly prescriptive but also highly discovery oriented. Client collaboration is mostly of Type 4, and the philosophy is very much compatible with the idea of the client as active self-healer.

Constructivist Therapies

Constructivist therapies (e.g., Neimeyer & Mahoney, 1995) start out with an assumption that humans construct their own realities. The models they construct are inherently incomplete, and individuals need to continually modify them as they encounter new experience. Psychological problems occur when there is a mismatch between personal constructs and the person's world and the person fails to adjust. This may occur because the person's core constructs are rigid, because he or she is protecting those core constructs, or because he or she is overwhelmed. The therapist and the client operate as a team. Problems represent developmental crises or conflicts that must be resolved and transcended. They must be understood in terms of the individual life trajectory of the client, rather than as discrete disorders with standard etiologies. Therapists use techniques that are in aid of client self-discovery and self-modification. Constructivistic therapies are discovery oriented and do not follow the medical model. Client collaboration is of Types 4 and 5.

Self-in-Relation Theory: Feminist Therapy

The self-in-relation approach of the Stone Center theorists (Jordan, Kaplan, Miller, Stiver, & Surrey, 1991) assumes that problems are relational, and therefore that therapy is relational. The therapist helps the client heal through his or her being in relationship. However, the relationship is not a medical-like intervention. Instead it is healing precisely because it is a healthy, real relationship of mutual empathy and dialogue. The client develops better relational skills and works through relational issues from childhood. The client has a chance to bring feelings into relationship and to "say his or her own truth." Therapy is not programmed or manualized. This is a discovery-oriented, non-medical-model approach. Client collaboration is of Type 5.

Motivational Interviewing

W. R. Miller and Rollnick's (1991) way of working with addictions overlaps considerably with our point of view. They said, "We believe that each person possesses a powerful potential for change. Your task as a therapist is to release that potential, to facilitate the natural change processes already inherent in the individual. In this approach, the client is treated with great respect, and as an ally rather than an opponent" (p. 62). For them, individuals with addictions have problems giving up the addictions because they are ambivalent. The goal of therapy is to help the clients resolve their ambivalence so that they become motivated to change. This is done through empathic listening rather than through confrontation of denial. However, the approach also includes various active strategies, such as goal setting. Collaboration is of Type 4 and Type 5.

Eye Movement Desensitization and Reprocessing

F. Shapiro's (1995) eye movement desensitization and reprocessing (EMDR), despite sounding as if it were a behavioral desensitization procedure, is almost entirely an active client self-healing approach. Both the procedure and the philosophy are generally compatible with the idea of the client as self-healer. In the most typical protocol, the therapist asks the client to focus attention on a traumatic memory, and then to follow the therapist's moving fingers. After a minute or so of this, the therapist stops and asks the client to report on "what is coming up inside." No matter what it is, the therapist then asks the client to focus on that while following the therapist's fingers. The unfolding process of the client is considerably more complex than simple desensitization. It includes the acquisition of insights, shifts in bodily felt meanings, the accessing of new emotional experience, appearance of new images, and generation of new perspectives and integrative solutions. All of these are entirely client generated. The therapist is a facilitator of the client's own natural self-healing process, and Shapiro's theory includes the idea that human beings have such a process. In fact, people have probably spontaneously used eye movements to self-heal for centuries, and Shapiro discovered the process on her own while walking through a park. The process is facilitated by what looks like a technological procedure, but Shapiro argued that it is not a technique but rather a method for promoting client self-healing. Collaboration in this method is of Type 4: The therapist directs the process, but the process is entirely one of client self-discovery.

Approaches That Can Be Practiced in Ways Either Compatible or Incompatible With the Client-as-Active-Self-Healer Perspective

We next turn to approaches that can be practiced in ways either more compatible with the medical model or more compatible with our view. The therapist can either play the role of the expert physician or play the role of guide, tutor, or mentor. In addition, there is often a discrepancy in these approaches between their theoretical descriptions of psychological problems and therapy and how they actually think therapy should be practiced. At the theory level, the process is often described in terms compatible with the medical model, whereas practice is advocated compatible with a belief in the client as an active self-healer.

Psychodynamic

Psychodynamic models vary in the degree to which they are compatible with the idea of the client as active self-healer. We first examine Freudian views and then modern relational views.

Traditional psychoanalytic theory. At the *theory* level, traditional Freudian as well as some modern object relational perspectives have a distinct medical-model flavor to them. Problems result from dysfunctioning internal mechanisms, such as toxic introjects, splits in ego functioning, weak ego functioning, and dysfunctional defensive organizations. Therapy works by "repairing" such mechanisms. In Freudian psychoanalysis, this occurs by lifting repression. In object relations theory, this occurs by healing "splits" in ego functioning and by replacing toxic introjects with benign ones. In addition, for Freud, psychological problems result from disturbances in how energy is regulated and discharged. Freud's model at this level is mechanistic, described in terms of energy, its channeling, its discharge, the dysfunctional workings of certain mental structures, and so on. Therapy is also described mechanistically at this level of theory. Therapy leads to new introjects, realigns the id, ego, and superego, and so on. Different disorders represent different dysfunctional internal organizations. Although these do not formally match up to the DSM system, nonetheless, diagnosis and assessment of the client's dysfunctional internal organization is a key part of classical psychoanalytic treatment. Psychotherapy is therefore treatment of a condition, not unlike medicine.

At the *practice* level, there are both compatible and incompatible elements with the idea of the client as an active self-healer. On the one hand, there is a crucial role for the client's own active self-healing efforts. It is only through clients' self-confrontation, ultimately, that change takes place. Even corrective interpretations by the analyst do not magically create change. It is only when clients rigorously make the discovery themselves, aided by the analyst's interpretation, that change will occur. Freud was of the opinion that clients ultimately cured themselves. Cure did not actually occur through the therapist's telling things to the client, despite the theoretical model that views interpretations as "strengthening the ego." On the other hand, there are major parts of traditional psychodynamic practice that are incompatible with the idea of the client as active self-healer. This has to do with the view of how powerful the forces of healing, growth, and reality adaptation (the ego) are compared with the regressive forces of infantile wishes and defense. Many traditional practitioners do not believe that the power of client self-healing can overcome clients' desires to avoid facing the truth about themselves without outside intervention. In therapy, change only occurs because in the battle between the ego and the id, the therapist aligns with the client's ego.

The therapist therefore assumes the more knowing role. Because the person is "diseased" in some sense (i.e., suffering from an internal malfunction in personality dynamics), the person needs outside intervention to most effectively self-heal or self-right. It is the therapist's eagle eye for subtle and unconscious maneuvers on the part of the client that provides the corrective feedback that allows the client's ego to win the battle. Self-healing ultimately comes from the client, but only with major guidance and intervention from the therapist.

Modern Relational Perspectives. Many modern relational psychodynamic perspectives are generally compatible with the idea of the client as active self-healer (J. R. Gold, personal communication, January 17, 1998). First, humans are seen more proactively than in traditional psychoanalytic theory. They have great capacities for growth, coping, and creativity (Jenkins, 1995). When they disown their experience, it is because it is a necessary survival tactic, given the dynamics of their early childhood family relationships. Defenses are also seen more proactively, as adaptive coping mechanisms. Kohut's (Rowe & MacIsaac, 1991) self-psychology sees the person as actively struggling to grow and to develop a strong, coherent self. Significant others can either aid and support or block and interfere. In therapy, there is a strong positive thrust on the part of the client to grow if he or she can get the proper nurturing conditions. Insight is important, but so is empathy, and clients have a sense of what they need in order to grow. According to Weiss, Sampson, and the Mount Zion Psychotherapy Research Group (1986), the client uses the therapy relationship as a site for testing out dysfunctional unconscious beliefs. If the therapist passes the tests, clients are able to acknowledge their unconscious beliefs and to modify them.

We particularly mention the work of Paul Wachtel and Dan Wile. Wile (1981) assumed that clients develop extreme or dysfunctional behaviors because they think they do not have a right to their feelings and desires. They have learned, from the culture, from parents, from psychology itself, that to have certain feelings, desires, thoughts, and beliefs is wrong. Therefore, when they have them, they block them off or disown them. When they do this, they express the needs in dysfunctional ways. The needs themselves are normal human needs, not infantile ones as in traditional psychoanalytic theory. The goal of the therapist is to facilitate clients' realizing they have the right to their needs and feelings. The therapy process not only includes interpretation but is also allowing, accepting, and supportive, which allows clients to reown normal parts of themselves. Wile's approach is a guided discovery-oriented approach. Client collaboration is of Types 3, 4, and 5.

Wachtel (1993) believed people carry from childhood dysfunctional coping strategies that set up self-fulfilling prophecies. A client learns in early childhood that feeling angry is not acceptable. Believing this, the client disowns any anger. This may lead to the behaviors of acting overly deferent, of self-blame, or of avoiding situations that can provoke anger. This kind of behavior can create dysfunctional relationships. The individual does not stand up for him- or herself. He or she allows him- or herself to get walked on, which leads to more anger, which leads to further self-disowning, in an endless vicious circle. What is disowned is not primitive infantile impulses, but rather normal empowering and enriching human feelings, such as anger, love, needs for support, and so on. These feelings are disowned because the individual is trying to be proactive in a self-protective way. In the context of the individual's family, he or she has learned that this is the right, acceptable way to be. The therapist's goal is to both provide insight through interpretation and to encourage behavioral experimentation to bring in corrective feedback. Clients are seen as proactive, as well as capable of and motivated to self-heal if given half a chance. For Wachtel, the therapist is an active guide. Client collaboration is primarily of Types 4 and 5.

In sum, many modern psychodynamic perspectives are generally compatible with the idea of the client as active self-healer. Problems are rooted in childhood experiences, and people are seen as disowning experience, but these are seen more proactively, and clients are seen as having a greater intrinsic capacity for positive growth and maturation. Next we consider specific psychoanalytic concepts and their relationship to the client as an active self-healer.

Unconscious Resistance and Transference

Several psychodynamic concepts are, on the surface, incompatible with our thesis. Most primarily, the concept of unconscious resistance would seem to be incompatible with the idea that the client can be an active self-healer. Some psychoanalysts believe that people are so locked in by unconscious resistance and self-deception that they could never find their way out on their own. They need the "objective" feedback of the therapist to break out.

It is here that one must make a basic philosophical choice about what one believes as to the basic nature of human beings. Are humans primarily and most fundamentally motivated to avoid and self-deceive, or are humans most fundamentally motivated by a proactive desire to approach life and to cope and adapt? It is not a question of either–or. Humans do both. There are plenty of examples of human self-deception. But which is more basic? Some psychoanalytic models, especially ones that retain aspects of traditional views, see the human desire to avoid painful self-knowledge as most basic. In these models, healthy behavior is based on defensive avoidance. It is essentially "adaptive pathology." Vaillant (1993), for instance, viewed humans as constantly and chronically engaged in self-deceit. Humans mature, but they do so by self-deceiving in more adaptive and less dysfunctional ways—they adopt "mature defenses." In essence, self-avoidance of truth is chronic, pervasive, and omnipresent. Such a view would seem to suggest that individuals would get locked into their dysfunctional behavior patterns and never find their way out without outside assistance. Yet even Vaillant has documented a natural growth and evolution toward more mature and functional behavior in the individuals he studied.

In contrast, we believe that individuals are more fundamentally motivated to act proactively, to learn, and to try to cope and adjust. Avoidance, defense, and self-deception certainly happen. In fact, avoidance itself is primarily an attempt to preserve a base for proactive functioning. People unconsciously avoid and self-deceive when they see no other way of maintaining a workable ecological balance. For instance, they may repress or dissociate memories of early childhood abuse because they have no viable way of coping with them in their childhood circumstances. They have no empathic listener around, the people who should help them are the very people who are posing the threat (e.g., the parents), and the experience is overwhelmingly confusing and painful. As Bandura (1986) noted, people act defensively when they feel inefficacious to do anything more proactive. Avoidance allows life to get on as best one can. However, people prefer proactive solutions. Psychoanalysis can work precisely because the "forces" toward growth, coping, and adaptation are stronger than the "forces" toward avoidance.

The issue is not whether clients may be unaware of key aspects of their experience. This can be the case. For instance, Wickramasekera (1998) wrote a paper entitled "Secrets Kept From the Mind, But Not the Body and Behavior." He gave an example of a man with significant somatic symptoms, including high blood pressure and headaches. This man had received extensive medical treatment, with only modest results. Psychophysiological measures revealed high levels of stress, although verbally the man reported little distress. The measures also revealed significant increases in stress when the man talked about his wife. Wickramasekera showed the client the data, and over a 3-week period the client became aware of intense rage at his wife. As he dealt with this, his somatic symptoms disappeared.

In a similar manner, one of us once had a client who was referred because of a chronic cough for which no physiological basis could be found. The therapist noted that the cough intensified every time the man spoke of his wife. The man was made aware of this, therapy switched to talking about the problems with his wife, and the cough disappeared.

The issue is whether, without external therapist feedback, clients such as these would ever become aware of what they are not aware of and self-heal. Do they have a built-in proactive self-righting tendency that, given the proper circumstances, might lead them to grow into awareness on their own or grow beyond defensive early childhood fixations on their own? We believe the answer to this is yes. In the case of these clients, even if the therapist had not confronted the men with the data about their wives, they might well have discovered these things on their own, given the proper facilitative environment. For instance, in an empathically based client-centered therapy, the client with the cough might first have denied any distress in his marriage. However, he might have found it rewarding to talk to an empathic listener. He and the therapist might have started talking about other things. Eventually, the client might have been able to gingerly approach the issues with his wife. He then may have accessed the distress he felt in his marriage, and even may have become aware of the relationship of his cough to that distress. Is this plausible? We have seen this happen.

Gendlin (1990) discussed an "order of steps" in personal problem solving. Clients may need to start with certain issues first, perhaps ones that they intuitively know they have some chance of mastering. In a safe environment, they deal with whatever is most available to them. First, they may deal with issues of safety and self-acceptance. Then, as they deal with those issues, they gingerly approach something more painful and threatening. And, as they master and resolve that, they approach even more painful issues. This process may happen in therapy or outside of therapy, if they are sufficiently motivated to grow. This process is usually not linear. It may recycle issues repeatedly, going deeper each time. Hofstader (1979), discussing recursion in computer programming, used the analogy of a push-down stack: As a person deals with one aspect of a problem, the next related thing pops up, and so on. Thus, if the person has a safe space to start he or she may be able to work his or her way down the stack sufficiently far enough to resolve the problem on his or her own.

We believe humans can operate intelligently at a tacit or unconscious level. Freudian theory also holds this. However, classical Freudian theory portrays the unconscious as only operating intelligently in its ability to hide things from consciousness and in its ability to find ways to covertly express infantile wishes. Some modern psychoanalysts (e.g., Weiss et al., 1986) portray the unconscious as operating in an intelligent, proactive way—clients unconsciously seek corrective information that will allow them to give up beliefs learned in childhood. The idea that people can unconsciously strive to grow and change is an idea that Milton Erickson, Carl Rogers, and Carl Jung would all find compatible. In client-centered theory, Gendlin (1964, 1996) did not really talk of the unconscious but instead of implicit, preverbal felt knowledge. It is from this implicit level that creativity arises. Given the right circumstances, people can be implicitly or unconsciously seeking, searching, exploring, and experimenting and may gradually move toward growth and change. Just because something is unconscious does not mean it is locked away forever and the behavior on which it is based is unchangeable unless a therapist helps the person access it.

Over time, humans therefore may gradually loosen up their defenses on their own. This may not be a conscious process of self-confrontation. Nonetheless, they may gradually expose themselves more and more to fearful situations and change without making a conscious effort to do so. A person who is afraid of anger may, if given the proper supportive circumstances, fearfully but courageously explore anger, slowly but surely, and gradually modify his or her behavior. This may be why defenses can "mature" without psychotherapy (Vaillant, 1993).

This will not spontaneously and naturally happen in all cases. Some life situations will keep people sufficiently on the defensive that they will not feel safe to explore, even tacitly. Some of these situations may inadvertently be set up by their own behavior (Wachtel, 1993). Other individuals may achieve an ecological balance sufficiently functional and satisfying that they are not motivated to change. People will be more spontaneously able to grow through their own resistances and avoidances if they have a relatively safe and respectful environment, in which they feel safe to experiment and there is some motivation to change. In sum, we do not believe that people are inevitably locked into unchanging defensive structures, unable to break out without the presence of the benevolent therapist.

We adopt a proactive view of transference as well. In one sense, transference is ubiquitous. Humans learn so that they can *transfer*, that is, use the past to understand and better cope with the present. Having learned how to solve one calculus problem, we transfer what we have learned to solving a new calculus problem. But transference of old learning can interfere with coping with a new situation. People are prone to conceive of new problems in terms of old problems, sometimes blinding them to new solutions (Ward et al., 1995). Ward et al. gave the example of the first railroad cars, which were patterned after stagecoaches. As on stagecoaches, conductors initially rode outside. This led to the deaths of many conductors before it was finally realized that it was not necessary to have anyone outside as had been done with stagecoaches. This sounds very much like transference. An old way of construing things was blindly transferred onto a new situation, and rigidly held onto for a while, before new learning finally changed it. Whenever people view a new problem through the lens of an old problem, they may "fit" the new one into the frame of the old one. This leads them to relate to the new one as if it were the old one. It may take them a while to correct this. This may be because the new situation may be ambiguous in its differences from the old situation. The therapy situation is sufficiently ambiguous (especially with a traditional blank-screen psychoanalyst) that it may take quite a while to detect that the therapist is not the same as significant others in one's past. Until one does make that detection, it makes perfect sense to use the frame of those significant others to try to understand this new situation. In fact, if all people were like one's father, transference would be a highly adaptive strategy instead of a dysfunction.

Thus, people transfer because they are trying to proactively understand and cope with the current situation. They are using the past to try to understand the current situation. They are not mechanistically and rigidly transferring the past onto the current situation. The use of the past to understand the present may be done reflexively and nonconsciously. But this is not unusual. People often use automatic proceduralized knowledge nonconsciously. If I see a hexagonal red sign with the word STOP, I may reflexively stop my car without thinking. This might be quite difficult to unlearn if for some reason *stop* came to mean *speed up*. But this too makes perfect sense. It is dangerous to speed up if one should be stopping, and it may take quite a while before the person believes that the sign now means speed up instead of stop.

It is true that some individuals will be more resistant than others to changing their impressions. This is most likely to happen when individuals perceive danger in the current situation. If they view the situation as dangerous, the safest, most conservative strategy is to not change their view unless they are absolutely certain the situation is truly different on all relevant variables. If one has been sexually abused as a child by an adult male, one may certainly transfer onto the male therapist the perception of him as dangerous. This may lead to being seductive (to buy him off and control him), to shutting down and dissociating, to viewing innocuous things he does as potentially dangerous, and so on. One may take quite a while before one is willing to "stick out one's hand and find that this is not really a fire that burns." This makes perfect sense from the perspective of the client as an active, agentic self-healer. In summary, transference is a proactive attempt to cope.

What the Client-as-Active-Self-Healer Perspective Has to Offer to Psychodynamic Perspectives

Viewing the client as an active self-healer could alert psychodynamic therapists to the client's positive, proactive self-healing potential underlying unconscious, defensive, and avoidant behavior. This should help the therapist work with and side with that potential in the client, even if on the surface the client seems defensive and avoidant. Siding with the clients' self-healing potential should help the therapist frame interpretations in a more proactive way that would simultaneously provide insight and support client's proactivity (see Wachtel, 1993). Psychodynamic therapists would also be alert to spontaneous and creative, generative moves on the part of the client, including self-challenges of defensive avoidance and possibilities of spontaneous acquisition of insight. Even when clients seem defensively unaware of the emotional bases of their problems, therapists should assume that there is a capacity for self-healing and that, at some level, there is an implicit understanding of what is needed for clients to move, albeit slowly and gingerly, toward awareness and more proactive solutions to life problems.

What the Psychodynamic Perspective Has to Offer the Client-as-Active-Self-Healer Perspective

Traditional psychodynamic theory probably has little to offer the client-as-active-self-healer perspective. However, modern psychodynamic perspectives, such as those of Wile, Wachtel, and the Mount Zion group cited earlier, offer a proactive view of client defense and avoidance that can help therapists understand and work with apparently non-self-healing behavior on the part of the client, as we have already discussed.

Cognitive Models

At a theoretical level, cognitive therapy (e.g., Beck et al., 1979) is not compatible with the idea of the client as active self-healer. However, at the practice level it is.

Theory Level

Cognitive theory adopts a mechanistic information-processing model (S. C. Hayes et al., 1995). Individuals' psychological problems result from dysfunctions in the information-processing system. This is due to the presence of dysfunctional information-processing structures, such as schemas. Dysfunctional feelings and behaviors result from information-processing errors. There is nothing in the theory to imply that the person is trying to do anything proactive by thinking dysfunctionally. Therapy becomes the mechanistic correction of errors in the information-processing system. Therapy is seen as an external force that "corrects" dysfunctional cognitions and schemas. Therapists restructure clients' dysfunctional cognitions. At this level, the client sounds like a passive recipient of corrective therapeutic interventions.

Practice Level

However, at the practice level, cognitive therapy relies heavily on the client as an active self-healer and on the client's collaboration. In fact, the process is described as *collaborative empiricism*. The therapist asks the relevant questions and provides helpful structured exercises (such as keeping a daily record of dysfunctional thoughts) but relies on clients' ability to think things through for themselves. The therapist has faith that simply by asking the right thought-provoking questions, clients can logically come to their own reasonable answers. The ultimate goal of cognitive therapy is to help clients think more clearly so that they can help themselves. In fact, when cognitive therapists ask questions such as "What is the evidence concerning your belief that no one likes you?" they are not trying to implicitly persuade clients that they are wrong but rather are actually encouraging them to consider all the evidence. It could turn out that, in fact, in the client's current life situation no one does like him or her. If so, the cognitive therapist would then help the client think through in a proactive way the implications of that.

The model is a teaching or tutorial one. Therapists guide clients to learn how to evaluate evidence and thereby to challenge their dysfunctional cognitions. In addition, the therapist encourages clients to practice thinking out more proactive ways of handling problems. The process is not unlike one in school where the teacher poses certain problems to the student, and the student learns the principles through thinking out those problems. In cognitive therapy, a series of problems is posed to the client, mostly in the form of "What is the evidence for that belief?" The client must develop his or her creativity in solving these problems.

Cognitive therapy relies heavily on client self-healing in another way by its use of homework assignments. Clients keep a daily record of dysfunctional thoughts and develop their own skills at challenging dysfunctional cognitions.

*What the Client-as-Active-Self-Healer Perspective Has to Offer
Cognitive Therapy*

Cognitive therapy can be viewed in two different ways. The theory makes it sound mechanistic, as if the therapist is replacing dysfunctional parts of the client. However, in practice most cognitive therapists see themselves as helping clients learn how to think through their beliefs in ways that free them up to attack life's problems in a more proactive, less self-defeating way. The perspective of the client as active self-healer is therefore compatible with the practice of cognitive therapy. One thing it can contribute to cognitive therapy is that it makes it clear that it is not really therapists, but rather clients, who restructure clients' cognitions. It can remind cognitive therapists that, as they already know but may have forgotten because of some of the mechanistic ways in which their theory is couched, therapy is really nothing more than education. The client must "get it," just as a student must really understand something that is being learned in order for it to be helpful. Mechanistically and rotely following what is being learned will not usually be helpful. Therefore, the perspective of the client as active self-healer can alert the cognitive therapist to when and why the procedures may not be working. In addition, it can alert the therapist to the possibility of client generativity—clients may inventively "ring" their own variations on what is being learned in productive ways, use the procedures badly but still profit, or make sudden productive leaps unexplained by the theory.

What Cognitive Therapy Has to Contribute to the Client-as-Active-Self-Healer Perspective

Cognitive therapy contains a whole set of highly useful tools that therapists can help clients learn how to use to take more positive charge of their lives. Clients can learn to think in ways that free them from pessimistic (Seligman, 1990) and self-defeating thoughts and feelings that hamper their potential for creativity and productivity. Good cognitive therapists also provide excellent models of how to relate to clients in ways that are respectful, are collaborative, and draw on clients' own abilities for thoughtful learning and understanding (e.g., Shostrom, 1986). Finally, cognitive therapy lends itself to the development of self-help materials. In fact, the most extensively used self-help materials have probably been developed by cognitive and cognitive–behavioral therapists. Burns (1980), Greenberger and Padesky (1995), and others have developed self-help books that have been highly successful and useful.

Behavioral and Cognitive–Behavioral Models

There are many different approaches to behavior therapy. Traditional views have evolved into modern cognitive–behavioral views and social learning views. Traditional views tend to be antithetical to the idea of the client as active self-healer, whereas most modern views are compatible with it in varying degrees.

Traditional Behavior Therapy

Traditional behavior therapy, as exemplified in the work of Wolpe (1990) and others, totally excluded any idea of an active, agentic organism who could either self-heal or serve as his or her own therapist. Using the metaphor of the conditioned reflex from Pavlov's studies, dysfunctional behaviors were seen as conditioned responses. The organism was viewed as a mechanism (Hayes et al., 1995), and behaviors were built in by reinforcement and practice. Thus, the organism was a kind of passive, inert material that was operated on by external events. To use Bandura's (1986) phrase, the organism was merely the site or host for responses. There was no theoretical mechanism whereby an organism could possibly self-right. When applied to therapy, this led to an entirely external model of the therapy process wherein the therapist conditioned new behaviors and de-conditioned old ones. For example, clients practiced relaxing in the presence of imagery of frightening scenes until the relaxation response was associated with the frightening stimulus. Insight as a change procedure was forcefully rejected. Acquisition of skills was also seen in a mechanistic fashion. Practice of assertion, for instance, built in the habit of assertive behaviors. There was no explicit appeal to thinking in the process.

When one watches a demonstration by a traditional behavior therapist such as Wolpe (1990), it is clear how much the client is in a passive role. The model is like that of a physician in that the therapist asks questions and gathers information. The role of the client is to answer the therapist's questions. But then it is up to the therapist to diagnose the problem and to prescribe a remedy. The therapist is not interested in the possibility that through talking to the therapist the client might have an "aha" experience and resolve problems him- or herself. The client is active only to the extent that he or she follows the therapist's directions. Client collaboration in this approach is of Types 1 and 2.

Modern Behavioral and Cognitive–Behavioral Perspectives

Modern behavioral and cognitive–behavioral perspectives vary in the degree to which they are compatible with the idea of the client as active self-healer. We first consider aspects compatible with the idea of the client as active self-healer.

Compatibilities between cognitive–behavioral and client-as-self-healer perspectives. In the 1970s and 1980s, most behaviorists became more cognitive and more oriented toward the view of the human as an active organism, capable of self-regulation. From social learning theory came the idea that beliefs such as locus of control and self-efficacy played a role in self-regulation. Albert Bandura was (and is) a major spokesperson for this point of view. Theoretically, Bandura (1986) challenged the traditional behavioral view by arguing for reciprocal determinism. Humans are agents. Not only are they operated on by the environment, but they also can initiate action and operate on their environments. Humans also are active learners. They learn through observing others (modeling) as well as through active behavioral experimentation and practice. Bandura (1986) said, "Behavioristic theories are reluctant to grant the organism a working memory and reasoning skills, let alone the capacity for consciousness of its own knowledge" (p. 110). In terms of what is learned—responses or generative conceptions—Bandura argued for generative conceptions: "Learning must be generative in nature, because skilled activities are seldom performed in exactly the same way; they must be varied to fit different circumstances. . . . It is because people learn generative conceptions, rather than specific acts, that human skills have remarkable flexibility and utility" (p. 111). Furthermore, Bandura argued that concepts of goals and intentions, concepts essentially barred as unscientific by traditional mechanistic behavioral models, were necessary if one is to really understand human behavior.

Bandura's (1986) concept of self-efficacy also is a concept of a goal-directed organism. It holds that a major variable in whether individuals behave effectively or not is their sense of whether they have the ability to perform the appropriate behavior. Self-efficacy does not mean that individuals believe they can control an event, but it does mean that they believe they are able to perform a certain behavior effectively. For instance, a surgeon may believe she is highly skilled and able to perform a complicated surgical operation, but she may not necessarily believe that it will save the patient's life. Bandura showed that those who feel efficacious operate in proactive ways: They take risks, they approach difficult tasks, and they persist in the face of failure. Bandura (1997) argued that feelings of low self-efficacy are at the core of many psychological problems, such as anxiety disorders, and that therapy operates by increasing feelings of efficacy and mastery. He believed, for instance, that exposure techniques work primarily by increasing clients' feelings that they can master their anxiety in a particular problem area.

Cognitive–behaviorists also have increasingly emphasized the training of skills over the idea of conditioning processes. Skills training was seen as helping clients assume greater control over their own lives. For instance, Goldfried (1995) argued for a coping skills model of behavioral methods. A traditional view of systematic desensitization is that it is essentially a passive procedure. The person passively undergoes this procedure, which "counterconditions" a relaxation response in place of an anxiety response. However, Goldfried argued that, instead, the person is learning an active coping method. This active coping method consists of using relaxation to cope with anxiety-provoking situations. Goldfried cited evidence to back this position up. For Goldfried, therapy is training clients how to be their own therapists.

Therapy practice is also more collaborative for many modern cognitive–behaviorists (Kanfer & Goldstein, 1986). There have been changes in how the behavior therapist relates to the client. There has been a shift from the traditional administrative model of treatment, in which the helper administers a treatment to which the client submits, to a participant model that emphasizes client responsibility (Kanfer & Gaelick, 1986). Goals are decided on collaboratively by therapist and client. Therapy is seen as a transitory support system that helps clients until they can take over themselves. The goal of self-management training (e.g., Kanfer & Gaelick, 1986) is to help clients acquire new behaviors that are viewed as temporary devices. These devices help the client while the client learns new behaviors. As the person develops new and more satisfying behaviors, they will be less and less needed. Kanfer and Gaelick suggested that "whenever possible the client be given decisional control over the nature of their treatment plan" (p. 299).

Finally, cognitive–behaviorists have been on the forefront of the development of self-help materials. Self-help books such as the one by Zilbergeld and Lazarus (1987) present a variety of strategies that individuals can learn to use to modify their own behaviors. Lewinsohn, Munoz, Youngren, and Zeiss (1986) wrote a self-help book on depression, and Barlow and Craske (1989) wrote one on anxiety. A book on self-directed behavior (D. L. Watson & Tharp, 1989) has been used in undergraduate classes and includes a whole program of self-modification skills. Watson and Tharp argued that students who have used this program have had considerable success in modifying given target behaviors compared with students who did not use them. They reported figures of 66%–84% success.

Modern cognitive–behavioral approaches are compatible with the idea of the client as active self-healer primarily in terms of Type 3 of client collaboration. In essence, the cognitive–behaviorist has a "curriculum" for the client to learn that will solve the client's problem. The cognitive–behaviorist is like a teacher in that he or she sets the agenda of what needs to be learned and the framework of how it is to be learned. Within that framework, active stimulation of the client's thinking and behavioral participation is a necessity. There is, however, no concept in these models of the client as an originator of ideas about change in therapy. Clients need to be instructed in skills and techniques for self-regulation. For instance, Bandura (1997) is skeptical that "undirected" client self-exploration can be anything but, by sheer chance, helpful. To quote Bandura (1997), "therapeutic outcomes remain uncertain when intimidated persons have to create by themselves the conditions necessary for their own change" (p. 141).

Nonetheless, learning is primarily through client self-discovery. For instance, as part of Craske and Barlow's (1993) treatment for panic, the client was encouraged to test hypotheses. One client, Jane, was asked to estimate how likely a feared event was so that she could test it out. In one case, she estimated that it was 60% likely that someone at a dinner she would be attending would comment on how weird she looked. At the next session, after the dinner, she and the therapist evaluated the evidence as to what actually happened. In doing this repeatedly, the client discovered that in most cases her dire predictions had not come true. The point is that while the therapist has structured the learning exercise, what is learned results from the client's active efforts and discoveries.

Ways in which some cognitive–behavioral views are not compatible with the idea of the client as active self-healer. Despite the many ways in which modern cognitive–behavioral viewpoints are compatible with the idea of the client as active self-healer, there are also ways in which some of them are not.

First, the model of therapy advocated by some cognitive–behavioral practitioners is more compatible with the medical model than it is with the model of the client as active self-healer. For those who follow the recommendations of the American Psychological Association's Division 12's Task Force on "empirically validated treatments" (Task Force on the Promotion and Dissemination of Psychological Procedures, 1995), most of which are cognitive–behavioral, the therapist is definitely the expert who decides for the client what the problem is and what the treatment will be. The treatment is applied to the client in a manualized fashion, based on what has been shown to work for a given disorder. There is no real room in such a model for creative dialogue between therapist and client leading to joint choice or ongoing development of treatment.

Furthermore, some of the techniques such as exposure and extinction are still viewed mechanistically by some cognitive–behavioral therapists. Extinction is something that happens *to* a habit or a response through repeated exposure to a stimulus without reward. There is no implication of an active organism learning something proactively for its own good. Foa and Kozak's (1991) description of how exposure works leaves no room for an actively thinking, evaluating client. Rather, the working of exposure is described mechanistically. A fear structure in memory is activated and corrected by repeated exposure to a feared stimulus. Habituation takes place. Nowhere in this description is there any mention of a client who not only is having his or her emotions reprocessed and his or her fear structures altered, but is also actively reevaluating meanings and restorying his or her life. Habituation may be taking place, but clients are actively thinking, learning, and restructuring their life narratives as well.

What the Client-as-Active-Self-Healer Perspective Has to Offer to Cognitive–Behavioral Therapy

The idea of the client as active self-healer is compatible with and supportive of cognitive–behaviorists who view clients as active, thoughtful agents and therapy as a process of increasing feelings of mastery and of raising skill levels. However, cognitive–behavioral approaches are limited in the converse of the way that traditional client-centered and psychodynamic approaches are limited. That is, they operate almost exclusively from a Type 3 collaboration and fail to incorporate the kinds of creative, dialogic learnings that can occur from Types 4 and 5 collaboration. Viewing the client as an active self-healer could add to cognitive–behavioral therapy in the same way that it adds to cognitive therapy: by alerting the therapist to the possibility of client generativity. Clients may inventively modify techniques offered by the therapist, or learn from procedures in their own productive and idiosyncratic ways. Clients may even generate their own techniques. Furthermore, as with cognitive therapy, the perspective of the client as active self-healer makes it clear that it is not therapists, but rather clients, who change clients' behavior. Therapy is education, and unless clients invest themselves in their education, "inhabit" what they are learning, and understand it and make it their own, it will not be helpful. Habits are not being implanted in clients. Clients are learning techniques and skills that they will adapt to their own unique styles and life contexts. No two clients will use relaxation or assertion in precisely the same way, any more than any two elementary school students practicing handwriting will end up with identical handwriting styles. It is the clients who make relaxation work for them, assertion work for them, and so on. Therefore, the client-as-active-self-healer perspective can alert the behavior therapist to when and why the procedures may not be working—when the client may be mechanistically doing them but at another level does not really believe in them or is not investing in them.

What Behavior Therapy Has to Offer the Client-as-Active-Self-Healer Perspective

As with cognitive therapy, behavior therapy, if viewed as helping clients acquire a sense of agency and mastery as well as coping skills, can be seen as offering a set of highly useful tools for helping clients free up their creative problem-solving capabilities. In addition, behavior therapists have contributed a host of self-help procedures.

IMPLICATIONS FOR DOING THERAPY FROM OUR POINT OF VIEW WITH RESPECT TO DIFFERING APPROACHES

In general, a therapist can do therapy from a point of view that honors the idea that the client is an agentic, whole person who is capable of self-healing if they see the client that way, regardless of what approach to therapy they follow. If they have some faith and trust in the client's own intelligence, that can be integrated in with whatever else they do.

In the main, adopting a belief in the client as an active self-healer will not significantly change the therapist's practice. Rather, it is more likely to affect the flavor or feel of how the therapist practices. However, there are cases in which it should make a difference. When clients "resist," there should be greater faith in the possibility that there may be some wisdom in the client's resistance to be mined and used proactively rather than to be overcome. When a client questions a strategy, it should be seen as an opportunity to enlist his or her intelligence in the process, rather than as an annoyance or challenge to the therapist's authority. Furthermore, it should be seen as a proactive sign that the client is actively thinking and creatively involved in the process. When clients are doing the work themselves, there should be greater faith that it is okay to just shut up and be there. Therapists should be on the lookout for creative client variations on techniques, innovative client ideas, self-initiated client changes, client initiative between sessions, preferred client alternatives for solving problems, client decisions to integratively use something from another therapy approach, and so on. When a technique fails, clients should be listened to as collaborators whose feedback may be used to modify the process. Techniques should not be applied mechanistically, and it should never be believed that a technique will ever "make something happen" in a client. Instead, techniques should be shared as tools for clients to use to make their own self-discoveries. The therapist should be interested in what they build with the tool, not what is mechanistically supposed to be produced. Clients may use the tool all wrong and still come out right. Therapists should value and enjoy dialoging with this intelligent other, the client, and show appreciation for him or her as a partner in the process. Therapists should eschew paternalistic attitudes that they know what is best for clients, although they certainly may have some good ideas to offer them. Even when confronting clients' resistance and denial, therapists should be aware that this will only work if the clients are ready to use the material. If clients are not ready to hear, they will not. Therapists should offer their confrontations as information they hope will appeal to the client, rather than as the stern, paternalistic voice of truth. If the confrontation is offered strongly but collaboratively, it has a greater chance of being listened to and used by the client.

CONCLUSION

In this chapter, we examined how different theoretical approaches fit with our model of the client as an active self-healer. In particular, we

- Delineated five different levels of collaboration, from Types 1 and 2, which were mostly compatible with the medical model and in which collaboration largely means client compliance, to Types 3 through 5, in which collaboration more actively depends on the client's intelligence and generativity.
- Explored approaches that were largely compatible with the

idea of the client as active self-healer. These included client-centered therapy, experiential therapy, strategic and solution-focused approaches, self-in-relation theory, constructivism, Miller and Rollnick's treatment for alcoholism, and EMDR.

- Explored compatible and incompatible elements in psychodynamic, cognitive, and behavioral approaches. At the theory level each has some incompatible elements, but many modern forms of practice are highly compatible. In particular, cognitive and behavioral approaches have developed a great deal of useful self-help material.

- Argued that one can practice from any of the major perspectives and still honor the client as an active self-healer if one keeps that in the forefront of one's mind.

III

THERAPY AS A
MEETING OF MINDS

7

WHEN THE ACTIVE CLIENT IS DIFFICULT

Clients do not always act proactively. They may be defensive, resist new ideas, and act in self-defeating ways. Some clients are easily offended or will not experiment with new behaviors that might help them feel better. Other clients focus on identifying what is wrong in the world, but not on what they can do to change their situation. They seek to assign blame for problems rather than solve them. Others think in rigid stereotypic ways and refuse to try out new ways of looking at things. They repeat the same failed patterns and seem not to learn from mistakes.

What is the difference between clients who have a helpful motivational set conducive to change and those who seem resistant to change? In this chapter, we suggest that often it is the clients' belief systems and the goals they are pursuing that can sidetrack their efforts. Goal-orientation research on motivational problems during learning provides a partial explanation for a variety of learning and motivation problems seen in therapy, as well as implications for how therapists might help clients overcome their problems. It explains many of the reasons the proactivity of the client can be suppressed.

GOAL ORIENTATION

One explanation for the problems encountered by therapists may be provided by the motivational model developed by academic achievement motivation researcher, Carol Dweck. Dweck found that when faced with difficult problems to solve, most students showed an adaptive mastery pattern of behavior. They persevered in their efforts and performed well. However, other students complained about the task, blamed their failures on their lack of ability, stopped working, and gave up. Diener and Dweck (1978, 1980) investigated this phenomenon and documented a form of helplessness in the classroom.

Dweck's description of how helplessness develops can be useful for therapists. Like students learning difficult lessons, clients enter psychotherapy because they are experiencing problems learning and changing (Tallman, 1996). Therapists can intervene to support effective coping (mastery behavior) and minimize helplessness in therapy as Dweck was able to do in the classroom. The benefits to be gained from using this research include (a) a framework for recognizing when a helpless condition has developed; (b) information that helps the therapist understand why the client is paralyzed in his or her situation; and (c) implications for how the problem can be corrected.

We suggest that coping with helplessness is a common factor across therapies and that all forms of psychotherapy function in ways to minimize helpless responses and maximize adaptive mastery approaches to problem solving and work. The goal of therapy is thus to provide clients with the conditions under which their ability to learn is maximized. What most therapies do is help remove the obstacles to effective learning, developing, and changing.

The Mastery and Helpless Behavior Patterns

Mistakes are a normal and necessary event in the process of learning. Young children are quite tolerant of their own errors and generally do not become discouraged. They persevere and, with time, they overcome obstacles. Some older children are not as resilient. Dweck and Reppucci (1973) observed schoolchildren to determine why some of them responded very poorly to mistakes. A subset of children became very distressed and gave up when they encountered difficult challenges. Dweck and Repucci identified this behavior as the *helpless* pattern, similar to the learned helplessness phenomenon described in animals by Seligman, Maier, and Geer (1968).

Dweck (1975) found that children who attributed successes and failures to unchangeable characteristics, such as ability, were likely to display maladaptive helplessness when confronted with failure. In contrast, the children who attributed success and failure to a changeable dimension, such as effort, were relatively unaffected by errors and were able to continue striving. This adaptive response was called the *mastery behavior* pattern.

In related studies, Diener and Dweck (1978, 1980) and Dweck and Leggett (1988) discovered and documented in detail the maladaptive helpless pattern and the adaptive mastery pattern (see Table 7.1). In these

TABLE 7.1
Two Patterns of Student Behavior Identified by Dweck and Leggett (1988) Following Failure Trials

Behavior pattern	Mastery pattern	Helpless pattern
Work intended to	Gain competence	Demonstrate competence
Goals established	Learning goals: gain skills	Outcome goals: show superiority or adequacy
Failure indicates	Task difficulty, need for increased effort	Lack of ability
Meaning of effort	Effort is needed to gain mastery of a worthwhile challenge	Effort implies low ability
Use of strategies	Improve strategies	Persist in using unhelpful strategies
Performance	Maintain or improve performance	Performance deterioration
Metacognition	Monitoring of strategies	Monitoring of performance
Affective response	Positive affect, enjoy task	Negative affect, dislike task
Evaluation of own performance	Accurate estimate of successes and errors	Cognitive distortion, underestimates own successes
Criterion for gauging progress	Compare with one's past skill	Compare with others

experiments, children were trained to verbalize aloud their thoughts and feelings as they worked on a concept formation task. The students were first given problems that were easily solved and were later presented with problems that were too difficult for their age. Before the difficult problems, the two groups were indistinguishable, but after a few failures, the differences in affect, behavior, and cognition were observed.

Affect: The helpless children, who previously appeared to be enjoying their task, started to complain that the task was boring and too hard. They appeared to suffer. Many of them could be described as anxious or depressed during that time. In contrast, the affect of the mastery children was generally unchanged. They reacted to the task in a neutral manner, although some of the mastery students seemed invigorated by the challenge and showed an increased interest in the work.

Behavior: Behavioral changes accompanied the shift from success to failure trials. The performance of the helpless group quickly deteriorated, and they stopped working. The helpless children spent little time on task. They sought to appease or distract the experimenter and some boasted of task-irrelevant skills or possessions. In contrast, the mastery students stepped up their efforts to solve the problems and stayed on task. They worked harder.

Cognition: There were a variety of cognitive differences between mastery and helpless children. After making a few errors, the helpless students immediately began making attributions for their "failure," concluding that their ability was low or they were otherwise defective. The mastery students occasionally attributed their mistakes to task difficulty or an unfair experimenter. More commonly, the mastery students made few or no attributions, presumably because they did not perceive their errors to be failures in need of explanation. The mastery students treated their errors as *information* they could productively use to adjust their problem-solving strategy and move forward.

The quality of the strategies used by the helpless students to solve problems deteriorated severely after they started to make a few errors. Some of them used strategies that were typical of much younger students. These were approaches that would never yield a solution. The mastery students continued to use effective strategies and often managed to teach themselves new methods of approaching problems. The metacognitive functioning of the mastery group was quite superior. They continued to monitor the effectiveness of their strategies and made adjustments as required. They were exemplary self-regulators.

The talk-aloud data collection technique revealed the many dysfunctional cognitions of the helpless students. They were handicapped by a pessimistic outlook. Their recall of past successes was distorted. They seriously underestimated the number of problems they had successfully completed and overestimated the number of failures. They had a dismal prognosis for future performance and even believed they could no longer solve problems that they previously could solve. In contrast, the mastery students were quite accurate in their estimates and optimistic about their future performance.

It is important to note that the helpless students were not less skilled or less intelligent than the mastery students. In pretests, their ability scores were actually slightly higher (Dweck & Reppucci, 1973). If not ability, then what distinguished the mastery and helpless students? M. Bandura and Dweck (1985, cited in Dweck & Leggett, 1988) suggested that the two groups of students operated under different implicit belief systems. They hypothesized that some students viewed intelligence (or ability) as a *fixed entity*; one only receives so much ability. In learning situations, if individuals believe intelligence is a fixed entity and not changeable, they will want to demonstrate that they have adequate (or superior) intelligence. They will *set performance goals* to perform well. These believers in entity will not wish to risk failure under any conditions. They will be conservative in their choice of tasks, aiming to guarantee a successful outcome. This kind of risk-averse approach will deprive students of the opportunity to learn and develop. The belief in fixed intelligence may be a common adult belief system. Children tend to become sensitized to these beliefs after the age of 11 or 12 years (Nicholls, 1992), although there is evidence that early grade-school–age children also hold these beliefs.

Other students hold *incremental* beliefs (see Figure 7.1). They implicitly (not necessarily in a conscious manner) believe intelligence is augmentable, and thus they can acquire more if they work harder. They prefer to *set learning goals*, aiming to gain knowledge and skill.

The meaning of effort and failure is different for incremental and entity theorists. In an entity belief system, the need for effort to complete a task implies lower ability. If another individual can perform the same task as well in less time, it reflects poorly on the "slower" person. Mistakes are equated with failure, and failure is an indictment of ability for the entity theorist, evidence that the person's permanent trait is inadequate. Thus, the entity theorist will strive to give the impression of minimal effort and abundance of "natural" ability.

However, for an incremental theorist, high effort is a strategy for success, and mistakes are useful because they provide information used for modifying strategies. Mistakes tell the learner which strategy does not work. Making an error is not equated with failure. People need to endure a large number of mistakes while they learn. Making and correcting errors is necessary in the schema-building process.

The importance of implicit theories of intelligence was demonstrated in the classroom as well as the laboratory (Dweck & Bempechat, 1983). These authors found that children who endorsed items reflecting an entity belief system ("You can learn more things, but how smart you are stays pretty much the same") were more likely to pursue performance goals to show they possess sufficient ability. Children who agreed with incremental theory items such as "Smartness is something you can increase as much as you want to" were more likely to set learning goals, hoping to gain skills.

E. S. Elliot and Dweck (1988) proposed that the behavior patterns are determined by the goals an individual establishes. If a person has set

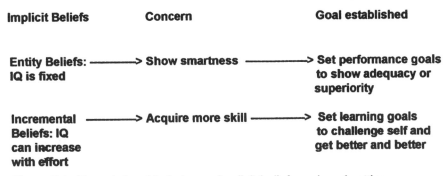

Figure 7.1. The relationship between implicit beliefs and goal setting.

performance goals to demonstrate competence, repeated failure is an indictment of ability and there is little reason to continue trying. They will give up easily. If a person is pursuing learning goals, failures are not disruptive. The individual just continues to learn and get smarter. The full causal sequence of goal-orientation effects was presented in Dweck and Leggett (1988). Their arguments are summarized in Figure 7.2.

Role of Perceived Ability

E. S. Elliot and Dweck (1988) manipulated perceived ability and goal orientation to demonstrate the relationship between goals (performance or learning) and the two patterns of behavior (mastery and helpless). They gave students bogus results of a pretest that suggested they possessed either high or average ability. They manipulated the choice of learning or performance goals by enhancing either the value of ability or the value of a skill. They found that when learning goals were set, students consistently displayed the adaptive mastery behavior pattern and performed well, whether they perceived their ability to do the task as high or just average. When performance goals were being pursued, and the students believed they possessed average ability, helpless responses sometimes occurred. If the students were pursuing performance goals and thought their ability was high, the mastery behavior pattern was maintained. This frequently overlooked finding may be the most significant outcome from the early Dweck research. To reiterate, *perceiving oneself as having lower ability was not detrimental for incremental theorists pursuing learning goals.* They knew they could get smarter. However, the students pursuing performance goals (the entity theorists) needed to believe their ability was high to survive challenges and function as well as the incremental theorists. Highly perceived ability (high self-efficacy or high self-esteem) is only important if one is pursuing performance goals. The implication of this finding is that setting learning goals is preferable whenever possible. In other words, set goals to improve

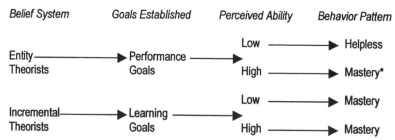

Figure 7.2. The role of perceived ability in producing mastery and helpless behaviors. From "A Social–Cognitive Approach to Motivation and Personality," by C. S. Dweck and E. L. Leggett, 1988, *Psychological Review, 95,* p. 259. Copyright 1988 by the American Psychological Association. Adapted with permission.

relative to oneself or to an absolute criterion but avoid indexing performance to others. Everybody can make great strides using this approach.

As shown in Figure 7.2, entity theorists with high perceptions of ability can maintain mastery behavior. However, there is evidence that the group of entity theorists with high perceptions of ability were actually exhibiting a *pseudomastery* behavior pattern because they were still relatively risk-averse like the helpless group. They preferred easy tasks, a choice that tends to place a ceiling on learning potential. They miss opportunities to learn. Dweck and Leggett (1988) noted it is difficult to maintain confidence when pursuing performance goals, even when students believe they are highly able. (The client who always seemed to function well until he or she had reason to doubt his or her ability may be exhibiting pseudomastery behavior.) Their self-esteem is vulnerable to attack.

Personality Can Be Viewed as Fixed or Changeable, Just Like IQ

The earlier Dweck research demonstrated the role of beliefs about intelligence in learning and behaving. Dweck (1991) argued that people tend to treat their self-attributes in general (not just intelligence) as if they are either fixed, unchangeable entities or incremental and improvable. People tend to see social skill, morality, and personality as either fixed or changeable characteristics. They display similar tendencies either to be optimistic, persist in thinking and improving strategies, and be successful or to become rigid and give up trying.

Dweck (1991) and Dweck and Leggett (1988) speculated that the powerful effect of implicit belief systems on behavior could be generalized from intelligence to other attributes. Dweck showed that people hold entity or incremental beliefs about personality, morality, and sociability, and it affects their behavior. The incremental believer sees personality as something that can be developed. In contrast, entity theorists (implicitly) believe personal characteristics are fixed traits. The entity theorists were shown to make more long-term, extreme, negative, global, and rigid judgments of themselves and about others (Erdley & Dweck, 1993). The entity believer tends to think about people in terms of traits, whereas the incremental theorist focuses on specific and modifiable factors, such as the situation, effort, and strategies.

If a person believes self-change is possible, the person focuses on what will be changed and how he or she will direct the ongoing process of self-modification (in other words, mastery behavior). Although success in bringing about the desired goals is not guaranteed by beliefs that change is possible, the probability of success is much higher if the person attempts modifications than if change is viewed as impossible. The self-change belief idea thus is a *gatekeeper* concept. If a person believes something is not possible, any further pursuit is halted. For example, if one believes that a problem such as clumsiness can be outgrown, there is no particular barrier to gaining coordination. In comparison, if one believes "once a criminal always a criminal," there is a large psychological barrier to considering that a criminal can change—it is not possible in one's framework. The expression "tigers don't change their stripes" is the epitome of entity theorizing about personality.

Goetz and Dweck (1980) found mastery and helpless responses to social rejection in experimental studies. People who believe their social skills are fixed entities tend to repeat ineffective social coping strategies when they experience a social failure. Those who believe they can improve their social skills examine their methods carefully and make adaptive changes likely to bring about positive social results.

Entity and incremental theorists may have different social experiences as a result of their beliefs. Erdley, Loomis, Cain, Dumas-Hines, and Dweck (1997) investigated the effect of holding entity versus incremental beliefs about personality on children's reactions to social rejection. The rejection took the form of initial nonadmission to a pen pal club. The entity theorists made more dispositional inferences about themselves, concluding they had general-level defects. Their responses were maladaptive, much like the helpless children in the early Dweck research (Diener & Dweck, 1978). The children tended to perseverate, repeating unsuccessful strategies in a manner that would not have helped them gain social acceptance. In contrast, the incremental believers modified their behavior in socially adaptive ways.

People who view themselves and others in terms of entity dispositions will seek to identify or "diagnose" these traits, for example, "Jerry is shy," "Marcia is a dummy," and "Matt is a tough guy." Dweck, Hong, and Chiu (1993) found that entity believers expect more traitlike behavior and greater consistency across situations in themselves and in other people. In contrast, incremental believers are more likely to perceive behavior in the context of situations and see actions as the products of states rather than enduring traits. After reading a scenario, an incremental theorist is more likely to describe the events, for example, "Jim is not telling the truth." In contrast, the entity theorist is more likely to draw a conclusion, such as "Jim is dishonest," classifying the information at an abstract trait level. The entity theorist decontextualizes behavior (Dweck et al., 1993). Similarly, Fiedler and Semin (1988) showed that abstract trait coding increases the likelihood that the respective traits will later be viewed as causal determinants of behavior. Situational explanations for behavior will occur infrequently.

Providing further data in support of the entity–incremental distinction, Gervey, Chiu, Hong, and Dweck (1993; cited in Dweck, Chiu, & Hong, 1995) asked participants to serve as mock jurors. When asked what the purpose of imprisonment was, significantly more entity theorists said it was for retribution, whereas more incremental theorists said it was for rehabilitation. Not only do entity theorists believe in behavioral invariance at the theoretical level, but they also quickly and easily apply the theory to specific settings.

Dweck et al. (1993) explained that implicit theories themselves are not fixed or dispositional. People do not invariably use entity or incremental theories in all situations. Belief systems are domain specific and not universal (Dweck et al., 1995). The intercorrelations among implicit beliefs about morality, intelligence, personality, and the world are very low. For example, people who hold entity beliefs about people's intelligence may hold incremental beliefs about the possibility of modifying other aspects of personality.

Beliefs about the modifiability of self-attributes are themselves modifiable. Bergen (1991) was able to manipulate implicit beliefs in an experiment by giving participants a "scientific" article arguing either for or against the correctness of the entity or incremental view of intelligence. After the inducement, people who read the entity paper were more likely to predict a character would show trait-consistent behavior in different settings. Conversely, those who read the incremental paper expected less behavioral consistency over time. This research demonstrates (a) the power of implicit beliefs to alter perception and expectations; (b) the changeability of belief systems, at least on a temporary basis; and (c) the ease of generalizing entity beliefs to a more abstract global level.

Theories about personality affect people's responses to other persons. Erdley and Dweck (1993) showed slides of a boy exhibiting rule-breaking behavior and asked how the boy would behave in the future. This behavior was seen by entity believers as indicative of an underlying trait. The entity believers were more likely to foresee a trait-consistent ending for the boy. They attributed negative global dispositions (mean, nasty, bad) to him and were unwilling to change their opinion of him when new, conflicting information was introduced. They recommended more punishment for the boy than did incremental theorists. Chiu and Dweck (1992; cited in Dweck et al., 1993) found that when a situation was described in which a person inflicted some harm unintentionally, the entity theorists produced more global and negative descriptions of the actor. Entity theorists also generated statements regarding the person's competency, using words such as *idiot*, *retarded*, or *stupid*, that the incremental theorists did not.

There is evidence that people who hold entity and incremental beliefs structure meaning differently (Chiu, Sacks, & Dweck, 1994; cited in Dweck et al., 1995). Participants were given comics that provided information about both the characters' traits and goals and were asked to determine how the characters were similar. Entity theorists identified traits, such as competence or morality, whereas incremental theorists perceived the similarities between people in terms of the characters' goals. The entity and incremental theorists frame the world differently through their respective lenses. The entity believers expect and seek information about human constancy (traits). They expect to find universals and consistency. They expect behavior to be predictable and invariant over time, which is consistent with entity or trait beliefs.

In contrast, incremental believers have a contextually sensitive lens and describe people in terms of settings. These differences are similar to the distinctions between individualistic and collectivistic perspectives, as described by Triandis (1989, 1996). One's beliefs are likely to become self-fulfilling prophecies. There are times when adopting incremental beliefs is more adaptive. Sometimes change is highly desirable. Can people who are not socially adept become entertaining? Can people become smarter or more moral? Can people change those things they consider basic about themselves? Can a person become more considerate or more punctual? Can a displaced worker develop new skills or an old dog learn new tricks? Can a pessimist become more optimistic? To some extent, beliefs about change can become limiting factors. If one believes change is not possible (for whatever reason), then change is more difficult.

Helpless and Mastery Behavior Patterns in Therapy

Like students with entity beliefs, if clients view their traits, their personality, or their problems as fixed and characterological, and they try repeatedly to correct the problems and fail, helplessness or a depressed response is a logical, albeit undesirable, response.

Other problems that are similar to the helpless pattern and that interfere with therapy include client's expectations of failure, negative self-evaluations, constant evaluation of self and others, and attempts to demonstrate superiority over others. Helplessness may be associated with polarization of important constructs in life, including dichotomous thinking and focusing on issues of right versus wrong or excellence versus incompetence. Life choices may also become polarized, giving the impression one has only a few options in a situation, which allows no room for consideration of alternatives.

Polarized, either–or thinking is generally restricted to evaluative dimensions, including these common polarities: good versus bad, moral versus immoral, perfect versus worthless, superior versus inferior, and strong versus weak. These are all terms associated with performance and judgments. They can be found at the base of the helpless condition.

Recognizing the Helpless Pattern in Clients

The following are some of the clues that suggest a client may be experiencing some elements of helplessness. The client

- Frequently interprets the therapist's comments as judgmental or negatively evaluative
- Attempts to distract the therapist from relevant issues
- Seems preoccupied with diagnosis
- Appears to want to "prove something," to assert his or her competence
- Provides lengthy lists of his or her imperfections
- Changes the subject
- Attempts to entertain or flatter the therapist
- Starts boasting of unrelated achievements or possessions
- Engages in dichotomous thinking (things are right or wrong, good or bad, successful or disastrous)
- Has a need to assign blame for most problems
- Wants to know how well he or she is progressing in therapy in relation to others or wants other social comparison information
- Perseveres in unproductive ways

Such a client is not necessarily resisting the therapist's efforts to help. A client who is an entity believer may simply feel threatened and will not be receptive to exploration or new ideas at the time. If the client is pursuing performance goals, the client will be using his or her energies, anticipating his or her own, the therapist's, or the world's praise or criticism. The client is pursuing different goals than the therapist.

These distracting behaviors are important as indicators that a client may be outcome-focused and unable to concentrate, and because these activities limit time devoted to more productive activities. These restrict the client's vision so he or she will miss new possibilities, overlook alternative courses of action, and generally think in a less effective manner.

Making self-attributions for shortcomings can also be a sign of the helpless pattern. Diener and Dweck (1978, 1980) found mastery students made few attributions for failure. Whereas the helpless students used their cognitive resources to make attributions for failure, the mastery students devised new strategies aimed toward solving the problem. In therapy, mastery clients may similarly attend to the immediate demands of the task and find conclusions about traits to be less relevant.

Helpless clients frequently make negative, destructive evaluations of themselves; they are also distinguished by their tendency to evaluate others. This is problematic in part because time and energy are spent judging and are not directed toward resolution of issues. The focus of attention is centered on attitudes, judgments, and the emotional reactions to these judgments. Resources are not available for assessment of complex causes and new strategies for improving the situation.

WHAT IS THE FOCUS OF THE CLIENT'S ATTENTION? THE LENS ANALOGY

The helpless and mastery behavior patterns can be conceptualized as being the products of different states of mind (Tallman, 1996). Used here, *state of mind* is defined as a moodlike configuration of thoughts and feelings that predispose one to respond with certain patterns of behavior. The state of mind can change in accordance with circumstance, including environmental demands, presence of social comparison information, and the nature of the task. Some people can be more chronically prone to one state over another. However, state of mind can also be produced by the situation.

The Process-Focused State of Mind

The state of mind associated with a process focus is fairly calm, with neutral or positive affect, good attention to the task, creative problem solving, task perseverance, and mastery behavior. The person gauges progress by comparing current skills to one's previous skills, not to other people. Being process focused increases the likelihood of mastery behavior. Being process focused means the client is focused on the "how to" aspects of the current situation (see Table 7.2).

The Outcome-Focused State of Mind

In contrast, the outcome-focused state of mind can be associated with concerns about evaluation. It is linked with agitation, fear, other negative affect, loss of effective use of strategies, reduced concentration, and poor performance. Negative assessments of past functioning and pessimistic expectations for future performance typify this state. This deterioration is caused by attention (limited cognitive resources) being diverted to performance (and other outcomes). Attention is focused on future outcomes, such as doing well or appearing successful. This state can lead to helplessness because the individual never attends to the problem at hand. The problem is poorly resolved or neglected entirely. Under this outcome focus, the attention is focused on the "how good" aspects of the situation rather than on the "how to" aspects. At some point in time, a person must attend to the how-to aspects to effectively solve most problems. Detailed examples of the outcome and process-focused patterns in therapy are provided in Table 7.2, illustrating the breadth of the classroom analogy to the therapy setting.

People seeking psychotherapy are not the only people whose attention drifts off to concerns about performance. For example, athletes have long struggled with the problem of maintaining their concentration. The nature of the athlete's competing thought is not particularly important. Regaining concentration is all that matters for performance. Performance

TABLE 7.2
Behavioral Consequences of a Process or Outcome Focus

State of mind: Focus of attention	Process focus	Outcome focus
Behavior pattern	Mastery	Helpless
Type of goal pursued	Learning goals to increase competence	Performance goals to demonstrate adequate or superior ability
Role of evaluation	Identify strengths and weaknesses	Establish competence or prove superiority
Affective responses	Positive or neutral affect	Negative affect (complaining, anxiety, depression) and surrender
Cognitive functioning	Consider and test new ways of responding	Perseverate with old, ineffective strategies
Meaning of effort	Task is worthy challenge; effort is required to master	Lack of ability, avoid appearance of hard work; one should be naturally good at the task
Meaning of errors	Information about what will not work	Errors mean failure, evidence of low ability
Response to failure	Curious examination of errors, generate new hypotheses, increase concentration, attend to task	Negative self-evaluation, attribution to low ability, give up trying, avoid more exposure to failure-prone situations
Success in therapy means	Current methods are effective	Client and therapist is "good at" therapy
Role of therapist	Give feedback, information, keep client process focused on task, provide extra cognitive space and support for thinking	Identify client disorders, fix defects, evaluate progress, provide praise for good choices
Attributional style	Success attributed to effort and strategies, attributions not relevant when process focused	Frequent attributions for failure to low ability, few attributions for success; successes are forgotten
Perspective on progress	Accurate self-perceptions of progress	Underestimates success and overestimates difficulty
View of future	Expects success to follow effort	Expects failure despite success in past

Continued

TABLE 7.2   (*Continued*)

State of mind: Focus of attention	Process focus	Outcome focus
Persistence	High	Low
Performance	High; makes changes, tries new methods of responding	Inconsistent, risk averse, protective of usual ways of responding
Rewards	Enjoy gaining skill, learning; some enjoy overcoming big hurdle	Avoiding appearance of inferiority, gaining superiority, risk reduction
Posture toward risk	Will risk mistakes and looking foolish to gain new competency or understanding	Mistakes must be avoided to protect self-worth and negative evaluations, find the "sure thing," choose easy tasks
Consequence of attitude toward risk	Gains opportunities to "stretch," increase effectiveness	Misses opportunities to learn
Beliefs about therapy	Client develops	Client is corrected, cured
Meaning of slow progress in therapy	Difficulty of task; need for more time or change in strategy	Lack of ability, failure, incompetence, presence of pathology; client is not working; client is not a "good" client

concerns will, of course, be a very common cause of lost attention and poor results. People can change their focus of attention in the moment. Athletes learn to keep a current process focus, and clients can learn to access their mastery behavior patterns. Reinforcing the process-focused state of mind may be especially helpful for clients with cognitive limitations or extreme emotional states.

The helpless pattern is the result of a state of mind, not just a dispositional or characterological attribute. Although a person may exhibit one state of mind more often than another, these patterns need not be considered traits, as situational elements have been shown to override individual dispositional states (Dweck & Leggett, 1988; Nicholls, 1992). These states of mind, outcome-focused versus process-focused, may be mutually exclusive in the moment. Each state may be a well-developed schema that is in place during the task unless another schema is more salient. A person either focuses on the task or on outcomes in any given moment.

An analogy for the state-of-mind view is the camera lens. If one is focused on an object located 30 feet from the lens, an object 1 foot away will not be in focus and vice versa. One cannot distinguish objects in the background when focused on a close object. The background objects do not disappear, but they are not accessible or salient. They seem less important. Similarly, a student or a client cannot focus and work on the task at hand when future performance outcomes are emphasized. In contrast, when the learner is concentrating on proximal, immediate issues such as assessing strategies, overall performance is less salient. A process focus may be the direct cause of the functional mastery pattern, and an outcome focus may be the cause of the helpless pattern.

For example, a writer cannot simultaneously perform while worrying whether his or her manuscript will be rejected. Test anxiety is another example of how the two states of mind are incompatible. Although concern for the outcome of a test can provide some motivation to study for a test, continuing to think about performance is disastrous during an exam. Similarly, in therapy, a client's belief that he or she is a failure blocks efforts to improve behavior. The brain does not function as a multiprocessor (Weil & Rosen, 1997).

It is not just contemplating negative outcomes that can be harmful. Overconcern with positive outcomes can also be debilitating. Overfocusing on perfection and competing to be the best can similarly interfere with effective work. The helpless pattern is associated with global evaluations of the self (such as "I'm no good") and is future focused or past focused in its perspective. The mastery pattern is associated with focusing on the immediate task. The evaluations of a person who is showing mastery behavior are focused on the effectiveness of one's immediate strategies. The mastery pattern calls for moment-to-moment adjustments to strategies. The more difficult the task, the more important it is that performance concerns can be set aside.

Metacognition

One distinguishing feature of human thought is metacognition, the ability to monitor how one is functioning and give oneself feedback (Flavell, 1979). Superficially, it may appear that the helpless person is using his or her metacognitive capabilities to excess, evaluating and checking instead of doing the task. However, it is not necessary or even desirable that people halt the process of self-monitoring. In fact, during effective process-focused work, metacognitive activities do occur. The important difference is between helpful and destructive monitoring. The helpless person is scrutinizing and evaluating his or her overall performance and sometimes his or her self-worth. In contrast, the process-focused person analyzes and critiques strategies. The relevant question becomes, "Is this approach still working?" In contrast, both the positive and the negative self-esteem self-talk of students with performance goals can be a distraction from the work.

State of Mind: An Additional Site of Intervention

Dweck's (Dweck & Leggett, 1988) model suggests that if therapists can change the belief from entity to incremental, change can occur. In Dweck's model, the way to reach the mastery behavior pattern is through trying to change beliefs or goals. In the state-of-mind model, one could also build mastery behavior by developing a process state of mind (with or without changing beliefs or goals). Anything that creates an immediate, here-and-now focus leads to a process focus and mastery behavior patterns. On the other hand, conditions that divert attention to performance, evaluation, or other outcomes will cause an outcome focus and create vulnerability to helpless responses.

Having incremental implicit beliefs is not necessary for supporting mastery behavior. Similarly, setting learning goals is not essential. What the idea of state of mind adds to the Dweck model is another point of entry for a pivotal intervention. The performance goal can remain in place if attention to the task can be trained. The loss of attention to the process is the reason the helpless state occurs. It might be useful to train clients in therapy to control and manage their state of mind. It is much more difficult to change one's beliefs or one's goals (see Figure 7.3).

Some helpless and mastery reactions may occur quickly or otherwise not be consciously mediated; some reactions may be automatic. Mastery behavior can occur even if the client holds entity beliefs about change, has low estimates of ability, and is pursuing performance goals as long as he or she keeps attention focused on the task. Effective therapies try to shift the client's attention from a judgmental frame of mind to attending to strategies for exploring and correcting the problem.

Setting performance goals can result in helplessness because the person may stop thinking about the task at hand and focus attention on evaluation. Attention to problem solving is lost and eventually performance deteriorates. This applies to effortful work in general: schoolwork, therapy, relationships, and the everyday problems of life.

The Pervasiveness of Performance Goals and Evaluation in Life

When people set long-range goals, make evaluations, or develop plans, it is appropriate to be outcome focused to some degree. Focusing on outcomes can be an effective motivator. For example, performance anxiety can make a student sufficiently uncomfortable that the student will study for his or her test. Concerns about personal effectiveness may lead a client to seek therapy. Outcome-focused states can be the initial motivators of behavior. The critical feature is that once the person settles down to do the work, practice, learn, or explore therapy, he or she must be able to switch states of mind away from an outcome focus and adopt a process

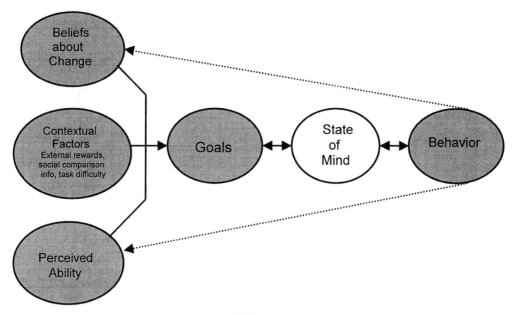

Figure 7.3. The state-of-mind model for therapy.

focus. The outcome focused states (which often include fear or anger) are very intense and self-perpetuating, so switching states is a challenge. Psychodynamic, behavioral, cognitive, and humanistic therapies all help create this shift. Their methods are described in a later section.

APPLICATION OF THE GOAL-ORIENTATION RESEARCH TO PSYCHOTHERAPY

The state-of-mind model for therapy appears in Figure 7.3. According to this model, when people stay process focused and gain successful mastery experiences, the positive experience feeds back into earlier parts of the system. Success (following sustained mastery behavior) makes it easier to maintain concentration (the process focus). Successful mastery experiences can change perceptions of ability, which helps people cope with performance goals. Successes also feed back and may change implicit or conscious beliefs about ability to change.

Intervene where it is possible. If the client's beliefs can be shifted toward the incremental direction, this will help the client. If perceptions of ability can be increased, this will help. If learning goals can replace performance goals, mastery behavior is more likely. But training a focus on the current task and strategies is also possible. We believe that all the effective therapies help train a process focus in clients in addition to intervening at the level of beliefs, goals, and beliefs about ability.

It is difficult to change ingrained belief systems, particularly when they are continually reinforced by the cultural environment. American values emphasize productivity, achievement, and "natural ability." If it is not feasible to change the beliefs, at least there may be another method of altering the system: by supporting a process-focused state of mind during working times. In turn, some experience in a successful mastery pattern could feed back into the system through increased self-efficacy, learning goals, and modified beliefs, which in turn could alter one's guiding strategies and one's goal choices.

IMPLICATIONS FOR THERAPY

There are several important implications for therapy. First, many client difficulties are aggravated or sometimes may be caused by excessive focus on outcomes. Some clients suffer in part from fundamentally the same kind of helpless condition afflicting Dweck's students. The corresponding changes in affect, cognition, and behavior are observed. The client feels terrible, shows distorted estimates of his or her capabilities, and seems to show reduced problem-solving capacity (in and out of therapy).

Second, an outcome-focused state of mind interferes with the process of therapeutic change. The client's efforts are diverted. Third, effective therapies such as cognitive, behavioral, humanistic, and psychodynamic therapies all increase a person's process focus and reduce outcome focus. Most progress is probably made when the client is in a process state of mind, so therapists foster attention to process to help the client do the work of therapy. When the client is pursuing outcome goals, therapy progresses poorly and the client might be perceived as defensive, passive, or depressed. An outcome-focused state of mind can be part of a client's difficulties before therapy, and it can be an obstacle during therapy.

Many clients will probably come into therapy feeling judged and negatively evaluated in some aspects of their lives. There is something wrong with them. They need therapy. They perceive themselves to be unable to cope effectively, and they are likely to be feeling helpless at this time. In an individualistic society, people are expected to "bootstrap," to meet their own needs. Receiving help from others becomes less acceptable, beginning in the early teens (Covington, 1992; Nicholls, 1992). As a result, many people are likely to feel they do not measure up, and they will be overly outcome focused at times.

Curious exploration is a necessary first step for all learners, those in school and those in therapy. It provides the raw material for later thinking. Early in therapy, extensive focus on outcomes can translate into inhibited client exploration. Psychological exploring entails venturing into unknown territory. Such exploration implies risk to self-esteem if one tends to focus on evaluation and outcomes. For the outcome-focused client, there is risk of failure and little opportunity for rewards because new activities and learning nearly always involve mistakes and a phase of incompetence—this is appropriate and necessary during the learning phase of competence development (Langer & Park, 1990). Clients may fear that too much venturing into uncharted territory could reveal additional weaknesses beyond the presenting problem. A person may be reluctant to be seen making mistakes either by themselves or by the therapist. Reticence to explore when one is in this state of mind appears natural. Effective exploration will not occur until the client can shift to a process state of mind.

What this means for therapy is that a client who is outcome focused and concerned with his or her performance will not be able to do the "work" of therapy as he or she is too distracted. When a client can focus on the immediate work (intervention, relaxation, exploration, relating to the therapist), he or she has a much better chance of progressing.

It is important to reiterate that helpless and mastery behavior patterns have both state and trait characteristics. Most people probably have a complex combination of process and outcome orientations in many aspects of their lives. In addition, their state of mind may change over time, according to contextual demands. So a person should not be depicted as generally helpless or outcome focused. The person is in one state of mind or other in the present. Helpless and mastery patterns should not be treated as fixed traits.

The Meaning of Errors in Therapy

Progress in therapy is not always smooth. Growth entails exploration, generation of new ideas, and experimentation with those ideas. Testing of alternative ways of behaving is needed to determine which is most effective. Often new tactics will not be great improvements over the established strategies, so errors will be made. Those strategies will be discarded and new lessons learned. There will be lots of errors, by both the therapist and the client. However, some clients may see unsuccessful attempts as failures. It is possible that a client might become discouraged and stop trying prematurely. Like any learning experience, therapy involves many failures, so it is desirable that both participants operate from a process-focused point of view for a reasonable proportion of therapy. When process focused, a client can tolerate setbacks long enough to acquire good strategies and gain skills and self-efficacy. Negative results are treated as information rather than condemnation. Progress is likely because then work promises possible rewards rather than the potential for failure.

The Pseudomastery Pattern

A particularly challenging situation for the therapist to work with is the pseudomastery pattern. As described earlier, students with performance goals and entity beliefs can appear to function adequately if they believe their ability is high, but they are actually risk averse and conservative (refer to the asterisk in Figure 7.2). These are the pseudomastery students. They seek only tasks at which they can excel and are reluctant to challenge themselves. This group appears to be vulnerable to pressures such as novelty, unfamiliar competition, and the threat of feeling ignorant. It is possible that these individuals may be much more difficult to help in therapy than those in the helpless group, who are more likely to be openly distressed and receptive to change. Outcome-focused clients with highly perceived ability may be highly defensive and easily threatened. They would be expected to resist interventions and new perspectives and want to maintain high self-esteem at all costs. They might appear narcissistic because they want or expect to be superior to others with no effort, and they boast of their accomplishments (B. Palmer, personal communication, February 10, 1996). Given their belief system, it would be important to their self-esteem that they maintain their belief in their high ability (or other positive attributes not related to effort). At times they may energetically oppose the therapist's challenges. It is probably unlikely this group would enter therapy without some inducement. They would not want to be challenged in any way. According to the state-of-mind model, they might enter therapy when their perceptions of ability have dropped and they are vulnerable to helplessness.

Self-Esteem (A Perception of Ability)

Often clients complain they have low self-esteem. Is raising self-esteem desirable? Emmons (1999) argued that acquiring high self-esteem might not be a productive goal. The process of seeking high self-esteem may be actually a search for positive performance evaluations, which could escalate the potential for helplessness. The therapist should attempt to eliminate negative self-evaluations. However, acquiring high global self-confidence or self-esteem might not be a wise goal. The reduced emphasis on self-esteem is consistent with the positions taken by Beck, Rogers, Ellis, and various Eastern religions and philosophies. High self-esteem is the flip side of helplessness. Clients with high self-esteem who seek high performance are vulnerable to becoming helpless if their competence is challenged and they fail (make a routine mistake). Instead, clients should set process goals to learn, to grow, explore, and gain skills whenever possible.

One thing that most clients have in common is their low perceived ability to overcome their problems. Diener and Dweck (1978, 1980) found that students with low perceived ability did not perform well if competitive or difficult conditions were present. However, students in the low-perceived ability group continued to function well and to tolerate errors while they were pursuing process goals. Clients too can function in a productive way despite a low self-evaluation (such as low self-esteem or depression) if they are pursuing process goals. If they can focus their attention on the task rather than on evaluation, they can stay in the moment long enough to do the work.

If clients could function as process-focused learners the way young children do, helplessness might not be a frequent problem. Young children are in a situation somewhat analogous to clients who perceive that they have low ability. Their experience is limited, they have many things to learn, and they make many errors, yet these children retain a mastery pattern and persist in trying.

The Effort Dilemma

American competitive values include a concept of ability not important in all cultures. In some situations, especially those involving social comparison, students believe that if a person must work harder on a task compared with other people, it reflects poorly on their ability (Jagacinski & Nicholls, 1987). Consider the expression, "If you have to work at something, you must not be very good at it." This kind of belief would silence the efforts of many people. It could be especially painful for clients coming into therapy in their time of greatest distress. People come to therapy to "work on themselves" and correct problems. Entity believers may reason one should not have to seek help. This creates shame for being in therapy. An example can be found in Ellis and Whiteley's (1979, p. 71) report of a woman who reported problems reaching orgasm. During the course of therapy, it became clear that one of the problems she was encountering was her belief that orgasm should be easy and she should not have to work at it. In this case, being outcome oriented almost guaranteed failure.

An outcome focus is evidenced in couples who believe something must be wrong if they have to work on the marriage. If the relationship were "good," it should come easily. In a similar vein, the other partner should be able to "just know" what the problem is, without explanation. The implication is the spouse should act properly without the effort of learning and discovering each other. In the United States, people expect to be "a natural" at performing well.

One might ask, why would clients enter therapy if they believe their characteristics are unchangeable? Some clients with entity beliefs could have concluded they lack the ability to change. They hope that the therapist can effect change for them. They could expect the therapist to do everything for them. They will need positive experiences to show them they can change.

An outcome-focused client may feel the need to demonstrate a variety of qualities. A client might wish to show the therapist he or she is a good person despite the client's problems or might want to show he or she can be a good client. The client could even ironically feel the need to show he or she really is depressed, anxious, unlovable, innocent, or a victim, so he or she deserves the therapist's time and attention. The client may become preoccupied with the outcomes of therapy, seeking to "be happy" or "have higher self-esteem." Such vague, global, and elusive aspirations make maladaptive goals. In part, it is difficult to determine when and if one has succeeded.

General Therapeutic Strategies

The therapist can learn to recognize the helpless state and not become discouraged with the client. The therapist can model effective process-focused responses to challenge and otherwise foster development of adaptive process-focused skills in the client. Learning methods to extricate oneself from a helpless state will be highly valued by the client.

The therapist also needs to be alert to the phenomenon and not contribute to the problem by creating or intensifying an outcome-focused state of mind. The values that are associated with belief in entity theories and the establishment of performance goals are ingrained values of American culture. It is easy to inadvertently support those values in a way that can interfere with therapy. A few issues that often affect state of mind in therapy are discussed below.

Potential Problems With Reinforcement

Too much focus on evaluation by the therapist can be harmful. Praise from the therapist may create overinvolvement in outcomes and contribute to an outcome focus. For example, a person may work energetically on a hobby but be derailed into a helpless state of mind if someone interrupts and evaluates the work. As Lepper, Greene, and Nisbett (1973) found, children who show intrinsic interest in an activity (such as drawing) will sometimes stop working following a reward, but children who are promised no reward will continue the activity. Muellar and Dweck (1998) found that praise for ability undermined performance but praise for effort did not. It appears that intrinsic motivation to work can be lost when the behavior becomes instrumental to obtaining rewards. This distinction can be important in therapy. There are potential problems in making judgments and giving too much reinforcement. Therapist approval could, under some conditions, reduce clients' commitment to their original course of action and distort clients' reasoning processes. Lessons learned while seeking to gain therapist approval may not be retained or may only be superficially understood. Well-intended positive statements such as "Good move" and "You did the right thing" can have a cumulative effect and, when used frequently, may shift the client's attention to outcomes.

Clients sometimes do their best work while looking away from the therapist, possibly suggesting a process-focused concentration on their problem. For example, the client could be asking himself or herself, "Is this approach working? What are the other options? How can I do this?" The focus and judgment should be centered on the process, on the way things are accomplished.

Note this does not imply that there is no value in ever praising the client's accomplishments. The client needs to feel supported, and praise for a person's efforts is natural. But the therapist needs to be judicious in its use. Even reinforcing a client for staying in process is likely to destroy the process-focused state of mind.

There are two potential problems with the use of praise. First, there is the potential reaction to being evaluated as good or right. Equally important is the cognitive shutdown that results. For example, a client has just reported how well she has successfully handled a complex business or social situation that has troubled her for months. Praise or disapproval by the therapist can be a dichotomous "good–bad" reduction of a complex problem to a simple result. The client had in mind a multidimensional problem and would greatly benefit from a moment to carefully reflect on and examine why and how events developed as they did. Which strategies helped and which interfered with progress? What insights and ideas may have assisted her decision making? What values guided her? What would she do differently in the future? This is an opportunity to revise strategies for future challenges. Therapist silence is priceless when clients are thinking and is often better than a simple praising remark. Therapists should be supportive of client successes but should not let judgments interfere with the self-healing process.

Another way the therapist can inadvertently introduce a performance outlook is through intake interviews and diagnoses, which tend to be evaluative processes. They create a focus on outcomes. It is possible to see why clients become defensive following these events. Global evaluations can be especially threatening if the client is already outcome focused. Even the client who entered the intake in a process-focused state of mind might become reoriented toward outcome concepts if, for example, the client is labeled with a diagnosis by the therapist or told that therapy might take years to complete.

The least productive response a therapist can give to a helpless client is to confront him or her with the fact that he or she is being outcome focused. This would simply be another judgment or evaluation. Many clients make too many evaluations of themselves already. The most positive approach is to support a process focus rather than try to eliminate an outcome-focused state of mind directly. Using the camera lens analogy, keep pulling the client gently back to the present problem, while tolerating the presence of performance issues in the background.

An effective method of encouraging the client's process focus is to closely attend to and sometimes participate in the client's exploration or testing of ideas. Such therapist responses will also model a process-focused state of mind.

Necessary Evaluations

The most clear and common way therapists inadvertently encourage an outcome focus is by using evaluative comments and positive or negative judgments. In the preceding subsection, we discussed the risks of overusing praising reinforcement. It is easy to imagine that negative evaluations of the client's behavior are also likely to put the client into a defensive outcome-focused state of mind. Yet we know that evaluations of behavior are a normal part of life. How can the therapist cope with the inevitable evaluations that occur in and out of therapy? The productivity of the session can depend on how well the client and therapist deal with evaluations, especially global evaluations (such as diagnoses or major interpretations). When an evaluation is presented may affect how it is used. The client will tolerate and integrate evaluative feedback better if he or she is in a process-focused state of mind. For example, if a therapist refers to clients' behaviors as evidence of denial, can the clients use information productively? Do they treat it as evidence of their global inadequacy, or do they treat it as information and develop new strategies? Learning to cope with such judgments (use them as data) will be a very important skill for the therapist to help the client acquire.

Evaluations of performance are not evils for the therapist and client to avoid at all cost. The external world makes performance evaluations and global judgments, even if the client and therapist do not. A necessary part of life is evaluative: choosing values and assessing one's strengths and weaknesses for life choices such as relationships, lifestyles, and careers. These require the client to focus (appropriately) on evaluation and outcomes. But the client will also need to accomplish or enact his or her values and choices. If the person remains in the evaluative state of mind, he or she may encounter problems. To implement choices, one must shift concentration to the details of the task. The attentional focus is what distinguishes the comfortable, effective learning state of mind from the helpless, frustrated state of mind. When process focused, the client still makes evaluations, but the client evaluates the task and strategy. When outcome focused, the client makes evaluations about the self.

Goal Characteristics

The use of process rather than outcome goals has been found to be more effective for improving performance in business settings, especially when the task is complex, difficult, or novel. Client problems routinely meet these criteria.

In his review of the goal research literature in management and psychology, Latham (1996) concluded that often it is better to stress learning goals (e.g., coming up with ideas or strategies for solving a problem) rather than outcome goals (e.g., completing a task or producing a certain quantity of something) until the person has mastered the requisite strategies. Then the outcome goals can be used to increase productivity. Exploration is thus a legitimate goal for most clients. A client who already has a skill can cope with an outcome goal.

Utman (1997) conducted a meta-analysis of the performance effects of motivational states. He found the advantage of setting learning goals over performance goals was larger for complex tasks and moderately pressured situations and when the participant was not with peers. This situation describes the therapeutic setting.

In the following section on common factors, we discuss the many ways therapists have successfully helped clients create a process-focused state of mind during therapy. It is presumed that experience in therapy with switching to a productive process-focused state of mind will be exported to everyday life and the client will transfer that learning to daily work and problem-solving situations.

STATE OF MIND AS A COMMON FACTOR IN PSYCHOTHERAPEUTIC CHANGE

The process–outcome state-of-mind concept is compatible with many psychotherapies. In this section, four major therapies are discussed: psychodynamic, behavioral, cognitive, and humanistic. These therapies deal with the helpless state and teach process-focused skills. We believe all effective therapies address the following issues:

- The various therapies all attempt to explain the helpless condition.
- Developing process-focused skills in clients is a common goal of therapies.
- The therapies have all developed techniques for treating an excessive focus on outcomes.

The specific manner in which these four therapies deal with outcome focus are described next.

Psychodynamic Therapy

Freud described the client's struggle with change in great detail, and he believed that much of the work of therapy must be devoted to overcoming resistance. Clients are inclined to defend themselves against full awareness and change. Therapists may sometimes feel as if they and the client are working toward different goals.

The psychodynamic approaches might describe a client's maladaptive, outcome-focused behaviors as resistance to the therapeutic process, a defense against exposing unwanted material. The state-of-mind theory would suggest that an excessive focus on outcomes and performance might be the force that leads to resistance.

Resistance and defensiveness may often be a sign of an outcome focus because the person's goals to demonstrate competence are at odds with therapeutic goals. The client may be operating under a different belief system from the therapist. A client may take an interpretation as a threat to the self, instead of as task-relevant information.

Therapists can inadvertently evoke an outcome focus. For example, Wile (1984) encouraged therapists to avoid "accusatory interpretations" when offering explanations for their clients' behaviors, as clients may become defensive. Some examples of poor phrasings that would be likely to create an outcome focus include the following (Wachtel, 1993, p. 72–73):

> "You are trying to avoid . . . "
> "You are denying how you . . . "
> "You are defending against feelings of dependency."
> "Behind your silence is a lot of anger."

Such judgmental comments would be especially difficult for a client with an outcome focus to use productively. However, a client in a process-focused state of mind might find something helpful in these remarks. In this state of mind, the client is less judgmental and may not react defensively.

To produce new ways of behaving, psychodynamic theorists use the transference relationship and techniques such as free association and dream analysis to access deeper levels of consciousness, outside the range of active, conscious resistance. One might argue that they move around outcome-focused evaluations to reach a different state of mind, one more open and less protected. In support of the process-focused environment, the psychodynamic therapist avoids conveying approval or disapproval or expressing judgments of the client's behavior. The use of free association very likely creates a state of mind in which performance judgments are temporarily suspended. The client does not even have the distraction of the therapist–client interaction. The client attends closely to his or her thoughts and is explicitly given permission to say anything that comes to mind, without fear of evaluation. Furthermore, this suspension of judgment by the therapist models nonjudgmental thinking for the client, so later the client may be more likely to think without judging himself or herself or others. This kind of environment would be a relief to a helpless client. It could encourage development of a mastery state of mind. It could also encourage step-by-step tracking, keeping the client in the present. Showing the client how to develop a process-focused state of mind will assist the client in approaching a goal of psychodynamic theories—making informed, rational decisions.

Another goal of psychoanalysis is to teach clients not to judge their impulses, but to learn to deal effectively with them. This is analogous to eschewing an outcome focus (i.e., that the client's impulses are bad) and adopting practical, coping mastery goals.

Finally, the therapist emphasizes development of a strong ego. The ego might be seen as the practical, "get it done" process-focused function of the self. It is relatively value free. It may problem solve, even when it is serving performance goal functions. The psychoanalyst encourages the client to suspend self-judgments and focus on the task of understanding. This helps the client practice having a stronger ego state. The psychodynamic approach changes behavior by altering beliefs and by changing the client's state of mind (see Figure 7.3).

Behavioral Therapy

Behavioral therapists emphasize specific behavioral changes through relaxation training, skill acquisition, strategy development, modeling, repeated practice, and feedback (Bandura, 1986; Kanfer & Goldstein, 1986; Linehan, 1993). These changes correspond to acquisition and strengthening of a process focus. Behavioral therapies focus on, and have their clients focus on, the task. The therapist needs to know specifically what the client wants to accomplish and what behaviors need to be developed or extinguished. The concentration of attention remains with the task and on specific behaviors, rather than on the person at a more general level. A behavioral focus is a process focus. An outcome focus is likely to be extinguished, as it receives little reinforcement. A helpless behavior pattern is extinguished or eliminated indirectly by adding process-focused behaviors.

When a person is engaged in activities that generate a process-focused state of mind, an outcome-focused state of mind is difficult to sustain. The helpful behaviors are reinforced repeatedly to increase the likelihood of occurring when they are needed.

Many features of behavioral therapy support the development of mastery skills. Relaxation techniques replace an outcome focus with a here-and-now focus. A relaxed client is less defensive and more able to function in a process-focused manner. Systematic desensitization builds mastery habits. The tasks are graded in difficulty, so the client does not consider confronting a feared outcome without preparation. In step-by-step approximations, he or she makes small manageable improvements. With each step, he or she practices being process focused and successful by attending only to the immediate task at hand.

One helpful aspect of a behavioral approach is the formulation of the problem. It is not necessary to think of the client as pathological, especially at the characterological (trait) level. Behavioral therapy is nonjudgmental in its view of all behaviors being learned and able to be unlearned.

The client may begin therapy with general goals, such as raising self-esteem and feeling better about themselves. The behaviorial therapist will soon guide the client to be process focused, requiring him or her to be specific about objectives and to create learning goals and subgoals and to avoid outcome goals. Evaluation is then based on the client's previous performance, not the performance of people in general. Clients who are in a process-focused state of mind use self-referenced evaluation to judge their progress.

The behavioral therapist construes challenges as learning situations. The client should not expect to perform new tasks with no effort. He or she should expect to progress through a learning curve, gaining skills slowly. Once the new skills are acquired, practice will be needed to reinforce the new behaviors. Behavioral therapy creates change through altering the client's state of mind and by changing the client's goals.

Cognitive Therapy

Cognitive therapy aims to modify dysfunctional cognitions. Some of the destructive assumptions that clients hold are values, goals, and beliefs that are difficult or impossible to achieve. When clients fail to live in accordance with their standards, they devalue themselves. For example, beliefs such as "I must parent well enough that my children will carry no hurts from childhood" will certainly lead to disappointment. This is an unrealistic performance goal.

Ellis (e.g., Ellis & Whiteley, 1979) identified self-evaluation as a major source of psychological problems and advocated making no self-judgments. Outcome-focused beliefs such as "shouldisms" are directly targeted for change. Shouldisms are outcome focused because they shift the attention to the absolute demand. For example, "I must win my partner back or I will never be happy" is a performance demand. Dwelling on this idea monopolizes the clients' cognitive resources, so they may overlook current opportunities, fail to observe how they are contributing the problem, and neglect activities that might help them to feel better.

Ellis (e.g., Ellis & Whiteley, 1979) disputed the client's absolutistic adherence to values. A client may behave in a way that violates his or her values and may become anxious and depressed about the action. Ellis replaced the extreme reactions ("I am a terrible louse!") with more tempered reactions ("I prefer not to act that way"). The behavior (rather than the person) is evaluated and found undesirable. Then the person does not continue to make negative self-judgments. Instead the person is encouraged to change the behavior and reevaluate the strategy leading up to it (typical of the mastery pattern). He or she changes the emotional reaction by changing the state of mind (primarily through the belief). The client learns to evaluate the strategy and the behavior rather than evaluate himself or herself. The client attempts to change his or her state of mind and shift attention away from self-judgment.

Beck (Beck et al., 1979) similarly sought to reduce harmful outcome-focused evaluations, such as perfectionism, dichotomous thinking, jumping to conclusions, excessive concern with the future, and global judgments of self. His techniques support a process focus. Clients keep process focused by recognizing destructive thought patterns and challenging them one by one. Clients are forced to examine their reasoning to see if they really accept their arguments. The catastrophizing process is slowed down and scrutinized. Beck worked on change at the belief level by teaching clients to be process focused about the belief.

An effective method to produce a process focused state of mind is Beck's (1987) use of graded task assignments. A seriously depressed client is not expected to move from a bedridden condition to a fully functioning state. Instead, Beck gives low-demand assignments such as just leaving the bed and showering that day. These assignments are given in a manner to reduce outcome focus. The assignment is "for experimentation only," and it is not important that it be completed. Even if the client fails to do it that day, he or she need not punish himself or herself for failing. Subsequent tasks are slightly more challenging. Beck keeps the client focused on the present task and the present goal, rather than the much more global and challenging task of getting a job and functioning at the client's previous level. Similarly, keeping a daily record of dysfunctional cognitions gives the client experience with being in the moment and process focused outside of therapy. If Beck can keep the client process focused, catastrophizing and self-blame are much less frequent and less urgent. The one-step-at-a-time approach may be effective because the client's attentions (and cognitive resources) are focused on the task.

Meichenbaum (1977) used positive self-talk to create therapeutic change. Effective self-talk may be one of the best methods for building process-focused skills. The therapist can model this behavior when he or she encounters an obstacle in therapy. A misunderstanding with the client is a good opportunity to demonstrate positive self-talk. The therapist models focusing on the task, not evaluating the self, and not becoming discouraged.

Meichenbaum (1977) used the self-talk technique with hyperactive children. He trained the children to attend to moment-by-moment task work, as modeled by the therapist. The following is an example of how he modeled positive self-talk:

> Okay, what is it I have to do? You want me to copy the pictures . . . with the different line. I have to go slowly and carefully, Okay, . . . draw the line down, down, good; then to the right, that's it: now down some more and to the left. Good, I'm doing fine so far. Remember, go slowly. Now back up again. No, I was supposed to go down. That's okay. Just erase the line carefully . . . Good. Even if I make an error I can go slowly and carefully. I have to go down now. Finished. I did it! (Meichenbaum & Goodman, 1971, p. 117)

This passage illustrates numerous process-focused elements. First, the self-talk is not concerned with either avoiding failure or what a terrific picture the child will produce, but *how* to complete the picture. One way Meichenbaum prevented an outcome-focused state of mind is by showing the child self-reinforcement for mastery of the component steps and focusing mental effort on training of follow-the-line skills. This allowed the child to learn a comfortable attitude and indirectly discouraged premature judgments about the goodness of the work. Through modeling, the child learned how to cope with errors. This self-speech also exemplified strategy development over time. Also, no global evaluations were modeled. The child had not lost knowledge of how to claim he or she was "no good," but had added many skills and strategies. With practice, he or she will automatically guide himself or herself supportively through drawing and other challenging tasks. In terms of the process model, the child learned how to direct his attention to the immediate task rather than let it wander ahead to the outcome and global evaluation. The cognitive approach helps clients through changing beliefs (as expected), but also through training a process-focused state of mind. Cognitive methods also help clients establish more functional (more process-focused) goals.

The cognitive therapies train effective process-focused responding. Yet, there is a potential problem with the philosophy of cognitive therapy. The therapist may believe that the client's various beliefs and assumptions are erroneous. This potentially judgmental quality could interfere with process-focused work in therapy by creating an outcome evaluation. It could also cause the client to attempt to appease the therapist. Focus on practical problem solving could be lost.

Humanistic Therapy

Rogers (1961) implied that a well-adjusted person stays "in the moment," which suggests a process focus. A humanistic view of the development of a helpless state of mind would be that when people are valued for their performance and achievements rather than themselves (conditions of worth), they are likely to develop performance standards for themselves and think of themselves as good or not good, able or inept, and superior or inferior. This could lead to chronically outcome-focused states of mind and the helpless pattern.

In practice, Rogers (1961) did not directly dismantle outcome-focused behavior and cognitions but concentrated on active listening and exploration of meaning, which aided the client's return to focusing on the process. Hearing one's reasoning in a reflection often makes clients want to revise their arguments. This method is immediate and process focused. Rogers focused on the active process of being in the moment, which teaches the process-focused pattern. Humanistic therapies attempt to keep the client changing and evolving. They help the client increase awareness of the many sources of information in their environment. They encourage the client to listen to his or her intuitive knowledge and integrate this information for better decision making. Client-centered therapies have been shown to enhance intelligent thinking (Zimring, 1990), which may be true of all effective therapies. The reflections used by humanistic therapists keep attention close to the client's experience and prevent both the client and therapist from racing ahead to conclusions or evaluations. They support a here-and-now process focus.

Empathic responding helps reduce outcome-focused reasoning. Clients who feel empathically understood are unlikely to feel the need to prove their superiority or adequacy. Empathic responding operates on a step-by-step basis. Clients are focused on communicating and clarifying their experience. They can create some distance from their problem, think about their role in troublesome situations, and reconsider the approach (strategies) they have been taking. New options can come to light and be evaluated. In contrast, prior to therapy, the efforts they might spend on the problem might consist primarily of "shoulds," "have to's," and self-criticism.

The concept of self-actualization is consistent with maintaining a mastery orientation to one's life, work, relationships, and one's relationship to one's self. Rogers (1961) talked about self-actualization as a process rather than an outcome. It seems a person is most likely to be in the process of self-actualizing when he or she is process focused. A process-focus may actually be what Rogers meant by self-actualizing, or it may be a precondition for self-actualizing. The humanistic approach works almost entirely through changing the state of mind to a process focus.

In sum, psychodynamic, behavioral, cognitive, and humanistic therapy function in ways that change behavior, build a process-focused state of mind, and reduce excessive focus on outcomes. They keep the client focused in the present rather than the future, and they minimize judgments and evaluations. Several of the approaches also directly change beliefs or goals.

DISCUSSION

Adaptive, process-focused behavior patterns can be generated through holding incremental beliefs, setting learning goals, *or* directly through the state of mind. Therapists can facilitate change by challenging dysfunctional entity beliefs, by helping clients set learning goals rather than performance goals, or by helping clients adopt a process-oriented attentional focus. Behavior is affected by the focus of attention on either outcome or process. In other words, attention consistently directed to outcomes might cause a helpless pattern, whereas attention directed to the process supports a mastery pattern. Therapists can foster this directly. A productive state of mind can be created in the absence of a focus on goals or beliefs.

The following summarizes how a therapist can use the state-of-mind model to support the client's agency and build effective coping skills, as well as to reduce outcome focusing and helplessness. There are four possible sites for intervention to support an effective mastery behavior pattern and reduce helpless behavior:

1. Attempt to change the client's implicit belief system (to incremental beliefs).
2. Change the goal: Set learning goals while simultaneously reducing the salience of social comparison information. Compare behavior to oneself, not others.
3. Change perceptions of ability (self-esteem, self-efficacy).
4. Change the client's state of mind. Focus on evaluating behaviors and strategies, not judging the self or others. Accept the outcome-focused state of mind as necessary at times, but be able to refocus on the task when needed.

Feedback from experience with a process or outcome focus will in turn influence a person's state of mind, perceptions of ability, and beliefs (see Figure 7.3). An advantage to using state of mind as a point for intervention is that there may be many dysfunctional beliefs to challenge. Targeting the state of mind may be a shorter route. As the client gains practice with a process-focused style and develops adaptive behavior patterns, a sense of self-efficacy and the experience of success will increase. In turn, successful experience may lead to refinements in beliefs.

Keeping attention focused on the process may be an important and learnable skill. One advantage that a process-focused approach can offer clients and students is how to use helpful and supportive self-talk. Clients who easily become process focused may have witnessed effective modeling in the home or from friends who know how to talk themselves through difficult times—to self-instruct and self-support. Therapists can help clients talk through problems so they learn the strategizing, self-coaching, and self-monitoring lacking in the helpless client. Relatively short-term goal setting is also process focused and supportive of sustained efforts to learn and change.

Clients who come in to therapy with a process focus or clients who easily reach a process-focused state of mind may be the "good clients" described by therapists. Such clients will be ready and able to do the work of therapy and seem cooperative. They get involved in therapy and respond to interventions. They appear open to suggestions rather than defensive and fearful. These clients are able to switch from the outcome-focused state of mind to the process-focused state of mind, and they also can switch back when needed. Optimal functioning occurs when the client is in control of the switching process.

How do therapists support a process environment? Modeling of effective process behavior may be one effective approach. Therapists can model an on-task thinking style, limit evaluations, and share their metacognition with their clients. Then the client will understand the "how to" of being process focused. Practice in thinking in a more process-focused manner is also needed, so that under pressure, clients will have access to this thinking skill and will use it to solve problems. Emphasis is placed on strategies rather than outcomes.

Clients do not just need emotional support. They need help becoming effective problem solvers to help them deal with challenge. They can accomplish this using free association, modeling of process-focused behaviors, empathic listening, examination of beliefs, rehearsal of effective coping strategies, focusing on the present, and avoiding evaluative thinking styles. When the client can switch to the process-focused state of mind, the client is again actively problem solving and developing.

CONCLUSION

- Experiments by Dweck demonstrated how implicit beliefs in fixed and unchanging traits (such as intelligence) contribute to the risk of developing helpless behavior in school children. When individuals hold these beliefs, they set goals to demonstrate competence. If they do not perform well, they sometimes give up and stop trying. (This is similar, but not identical to, Seligman's learned helplessness.)
- Belief in the ability to augment one's ability and improve leads to the establishment of mastery goals to increase competence and ability. For persons pursuing goals to learn, fail-

ures are informative and not discouraging. They do not surrender. They develop effective new strategies.

- Defensive clients may implicitly believe their personal characteristics are fixed and not changeable. They may be setting goals to demonstrate competence, which will distract them from pursuing goals to learn, explore, and experiment. They will easily take offense and may avoid trying new things that could help them develop.
- Sometimes the client does not appear to be an active problem solver. Client behavior may appear defensive and rigid. Defensiveness, demoralization, dichotomized thinking, and helplessness can be caused by an excessive focus on outcomes (such as being good, OK, perfect, right, smart, or the best).
- Clients need to be in a process-focused rather than outcome-focused state of mind to benefit from therapy.
- Believing personality is fluid, pursuing goals to learn, concentrating on the task at hand, and using effective problem-solving strategies all contribute to a process-focused state of mind.
- Evaluative conditions trigger development of an outcome-focused state of mind and can derail efforts to learn and change.
- The major therapeutic approaches all reduce excessive focus on outcomes and support and train a process focus. Methods such as self-talk, empathic listening, following a stream of consciousness, modeling, practicing effective responses, and addressing problems one at a time encourage the client to pay attention to the task or issue at hand rather than use judgments and evaluation. A person cannot learn while thinking about how well he or she is doing.
- Therapists are encouraged to minimize positive and negative evaluations.
- People are not outcome focused or process focused in all settings. One changes according to past experiences and current conditions.
- People need not be process focused all the time. People need to be process focused when they work, so they can explore, learn, and think through problems.

8

ENGAGING THE CLIENT'S INTELLIGENCE: THE CONSTRUCTION OF MEANING

Raymond Corsini (1989) reported a case when he was working at a state prison. One day an inmate came into his office and told him that he was leaving on parole in a few days, but that he wanted to thank Corsini for what Corsini had done for him. The man said, "When I left your office about two years ago, I felt like I was walking on air. When I went into the prison yard, everything looked different, even the air smelled different. I was a new person. Instead of going over to the group I usually hung out with—they were a bunch of thieves—I went over to another group of square Johns" (p. 3). In addition to this, the man reported that he had begun to learn a trade, had taken a correspondence course, and had a job waiting for him when he left. He had started back to church, and he had completed a high school diploma through a correspondence course. He said that he was planning to go to college, and he thanked Corsini for changing his life.

The problem was that Corsini could not remember ever having spoken to him. Corsini looked through his folder and noted that he had given this man an IQ test about 2 years before. So Corsini asked the man what he had said that had changed the man's life. The man reported, "You told me I had a high IQ" (p. 4).

This chapter is about how clients actively construct meaning in their lives (along with help from therapists). People fail to self-heal when learning processes get blocked or go awry. Therapy works by supporting, amplifying, and focusing naturally occurring client learning and meaning-making processes. Given a client who is able to focus efforts on the tasks at hand (see chapter 7), clients explore, learn, and change by *thinking* (in a productive fashion) about their problems; *experiencing* aspects of problematic behavior as well as new ways of being and behaving; and *behaviorally experimenting*. We examine these processes in detail.

THINKING, EXPERIENCING, BEHAVING

Thinking, experiencing, and behaving are three interrelated learning activities. They feed into one another in a cyclical fashion (e.g., Kolb, 1984; also see Figure 8.1). For instance, individuals may first try new behaviors. They experience their effects, and then think and reflect on these experiences. What they learn from their reflection may then lead to the development of new hypotheses to try out in behavior. Or they may begin by paying attention to their experience and formulating it in words. This leads to thinking and reflection, and then generation of new behavioral alternatives to try out. The process cycles until problem resolution is sufficient so that the individual can move on to other problems. This cycle can be abbreviated as the thinking–experiencing–behaving cycle, or TEB cycle. The processes of thinking, experiencing, and behaving encompass those emphasized by the major brands of therapy. Psychoanalysis focuses primarily on thinking (self-reflection and self-understanding) and secondarily on experiencing; humanistic therapies focus primarily on experiencing (exploration and accessing of inner experiencing) and secondarily on thinking; cognitive therapies focus on thinking and behaving; and behavioral therapies focus on behaving and experiencing (in the form of having new experiences).

Thinking, experiencing, and behaving are processes that lead to certain outcomes or products. The products, in turn, lead to problem resolution and personal change. These products are shifts in perspective, bodily

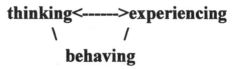

Exploration, learning, and meaning-making through

thinking<------>experiencing
            \\   /
            behaving

Figure 8.1. The thinking–experiencing–behaving cycle.

felt shifts, and the development of new behaviors. We give a case example below, and then consider both the TEB cycle and its products.

The Case of Hugh

Hugh, age 65, was a recently retired business executive who came into therapy because he was having trouble attaining erections with his girlfriend Dora. Hugh had been married once but mostly had lived the life of a swinging bachelor until he retired. Then he met Dora. He now no longer felt that he wanted to play around and was growing increasingly attached to Dora, although they did not live together. His problem was not organic—he had seen a urologist. Moreover, he was able to attain erections when he masturbated.

Hugh's initial goal, as he defined it, was to be able to attain erections during sexual encounters with Dora. He said he got very nervous about performing with her. Hugh, however, did not want to bring Dora into therapy. Therefore, because he lived by himself, it was suggested that he try some masturbation exercises (Zilbergeld, 1992) to help him overcome his performance anxiety.

Although these behavioral experiments did not resolve his problem, they did lead to experiential exploration and clearer problem definition. Hugh became experientially aware that his problem was not really performance anxiety but rather that he did not find sex with Dora that exciting. He was used to sex in noncommitted relationships, and he had frequently found partners who, like himself, enjoyed incorporating pornography and sex games into their sex life. However, Dora seemed too proper for him even to suggest these things. It was no wonder that he felt anxious about performing. He realized through the masturbation exercises that he really enjoyed sex that incorporated pornography and sex games. He revealed that he had a large collection of pornography. He did not find sex without such aids interesting, although he thought he "should."

The therapist and Hugh thought together about the meaning of this discovery. They discussed the possibility of Hugh's disclosing it to Dora. Hugh did not want to disclose everything, but he did think of a compromise. He would ask Dora if they could watch a pornographic movie together before sex, without revealing this was one of his major preferences. When Hugh returned the next week, he reported that he had tried this and Dora had been surprisingly receptive. However, it still had not led to his having an erection for intercourse. Instead, Dora had masturbated him (which he had enjoyed), and he had masturbated her.

In thinking about this, Hugh accessed several reservations about being in a committed relationship that had heretofore been implicit. As he began to think about his reluctance to bring Dora into therapy and to fully disclose to her, he began to articulate in words his uneasiness about being in the relationship at all. This led to a period of therapy in which Hugh thought about and evaluated his relationship with Dora.

Through this evaluation, Hugh gradually realized that he did experience the relationship as fulfilling; he finally decided to take the big behavioral leap of inviting Dora into therapy. In the therapy session, Dora was open and receptive to Hugh, although Hugh still did not disclose at that time his sexual preferences. Dora was open to trying sensate focus exercises, so they went home to do that.

The sensate focus exercises did, over a period of a week or so, lead to Hugh's having successful intercourse. However, more important, it led to Hugh's finally disclosing his sexual preferences to Dora. Once again, she was accepting of this, and they began to work out a sex life that incorporated his preferences. The biggest benefit Hugh said that he got from therapy was taking the chance to self-disclose to Dora. In addition, he realized that he did want to maintain his relationship with her, and he became more accepting of his sexuality.

This case illustrates the intertwined contributions of behavioral experimentation, experiencing, and thinking in the change process. Hugh learned both through accessing and articulating his implicit knowledge of his problem situation and through direct experiential encounter. He thoughtfully evaluated his relationship and considered alternative possibilities for action. Behavioral experiments led to both behavior change and to new experiential recognitions, as well as to new thinking.

One other point worth noting from this example is that problem resolution is an ongoing process. Complex, ambiguous, difficult problems do not usually yield all at once to some preset "neat" logical solution, even if that solution seems in advance to be the right one. Note that the process in this case was a nonlinear one. Things did not flow neatly from one thing to another, but rather recursively fed back into one another. Furthermore, there was no one resolution. The process demanded continual tinkering, as well as continual hypothesizing and exploring. Even when therapy terminated, things were not magically and neatly all wrapped up, though generally reasonable accommodations had been reached so that life could continue to chug along for Hugh and Dora (who undoubtedly encountered new and different problems after therapy terminated).

Next we consider each of the three processes in more detail. Despite the fact that we have listed thinking first (primarily because it makes for a nice acronym: TEB), experiencing is actually the most basic way humans know the world, so we first consider experiencing.

Experiencing

We start with experiencing because it is the most basic mode of knowing the world (Bohart, 1993; Gendlin, 1964; Lakoff, 1987)—knowing that comes through direct interaction and encounter. Clients actively use their experiencing in therapy because, first, much of what they know about their problems they know implicitly and intuitively. Clients implicitly know many of the factors involved in their problems, and often have a sense of what possible directions the solutions lie in. Helping them access their implicit experiential knowledge and articulate it in words can lead to productive insights into their problems, as well as to the generation of creative solutions. (As an example in another area, Einstein once said he was following a "feeling" in developing relativity theory. His creative work developed from articulating that feeling in words and mathematical symbols.)

Second, clients learn much better when they experience new ways of being and behaving. Possibilities generated by thinking need to be fleshed out and "made real" through experiential encounter.

Third, experiencing is bodily and also includes emotion. Paying attention to the emotional aspects of experience is particularly important in therapy because emotion is a key component of so many problems. In many cases, clients must involve their emotions in the learning process for any significant change to take place.

Nature of Experiencing

Experiencing has tacit, bodily, and perceptual components. We look at each of these in turn.

First, much of experiencing is tacit. Infants learn through direct experience before they form verbal concepts (Neisser, 1988; Stern, 1985). People know things through experience that are not "thought." They do this by intuitively extracting patterns from their direct experiential encounters and interactions. Much of what young children learn, for instance, is implicit and tacit (e.g., the rules of grammar).

People often have the experience of recognizing relationships among events that they may have trouble describing. Amateurs may "know" when a piece of music has been well performed, by sensing or perceiving the smoothness of its flow and the facility with which complex passages are performed. Individuals may "know" when a relationship is clicking, from perception of the rhythms of the relationship—how smoothly transitions are managed, problems resolved, commonalities found, resonances in experience shared, and so on. Their words for this may be rather global: "We are soul mates" or "We think alike," but these words are crude and simplistic summaries of the complexities of the perceptions on which they are based.

Along these same lines, the cognitive linguist George Lakoff (1987) proposed that all knowing is first and most primarily experiential and non-conceptual in nature, and that concepts are derived from experience. Concepts are an attempt to articulate experience in words. Concepts are not so much "there" in the mind, forming the structure of how one experiences the world, but rather are things one creates as one tries to understand the experience.

Second, experiencing has a bodily component. Several cognitive scientists have argued that the basis of all cognition is bodily experience (Gibbs, 1997; M. Johnson, 1987; Lakoff, 1987). For instance, Gibbs (1997) argued that the concept of *balance* is based directly on bodily experience and could never be defined in words that would make any sense unless one had had this bodily experience of being balanced or imbalanced. The concept of balance is abstracted from the bodily experience and metaphorically generalized to things such as justice, forming a balanced opinion, or having balance in a relationship.

Third, experiencing is grounded in perception. Perception has more of a direct and immediate quality than does thought. Things are given to people directly in perception. They are recognized and the experience of recognition is different from that of conceptualization. To recognize or to actually "see" how to do something is a much more powerful learning experience than merely acquiring a concept about it. Some cognitive scientists now believe that how people know the world is first perceptual and experiential, and that the acts of conceptualizing come later. Barsalou and Prinz (1997) said, "psychologists are beginning to propose that the human conceptual system is inherently perceptual" (p. 276).

Experiential Understanding

It is when people recognize (i.e., directly experience) relationships that they "really understand" them. In therapy, abstract conceptual knowing without recognitional knowing is unlikely to lead to change. Change occurs when a person attains an experiential recognition of meanings. True insight is perceptual and recognitional (Bohart & Associates, 1996; Schooler, Fallshore, & Fiore, 1995) and only secondarily conceptual.

The fact that true insights occur only when clients see and experience for themselves means that therapists cannot simply tell truths to clients. All truths discovered in therapy ultimately must be discovered by clients themselves, even if they were pointed in the direction by the therapist. Simply telling solutions to clients is not likely to be useful (Dominowski & Dallob, 1995), unless clients are able on their own to go out and use the solutions to see if they are useful.

Therefore, in therapy clients ultimately make their own discoveries, even if they were guided to them by the therapist. Even two different clients practicing "the same" assertion skills will have their own unique experiences as they practice, and will therefore end up with somewhat different perspectives on what assertion means to each of them.

Experiencing and Change

When clients are actively trying to change themselves, they need to be able to experientially explore as well as conceptually explore. If they merely think about their lives in a distanced intellectual fashion, nothing seems to happen. Concrete images of experiences in the problem situation need to be accessed, re-presented, and reexperienced. It helps to be experientially present in the problem situations to begin learning how to handle them differently, either in actuality (in vivo) or in imagination.

There are two dimensions of experiencing. One involves having experiences in the external world. This occurs primarily through behaving in the external world. Clients learn through directly encountering experiences provided by trying out new behaviors and by confronting fears. This is the kind of experiencing most typically emphasized by cognitive–behavioral therapists. A vicarious form of this is exposure or confrontation with experience through the use of imagination.

The second kind of experiencing is internal. This can include tracking one's own experience as one talks to the therapist, vicariously reviewing experiences one has had in one's life, or vicariously experiencing through imagination. Tracking one's own experience, "listening" to it, trying to articulate it and put it into words, and trying to access one's experiencing (including emotions) are all characteristic of humanistic and psychodynamic approaches to therapy. People struggle to articulate their experience in words. That is because experience is often not sharp and easily categorizable (Buck & Ginsburg, 1997; Gendlin, 1964; Leitner, 1994) or explainable.

A key part of some humanistic therapies, as well as of methods like eye movement desensitization and reprocessing (EMDR; F. Shapiro, 1995) is to follow the flow of internal experiencing. In client-centered therapy the client follows the flow of internal experiencing, articulates it in words to the therapist, who tries to empathically resonate with it, and then returns to further internal tracking. Gendlin's (1981) focusing procedure consists of practicing a kind of internal listening and following of the shifts and changes in inner experiencing as one tries to articulate it in words. In EMDR, the client follows the internal flow of experiencing, paying attention to it while also paying attention to the therapist's moving fingers. What seems to be common to these processes is a move into a mental state of observing and listening, rather than over intellectualized self-analysis.

A particularly important part of experience for therapists and clients alike is emotion. There is increasing evidence that experience is constructed emotionally first before it is constructed cognitively (Greenberg & Paivio, 1997). Emotion is therefore important in solving personal problems because personal problems are so intimately tied to emotions. Part of the internal openness and awareness process that seems to be needed for the problem-solving process involves the active experiencing of emotions. This is not surprising because emotions are intimately tied to most major personal problems. To be really exploring the problem, to be really confronting it, is to also be open to and experiencing the emotion. However, the experiencing and expression of emotion per se is not the only healing element. Exposure to the emotion is also exposure to the impact the problematic experience is having on one's self; one's beliefs, values, and goals; and one's body. Emotion is a part of the gestalt of the problem. To explore a problem with one's boss is to experience the emotion of anger and frustration that one feels toward him or her. Experiencing one's emotions, then, is a part of accessing the meaning of experience.

In the following and tracking of internal experience previously mentioned, allowing and experiencing of emotion appears to be an important component (Greenberg & Paivio, 1997). Humanistic therapists, behavioral therapists using exposure, and therapists using EMDR encourage clients to "stay with" the emotion, experience it but not get lost in it, until there is a shift and a change. The changes vary as a function of the theory and the method. For behavior therapists, the change is usually a decrease in the intensity of the emotion; for humanistic therapists and for those using EMDR, there may also be associated shifts in meaning and the gaining of new perspectives. Allowing and experiencing of emotion, therefore, is not necessarily cathartic, but rather leads to shifts in personal meaning.

In summary, the importance of experiencing to the client as an active self-healer is that it is through the client's own confrontations with experience, and through his or her own experiential self-discoveries, that change ultimately takes place. Clients can encounter experience through trying out new behaviors in the world or through tuning into their inner experience, including their emotions.

In the case of Hugh, Hugh used both kinds of experiencing. He paid attention to his vague, uneasy feelings about his sexuality and his relationship, and that helped him articulate in words what both meant to him. This then facilitated cognitive reflection. Hugh also tried out new behaviors and learned through direct confrontation with experience. His experience doing some of the sex therapy exercises, for instance, helped him sharpen his sense of what he wanted.

Thinking

With very few exceptions (e.g., Jenkins, 1996), the client as an active, generative thinker does not exist in current theories of psychotherapy. It is as if, in therapists' eyes, clients have become lobotomized when they enter therapy. A perusal of the indexes of most books on psychotherapy either have no references to client thinking at all or have references only to clients' dysfunctional thinking. Clients are not granted the ability to think in the same active, generative way therapists do.

There are certainly dysfunctional ways clients can think. Cognitive therapists identify a number of cognitive errors that clients can engage in, such as overgeneralizing (Beck et al., 1979). Rational–emotive therapists (Ellis & Whiteley, 1979) identify *musturbatory thinking*—thinking in terms of absolutistic shoulds and musts. Both psychodynamic and humanistic therapists have talked about overly intellectualized thinking, that is, highly abstract analytic thinking about oneself not connected with bodily experience. Many clients exhibit such dysfunctional thinking patterns as rumination—going over the same grounds over and over—and dichotomous thinking—thinking in terms of either–or.

However, despite dysfunctional thinking, clients also think productively and generatively. In fact, as we have discussed in chapter 7, much of client dysfunctional thinking is a product of their being helpless, overwhelmed, and stressed. The job of the therapist is to support and promote the clients' capacities for productive and generative thinking. Next we consider what this is.

Functional, Generative Thinking

Clients actively use thinking in therapy to (a) observe and track their own experience, (b) struggle to articulate their experience in words, (c) apply concepts to understand and analyze problems, (d) try to "make sense" of experience through narratively restorying it, (e) run mental simulations of events to try to understand them, (f) think dialectically to generate new alternatives and possibilities and then evaluate them, and (g) suspend old ideas to search creatively for new patterns and insights. Thinking provides a good deal of freedom for exploration. The person can scan alternative possibilities, try out various ideas in imagination, and pose hypotheses for testing. Thinking is somewhat removed from experience, and largely generates *possibilities*.

Thinking as observation of experience. Thinking seems to be most productive when there is a lively dialogue between thinking and experiencing or between thinking and behaving. Thinking that results from direct encounter and observation of experience seems to be particularly important. Clients observe their internal and external experience and behaviors or engage in exercises in which they have a direct confrontation with experience, and thoughts just naturally emerge from these observations. Such thoughts are grounded in experience and seem particularly useful in change, in contrast to thoughts that are derived from highly distanced intellectual analyses. Such observations lead to the articulation of experience.

Thinking as articulation of experience. Thinking begins with the articulation of experience into words and symbols (Gendlin, 1996; Lakoff, 1987;

Pennebaker, 1995; J. C. Watson & Rennie, 1994). The articulating process is one of trying to fit concepts and words to experience. This includes the process of trying to identify what is going on. Much of experience is nonverbal, and clients often must search for the right words or concepts. Frequently, they have to invent concepts or use metaphors to articulate what something was "like" for them. Describing experience is an active synthetic process, not merely a reporting one. Therapists can actively help co-create the words and concepts clients use to capture their experience by making their own guesses as to what the client is experiencing and trying out their own words. One example of this is the use of empathic reflections in client-centered therapy.

Use of concepts. Clients try to understand their experience by looking for some organization in it. They try to identify what type of event a particular experience is (e.g., "Am I being cowardly here?"), and they look for patterns ("I seem to be avoiding making a commitment to her"). Furthermore, they use concepts to suggest solutions.

This is an active, synthetic process. A number of cognitive scientists now argue that concepts are not fixed structures through which information is filtered mechanistically, but rather are things that people continually modify and create to deal with new situations (e.g., Glucksberg & Keysar, 1990). People do not really ever use exactly the same concept twice. Instead, whenever they use a concept, they are extending it and fitting it to a new situation. To quote Ward et al., (1995),

> [T]he way you think about any concept may be slightly different every time you think about it. This is partly related to the fact that the exact concept you bring to mind depends on your immediate situation, and no two situations, no matter how similar, are ever identical. . . . Research verifies that the exact concepts we construct change from one time to the next. Francis Bellezza of Ohio University had people provide definitions for a set of words, and then return a week later to define the same words a second time. He found that people's definitions changed greatly from one week to the next. In other words they constructed their concepts differently on the two occasions. (Bellezza, 1984, cited in Ward et al., 1995, p. 37)

Ward et al. went on to note,

> [I]t is unreasonable to think that you have an infinite supply of fixed, prestored structures ready to go in anticipation of every possible situation in which you will need to dredge up every concept you know. It is more reasonable to believe that you have the ability to construct exactly the concept you need when you need it. (pp. 37–38)

This is not to say that people do not use their old concepts, bending and modifying them to fit with each new situation, but that the act of conceptualizing in any given situation is a continuously creative and generative one. The process is not a mechanistic one of incoming information being fit into preset, neat conceptual boxes or schemas.

In many cases, when people apply a concept to a new situation, they are engaging in a process of *metaphorical extension* of an old concept to a new situation. Thus, they may use a solution that worked in one situation in a new situation because the new situation is "like" the old situation.

Consider Hugh. Hugh had to decide if it was acceptable that he prefer pornography as a part of his and Dora's sex life. To evaluate this, he had to dredge up old ideas and concepts about what is acceptable and unacceptable sexual behavior that he had learned in the past. Then he had to "tweak" them to see how they fit with his current situation. He also had to decide and evaluate what was acceptable in terms of this particular relationship. In so doing, he eventually decided his behavior was acceptable. But Hugh did not apply some well-defined concept of acceptability to his experience like a cookie cutter. Rather he had to bend it and stretch it, see if it fit, and eventually modify it. Later on, Hugh might have to creatively struggle again with deciding on the acceptability of a certain behavior. Hugh was not mechanistically using a "should" about what was acceptable to understand his experience; he was actively using concepts to try to figure out for himself what was the most effective way to be.

Therapists can facilitate this process by offering concepts (insights and interpretations) that may help clients capture and organize their experience. However, these must be offered tentatively, and the client is the ultimate authority on whether they fit or not.

Developing and reworking narratives. In addition to using concepts to understand experience, clients also make sense out of experience by forming narratives about it. Telling a story is a form of organizing an experience. How one tells the story highlights what one thinks is important; who one focuses on as the "main character"; how motivations are directly or indirectly portrayed in the narrative; the role of emotion in the narrative; and how themes of jealousy, achievement, heroism, courage, cowardice, betrayal, and so on are all portrayed. Narrative may be closer to how people actually experience life than formal conceptual understanding.

Many approaches now argue that therapy is primarily a matter of the narrative restorying of life (Gold, 1996a; Neimeyer & Mahoney, 1995; Omer & Alon, 1997; Schafer, 1992). Helping clients tell and reorganize their story so that they see new possibilities and gain a sense of empowerment is one way therapists help clients self-heal.

Running mental simulations. People run mental simulations all the time. It has even been argued that our liking for stories is because they provide "what-if" worlds for us, that is, mental simulations (Oatley, 1996). Taylor, Pham, Rivkin, and Armor (1998) argued that running mental simulations is a primary way of coping, and they demonstrated empirically the use of mental simulations for improving studying. Hugh ran several mental simulations trying to imagine what it would be like to suggest to Dora a change in their sexual practices.

The running of mental simulations has been explicitly used in therapy. A favorite mental exercise of strategic therapy is to use the "miracle question," in which the client is asked to imagine the future where the problem is completely resolved and then is asked, "What is different?" Running this simulation helps the clients focus on what exactly is important to them, so it helps them sharpen their goals and provides a target for them to move toward. Running such a simulation by itself seems to be therapeutic (De Shazer, 1985) in a fairly large number of cases.

In a similar manner, Zilbergeld and Lazarus (1987) presented a series of guided imagery exercises for positive performances. Systematic desensitization could be thought of as a kind of mental simulation of a positive performance. Role-playing exercises in various forms of psychotherapy could also be thought of as kinds of mental simulation, although they include behavioral and enactive components. Finally, behavioral practice exercises, such as role-playing assertion with one's therapist, is a form of simulation.

However, not all mental simulations will be positive. Zilbergeld and Lazarus (1987) pointed out that sometimes clients mentally simulate things going wrong, and thus repeatedly "indoctrinate" themselves with negative images. Similarly, ruminative worrying could be thought of as a kind of repetitive dysfunctional mental simulation. Thus, although mental simulations can be helpful, they are not always so. A goal of therapy is to support and promote the client's running a positive mental simulation. Therapists can facilitate this by encouraging clients to imagine not only what a positive outcome will look like, but also the processes by which the outcome will be achieved (Taylor et al., 1998; Zilbergeld & Lazarus, 1987).

Dialectical thinking. We have previously mentioned the idea of dialectical thinking. Jenkins (1996) discussed how therapy can promote this kind of thinking. Jenkins's work is based on the work of Rychlak (1994), who said "dialectics recognizes that in deriving the meaning of a situation people are inherently able to appreciate the alternative. . .ways of construing what seems to be firmly structured social or physical circumstance" (p. 3). In other words, thinking dialectically allows individuals to generate alternative possibilities. Jenkins believed that individuals can be creative and flexible in their everyday lives if they keep their ability for dialectical thinking available. He sees psychotherapy as helping to reinstate the dialectic process in areas where the person is stuck.

Dialectical thinking consists of posing one alternative, and then moving back to consider an opposing alternative. Thus, if the client is thinking that something "must" be one way, it is standing back to at least consider the alternative possibility that it need not be that way. This leads to the generation of productive syntheses that move the client beyond either–or thinking.

Dialectical thinking is to be contrasted to syllogistic thinking, in which certain premises are held to be true and then implications are derived from them. This kind of thinking is perfectly appropriate once one has decided on premises. But when one has psychological problems, one must move back to a preaffirmative position, suspend premises, and reopen up new possibilities. Dialectical thinking therefore is an important part of creativity.

A dialogical atmosphere would seem to be an ideal format to promote dialectical thinking. Genuine dialogue involves a back-and-forth exchange between two intelligences. It involves each person being willing to listen to the other and to have one's ideas affected by the other. In contrast, unproductive or unhelpful thinking is nondialogical, or nondialectical. In therapy, this is characterized by clients who simply express, without thinking along with it, or simply describe and report. It is characterized by therapists who may listen respectfully to clients but who fundamentally adopt the expert stance of authoritatively imparting truths to clients. This may encourage the kind of passive reporting by clients that is antithetical to dialectical thinking.

Thinking creatively. Creativity is an important part of problem solving, particularly in psychotherapy. Ward et al. (1995) noted that creativity is particularly needed when problems are ambiguous. Many of the problems of life are ambiguous, and that is why they are not immediately and easily solved. Thus, creativity ought to be crucial in just the kinds of problems that are brought to therapy.

Ward et al. (1995) noted several ways of thinking creatively. One way is to combine two ideas to produce a new idea. Another way is to extend old ideas to deal with new situations. A third way is to use metaphorical extension to understand new situations. Therapists may facilitate clients struggling with contradictions (as in the dialectical thinking process previously described) until they come up with a synthesis that produces a new idea. They may also help clients extend ideas to deal with new situations. This may include learning how to apply ideas taught by the therapist, such as helping clients learn how to creatively apply ideas from cognitive therapy to everyday life situations. Therapists may also facilitate clients' development of new ways of being and behaving through the use of analogies and metaphors (Kopp, 1995).

Things that get in the way of creativity are stress, getting hung up on old solutions, and getting hung up on the initial way one conceptualizes a problem. Seifert, Meyer, Davidson, Patalano, and Yaniv (1995) argued that when the person's information-processing system gets too overwhelmed with too many problems, his or her ability to creatively solve problems deteriorates. They suggested that one may not be able to attain useful and creative insights into problems if one is too overburdened with pressing problems. Thus, therapists' facilitating stress reduction can support clients' creativity.

Therapists can encourage a creative atmosphere by helping clients suspend their initial way of viewing the problems so that they can stand back and generate new possible solutions. This can be done by promoting an open, nonjudgmental atmosphere that encourages novelty and exploration (Sternberg & Davidson, 1995). Lubart (1994) suggested that the needed environment for creativity is sufficient time to think, freedom over one's work, and sufficient resources to develop ideas. He also suggested that encouragement of intuition can facilitate creativity. These are all qualities that a good therapeutic atmosphere should foster.

Creativity also needs some structure on which to operate (Finke, 1995). When individuals are asked to be completely creative without any structure, paradoxically they are less creative than if they have to work within certain constraints. Structures that facilitate creativity are ambiguous, yet have some underlying sense of meaningfulness, are novel, and allow for different uses (Finke, 1995). Good therapy situations have these properties. Procedures like free association, empathic responding, and using experiential exercises such as the gestalt two-chair technique all have these properties. A procedure like challenging dysfunctional cognitions can have these properties if done in the socratic, open-ended way that Beck uses (Beck et al., 1979). A procedure like assertion training can have these properties if done in a way that encourages client novelty instead of mechanistic repetition of canned "lines." In sum, it could be said that good therapy situations provide the structure to encourage creativity.

How Thinking and Experiencing Go Together

How do clients think things through? J. C. Watson and Rennie (1994) conducted a study in which a procedure designed to help clients resolve problematic reactions was used (Rice & Saperia, 1984). A problematic reaction is when a person has a puzzling reaction to something, such as feeling a sense of relief when an old friend decides not to come to town to visit, or when one reacts with unexpected anger to something. The procedure consists of helping the client relive the incident in a focused way, all the while exploring it. Watson and Rennie had clients listen to tapes of their sessions and had them report on what was going through their heads at various points. Then a qualitative analysis of the clients' reports was done. Basically, Watson and Rennie found that clients engaged in the following.

Clients first searched their experience, trying to find words to symbolize it. When they were able to represent their experience in words, they were able to identify the impact their experience was having on them. For them, representing their experience was done in a narrativelike fashion. As clients tried to recollect their experience, most retrieved associated feelings.

As clients searched their experience, they began to see things they had not noticed before. Things became clearer. Furthermore, as J. C. Watson and Rennie (1994) noted,

> Occasionally clients discovered what they wanted to say as they were speaking. In the act of sharing their experience and confessing their difficulties and disturbing material to another person, their problems became more concrete and real, so that their problems had to be confronted and given attention. As one client said, "It's more concrete. If I just kept it in my mind, I could push it back and forget it; now it will have to be dealt with." (p. 503)

Sometimes the attempt to represent their experience in words required repeated efforts, before clients were able to distill its essence.

Once experience was represented in words, clients began to engage in *reflexive self-examination*. Now that the experience was represented, clients were able to explore it and critically evaluate it in a way that they had not been able to do before verbal articulation. New realizations prompted further questions and further exploration. Clients then stepped back to compare their formulations to their experience in a kind of validity check. J. C. Watson and Rennie (1994) noted, "as the clients examined, questioned, and evaluated themselves and their behavior, they sought to understand its origins and whether it facilitated or was congruent with their current needs, values, and goals" (p. 503). This led them to be able to decide whether they wanted to act differently in the future.

Watson and Rennie's (1994) work provides a model of active client self-generative thinking. Although it was done in a client-centered/experiential framework, we believe that the process is representative of the active generative thinking process that can occur in any therapy situation, as well as how clients can spontaneously generate change themselves outside of therapy.

Behaving

Behaving consists of behavioral experimentation and practice. In therapy, clients try out new behaviors to learn through experience. Behavioral experimentation consists of (a) trying out new behaviors in the world and (b) practicing and learning new skills for self-management and for coping in the environment. Behavioral experimentation in the real world can bring in corrective data or open up new possibilities, which has a much more potent, experiential effect on the client than does simple cognitive insight or explanation. As Bandura (1986) noted, what he called *verbal persuasion* is not as potent a way to increase feelings of self-efficacy as is having actual behavioral experiences of efficacy. One may decide through conceptual exploration that one has the right to be assertive. But it may take practice in actually acting assertive to get the experience that leads one to get a "feel for" what effective assertion is and how to do it. Furthermore, as practicing assertion occurs, new possibilities open up. The individual gets a clearer sense of how he or she can flexibly respond to situations. In addition, the individual may realize that, in a broader sense, he or she has a right to his or her own feelings, desires, and motives. Response prevention, exposure, and other kinds of skills training are not only ways of developing certain ways of responding, but also ways of exploring one's ability to master and have some control over one's life (Bandura, 1997).

Behavioral practice leads to the development of fine-tuned behavioral skills. However, practice of new behaviors is really a form of behavioral experimentation. Complex operating knowledge is not learned in a rote fashion. Skills training is not the mechanistic implantation of habits. Bandura (1997) talked about the need to develop *generative* skills, that is, skills that can be flexibly and creatively applied. In virtually all cases, repetition and practice involve trying out some schema or sequence in the world, and practicing it so that one can come to really understand it and enact it from that understanding. Practice provides experiences leading to new recognitions and increasingly deepened knowledge of a skill domain. Clients who apply assertion skills in a rote, mechanistic fashion will not fare well. Learning that is rote and algorithmic does not generalize well to new situations (Nickerson, 1994). Therapists can facilitate the learning of skills in a generative fashion by asking clients to improvise and vary the skills as they do them and to encourage their use in novel situations.

Now that we have considered the three processes of thinking, experiencing, and behaving, we take a look at how these processes produce various positive products in therapy.

THE PRODUCTS OF THE PROBLEM-SOLVING PROCESS

The thinking–experiencing–behaving process can lead to the following products: development of new behaviors, insights and perspective shifts (shortened to *perspective shifts*), and bodily felt shifts.

Development of New Behaviors

The process of exploring can lead to the development of new behaviors. For instance, Hugh developed his skill at talking about personal matters with Dora. This was one of the biggest learnings from therapy for him.

As part of this, he practiced being productively assertive in an interpersonal situation.

There are a wide variety of new behaviors that clients can develop as a function of therapy. Because these are well cataloged by behavior therapists (e.g., Linehan, 1993), we do not consider them extensively here. However, they include communication skills, self-regulation skills, emotional management skills, and stress management skills.

Perspective Shifts

Perspective shifts include insights and changes in awareness. In psychotherapy, insights are typically thought of as acquiring a new way of understanding something ("Oh, I see! I've been thinking dysfunctionally!"). Perspective shifts can be primarily cognitive or primarily perceptual, such as in suddenly seeing the old woman in the gestalt figure as a young woman. Changes in awareness are more nonverbal. Corsini's client (at the start of this chapter) did not report gaining any insight, but did report "feeling differently" and that "everything in the world seemed different" after hearing that he had a high IQ. This is more of a change in awareness than it is a specific insight.

A concrete example of a perspective shift happened with Steve. Steve came into therapy complaining of erection problems. Steve was a 35-year-old man who had recently gotten involved with a 25-year-old woman, Toni. Steve reported that he had been quite a womanizer until his early 30s, when, after a bad experience with a woman, he had remained celibate for about 3 years. During that time he had not dated. Recently, he became interested in Toni. He was having trouble gaining erections with her. After a consultation interview, Steve and Toni scheduled a second appointment. The therapist recommended sensate focus and gave them a self-help book. At the next meeting a week later, they reported that the problem had resolved itself. They thought it was not necessary to come in again.

However, about a month later, Steve called again. The problem had recurred. The therapist had him come in alone. The therapist wondered if it had to do with the problem that had turned him off women for the 3 previous years. They talked about his previous relationships for a while, and then they talked about his relationship with Toni. Steve talked about how much he wanted the relationship, even though there were several problems. One was that Toni had a tendency to say sarcastic, critical things, which he did not like. The other was when they went to visit his family, she tended to hang back. His family was big, warm, and outgoing. At one point, quite innocently, trying to elicit the reasons the relationship was important to him, the therapist asked "Why do you want the relationship?" Steve answered somewhat vaguely, saying he really liked her. After discussing the problems some more, they terminated for the night, and scheduled another appointment for the following week.

At the next session, Steve reported that things had completely changed. He said that it had been the question that the therapist had asked: "Why do you want the relationship?" He had gone home thinking about that: Why did he want the relationship? Why was he so desperate to make the relationship work? He remembered that he had never been like that with women before. In previous relationships, he had always felt in charge of himself. If he felt a woman was mistreating him, that would be it for the relationship. What had happened in this relationship? Why was he so desperate to make this one work? As he thought about this, he said, he realized that he had lost himself. He had never been like this before, so dependent on a woman's approval and presence to feel good. He began to wonder, did he want the relationship? As he thought about that, he began to feel his own power. He began to feel himself come back. He began to feel, "If this relationship isn't right for me, I'll leave. I'll give it a chance. I'll talk to her about the criticism, but I don't need this relationship." As he began to feel some of his old power, his sexuality returned. He now was having no problems attaining erections.

This was basically the turnaround session. A subsequent session, during which Steve and Toni came to try to work out their differences, confirmed that the sexual problem had resolved itself. About 8 months later, Steve contacted the therapist to update him and to finally settle his bill. He reported that sexually everything had been fine ever since that one session.

True perspective shifts, even ones that are primarily cognitive, are not merely intellectual exercises. To be effective, they must ultimately be "felt" or "experienced," and even cognitive therapists like Beck (1987) talk about gaining understanding at an experiential level. True perspective shifts or insights have a perceptual component to them, a genuine "aha" experience (Bohart & Associates, 1996; R. Elliott, 1984; Sternberg & Davidson, 1995). Next we take a closer look at how true insights and perspective shifts work.

A Closer Look at Insight

To discuss the importance of insight in therapy, we must distinguish between what we call *true insight* from intellectually manufactured insight. In some circles, insight has a bad name. Behaviorists have long contended that insight is not the primary determinant of behavior change, rather behavioral practice, exposure, and so on, are. The anti-insight sentiment can also be seen in experiential therapies such as Gestalt therapy, in which Fritz Perls called intellect (and intellectual understanding) the "whore" of intelligence. Finally, many strategic family therapists (e.g., Watzlawick, 1987) are skeptical about the usefulness of insight.

What all these writers are objecting to, however, is *sheer intellectual insight* (Bohart, 1993; Todd & Bohart, 1994). Going back to Freud, there has been a recognition that sheer intellectual insight is not useful in creating change. There is an important difference between intellectually derived insights, no matter how plausible, and directly experienced and recognized insights. Only the latter have a true "aha" quality to them, and it is only the latter that are truly powerful in facilitating change. They are compelling because one *sees and experiences* the connection, or the new perspective, one does not merely imagine it or think it.

Karen is reminded of the days when she was studying for her master's degree in statistics and measurement. In an intermediate statistics class, she suddenly saw how all the parametric statistics were related. She got a feel for how each statistic colors the data, and how it is all tied together by the idea of variability. In a similar manner, Art remembers his undergraduate days when he was studying physics and mathematics (at that time planning to become an engineer). In a physics class, he was struggling to solve a physics problem, and the instructor told him that he needed to learn to "think like" a physicist. After repeated struggles, he suddenly "saw" what the instructor was talking about, and then was able to think like a physicist from then on. When he was initially learning to do proofs in advanced mathematics, he rotely applied the proof method, but at one point suddenly saw the logic underlying it, and from then on was able to more creatively do proofs.

Our view of insight is backed up by experts in the field. For instance, Perkins (1995) suggested that insight has a suddenness to it that has little to do with cognition. It is achieved rapidly and is a kind of falling into place. Schooler et al. (1995) suggested that insight involves pattern recognition, and that the nature of insight is perceptual. Recognizing out-of-focus pictures is the best empirical predictor of insight in their studies.

A client, Le Ann, had repeatedly "understood" at an intellectual level that her self-esteem problems were associated with her father's critical tendencies. However, one day, in recounting an experience with her father, it was as if she suddenly saw the relationship between her father's criticism and her self-esteem problem. It was no longer merely an intellectual formula. She said, in an "aha" kind of way, "Oh! It's my father!" and burst into tears. This was a turning point in therapy.

Nevertheless, true insights do not magically transform people without work. Sometimes even a true insight needs to be reexperienced several times before it takes. Furthermore, even if it is a real "aha" experience, if one does not seize the moment and begin to make changes, it will lose its power. As authors, we have had the experience of having an insight into psychotherapy that we wished to write about. But because we were too busy, we simply wrote a note down about it. Later when we returned to it, it was "cold" and we did not easily recapture the feel of the insight in such a way that we could easily write about it. Thus, insights may need to be implemented soon while one still has the direct recognitional quality, or one loses the sense of them, and one has to start over. Corsini's client immediately started making changes after his perspective shift, which is probably one reason it had long-lasting effects.

True insights are not easily or routinely produced in therapy. Clients may have to work and work to understand, and insights then "come when they come." This is not surprising. This is also true in intellectual pursuits, such as in physics or mathematics. In therapy, conditions that appear to make true insights more likely, however, have to do with vividly exploring experience. That is, when one is really in an experience and not just intellectually talking about it, one is more likely to have the kind of "aha" recognitions that constitute true insights. This can happen in structured experiential exploration such as through the gestalt two-chair procedure (Greenberg et al., 1994), or it can happen through getting deeply and experientially involved in reflecting on one's childhood or current circumstances. It can also happen as a result of behavioral exercises.

Bodily Felt Shifts

Change also has to occur at the body level. If simple intellectual understanding were enough, clients could tell themselves what to do and do it. People with obsessive–compulsive symptoms, for instance, could simply say "I know these rituals and fears are irrational. Therefore I will stop them" and have it work. Yet people come to therapy because this usually does not work.

In addition to insight, there must be a bodily shift in understanding or in reacting. The obsessive–compulsive person must not only intellectually understand that his or her symptoms are irrational, but must also come to understand through direct experience at a bodily level that it is not dangerous if he or she touches, for example, door knobs, and so on. The cognitive–behavioral treatment for posttraumatic stress disorder (e.g., Foa & Rothbaum, 1997) relies heavily on an extinction–emotional reprocessing model in which clients repeatedly tell their traumatic stories over and over, not primarily to gain intellectual insight, but to directly change their emotional experience. Eye movement desensitization (F. Shapiro, 1995) is another treatment whose goal is to create a distinct bodily felt experiential shift. There are probably many paths to the final common outcome of a bodily felt shift: extinction; behavioral practice and rehearsal; engaging in experiential search activities through homework assignments, through repeatedly comparing one's actual experiences with one's dysfunctional cognitions, through repeatedly reviewing the connections between one's childhood experiences and one's present experience, through articulating one's experience in words, through accessing emotion, through extinction procedures, or through eye movement desensitization.

CONCLUSION

Clients make change through the normal processes by which people make changes in everyday life—through thinking, experiencing, and behaving.

- Productive thinking can articulate experience in words, lead to perspective shifts, generate new solution ideas from the running of mental simulations, create order in experience through narrative restorying, and produce creative solutions through dialectical thinking.
- Behavioral experimentation and practice can lead to the development of effective and more finely tuned skills and can lead to bodily felt shifts in experiencing. It can also produce feedback leading to new understanding.
- Experiencing is often the source of both implicitly felt understandings of problem situations and creativity. Accessing emotional experience is important in facilitating bodily felt shifts and emotional reprocessing. Learning that includes experience is the most powerful way to achieve genuine understanding.

Ultimately the learning that occurs in therapy is a product of the active, creative efforts of clients, facilitated by the therapist.

9

FACILITATING THE MEETING OF MINDS: A "MANUAL" FOR PRACTICE

Duncan et al. (1997) described a case in which a woman was referred who had multiple personalities. The client's previous therapist had told her that she needed to work toward integration. However, this was not the client's personal goal. In fact, she had reentered therapy because she had lost the ability to contact her alter personalities. For her, success was not elimination of her multiple personalities but being able to access the other personalities. Instead of setting a goal for this client, the therapist stayed with her goal. Together they explored all the advantages of having multiple personalities, and the client began to gain access once again to her alter personalities. They then proceeded to focus on specific problems the client had, and different alter personalities would emerge to help with particular problems. Finally, the client announced at one session that she was integrated.

In this chapter, we present our personal view of therapy. One could think of this chapter as a "manual," but it is a manual for a mind-set, not for specific behaviors. Our view is an attitudinal framework that allows us to incorporate a wide range of ideas and procedures from different approaches. It is not a step-by-step cookbook for doing therapy. It makes no sense to ask, "What would a therapist operating from your perspective do to help a panic-disordered person overcome their panic?" We might do the same things another therapist would do to help. Instead of looking at therapist competence as a set of precise techniques, we look at how the therapist thinks about clients, specifically what fundamental beliefs about human nature and therapeutic change are being held. We want therapy to be a mutual, equal, active collaboration between two intelligences in which two streams of expertise enrich one another and blend. We think of the client as a co-therapist. For us, this optimizes use of both the therapist's and the client's resources.

There is no specific research to back up the frame of reference that we are going to suggest. However, as we have reviewed in chapter 2, there is a good deal of research compatible with the premises under which we operate.

For us, therapy is the meeting of minds. Two active minds in relation to one another have the potential to form an intelligent partnership, such as might be found in coauthors working on a book together, a good parental dyad working together, or a creative relationship between two research colleagues. This meeting of minds creates an interactive, intelligent, back-and-forth process in which both persons' resources can blend synergistically. Problem solutions can be generated, and creative ideas can emerge. Such a relationship provides the optimal opportunity for resources of both parties to be used.

Through this mind-set, we approach therapy as a relationship with the potential for fully equal, collegial collaboration. In our therapist–client dialogue, each party's ideas and perspectives are valued as potentially useful contributions. Each party listens to and is influenced by the other. The client is an expert on his or her life and is struggling to "right the ship" and to keep it afloat as best as he or she knows how. The client is intuitively aware of the constraints creating the problems and may have an implicit idea of the points of "give" where solutions might be achieved. As therapists, we are experts on "being with" another person in a facilitative, problem-solving way, are good at listening and understanding, and have expertise on various procedures that may be of use in our mutual endeavor. Recommendations are made through consultation with clients. After appropriate dialogue, clients can decide that a particular recommendation may not be wise for them. We value clients' input in terms of creative ideas, hunches, objections, and thoughtful alternatives. Objections are not automatically treated as resistance. We will change our minds and alter our plans in thoughtful response to the client and will be open to getting good ideas for how to proceed from them. On the other hand, if we feel strongly about something (such as the value of a procedure or an assessment of the problem), we will disclose that, while allowing the client room to disagree. In many cases, the final strategy chosen will emerge from a blend of the two expertises. Solutions jointly developed should have a higher level of success.

The time spent in "meeting" is not inefficient. Improvements in communication speed up therapy and eliminate dead-end time and time lost to resistance because we know who we are working with and what the clients value and think.

THE COLLABORATIVE MIND-SET AND PSYCHOTHERAPY

Psychotherapy is a situation in which two people meet for the purpose of helping one person remove obstacles to living a more personally satisfying and socially productive life. The core process of psychotherapy is that of *intelligent conversation*. Together therapist and client fix problems, not the client. Within that, the goal can be as specific as symptom removal, or can be far more general, including self-actualization, working through childhood issues, or dealing with general philosophical or value considerations. The goals chosen depend partly on the setting in which this relationship takes place. In some settings, such as health maintenance organizations, the goal is more likely to be symptom removal. In private practice, the choice of goal may be more general, and there may be multiple goals. In some cases the client's goal may be nothing more than to use the relationship to examine life in general. Choice of goals depends on what the client wants. Goals will evolve and develop during the intelligent conversation.

The client is really a co-therapist because both the therapist and the client are working on the client's life. This means we want the way we relate to the client to empower the client. This is misspoken: *We are not empowering them*—we are simply respecting, recognizing, and responding to the client's power. We recognize that the locus of power to cause therapeutic change resides in the client, and we need the client's active collaboration and input. We do not just want compliance with a treatment regimen.

It is important to have intelligent conversations with clients because therapists are working with whole persons, not just with isolated symptoms. Even if the goal is symptom removal, symptoms are interconnected with other aspects of the client's life. At times symptom removal may be sufficient. Symptom removal may free up clients and lead to positive changes in other areas. At other times symptom focus may obscure important relationships with other aspects of the person's life, as predicted by psychodynamic and systems theories. In those cases, simple symptom removal may be counterproductive. Therapists need to be in dialogue with clients because only clients know, at some level, how things are interconnected in their personal ecologies.

As an example, a middle-aged couple came for counseling because of marital problems. Exploration revealed that they both loved one another, but the husband felt his wife was too critical; the wife felt her husband was not understanding. Their arguments had been growing over the last year, for no apparent reason. They were older now and did not have the children at home, but that had been the case for a number of years. Defining the problem as the arguments might have led the therapist to use a simple symptom approach, focusing on teaching the couple communication skills. The husband could learn how to empathically listen and reflect; the wife could learn how to express her desires in "I" statements instead of attacks. This was actually suggested to the couple, and some role-play demonstrations were done. The husband unexpectedly said he did not think it would solve the problem. The wife agreed. This sparked an exploratory conversation, which eventually revealed that their distress had begun when they had moved about a year and a half before. They had given up their old house because they no longer needed the space with the children gone. They had moved into a condominium, but had left behind a neighborhood full of friends and familiar places. They had also had to leave behind their pets, which were not welcome in the condominium unit. Both were feeling disgruntled and out of place, although it had taken about a half year after moving for the arguments to start. This information led therapist and clients together to shift focus. Counseling helped them, not by focusing on communication skills, but by facilitating their adjusting to their new situation.

Adopting a collaborative mind-set means going into therapy with the expectation that the client wants to find ways of proactively enhancing life, and will want to cooperate if he or she senses that the therapist is on his or her side. There is some old social psychological research that shows that in situations of potential cooperation or competition, those who initially approach the other person with a cooperative attitude cope better than those who go in with a competitive attitude. Those who go in with a competitive attitude inevitably end up in competition with the other person, even when cooperation to their mutual benefit was possible. Those who go in with a cooperative attitude are able to establish a cooperative relationship with potentially cooperative partners, but can switch to competition if need be with competitive individuals. We believe it is important for therapists to enter therapy with the premise that clients will be cooperative, and that the job of the therapist is to find ways of working with them cooperatively.

Therapy literature is replete with metaphors of conflict and resistance. Therapy is sometimes portrayed as a battle wherein the therapist must overcome client defenses. Going in with the idea that clients will be resistant and defensive can create a self-fulfilling prophecy. Research done with alcoholic clients shows that therapists who go in with the idea that they must confront denial, for instance, create resistance in clients and produce poorer outcomes (W. R. Miller & Rollnick, 1991).

We have previously referred to Monty Roberts's (1997) work on "starting" rather than "breaking" horses. Believing that horses will resist domestication leads to the idea that one must use force to overcome their resistance. Operating from this attitude, it often takes several weeks to break the horses and win their cooperation. However, if the horse trainer bothers to learn how to listen and communicate with the animal and respects the animal's initial desires to resist and shy away, the horse trainer can "join up" with the horse and foster a good working relationship quickly, often within 30 min.

As a concrete example of this, some of our clients have been very mistreated by both people in their lives and previous therapists and are fearful of the next therapist repeating the injury. Karen met two new clients in 1 week who warned her that they were very difficult clients and that their previous therapists had rejected them. Could she "handle" them? These clients did prove to be a little more troubled than the average client, but neither deserved to have been summarily "fired" from therapy for being uncooperative and resistant. These clients really appreciated being understood from their own perspective. Each initiated many self-improvements over time once they felt they were in a safe environment.

Most clients who come to therapy voluntarily want to overcome their problems. They have no reason to set out to overcome the therapist. The battle metaphor is a very negative belief to adopt. We believe the metaphor of therapy as a journey together is a better one. Fighting a battle between therapist and client is a terrible waste of client and therapist resources.

Therapist behaviors follow from a respectful, collaborative attitude. However, there are some specific therapist skills involved. First, the therapist must be able to create a safe environment. Open exploration, willingness to try new behaviors, and creativity are more likely to flourish in a safe environment. This is created by earning the client's trust, by the stability of the way the therapist relates to the client, by the therapist's honesty within certain reasonable constraints, by a willingness to listen to the client's feedback, and by a willingness on the part of the therapist to own up to his or her mistakes. The main skill is a sensitivity to clients' process, as well as skills in helping clients explore their goals, find meaning in their life and in their behavior, and develop coherence in their behaviors. The therapist shares information, data, and raw material with the client for experimenting in the real world and in therapy. The therapist also shares practical knowledge, such as of social skills, and of what is considered socially normal.

Implementing the Principles of Client Self-Healing

In chapter 4, we specified some principles of client self-healing. We now explore what they mean in terms of engaging in psychotherapy from our point of view.

Respecting Clients' Agency

To respect clients' agency means first to share responsibility for therapy with the client. Clients "nix" some of our ideas, suggest ideas of their own, and suggest creative modifications on procedures that we have proposed. We do not abdicate our own wisdom. If we do not like the client's modifications, we present our disagreement. Sharing responsibility also means that when clients are "on a roll," doing a lot of the work of self-exploration themselves, we are willing to primarily adopt a companionate, listening role.

Second, respecting clients' agency means looking for the proactive, agentic "thread" in their actions. We consider this next when we consider clients' wisdom.

Believing That Clients Are Wise

Believing that clients are wise means first that, as therapists, we respect them as capable of making intelligent observations on their own condition and on our suggestions or ideas. Despite their lack of "expertise," the clients might be right about some of our ideas. Second, it means looking for the grain of wisdom in whatever the clients say or do. Often therapists get so focused on the dysfunctional aspects of client behavior that they miss the "grain of truth" in what clients are saying or doing. We address the issue of tuning into the wisdom in clients' dysfunctional or defensive behavior later when we consider adopting an empathic attitude. Third, believing that clients are wise means that we actively elicit their wisdom—their ideas and intuitions. This includes helping them explore and clarify and define what they want to change.

Supporting Clients' Generativity

We have already mentioned some ways of supporting clients' generativity, such as through taking their ideas seriously. In addition, we support clients' generativity by not trying to prematurely bring closure in a problematic area. We need to give the clients time to think things out, especially when they are on a roll. Part of dialectical thinking is to stay with seemingly irreconcilable contradictions until some higher order integration emerges. There are times in therapy when we must be willing to patiently stay with a complex problem in an open-ended discovery-oriented fashion. It is as if we and the client are collaboratively brainstorming together as colleagues might work on a complex problem in government or business. Building on suggestions for nurturing creativity made by Ward et al., (1995), we (a) support flights of fancy and play with ideas, (b) encourage clients to generate alternative perspectives to both their old perspective and even our perspective, (c) encourage clients to scan the situation for novel or neglected aspects that neither they nor we have previously noticed, (d) encourage clients to stay with ill-formed ideas and concepts until they become clearer, and (e) encourage their struggle to articulate implicit or vaguely sensed ideas and perspectives not easily put into words. We do not bring premature closure by rushing in authoritatively with "the explanation" for them; that is, we do not stop the process by judging the ideas too quickly. Otherwise, clients will become outcome focused and shut down. They may also become defensive.

In addition, we support clients' generativity in how we propose exercises to them. For instance, when proposing some kind of behavioral experiment, we are not mechanistic about it, as if there were only one "right way" to do it. If, as the clients are practicing assertion skills they deviate from the script in a novel and interesting way, we treat that as an opportunity for discovery. If clients are resisting doing an exercise our way, we encourage them to try their own interpretation of it, *and* later, perhaps, our interpretation. There are multiple routes to success.

Finally, simple empathic recognition of clients' experience and giving them a chance to talk is often all that is needed to support their generativity. For instance, a couple came in because the wife was no longer feeling sexual or affection toward her husband, even though she did not want to leave him. To the therapist, the wife looked depressed and sad, and the therapist said this to her. She said that she indeed felt sad, did not know what was wrong with her, and felt that her life was empty. It was as if this was the first time that she had been recognized as feeling depressed, and that might be why she no longer felt sexual and affectionate. After an exploration of other aspects of the relationship, the first session concluded with a plan that the therapist and the couple together would work on the wife's depression.

The next week the woman already looked significantly better. On her own, she reported that she had decided she needed some friends and had joined a woman's group at her church. The remainder of the session was spent in exploration of one of their major problems. The husband ran an accounting business out of their home. The wife helped out with this by doing filing and other clerical activities. The wife had originally herself been trained as an accountant but had decided she did not like it. Instead she helped him out and spent the rest of the time raising their three children, all of whom were in school. In the therapy session, however, she disclosed that she did not like doing the filing. This was a surprise to her husband. They then engaged in a dialogue–debate over what this meant. He was willing to let her give up the filing and clerical activities, but that meant he would have to hire someone to do those things, and that would be a financial drain on the family's resources. He felt that if she did not help out with the filing, she should go get a part-time job to replace the lost income. She said she was willing to consider this. The therapist thought this might be a good solution because her complaint was that her life felt empty and she seemed to be feeling that she needed to be doing something she found more personally meaningful than filing. The solution at the end of this session appeared to be that she would look for a part-time job and he would hire a clerk. Other aspects of this solution, such as his disappointment that they would not be working together, were explored.

At the next session, they reported that they had come up with a new idea. She had gone looking for waitressing work, which she had once done, and had discovered that she could make, along with tips, $15 an hour. Using this figure, the two of them had negotiated the following. First, he would write a job description of all the tasks he would hire a clerk to do, and then he would pay her $15 an hour to do them. She would continue to work for him. Then he would not have to hire someone, and the money would not flow out of the family. This seemed to please her, and they were going to try it out.

This was an example of an unexpected, creative, emergent solution and of a second-order shift, not only for clients but for the therapist. In the previous session, the couple, as well as the therapist, had been seeing the problem as that the woman did not want to do the work of filing and other clerical tasks because they were not meaningful. However, the creative solution revealed that the problem had more to do with her wanting a *defined role* and a sense of her own identity. What worked for her was being treated differently by her husband in the work relationship, rather than finding work that was supposedly more meaningful.

The therapy process undoubtedly facilitated this shift by allowing the clients to air their feelings and perspectives. However, the shift was a creative one by them, not seen or anticipated as a solution by anyone at the previous session because of how all were defining the problem.

Believing Clients are Capable of Learning

First, this means we believe that while clients may be stuck in old habits and scripts, or defensively stuck, they are capable of approaching new learning. Even if they are stuck, they are still actively learning, only around the stuck point. Believing this, we look for "doors" into the clients' learning potential, rather than focusing exclusively on how they are blocking new learning. This means that sometimes it may work better to "do it the client's way."

Another thing we might do is to reframe problems in such a way that obstacles to learning are circumvented. As a simple example, focusing on "promoting a healthy lifestyle" sometimes works better than focusing on "overcoming resistance to dieting." Finding the positive in a client's deeply engrained trait of shyness and reframing it as "interpersonal sensitivity" may allow the client to develop a receptive, empathic, outgoing style instead of the client trying to overcome his or her shyness by trying to develop a more aggressive, assertive, outgoing style that does not fit with the client's personality.

This may also mean to look for small signs of learning and change, and to amplify those, along the lines of solution-focused therapy (De Shazer, 1985). It can also mean to focus on the positive: Find positive examples in the client's own life of when he or she has coped effectively and use those as models for new learning.

Finally, believing that clients can learn means that we are willing to "see it out" even if the process of change is long, frustrating, and difficult. Some new learnings may be complex. A trial-and-error process may be needed, as often is the case in areas in which complex new solutions are required. We are willing to proceed in a process-oriented fashion (see chapter 7), staying with ambiguity, frustration, and failure, until we and the client together finally begin to see light at the end of the tunnel. In so doing, our work together provides a model of how to collaboratively solve problems within a relationship as well. Learning how to "hang in there" when the going gets tough with another person may generalize to the client's relationships with partners, colleagues, and children.

Supporting Clients' Capability for Thinking

Supporting clients' capability for thinking means being receptive to clients' ideas. It also means being supportive when clients are thinking. This includes silently listening when they are thinking out loud. It also means that when we ask the client a question, we listen carefully to see if the client is willing to elaborate on his or her answer. If the therapist is in a "data collection" or a diagnostic mode, he or she may become impatient if the client takes a roundabout path to answering the question or if, in answering the question, the client thinks of something emotionally important but off the path of the question. The therapist may subtly signal to the client to simply answer the question, be quiet, and then wait for the next question. However, this can discourage one of the most important healing processes in therapy: the client's own unfolding process of active elaboration and thinking. Such a thinking process may not always proceed in a perfectly linear fashion, but may proceed through sidetracks and digressions. The therapist must be willing to follow this thinking process, as long as it seems to be going somewhere, rather than impose his or her agenda on the client, if the therapist wishes to promote this kind of client generativity.

Supporting clients' capability for thinking also means paying attention to the clients' fledgling efforts at autonomously thinking with us rather than simply following our lead. We intently listen to help catch the clients' meaning, even if they are having trouble articulating. We follow up on the clients' train of thought to see where it goes, drawing out implications and following them, even if at first they do not seem promising, before sharing our observations.

Part of facilitating thinking is to *respond*. This means to respond in a way that addresses the implications and meaning of what the client is talking about in a way that helps draw out and clarify these implications and meanings. In a dialogue between two colleagues, this might mean that Person B responds to Person A's communication with his or her own complementary thoughts, questions if he or she is unclear about something, the insights that were stimulated in him or her by Person A's communication, empathic reflections to convey his or her understanding of what Person A is saying, and self-disclosures of similar feelings or experiences. Therapists can respond in a similar fashion. Like two good jazz musicians building on each other's solos (Bohart & Rosenbaum, 1995), we pick up on clients' themes, add to them, and amplify them in productive ways. The therapist can promote thinking in conjunction with other activities in therapy by asking what clients thought about during the week and by asking them what they thought about exercises they engaged in. If clients appear not to be thinking as they talk to us, we might ask them about areas in their life where they do think—their opinions on political things, sports, and so on. We believe that it is better to be actively engaged together, thinking and talking together, even if the topic is not formally a therapy topic. This often gets the process started, and it usually gradually evolves into therapy-type issues anyway (because virtually anything ultimately has connections to important personal meanings).

Supporting Clients' Capability for Exploration

To support clients' exploration, the therapist must first realize that clients usually are exploring. Because living is exploring (see chapter 3), clients will have been exploring during the week. As clients leave sessions, they think about what they have experienced. They also think about it during their daily activities, particularly the ones that are problematic for them. They are not standing still, no matter how stuck they seem. This means that we are open to the possibility that clients will enter the session with new ideas. They may also come in with feedback on how something has not been working. As a technique, it can even be helpful to ask clients how much, if any, their problems have improved during the week, and how that came about (De Shazer, 1985). Or it may be useful to ask what the clients have done to try to solve their problems during the week.

Second, we are aware that clients are continually exploring in therapy as well, even as they seem to be only sitting and passively listening. They are thinking: turning ideas over in their head, deciding whether to self-disclose, deciding how to get us to go in the direction they think would be most helpful, and so on (Rennie, 1997). Being open and receptive to client feedback will create an atmosphere in which the client will be more likely to share this material with us, and some of it may be important and relevant to what we are doing.

Third, supporting clients' exploration means that we do not bring premature closure to things by assuming the authoritative role and "telling clients the truth." This may seem obvious, but many therapists think it is their job to give clients "corrective feedback," and they do it as if their perspective is the true one. In contrast, we believe therapists should share things more tentatively than that, as "grist for the client's mill." Client discoveries seem to have little meaning unless they make them by themselves (see chapter 8), even if guided by the therapist. In school, the student must discover and understand the logic of a solution for it to be of use. Good therapists know this, and do not merely tell clients things but stimulate them to explore for themselves in order to find the answers.

Telling clients "the truth" not only shuts off their exploration, but may also cause clients to shut up altogether. One of our clients, Mel, had previously gone with his wife to a couples therapist. The couples therapist had them do a dialogue exercise during which they discussed a problem while the therapist observed. On the basis of this one exercise, the therapist told Mel that he had a need to conform. This jumping to a conclusion caused Mel to lose faith in the therapist, because Mel was a highly successful businessman who did not view himself as having a need to conform to anybody. By *telling* Mel something rather than by offering it as a tentative hypothesis for exploration, the therapist lost Mel and facilitated the opposite of what he probably wanted—Mel's exploration of his own stance vis-à-vis his wife. (After getting to know Mel and his wife, we disagreed with the therapist.)

On the other hand, there are some clients who want the therapist to tell them what to do. Many people love radio talk show therapists precisely because they operate in this manner. This is fine if (a) clients are willing to wholeheartedly buy into the therapist's agenda and to enthusiastically follow the therapist, (b) the solution offered by the therapist happens to fit the client's problem well enough, and (c) the client is able to implement the solution. If one is working collaboratively, there may be times when the client demands, "Tell me what you think, or what you think I should do." In such cases, we are willing to tell the clients what we think or what we think they should do, but this is grounded in a relationship in which the clients know that if what we say doesn't make sense to them, they do not have to follow it.

Believing That Clients Prefer Positive, Proactive Solutions Rather Than Defensive Solutions and Are Motivated to Restore Their Functioning to as High a Level as They Can

Working from a collaborative mind-set, we do not find it helpful to see our clients as "wanting" to be sick, either to avoid inner truths that they are unwilling to face or to keep themselves dependent on caretakers and not have to take responsibility for themselves. When clients apparently act like this, it is because they see no alternative to making this kind of ecological adjustment. We believe that they would prefer to have more behavioral freedom to make more full accommodations to the world. If they are acting as if they want to be sick, or as if they are unwilling to face up to a truth, or as if they are "trying" to keep themselves dependent, it is because they see no other way to maintain some minimum acceptable level of functioning. We need to help them gain a sense of possibility. As active intelligent thinkers, seeing no way out is the first step dialectically to finding its opposite—some new way of looking at the problem that provides a way out. Thus, we empathize with the client's sense of stuckness and understand all the constraints that make change difficult, and listen for the client's own intrinsic capacity to generate the opposite perspective. Surprisingly, genuinely empathizing with what makes change difficult often seems to free the client up so he or she can consider what is needed to make change happen.

Believing That Clients Do Not Always Necessarily Need Our Guidance

Clients may come up with creative solutions on their own. This means that at times we simply empathically listen, without the need to "help." It also means that at times we "stay with" clients through the moments of confusion and their sense of being lost when no solution appears to either us or the client. It also means (a) to listen carefully to all client-offered solutions, even ones that on the surface sound inadequate or ill-conceived; (b) try to glean something useful from a client-offered solution; and (c) be aware of client-offered solutions that have worked in the past.

Being Aware That Clients Have Widely Differing World Views

The nature of collaboration is to hold respect for differing points of view and differing experiential worlds, as if the therapist is an ambassador visiting another country and consulting with one of its representatives. This means that in the therapeutic dialogue therapists respect the cultures and different experiential backgrounds of their clients and try to understand them. They are aware that radically different world views do not correspond in a one-to-one fashion to race, ethnicity, or national origin. Variation within groups is enormous. This is taken into consideration not only so that the therapist can cleverly tailor interventions to be more effective, but because the therapist might learn something new about him- or herself and the world. In addition, interventions may need to be contextualized within the client's world view and be modified to fit and honor aspects of that world view. Therapy is not like Western medicine, which might profitably be administered in a mostly unaltered form to people in vastly different cultures. The very essence of therapy has to do with personal issues of how people view and treat themselves and others. Thus, culture will be a central and intrinsic part of the construction of therapeutic solutions. This means that, working collaboratively, the therapist might even use folk methods (Comas-Diaz, 1992).

Being aware of widely differing world views also means respecting those clients who, because of their cultural backgrounds, treat you, the therapist, as the expert who is going to tell them what to do. We have previously discussed the possibility that some clients will want this. Since the therapist is in the client's hire, if this is the role clients want the therapist to adopt for their purposes, the therapist should be willing to do so. As an analogy, consider hiring a home-decorator consultant. You might want to actively collaborate with him or her, blending your input with the home decorator's expertise, or you might just want to say, "Tell me what to do." There is nothing wrong from a collaborative point of view in taking the lead if that is what the client wants, any more than it would be with the home decorator. At the same time, this will only work when clients are able to invest themselves wholeheartedly in the therapist's agenda. If they find that they are unable to, therapists must then be able to dialogue with them to find out what went wrong and to help create ideas for moving in a new direction. Furthermore, even in taking the lead, we would never lose sight of the fact that the power to change and the power to say yes or no to our suggestions ultimately lies in the client's hands.

With these principles in mind, we take a look at three basic aspects of how we do therapy.

THERAPISTS' OPERATING PRINCIPLES

Building a Collaborative Relationship

Because therapy is a meeting of minds, the relationship between ourselves and our clients is the most important part of therapy. We relate to our clients as people, and let them relate to us in the same way. This may seem obvious, but we believe that the relationship in therapy is a real one between two human beings, not primarily an intervention.

Some therapists see the relationship as an intervention and that it should be deliberately "provided" in different ways to maximize therapeutic impact depending on what they think different clients need. We do not believe we "provide" a relationship like a physician provides a prescription. Instead, if we are really relating, we are relating, not providing. We do not believe in using empathy to "open up" clients so they can be influenced. In fact, to deliberately be warm or empathic to create a therapeutic effect strikes us as unethical—in effect, it is providing the facade of a relationship and deceiving our clients.

We would not provide empathy to a collaborator on a research project. We would be empathic because we really wanted to understand them and meet with them. In a similar manner, we try to really relate to clients because we really want to dialogue with them. This means we naturally will be different with different clients. This is what happens in everyday life. People are different with their spouses than they are with their children, different with one child than with another child, and different with one friend than with another friend. They adjust to fit what is needed for a particular relationship in a particular situation. Sometimes, your spouse wants a friend who just listens and is very empathic, other times a cool, logical advisor, and at still other times a partner who is seen but not heard. To *be in relationship* means to be in genuine dialogue with another person such that the side of you most relevant to your meeting together in that time and place comes out.

This means that in therapy some relationships will be very business-like, perhaps relatively cool and practical. Others may be more emotional, with more active expressions of empathy. Some will be very formal and agenda driven. Others may be more informal and improvisational. In some, the therapist will act more like a tutor or mentor, in others more like a companion.

In some relationships, the optimum therapeutic distance (Leitner, 1995) between therapist and client may be relatively large; in others it may be smaller. Optimal therapeutic distance has to do with establishing and respecting limits with clients, while still staying close enough to empathize and join with them. This will vary from client to client, and from moment to moment within a relationship with a client, just as it does with everyday relationships. Sometimes, a person needs to respect the privacy of his or her spouse or best friend and not intrude when he or she feels bad; other times the person may want to move closer and be available for the loved one when he or she wants to open up. Along with this, at some times the therapist may feel it is appropriate to self-disclose; at other times self-disclosure may not seem appropriate.

Treating Therapy as an Intelligent, Two-Person Group

In a good therapy relationship, the contributions of both parties should blend in a dialogue from which creative solutions can emerge. The therapy relationship should look like Figure 9.1.

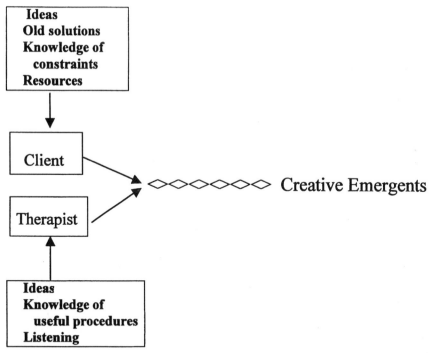

Figure 9.1. Therapy as an empathic meeting of minds.

Therapy can operate as an intelligent two-person group. There is evidence that groups can operate intelligently (Hinsz, Tindale, & Vollrath, 1997). Groups can increase the probability of a functional use of attention; groups notice important and relevant information and store and retrieve more information. Conflict between perspectives can lead to creative solutions. On the other hand, groups can function worse than individuals. One of the major dangers, applying Janis's (1982) work on group think, is when the leader of the group exerts too powerful an influence, leading to conformity and compliance among group members, rather than an atmosphere wherein they can voice their disagreements and alternative positions. Thus, therapists who adopt too much of an expert stance may silence the voice of their "critic" in the group—the client—even if they are not overtly being oppressive. We have already seen research by Rennie (1994a) which shows that clients indeed defer to therapists, keeping their opinions to themselves, and then working around therapist positions they do not agree with.

There is evidence for the idea that therapists and clients are involved in a collaborative, co-creative process (Angus, 1992). Angus found that clients engage in many of the same processes therapists engage in, making, for instance, 20% of the interpretations and 25% of the restatements and summarizations. Also, providing evidence for the co-creative nature of therapy, she found that clients seeing different therapists focused on different topics.

Building a Collaborative Frame of Reference

We work toward developing a collaborative frame of reference with our clients. A collaborative frame of reference is a kind of joint platform of shared understanding from which to operate. As we dialogue with our clients over time, we develop a set of common referents for communication and a common storage bank of shared experiences. These help both ourselves and clients know what the other means in a given moment. Several analogies are apt. One would be two people from different cultures trying to teach each other about their respective culture and language. Another would be two collaborators working on a problem together. A third would be two people getting to know one another. In all these cases, each person works to understand what the other is trying to communicate and to begin to develop a joint perspective from which to view a problem. The client must empathically understand where we are coming from, as much as we must understand where the client is coming from. Otherwise our suggestions, comments, and interventions will be misunderstood. We can facilitate the development of a collaborative frame of reference by (a) empathically listening to and working to understand the client's frame of reference and (b) empathically using and sharing our frame of reference.

Empathically Understanding the Client's Frame of Reference

What therapists mean by empathy is different from what developmental psychologists typically think of as empathy (Bohart & Greenberg, 1997). In developmental psychology, empathy is primarily having an emotional reaction similar to another's. Such empathy is thought to mobilize prosocial behavior in the empathizer and to be comforting to the person being empathized with (Bohart & Greenberg, 1997; Feshbach, 1997). For psychotherapists, empathy is primarily a matter of understanding the client's moment-to-moment experience, perspective, and subjective world (Bohart & Greenberg, 1997). It is not even necessary for the empathizer in therapy to share the emotional reaction of the client (Greenberg & Elliott, 1997). Carl Rogers, for instance, is often misperceived as responding primarily to emotion, probably because his manner of responding was mislabeled *reflection of feeling*. Yet several studies have found that the majority of Rogers's responses were to cognitive, *meaning* aspects of clients' experience. Feelings were the primary focus only about 25% of the time (Brodley, 1996). Thus, empathy in psychotherapy is really a form of understanding or comprehension (Shlien, 1997), based on trying to view things from within the client's frame of reference. Empathy parallels what

Belenky, Clinchy, Goldberger, and Tarule (1986) described as *connected knowing*, in contrast to *separate* (or external, analytic) *knowing*.

To try to understand someone empathically is to try to place oneself within the person's experience and to try to grasp the "sense" in it. In contrast, separate knowing looks at the client from outside, usually in terms of a particular theoretical point of view. A man is "unreasonably" refusing to give up on a relationship although the woman involved has made it abundantly clear that she wants to break it off. From a rational–emotive theoretical perspective, for instance, we could analyze his behavior as reflecting absolutistic "shouldistic" thinking. This is not an empathic way of understanding his behavior, however. It is highly unlikely he experiences himself as thinking absolutistically. Empathically trying to understand him might lead to understanding *his* thinking and reasoning process: From his point of view, he cannot see why the woman wants to leave. Wasn't he good to her? Didn't he provide for her? So what if he didn't talk a lot? Can't she see that he loved her in his own way? If she could only see the logic in his point of view, she wouldn't leave! So he must keep trying, because he just knows he's right! In essence, empathic knowing is an attempt to get in touch with how the client is thinking and feeling about the situation. It includes how the clients are construing it, what they see as reasonable and unreasonable things to do about it, their sense of justice or injustice in regard to it, and their own metacognitive thoughts about their own experience (their thoughts, for instance, that "maybe I am overreacting").

We have more to say later about the contrast between an external vantage point on the client and an internal, empathic one as well as the value of each. For now, we want to clarify what adopting an empathic vantage point means.

Believing in clients' intuitive or "ecological" wisdom. A key part of honoring clients' frame of reference is to value them, prize their ideas and thoughts, and understand their frame of reference. A core principle is that the client is *intelligible*. There is some reasonable component to their behavior patterns from within the clients' understanding of the world. There is some coherence and purpose to their dysfunctional behavior. Listening to the client's point of view means being willing to dig for the "inherent wisdom" in it (Linehan, 1997).

This concept has been discussed by a number of writers. From a client-centered perspective, Gendlin (1968) discussed the idea of a *positive thrust* underlying dysfunctional behavior. From a psychodynamic perspective, Wile (1981) assumed that normal adult needs underlie apparently dysfunctional behavior. From a cognitive–behavioral perspective, Linehan (1997) thoroughly explored this idea in terms of her concept of validation. Linehan argued that in every dysfunctional behavioral act there is a "nugget of gold" or wisdom. In her *levels of validation* model, Level 4 is where the wisdom in a behavior lies in the fact that it was once wise in the past. Level 5, however, is that, no matter how dysfunctional, there is a grain of wisdom in it in the here and now. The client is trying to achieve something proactive through whatever dysfunctional strategy he or she is following, no matter how dysfunctional the behavior. From a solution-focused point of view, Duncan, Solovey, and Rusk (1992) also support this idea.

We call this *ecological wisdom*. A client's behavior is ecologically wise within the constraints of his or her subjective world as he or she perceives it. We need to try to understand the ecology of the problem. Plus we need to take the time to let clients explore the contextual factors that keep them stuck. It is important to understand the meaning of clients' symptoms to them. Unless we understand their existence and impact in terms of the clients' perceptions, we may be "treating" the wrong problem.

Often clients themselves are not aware of or do not take seriously the ecological wisdom of their own behaviors. It is often implicit and tacit. They have been too busy defending themselves or criticizing themselves to access it. When individuals are being self-critical, they do not pause to reflect in a way that leads to accessing the behavior's implicit logic. If they can access their own logic, they often spontaneously reevaluate and then shift their position or beliefs toward their situation. We have previously noted the example of a woman in an abusive relationship who may choose "dysfunctionally" to stay because, from her point of view, to leave would be more chaotic and harmful than it is to stay. If she has children, no money, no job, and is living in a city far away from friends and relatives, leaving would seem to present insurmountable problems. Intuitively she knows this. Yet she engages in self-criticism because she knows she "should" leave. This self-criticism gets in the way of her taking seriously the "wisdom" in staying (i.e., the forces in her ecology that are conspiring against her leaving). The first step in transcending these forces is to acknowledge their existence and to take them seriously. In other words, she has to validate herself for the wisdom in staying before she can transcend that and find a way to leave.

An example of the implicit ecological "logic" underlying a dysfunctional behavior has previously been presented (Bohart, 1995b). A male client was court-ordered to therapy because he had exposed himself to his 13-year-old stepdaughter. He had married his wife only a few years before, and the stepdaughter had never accepted him. After an evening of her disobeying and treating him with disrespect, he exposed himself to her. She reported him to the police. Exploration of what he was feeling at the moment he exposed himself revealed feelings of helplessness and impotence to stand up for himself. In effect, exposing himself was a graphic form of giving her "the finger." Understanding the grain of wisdom in this dysfunctional behavior led to the therapist's successfully helping the client learn how to be more appropriately assertive. Setting a goal to understand had the additional benefit of not mobilizing his resistance.

To explore the inner logic of the client's perspective means to take it seriously. We do not mean here a hidden inner logic in the classic psychoanalytic sense in which the client's conscious frame of reference is a compromise formation hiding the real workings of the client's mind. In that frame of reference, understanding the inner logic consists of understanding how clients are avoiding truths about themselves, and how their overt behavior is an expression of disowned infantile wishes and needs. We agree with Wile (1981) and Wachtel (1993) that if there are disowned needs and emotions, they are normal human needs and emotions.

Nor do we mean that the inner logic consists of a wish to avoid painful truths about the self. Theories that assume that clients are avoiding painful truths do not go far enough. Why are clients avoiding painful truths? We believe it is because from their point of view it is "ecologically wise." It is the best compromise. This means that to face up to certain truths may vastly complicate and disrupt their lives. For a child to acknowledge that he or she hates his or her father when the family structure makes such acknowledgement exceedingly dangerous makes this an unwise thing to do. Better to devote one's energies to believing the father is lovable and finding proactive ways to survive within the structure of that belief system.

In this regard, the clients are the ones who have to live with the consequences of any action they take. A clever solution to a problem (from our perspective) may not be something that clients can actually implement immediately. If the client accepts our advice and implements it without consideration (because the therapist is a trusted expert), the client may be hurt. Understanding the grain of truth in clients' perspectives allows us to tailor our suggestions to coordinate with clients' sense of what will work for them. If a client says "yes, but," it might be because an idea will not work as presented in his or her world. Clients are not stupid; they are just having troubles.

When clients are heavily involved in criticizing themselves, or justifying themselves by criticizing others, it may be difficult for them to access the intuitive or ecological wisdom underlying their behavior. At those points, it is helpful to try to access the wisdom underlying the self-criticism or blame of others. For instance, seeing self-criticism as nothing but dysfunctional thinking misses the possibility that the client is actively trying to do something by thinking this way. In particular, the wisdom underlying this act is often that clients want to be honest with themselves, believing that by so doing they are avoiding something even worse than the pain generated by self-criticism: self-deception. Realizing that they are actually trying to be therapeutic with themselves by self-criticizing can help the therapist understand why it might not always be easy to give up dysfunctional thinking.

Understanding the ecological wisdom in the client's perspective may take considerable exploration. Because clients may not immediately articulate it, it is often easy to interpret their behavior from our frame of reference, either through the lens of our personal experiences or through our theory, despite all the cautions we have heard about countertransference. We have been trained to assume that we have the "objective" perspective on them. This may lead us to think we know what is going on with the clients when in fact we do not really understand the subtleties of their experiential world. A real, subtle, empathic understanding is frequently not easily achieved and takes considerable patience, nonjudgmental open listening, suspension of our theoretical notions as well as of our personal experiential frames of reference for interpreting experience, and sustained inquiry.

Understanding the client's point of view does not mean that we agree with or validate the behavior that flows from it. To the contrary, to use Linehan's (1997) phrasing, we do not want to validate the invalid. Thus, we need to be able to recognize the grain of truth while also offering feedback on the parts of the behavior that are unwise or dangerous. One can certainly understand why a person with bulimia might want to use self-induced vomiting as a weight-control measure. It allows the person to balance steps toward weight control with indulgence. It would not be hard to say, "Of course, you think of vomiting!" At the same time we do not want to validate or support the behavior that flows from the understandable motive.

In the extremes, while understandable, some behaviors are so dangerous that we will be motivated to impose our will on the client. We can understand the wish to escape the terrible pain of breaking up with the person who, at the time, seems to be "the only one I will ever love." We can even understand how, temporarily, that pain may seem so inescapable that one contemplates suicide. At the same time, we may choose to have the other person—friend, relative, or client—hospitalized if we think they may actually engage in suicidal behavior.

Empathic listening: Having a goal to understand. Careful, sustained listening is the single best thing we can do to establish a collaborative frame of reference. Good listening means we take seriously clients' ideas and communications. We do not listen to them to collect their communications as "specimens" of their condition or disorder. To take clients' communications seriously means we respond to them as if they had weight, as if they had matter, as if they had some substance, and as if they were worthy of consideration and thought. It means to listen to the client as we would like to be listened to when saying anything of personal importance to another person. It means being willing to let the client correct us until we really have the total picture. It means to respond in a way that makes the client think, "Yes! That's it! That's what I meant to say!" Once again, this is not so easily achieved.

Listening with a goal to understand has an inherent sense-making function. If we try to ferret out the sense in the other person's communication, that helps the other person literally "make sense." People do this all the time with children as they learn to communicate. People patiently try to understand, and through their joint efforts with the child, the child comes to communicate more clearly. This can also be done with clients, even with clients who apparently make no sense, such as clients with schizophrenia. But one must be willing to assume that the other person is trying to make sense and to communicate something.

Treating the client with respect. We treat our clients with respect. In addition to other things we have mentioned, this means that (a) we view them as equals and (b) we view ourselves as jointly working on problems *with* them, rather than working *on* them.

We want to view clients as equals. They may not feel like equals. Nonetheless, it is important for *us* to view them as equals. We relate to the inherently equal part in them, even when we are taking the lead. Also, we work with them on the problem, and not on the person. The medical metaphor of therapy leads therapists to view their enterprise as working on and fixing broken or dysfunctional parts of the person. This is an unfortunate metaphor and mitigates against the kind of collaboration we value. To think that way is to focus both therapists' and clients' attention on what is wrong with *the clients*—their dysfunctional dispositional attributes—and this is liable to contribute to both therapists and clients viewing the client as dysfunctional. This attitude gets in the way of proactive problem-solving on both therapists' and clients' parts.

Empathic understanding. There are several components to empathic understanding. The first component is that we try to understand how the client is viewing and experiencing his or her problem. A superficial understanding of the problem from the client's perspective is often easy to attain. However, attaining a deeper understanding from the client's point of view will sometimes be difficult because clients themselves often cannot articulate the problem. In fact, part of the problem may be their frustration, fear, and worry that they cannot clearly identify exactly what is going wrong.

Consider Andy, who presented with mild but persistent and troubling obsessive–compulsive symptomatology. It was easy for the therapist to empathically identify Andy's distress at his symptomatology. However, Andy also felt that neither his social nor his professional life was going as well as he wanted it to, and he could not identify what was going wrong. His frustration at not knowing why things were not going well was also easy to empathize with. But it was harder to get a feel for what he was implicitly thinking and feeling about himself *because* his life was not going well.

Gradually, the therapist was able to get a feel for the fact that Andy had great difficulty trusting his ability to be assertive and to take care of himself and protect his interests while still remaining socially appropriate. As this became clear and as the therapist and Andy together began to articulate this struggle and clarify it, Andy began to develop more differentiated and effective ways of handling social situations.

Second, obtaining an understanding of what the problem is from the client's subjective point of view also means getting a feel for the client's goals and values. This does not only mean identifying what the client's values are. It also means getting a sense of how they actually experience them, how important they are to them, and how they fit into their life scheme. It is considerably more difficult to really empathically understand clients' values than it is to understand how they are feeling. This is particularly true when the client's values lead to behavior that to us appears self-destructive, harmful, or offensive. It might not be hard to understand that a man is angry because his daughter is marrying someone of another ethnicity. It may be considerably harder to suspend one's own point of view enough to empathically "inhabit" those values to really get a feel for what it is like to see things as that person does.

Third, obtaining a sense of what the problem is from the client's point of view also involves attaining a subjective map of the client's current life experience. Where do the problems lie? Where are the constraints? Where are the opportunities? What are the rewards? Therapists sometimes substitute their objective perspective for empathic understanding and try to tell the client to see things differently. This is frequently to little avail. For example, a teenager is running around with a bad crowd. The therapist tells her how rewarding it would be to be independent and think for herself. This probably makes as much sense as telling her it is fun to wear geriatric shoes. The teenager, naturally, reacts to this with an increased defense of what she is doing, or with silence, and is then accused of resistance by the therapist. Such input from the therapist will only be listened to and considered by the teenager if an empathically based shared frame of reference has been established.

Fourth, obtaining a sense of what the problem is from the client's point of view can also include getting a sense of how the problem fits into the person's subjective life stream. This can include historical exploration such as in psychoanalysis. It can also include getting a feel for how the problem fits in with the flow of the person's personal evolution. Losing a relationship "now" may feel much more traumatic to someone if that person had been working for 20 years to establish a stable life structure. Then, just when the person thought he or she had it, the partner walks out.

Fifth, understanding the client's frame of reference also includes attaining an understanding of the client's theory of the problem. Therapists' beliefs that clients are resisting are frequently based on the therapists' failure to understand and work with how the clients are viewing the problem. Instead, if they bother to understand clients' theories at all, they dismiss them as unrealistic and then try to work against them, generating resistance. Therapists need to be careful not to let their theories of what the client is doing get in the way of really listening to the client.

There are numerous examples of this. These include a client who went to a psychiatrist because he was troubled by anxiety symptoms that he was convinced had something to do with significant psychological issues, and he was told it was biological and all he needed was medication. Another client was convinced his depression had roots in early childhood experiences, but was told by his here-and-now-oriented therapist that focusing on the past was a waste of time. Still another client just wanted to work on her problems in a here-and-now way, but the therapist kept insisting she had to deal with early childhood roots if she wanted to heal.

Two specific examples follow. In one case, a woman came into therapy for depression. After the therapist worked with her in a combined cognitive–humanistic way, her depression lifted. At that point, she brought up a new problem: She thought she might be a sexual addict. The therapist explored her sexual behavior with her and did not find anything in his opinion to support this. She had a history of being sexually active, but not to an unusually high degree. She actively liked sex and sought it out, but did not seem to jeopardize her life situation in so doing. The therapist was of the opinion that her problem was really one of excessive self-criticism and lack of self-acceptance, a problem that had previously surfaced in considering her depression. The therapist's attempts to convey this to the client, however, clashed with the client's theory that she was a sexual addict. She decided to terminate therapy and find help for that problem elsewhere.

A second example is the case history discussed in Duncan et al. (1997), presented at the start of this chapter. The client was a woman with multiple personalities who had been in therapy after therapy where the goal of the therapy (for the therapist) was to get her to unify all her personalities into one. However, *she* did not hold this goal. Her goal was to increase communicative collaboration among all her personalities. She was seen as resisting by prior therapists who failed to understand the logic in her point of view and who held to their goal that the "healthy" solution was unification. (It is interesting to note *who* is resisting change here— the client who refuses to adopt the therapist's frame of reference or the therapist who refuses to listen to the client.) Duncan et al. took her at her word and worked with her in terms of her goals, and, interestingly, she spontaneously arrived on her own at the integrative solution.

Not only do we try to understand clients' theories of problems (if they have any), but we try to understand their theories of change as well. How do the clients see change occurring? How have they made changes in their lives in the past? Do they think change is changing their character, their life circumstances, others around them, their own behavior, their emotions, their values, their thoughts? Do they think change comes through practice or insight? Do they think change is a product of willpower? Is it a product of logically arguing with oneself or with those in one's world? Should one be able to do it oneself? Or does one need help? Is God involved? What about prayer? How about the elders in one's community? What about shamans or witchcraft? Is change a matter of accessing one's true self? Of accepting oneself as one is? What things, from the client's point of view, are changeable, and what are not? Clients may hold many different ideas about change and how it comes about. Understanding their theory of change is crucial if one is to help them use their own capabilities for self-change.

All of the things we come to understand about the client through empathic listening help us and the client "localize" the problem and help us understand what to do.

Empathic attunement. Honoring the client's frame of reference also means being attuned to them in the moment. This means we try to be aware of how they are construing a problem in the moment, how they are construing our relationship with them in the moment, how they are construing what the two of us are doing in the moment, how they are reacting to us in the moment, and how they are evaluating and reacting to themselves in the moment. It also means we try to be sensitively attuned to their emotions. Finally, it means being attuned to their rhythms: Do they move slow or fast, do they enjoy a laugh, can they "play with" problems, or are they always serious and businesslike? Do they enjoy imagination, or are they very logical and practical? For instance, with Andy, the obsessive–compulsive client previously mentioned, therapy began to go better when the therapist realized that Andy enjoyed ironic humor. Because the therapist also enjoyed ironic humor, this came to be a natural way for the two to communicate.

We try to be honest and genuine in our attunement. As we have previously noted, we do agree that the therapist should establish different kinds of relationships with different clients, but we do not agree with the idea that this should be thought of as a deliberate therapeutic intervention. We reject the idea of the therapist as a master puppeteer who deliberately pulls the strings of the client. Instead, we try to adjust our style of interaction to "meet" the client because we honestly and genuinely wish to meet the client.

Empathically Using and Sharing the Therapist's Own Perspective

If we wish to meet the mind of the client, we must share what is on our own mind. Our perspective or our frame of reference needs to be available in the dialogue for both ourselves and the client to use as a resource.

Therapists' frames of reference include ideas from their professional knowledge, training, and experience, as well as from their own observations and reactions. The trick is to achieve a workable balance between sharing observations and ideas from the therapist's frame of reference and working with the client's frame of reference, or between what Belenky et al. (1986) called *separate* and *connected knowing*. Professional training has tended to privilege or emphasize the therapist's external perspective as the basis for decision making. However, if we can balance the two perspectives, then we can collaboratively offer ideas and feedback as part of the dialogue, without adopting a paternalistic "I know better than you" stance that works against collaboration.

Assessment of the client's dynamics or problems in terms of any given theory (e.g., the client's ego strength in psychodynamic theory, the client's dysfunctional cognitions in cognitive theory, and the client's dysfunctional behaviors in behavioral theory) is an example of a separate or external perspective. Behaviors that flow from the therapist's frame of reference include suggesting interventions, self-disclosing, confronting, giving advice, and interpreting. These can all be useful if given with an eye toward maintaining a collaborative relationship with a client.

It is important that therapists provide their own "external" perspective. Many clients explicitly want this. One of our values is our potential for providing corrective information. The issue is not *whether* we give it, but *how* we give it. We can even give corrective information rather forcefully and strongly if we believe in the importance of what we are saying. However, even then we try to convey an attitude that we want the client's input in response to what we say—that we recognize that unless they see some sense in what we are saying, it will be of little use to them. Furthermore, we are willing and interested in looking for compromises that turn either–or situations into win–win situations.

To use our frame of reference empathically means that we try to align whatever we are going to say or suggest so that it is responsive to the client's frame of reference. For instance, interpretations are given in a way that supports the client, rather than accuses him or her (Wile, 1984). Wachtel (1993) discussed this in some detail. He gave the following example:

> *You seem to expect something terrible to happen to you if you have any wish to be taken care of.* [instead of "You're defending against feelings of dependency."] (Wachtel, 1993, p. 73, italics in original)

The former response is an empathic interpretation that tries to connect with the client's frame of reference, whereas the latter is given from an external, separate knowing perspective (in addition to which it is an overgeneralization and an entity attribution; see chapter 7).

Similarly, advice, self-disclosures, and the suggestion of interventions are given in a way that are sensitively relevant to the client's perceptions of what is needed. They are also attuned to what the client believes he or she can do. We try to suggest procedures in a way that makes them sound interesting to clients to try. We discuss empathic intervention more fully in a later section.

In terms of confrontation, one can disagree with clients in a respectful way, without assuming that they are up to no good. Some therapists adopt a suspicious attitude toward clients, viewing everything the client says with skepticism and distrust. This leads to a manner of expressing disagreement or an alternative perspective that is harmful to the support of the client's self-healing potential. In contrast, we adopt the attitude that clients are intelligent and capable of hearing us, if not now in the immediate moment, at least at some time in the future. We do not have to brutally confront them with the truth, call them on their game, and so on, although we may want to point out to them that we do not always agree with them. We do not believe that if clients resist what we say now, they are forever locked into their resistance unless we batter down their defenses. Clients hear us, even if they must resist in the moment. But they go away and argue with us in their heads, and that means they are thinking about what we say. Often clients come, through their own internal process of arguing and considering, to eventually see some truth in what we were saying.

This does not mean we are completely gullible. Clients do fool therapists, though we think this is less common than some suppose. To gullibly accept everything the client says is to abdicate the use of our intelligence, and one of the reasons therapy is helpful is that it is the joining of two intelligences. Thus, while holding a fundamentally respectful attitude toward the client process, we still realize that, from the clients' point of view, for their reasons, and following their agenda and priorities as they see it, they may believe they have to fool us at times. In these cases, we give our alternative perspective. Furthermore, we may need to set workable limits at times. For instance, we might not want to work with clients who have been drinking. They may deny it. Nonetheless, we may send them home and tell them to come back when we can be more convinced that they have not been drinking.

We reject the idea that the therapist's perspective is the more objective one, implying that our perspective is necessarily superior in truth value to that of the client. Therapists' perspectives reflect their points of view, based on their experiences, their cultural backgrounds, the theories and ideas they have learned, and the dominant models of psychopathology of the time (now it is cognitive–behavioral; 30 years ago it was psychodynamic). Therapists' perspectives are as colored by their experiences as much as are clients'. It is a moot point who is in greater possession of "the truth." Rather than debate this issue, we believe it is best if therapists realize that, at least most of the time, they are reflecting their own perspectives and not truth. This leads to collaborative dialogue more often than if the therapist thinks he or she is a guardian of the truth and the client is in a state of error. We should be humble and realize that our truths of the present moment were not the truths of 50 years ago and probably will not be the truths of 50 years in the future.

Furthermore, the client has lived in his or her world for decades. The therapist has known the client for a limited span of time and only in one context. How could a limited acquaintance claim greater objectivity and knowledge? The therapist may recognize symptoms of a syndrome, but the disorder label will not capture the essence of the person or the problem. DSM labels, especially, do not capture the richness and complexity of the person's life history and life structure, the "game board" on which the client must operate. Thus, although therapists' perspectives are valuable, we question the contention that they are more objective. Nonetheless, the therapist's perspective is an alternative one that often catches aspects of the situation that the client may be overlooking.

Therapists' Use of Their Intuition. Therapists' intuition is an important basis for therapeutic response. Intuition is the therapist's "sense" of what is going on with the client and with the relationship. It is based on the therapist's tacit, experiential knowledge of what is going on in the interaction. There is nothing magical to intuition; it is based on humans' "animal" ability to pick up emotional information from others (Buck & Ginsburg, 1997) and to notice nonverbal configurations in their behavior. Intuition is important because it is a more context-sensitive knowing than the kind of external knowing that occurs through cognitive analysis. Humans are built to be attuned to subtle but important changes in their relationships, which they may notice and process at a tacit level. In relations with other people, a person often "knows" before he or she can put into words that something is going on (Browner, et al., 1993). Often intuition can tell us when something is not working for the client, when something else might be involved, or even when something is going wrong between ourselves and the client.

Intuitions can be used to guide therapeutic response. Intuitions sometimes allow us to make subtle fine-tuned adjustments. However, intuitions are not always, magically, correct. Often we are picking up something real, but the words and concepts we use to articulate it to ourselves are wrong. Furthermore, there is reason to believe that decision making is most effective when it combines both intuition and cognitive analysis. Intuition as a basis for decision making has become a topic of interest in medicine, business, and other areas (Agor, 1989; Davis-Floyd & Arvidson, 1997). Some research there has found that those who use both intuition and cognitive decision-making processes make better decisions than those who rely on either one alone. There is also some evidence for this in terms of psychotherapy (Caspar, 1997). Therefore, we listen to our intuitions, but we also think.

THE PROCESS OF THERAPY FROM A COLLABORATIVE POINT OF VIEW

In the initial sessions we think it is useful, as in strategic therapies, to explore what clients have already done to solve their problems, and to look for any evidence of prior signs of success. We also expect change. Expecting change, we are attuned to signs of small changes that can potentially be amplified into large changes. If we go in believing clients have deeply ingrained, fixed, unchangeable problems, we are likely to overlook small flourishing seedlings that can be nourished into larger plants. The point is to not miss progress that occurs in small approximations. The client who tends to react negatively to social interactions might report pausing a moment to consider the other person's intent, but still become angry. This may be a useful new behavior, even if the final outcome is still negative. If the therapist catches this and dialogues with the client on it, the next week the client might pause again and choose to clarify issues with the other person instead of simply reacting with anger.

Second, we initially rely on clients' resources and self-healing potential on their own rather than rush in with interventions. Instead of the popular saying "Don't fix it if it isn't broken," we say, "Don't fix it (so to speak) if it is fixing itself." We have had a number of cases in which simple empathic listening is sufficient. If clients function well without our input and seem only to want our physical presence, then we are open to the possibility that our input is not needed much of the time. There are highly active clients like this both among high-functioning and low-functioning groups. If clients can generate their own solutions, then minimal therapist intervention is the "treatment of choice." One client, Lucille, presented as having major depressive disorder in the first session. The depression was tied to a difficult life situation. Her aged mother, who had Alzheimer's, had come to live with her and her husband and was demanding all her time. She felt trapped by her own sense of responsibility into taking care of her mother, but it was wrecking her marriage. The therapist did nothing but empathically listen and take notes in the first session, while preparing to suggest either cognitive therapy or medication for the client at the end of the session. However, by the end of the session the client reported feeling much better. A second session was scheduled anyway. However, during the week the client took the initiative to find a nursing home she could afford not too far away for her mother and began to patch things up with her husband. She reported feeling much better and did not need further therapy or medication.

If simple empathic listening does not seem to be sufficient, or if the client right from the start expects us to offer more active interventions, then we may do so. We present a chart of how we approach therapy in Figure 9.2. This suggests how the five learning opportunities discussed in chapter 5 fit together. We turn to the collaborative use of techniques and procedures next.

Collaborative Use of Techniques and Procedures

Although in general techniques and procedures may not play a large role in why therapy is helpful (see chapter 2), both clients and therapists often want them. Procedures can be useful for some problems. In addition, clients may want them because, after all, they have come to see the doctor, and doctors should do more than just converse. Therapists may want the procedures to allay their own anxiety (Rosenbaum et al., 1990) and to give them a feeling that they are doing something. On the other hand, we have met many clients who resist the use of procedures.

We would like to learn as many procedures as we can and use them skillfully. Furthermore, we would love it if researchers could tell us which procedures are more likely to be helpful with which types of clients (e.g., Beutler, 1996). We firmly believe different clients have different learning styles, different world views, and different ways of self-development. We want to maximize our chances of offering to clients the best tool for them at the right time.

Choice of Procedures

In our own practice, we are liable to provide a wide range of techniques from a wide variety of approaches. Because we believe the healing power lies in the client and not in the procedure, we do not think it is so crucial to choose "just the right" procedure at just the right time. Often, several different tools might do, which is why there is evidence that both systematic desensitization and gestalt techniques can help clients overcome anxiety (W. R. Johnson & Smith, 1997), both experiential techniques and cognitive techniques can help clients overcome depression (Greenberg & Watson, 1998; Hollon & Beck, 1994), and both cognitive–behavioral and experiential techniques can help clients overcome posttraumatic stress disorder (Foa & Rothbaum, 1997; Paivio & J. Nieuwenhuis, 1998).

However, therapists need a heuristic for choosing which procedure to use at a given time. Following research is certainly one important heuristic that can be used, and this is one that we often use. The research on empirically validated treatments (Task Force on Promotion and Dissemi-

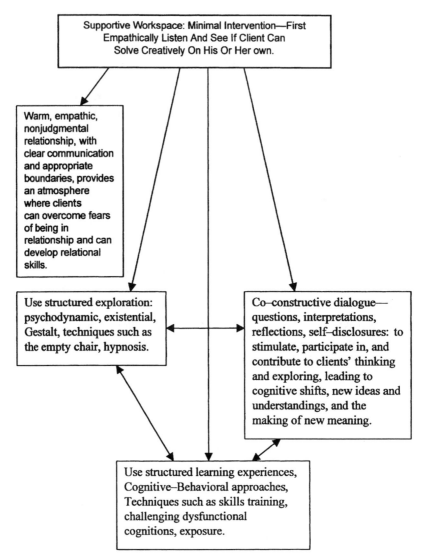

Figure 9.2. A chart of therapy: starting with a provision of a basic workshop and connections with the other four learning opportunities (as discussed in chapter 5).

nation of Psychological Procedures, 1995), while flawed in important respects (Wampold, 1997), provides a heuristic that matches treatment to disorder, for instance. If a client is experiencing panic, we would be very likely to offer the client ideas from the cognitive–behavioral approach (e.g., Barlow, 1988). Another possible heuristic to use is to take into account the match between procedure and personality (e.g., Beutler, 1996). For instance, some clients are highly reactant—they do not like someone having power over them and telling them what to do. For them, procedures that protect their autonomy may be more useful. A third heuristic to follow is the dictates of one's theory or point of view. Needless to say, for us, choice of procedures is made in consultation with the client.

Decision to Stay With or Change Procedures

It is not unusual to find that a procedure is not working. The therapist and client must then decide what to do about it. Therapists and clients must choose between rigidly staying with a procedure that is not working and desperately jumping from procedure to another, hoping to find one that does work. Part of the problem here is the medical model and its encouragement of the idea that it is the procedure, and not the interactive process between client and therapist together, that is therapeutic. This leads therapists to adopt the mind-set that they must select just the right procedure at just the right time. If a procedure does not seem to be working, they either rigidly hold onto it, because it must be "the right" procedure, or flail about, looking for another procedure. This results from having too much faith in procedures and not enough faith in the process between therapist and client together.

In all cases, we think it is important to listen to the client. Clients will tell us, over time, not only that a procedure may not be working, but why. It is the ability to listen to this that makes us able to creatively modify the program when needed. For instance, it was this ability to listen that allowed Heinz Kohut to hear that empathy might be more important than traditional analytic interpretation with some clients, and then to modify his views accordingly (Kohut, 1979).

In many cases it may be better to stay with a procedure than change, but to try to sharpen how the procedure is used. A procedure may not be working because (a) the problem is complex and does not easily or initially yield to the use of the procedure or (b) the client is having a hard time implementing the procedure but does want to learn how to use it. In these cases, "staying with the program" is probably the best thing to do. Both the therapist and the client need to patiently work together to modify the program or how the client is using the program so that it will be more useful. Jumping from one strategy to another too early is a good way to guarantee that nothing will work.

On the other hand, if the signs are that the procedure is not working because (a) the client is only half-heartedly doing it or (b) the client is trying very hard but is trying to make something work that really does not fit, it may be useful to consider changing. Therapists and clients also have to be alert to the possibility that they are working on the "wrong" problem. Sometimes in using procedures the most important thing that comes out of them is a redefinition of the problem, which leads to choice of a different approach. We gave an example in chapter 5 of a client with whom we wanted to use systematic desensitization. However, in trying to teach him the relaxation procedure it became obvious that a major problem to work on was that he felt too unsafe even to let himself learn how to be relaxed.

In any case, if therapists view the major work of therapy as being done not by procedures but rather by people using procedures, then therapists will worry less about choosing the right procedure and more about how the client is using the procedure and how the procedure furthers the ongoing therapist–client conversation. If we think of procedures (such as the gestalt two-chair technique) as facilitating exploration, then there is no such thing as saying that they are not working anyway, because the very attempt to do them will lead to new information.

Being Aware That Clients' Needs Change Over Time

Another reason for changing procedures is that clients' needs evolve over time. This is one reason why mechanistic adherence to a manualized therapy program is a bad idea, and why we think therapy should be an ongoing intelligent conversation. Gold (1994) documented a number of cases in which clients wanted different things at different times. Some, in cognitive therapy, wanted an experience of psychodynamic therapy before returning to cognitive therapy. Therapists should be willing to listen to clients—they often do know what they need and what is working for them. The therapist should then be willing to try new things out or, if he or she feels incapable of offering those things, refer the client.

Empathic Problem Solving

A good model of empathic problem solving might be how a good teacher coaches a student to figure out an algebra problem. The teacher tunes in to how the student is thinking about the problem, and then asks questions or makes suggestions to prod the student's own understanding, so that the student thinks it out with the teacher. The student moves in understanding through an empathic dialogue. In therapy, the therapist is an empathic coach, going along with the client step by step and facilitating the client's thinking it out. A good coach would also take a client step by step through a behavioral exercise. The therapist does not give "the answer" until the client has thought it through to the point at which the therapist's answer will make sense to the client.

An example of empathic problem solving (and working from a cognitive–behavioral point of view while honoring the client's frame of reference) is Donald Meichenbaum's work with Richard (Shostrom, 1986). Richard is a 47-year-old man who is depressed over the breakup of his marriage. In addition, he has problems managing his anger. Meichenbaum works from within Richard's frame of reference to get Richard to think out new alternatives. For instance, Richard reports feeling suicidal. Meichenbaum empathically listens while Richard unveils a detailed plan for committing suicide that includes a "clean-up strategy" so that minimal mess is left for others. Meichenbaum empathically validates and prizes the positive thrust underlying this—that Richard cares about others—and then moves on to help Richard assess his own reasons for not committing suicide.

> Meichenbaum: Let me ask you something unusual. What prevents you from doing that [committing suicide]?
>
> Richard: That the people I leave behind will think I'm weak. That there are people that care about me and they've told me this. And I don't want to leave this world that way.
>
> Meichenbaum: I wouldn't want you to leave that way either. . . . You've been through an awful lot. . . . And I am seeing that some of the reaction that you're having, the depression, the sadness, the feeling of hopeless and at times even helplessness, may in some sense even be a natural reaction to what you've been through. . . . I feel a kind of, how shall I put it, a real desire to live, a sense of realizing new potential, of wanting to change. (Shostrom, 1986, p. 53)[1]

We consider this an example of empathic problem solving because Meichenbaum clearly wants to help Richard manage his suicidal feelings. However, Meichenbaum does not merely assess Richard's suicidal feelings and make a contract with him. Instead he validates Richard's feelings and draws out Richard's own reasons for not killing himself. When he does give feedback, he normalizes Richard's feelings in an empathic way and responds empathically to the positive side of Richard.

This is very much antithetical to the idea that a treatment is being "applied" to a condition that the client "has." In fact, thinking about it that way could lead to mechanistic application, rather than sensitive interaction.

Empathic Intervention

The idea of the empathic intervention—suggestion of procedures and strategies—follows from our consideration of empathic problem solving. Good therapists use strategies and procedures as a context for sensitive interaction. We have previously mentioned the example of Meichenbaum with Richard. Another good example is that of Aaron Beck with the same client (Shostrom, 1986). Beck uses his standard strategy of challenging Richard's dysfunctional thoughts. But the essence of Beck's approach is to do this while honoring Richard's frame of reference. In fact, Beck works

---

[1]From *Three Approaches to Psychotherapy III* (Transcript), by E. L. Shostrom, 1986, Corona Del Mar, CA: Psychological & Educational Films. Copyright 1986 by Psychological & Educational Films. Reprinted with permission.

very clearly from within Richard's frame of reference. In essence, he uses the materials of Richard's frame of reference to help Richard devise his own challenges to beliefs that are getting him down.

For instance, at the start of the interview Beck uses Richard's experience to help him challenge his dysfunctional thoughts.

Beck: What do you feel about being here?

Richard: Very nervous.

B: Anything else?

R: My stomach is turning and I think my palms are starting to perspire a little bit and I am concerned about how well I'll come across. If I can maintain my faculties to communicate, keep a good conversation going.

B: Now then, do you remember having thoughts of that nature? "Will I come across well, will I be able to carry on a conversation, will I be able to perform properly?" Did you recall having had those thoughts?

R: The closer I got to your office, the more severe the thoughts got.

B: And as the thoughts got more severe, what happened to your symptoms; the anxiety, the stomach, the sweaty palms?

R: My stomach started to churn more and more, I felt a lump in my throat, I find it very difficult to breathe. . .

B: Now, can you see any connection between these fearful thoughts that you had and the symptoms that you are experiencing?

R: They run together. . . . (Shostrom, 1986, pp. 64–65)

Beck goes on to help Richard see that the therapy situation is not a situation in which he has to perform. All he has to do is be honest, and Richard realizes that he can do that while still feeling anxious. This helps Richard relax. Beck does this by carefully working with Richard's frame of reference. He helps Richard access the dysfunctional thoughts he is having, in the context of his bodily felt experience, and then leads him in a way that makes sense to him to seeing an alternative way of looking at the therapy interaction. He does not merely tell Richard that it is his dysfunctional thoughts that are making him anxious, and then tell him that the therapy situation is not one where he has to perform. He helps Richard see these things himself by being sensitively attuned to his frame of reference.

We want our "interventions" always to be empathic and always to honor the client's frame of reference. In essence, good intervention always speaks the language and culture of the client. This makes sense if therapy is the mobilization of the client's own resources for self-healing.

Another example of empathically honoring the client's frame of reference in formulation of interventions is that of a case reported by Heide (1989). A female Asian college student came to therapy feeling suicidal because she was not doing as well in school as she thought she should be. She felt suicidal because she felt she was bringing shame and dishonor to her family. The therapist initially tried to work with her in a standard cognitive way, challenging her "dysfunctional beliefs" that she must do well in college, and so forth. This was to no avail. What did work was to shift gears and help her think through the consequences of suicide, realizing that that would bring more shame and dishonor to her family than doing poorly in school.

Honoring the client's frame of reference in terms of empathic intervention is particularly important when working with clients from cultural backgrounds that differ from the therapist's. It may be particularly helpful in such instances to learn the client's language and to intervene in ways that make sense in the client's culture. Thus, Comas-Diaz (1992) advocated the use of folk methods with clients from rural Hispanic backgrounds, and *curanderos* (folk healers) have been successfully used in some Los Angeles area hospitals with rural Hispanic clients.

CONCLUSION

In this chapter, we tried to give the reader our view of therapy as a meeting of minds. Our model is a full-fledged, mutual, collaborative model of a relationship. This model is an extension of the idea that clients self-heal. One could accept the notion of a self-healing client, but not accept all of the ideas of the collaborative view described here. As we discussed in chapter 6, there are other types of collaborative relationships, such as the tutorial model used by cognitive–behaviorists. However, we believe a collaborative model such as ours is more likely to be able to use all resources of both therapist and client.

10

PROBLEMS AND ISSUES OF
THERAPEUTIC PRACTICE

In this chapter, we consider various problems of therapeutic practice from our point of view. First we examine resistance. Next we consider the topic of assessment. We follow that with a discussion of obstacles to adopting an empathic meeting-of-minds perspective. Finally, we conclude by answering questions we have encountered when we have presented these ideas at conferences.

DEALING WITH RESISTANCE

No matter what point of view the therapist works from, client resistance is one of the biggest problems therapists have to confront. There are clients who seem to resist all efforts to help, even when it is clear to everyone else from outside that their behavior is harmful or self-destructive. As an example, a colleague was involved in a case of a woman whose son was having difficulties in school. It was obvious to all the professionals involved in the case that the son both was mildly retarded and met the criteria for attention deficit hyperactivity disorder (ADHD). Yet the mother (a) refused to admit that there was anything wrong with the child other than that he needed some help with his social skills and (b) refused any suggestions that he be placed on medication or receive special educational help. She came from a culture in which to admit that she had produced a "defective" son would be a matter of great shame. In a consultation meeting, she brought a lawyer along from the same cultural background who defended her point of view. The woman showed great inventiveness in deflecting attempts to get through to her. When one of the professionals present at the meeting tried to speak to her in her language, she claimed that she did not understand that dialect, although at other times she did appear to understand it.

Resistance is a multidimensional concept. There are many different reasons why clients resist. Some resist because they do not agree with the therapist's agenda. In fact, they may be reluctant clients, in therapy either involuntarily or dragged by a significant other (a parent or a spouse). Some may be convinced that what the therapist is suggesting is not the right way to go. Some may disagree with the therapist on philosophical grounds. Some may resist because they do not have the same vantage point on the problem as does the therapist. They cannot see their behavior from outside. Or they come out of a different cultural background and have a different perspective on things. They may resist because they are intimately and intricately aware of the interweaving of factors in their life and know that what the therapist is saying or suggesting is unwise or wrong given that vantage point. Some resist because they experience the therapist as attacking them (and they are sometimes right in this). Some resist because they do not understand the therapist's agenda. Some may be unable to do what the therapist requires them to do. Some may feel misunderstood and misperceived by the therapist. Some may feel helpless, discouraged, and demoralized. Still others may be afraid to disrupt the delicate ecological balance of their lives. Finally, still others resist if they are asked to change what they have been doing for years, and what has worked at least reasonably well from their point of view in the past. It is not easy to abandon an old way of being that has to do with one's survival in order to learn a new way that one is less sure of.

We want to reiterate the implicit proactivity in most cases of resistance. People try to solve problems from within their point of view. They may resist solutions offered from outside if those solutions do not fit their view of the problem, or if the solution threatens the whole set of connections and interrelationships they have established in their personal worlds. The case of the woman and her son illustrates this. From her point of view, it was simply inconceivable that her son was "defective" (as she regarded diagnoses of retardation and ADHD). Such an admission would have brought such great shame that she sought every other possible solution. We can accuse her of resistance and denial, but from within the constraints of her experience and her cultural background, her behavior makes perfect sense. Furthermore, she showed great inventiveness in deflecting what undoubtedly felt from her side of things to be attempts to impose a solution on her.

Thought of this way, resistance is a perfectly sensible reaction from the standpoint of the client. Because our primary job as therapists is to create a good learning climate, we must find a way to get clients interested and involved and to look for win–win solutions. First, we need to show that we respect their desire to avoid us and to defend themselves against us. We have to find a way of showing them that we understand and respect them. Empathic listening is a major component of this, as is anything else that conveys to clients that we are truly interested in their point of view. Furthermore, we need to convey to clients that we are really on their side; we are not just acting as agents of society, or of parents, or of whomever. We need to convey to them that we believe they have something of worth to say—their perspective has its own validity. We need to take seriously when they say they do not want to do something (either in so many words or behaviorally) or when they say "I can't" or "It doesn't make sense to me" and find some other way of helping. That is why it is actually an advantage that we have different techniques and different therapeutic approaches, and that it is not so crucial to fit just the right technique to the problem. Finally, we need to be able to provide specific help at specific times as clients struggle to master new and difficult ways of being and behaving. We need to be able to deal with temporary discouragement and be able to shift gears if their discouragement with, or dislike of, a procedure runs too deep.

In the case of the woman and her son, the professionals needed to find a solution that showed they understood and respected her frame of reference, while still solving the problem. Our colleague suggested an analogy to her of diabetes. The woman admitted that taking medication for diabetes was not shameful in her culture. Using that as an analogy, she became more receptive to the idea of medication for the ADHD.

ASSESSMENT

From our point of view, whether the therapist does a formal assessment or not depends greatly on the therapist's point of view. Therapists practicing, for instance, from a client-centered point of view will not wish to do a formal assessment. Nonetheless, following are possibilities for assessment that are more likely to facilitate a collaborative meeting of minds.

We believe that matching therapy approach to client personality is a more potentially fruitful way than matching therapy to diagnosis. Part of the theory of the client as self-healer is that different clients may prefer different modalities or strategies for self-healing. Thus, therapy needs to be individualized in this sense. We do not have space to consider their work, but refer the interested reader to the research of Beutler and Clarkin (1990) for a useful scheme for matching.

The research of Prochaska and his colleagues (Prochaska, 1995; Prochaska et al., 1992) provided yet another framework for matching therapeutic procedure to client. In this case, the matching is made on the basis of the stage of change the client is in. Prochaska and his colleagues have identified five stages of change: precontemplation (the individual does not recognize the existence of a problem), contemplation (the individual recognizes the existence of the problem but deals with it by thinking and analyzing without taking action), preparation (the individual recognizes the need for action and is preparing to take it), action (the individual implements an action strategy), and maintenance (the individual takes steps to maintain the gains he or she has achieved). We eschew the idea that the therapist decides for the client what stage the client is in and then unilaterally chooses procedures and strategies based on that decision. However, Prochaska's model could be used to help the therapist and client together understand where the client is in the change process, and thus what the client might find most useful.

There are other diagnostic systems that therapists can use to more sensitively and empathically tailor their therapeutic suggestions to the actual doing of therapy. Leitner, Faidley, and Celentana (in press) developed a system that is based on a taxonomy of the kinds of life problems people encounter. Their system can be used both to sharpen therapists' empathic understanding of the client and as a focal point with the client for collaborative discussion. Their diagnostic system in part has to do with categories of optimal functioning, such as flexibility and creativity, and interpersonal struggles, such as distancing and dependency. Greenberg and his colleagues (Greenberg et al., 1993) have engaged in *process diagnosis* of the moment-to-moment interactions in therapy. Process diagnoses are assessments of the particular types of issues the client is struggling with and lead to the suggestion of procedures that will be helpful. There is a difference between diagnosis that focuses on client states or transitions, such as in the Prochaska system, the Leitner et al. system, and the Greenberg et al. system, and those that are global and characterological, such as the DSM. The former would seem more specifically useful in suggesting strategies the client would find useful for a given problem at a given moment in time.

There is a naturally occurring assessment process when clients come into therapy that follows from our perspective of the client as active self-healer. Basically this consists of asking the question: Why are the clients coming to therapy, given that they have a basic capacity for self-righting and self-healing? The answer is that they are either not using that capacity or they are having no luck in using it. We then want to know what is getting in their way. This may help us decide where best to devote our energies.

When clients come into therapy, we assume that they have already been trying to solve their problems. The catch is that what *they* see as their problems may not be what we and others see as their problems. For example, a man who is court referred for sexually abusing a child may not see his behavior as a problem. Nonetheless, he has been active in trying to resolve his problem from his point of view (though the problem as he sees it might consist of how to avoid legal sanctions). Therefore, one of the first things we might be interested in is identifying what the problem is from the clients' point of view, and what they have already done to try to solve their problems (as they see them).

Thus, the first thing we might want to know is, does the *client* think he or she has a problem? If not, who does? It will not be surprising that clients are not mobilizing their natural self-healing processes to solve a problem if they do not recognize the existence of a problem. Like trying to get the oil industry to recognize the threat of global warming, the impoverished people in Brazil to recognize the danger in cutting down all the rain forests, and people worldwide to recognize the danger of overpopulation, clients who do not acknowledge or see a problem will not be mobilized to solve it. This will be a first obstacle to client self-healing.

Then, using our discussion in chapter 4, we might assess other obstacles to self-healing, such as how the client's self-critical thinking may be getting in the way, how the client's environment may be blocking self-healing, how the client may be prematurely giving up, or how the client is blocked by feelings of helplessness and hopelessness. Once we have assessed what has gotten in the way of the client's self-healing efforts, we may be in a better position to provide assistance.

OBSTACLES TO THERAPISTS OPERATING FROM A COLLABORATIVE MEETING-OF-MINDS PERSPECTIVE

Several aspects of our field create obstacles to therapists adopting a meeting-of-minds perspective. First, the medical model is philosophically antithetical to this perspective. Believing oneself to be the doctor who has the answer for the client not only puts the therapist in the position of responsibility but also creates a climate antithetical to a collaborative mind-set. It is no surprise that clients sit and passively await their therapists' pearls of wisdom.

In medicine, physicians traditionally were trained to present as the experts. They were taught to appear completely confident and sure of their "verdicts" to gain patient compliance. If they were to express uncertainty or doubt, it was feared that patients would not comply with what the physician ordered. This surely is true in some cases and is probably true for some clients in therapy as well. It may well be that some clients do better "borrowing" their therapists' certainty and energy to use in their self-healing efforts. There are some clients who enthusiastically comply with the therapist-as-expert role, look up to their therapists, and actively and overtly comply with the therapists' prescriptions. Using their therapists' certainty, they throw themselves enthusiastically into the activities that the therapist has provided and, by so doing, self-heal.

However, in medicine, as a general rule, gaining behavioral compliance may be all that one needs to achieve. A patient can productively comply with the physician's prescriptions in a rote, mechanical way. Patient thinking and understanding is not an intrinsic part of the process of how the treatment operates. This is not true in therapy (witness the research showing client involvement to be the major factor in whether therapy works or not). The client needs to enthusiastically "inhabit" and actively use therapist-prescribed procedures in order for them to work. Mechanically going through the motions in therapy usually does not work. Thus, gaining compliance is really not the goal in therapy. Rather, active understanding is what is wanted. Thinking is intrinsic to the process. Many clients will think about what is going on and not necessarily blindly accept the therapist's perspective. More of a collaborative relationship is what is needed. We therefore do not believe that the therapist as physician–expert is the optimal stance, even though it may work in selected cases.

A second obstacle is a fundamentally negative attitude toward clients. Just walking in the door, the clients take on a degraded social identity. They are assumed to be incompetent in their decision making, just because they are "patients." Wile (1981) noted the pejorative ways our theories lead us to view clients. They are seen as narcissistic, manipulative, borderline, paranoid, dependent, avoidant, thinking dysfunctionally and irrationally, out of touch with feelings, alexythymic, grandiose, feeling entitled, defensive, rationalizing, denying, projecting, splitting, collusive, and so on. Such labels are hardly designed to create a collaborative attitude in the therapist. Rather, such labels are much more likely to create a paternalistic attitude in which the poor, deluded client must be "corrected" and set on the right path by the more healthy, knowing, in-touch-with-reality, sane-thinking therapist. As an example of this kind of attitude, consider this quote from Gediman and Lieberman (1996): "Patients are deceptive in the therapeutic encounter. . . . The patient fools himself or herself in an effort to protect self-esteem" (as quoted in S. D. Miller et al., 1997, p. 141), as well as to put one over on the therapist. Although we do not deny that clients sometimes do this, if therapists believe that patients are *generally* and *usually* being deceptive, then it will be hard to adopt a genuinely collaborative attitude toward them. Clients may have only a few weaknesses and have many areas of competence, yet what therapists are taught can encourage them to view the whole client as deficient and disordered. We invite therapists to think about this: As you encountered a life struggle and you sought help, would you have wanted your therapist to assume that your views and strategies are defective simply because you have taken on the client's role?

The models in the field of therapy also disempower clients. By calling everything therapists do *interventions*, while if clients do the same things they are *responses*, therapists make clear who is in the driver's seat. For instance, in discussing a rating system developed by herself and a colleague (Marziali & Angus, 1986), Angus (1992) observed:

> It is evident that this rating system is based on the implicit assumption that the therapist's job is to provide direction and offer interventions in therapy while the client's job is to follow and respond. This assumption is challenged by the results of the qualitative study. . . . At different points in the verbal interaction, all clients and all therapists in this study were found to initiate topics, make interventions, and follow the lead of the other participant. Had the four sessions been rated on [this coding system] . . . the activity and reflexivity . . . of the clients would have been rendered invisible by the a priori decision to classify client statements as responses to therapists' interventions. (p. 201)

Traditionally, therapy has privileged the therapist's frame of reference. Our field trains us to adopt an outside observational perspective on clients in contrast to an inside or jointly shared empathic perspective. We are taught to observe our clients, to take notes on their behavior and what they say, and then to form diagnostic pictures of them. Far more time is spent on this than on emphasizing the importance of connected knowing or trying to grasp a sense of the clients from within their frame of reference. If we are taught empathy, we are taught it as a response skill, as a technique (Carkhuff & Berenson, 1967; Egan, 1982). Empathy is taught primarily as a therapeutic strategy to build rapport and to gain the clients' trust. To judge clients as manipulative, for instance, is to make an external judgment of their behavior. It is unlikely that they are *feeling* manipulative. In fact, clients who are acting manipulatively are often feeling desperate and scared.

An example of the problem of judging a client's behavior from outside, *without* taking into account the potential wisdom in it from the client's point of view, is Norem's (1996) research on defensive pessimism. It is almost an article of faith in Western culture that being optimistic is healthy and being pessimistic is unhealthy. Congruent with this is a wealth of research showing that those who think optimistically (Seligman, 1990) function better.

Thus, a client who comes to see a therapist, catastrophizing about her upcoming exam, may seem unrealistically pessimistic and a product of "dysfunctional thinking." She says, "I'm studying hard, but I just know I'm going to fail this exam," and she is in an obvious state of tension and anxiety. From a cognitive perspective, this is a distortion: As the therapist interviews her, the therapist discovers that she routinely gets A's, she got an A on the last test, and she has studied just as hard for this one. An "objective" review of the evidence would lead the therapist to conclude that the data do not support her catastrophic expectation.

Yet, on the basis of Norem's (1996) research, trying to argue the client out of her belief might actually be *harmful*, not helpful. How? Norem found that there is a certain class of pessimists, labeled *defensive pessimists*, for whom pessimism is actually a proactive coping strategy. Catastrophizing is a way of managing anxiety and actually helps the client's coping. When the catastrophizing is interrupted or interfered with, the client's performance *deteriorates*. Thus, challenging this client's dysfunctional cognitions in an attempt to stop her catastrophizing may itself have catastrophic consequences. She may actually deteriorate in her performance.

A number of findings of Norem (1996) are illustrative: Defensive pessimists do better when they can "worry" or ruminate over their problems; optimists do worse. Also, defensive pessimists are better in situations in which they have to think about negative possibilities, whereas optimists are better in situations in which they can be "oblivious." We can imagine our client, brainwashed by society, coming to a therapist believing there must be something wrong with her for worrying about her grades so much when she is doing so well. She "shouldn't be that way." In fact, she has recently read in a book that "the healthy" way to be is to be optimistic. This makes her feel very pessimistic about her pessimism. The therapist agrees with her, based on the "local wisdom" of the time, and sets out to cure her of her pessimism. As the therapist does so, the client's grades begin to suffer. She becomes even more pessimistic. She is now seen as resisting treatment. Perhaps she will now even be given a personality disorder label. She is perhaps dependent or histrionic. All of this could be avoided if the therapist had truly respected her frame of reference and assumed there was some sense in it. The failure to really access her frame of reference then leads to a major therapeutic mistake.

QUESTIONS AND ANSWERS CONCERNING OUR POINT OF VIEW

In this section we consider questions we have been asked concerning our point of view and provide answers from our perspective of the client as active self-healer.

Q: My clients come from lower class backgrounds and are usually either court referred or referred by various family service agencies. A typical case would be a husband, wife, and two children, referred because one child is acting up in school. The parents do not want to come; their attempts to discipline the child are, by middle-class standards, punitive and nearly abusive. They want an answer. They do not want to talk. Yet when I try to educate them on more effective parenting strategies, including communication strategies and reward strategies, they do not really get the underlying idea. Furthermore, they have couple problems: They fight and argue with one another in verbally abusive ways. Is this not a case where the therapist must be more like a physician, intervening from outside? These individuals show little capacity for self-healing or self-change. Certainly I have not found that I can have an "intelligent conversation" with them. I must provide the structure; I must intervene. What do you say about that?

A: We still believe the clients are trying to solve problems and "right the ships of their lives" from their point of view. Furthermore, they are probably using considerable inventiveness in the dysfunctional ways they are doing this. The problem is not that these people are not capable of self-healing and self-righting, but for many different reasons they are not succeeding in doing it now. If we do not understand what the clients are doing, we know we need to listen more. From their point of view, the ways the middle-class therapist suggests for dealing with problems probably sound like nonsense to them. It may not be easy (no one ever said therapy was easy), but again the ultimate strategy is to build lines of communication so that they will be curious about and interested in what we have to say. Or if we are clever strategic therapists, we could use a clever intervention to release their own self-healing potential to operate in a more proactive direction.

Q: Some of my clients act just like you say. They actively participate, think, try things out, and learn. Others just sit there, waiting for me to fix them. They are not court referred; they have come voluntarily on their own. But they take no active role at all. I empathically reflect; they say "yes" or "no" and stop talking. I ask questions; they answer in a few words or sentences and then wait for more questions. They seem to passively resist doing exercises, though they may go through the motions. What do I do?

A: Not all clients proactively invest their energy and involvement in making therapy work. And we all know that the clients we like the best are the ones who actively volunteer information, are willing to try exercises out, think and self-explore, and are open with their feelings.

Once again our answer is to try to understand things from the client's point of view. Many clients come into therapy feeling frightened, helpless, and humiliated. They do not understand what is going on with them. They naturally do what is safest in a new situation they do not understand: follow the expert's lead and try to figure out what one is supposed to be doing. It may seem to them that what one is supposed to be doing is answering questions so that the "doctor" can figure out the answer. Thus, they may just be being polite by answering a question or a reflection with a few words. They do not know they are supposed to continue to talk and think. They have been taught by our profession that we are physicianlike experts. Therefore, they sit there passively and wait for us to direct them, just as they have learned to do with physicians. If they passively resist, it is because privately what we are suggesting does not entirely make sense to them, or they have a feeling that it is wrong for them, but they do not feel that they have a right to say what they think. So they comply and resist at the same time and nothing works.

We still say that the number one chore of the therapist is to get clients actively involved. If they get actively involved, then all our brilliant insights and wonderful interventions can be helpful for them. Otherwise they fall flat. How do we get such clients involved? It does not usually work to simply explain to them that therapy is a process in which they have to be actively involved. They will passively accept this information and then wait for us to direct them as to how to do it. We must find ways of involving them. First, we need to understand how they are viewing and experiencing the therapy situation and how they see their world. They may be very uncomfortable with the idea that they are supposed to be anything but a passive participant. After all, *they* don't know what to do—that's why they have come to us! We might tell them that therapy is like exercise: Athletes who really invest themselves in their exercises do better than those who do them half-heartedly. We might self-disclose (within appropriate limits, of course). Sometimes self-disclosure can create a climate in which the clients take the chance to become more actively involved. We might talk with them about things that do involve them and gradually segue the conversation over to personal matters (almost everything ulti-mately connects to personal matters). We might try all the various things experiential therapists do to get clients emotionally involved (see Greenberg et al., 1993; Mahrer, 1996, for examples). We might provide a lot of structure and follow our agenda, taking the "doctor" role that they seem to want us to take, and hope that eventually they will get involved. Or we might simply stay with them, work within their frame of reference, and be patient. We have found that such clients are learning nonetheless (they are active at a covert level) and that, with time, they usually become more involved.

Q: I work with severely disturbed clients. You are not saying that people with schizophrenia and borderline personality disorder can self-heal on their own, are you?

A: Yes, in fact we do believe people with schizophrenia and borderline personality disorder have as much self-healing potential as you do. They just face more difficult and complex problems. Some do manage to self-heal and self-right on their own, if by that we mean that they gradually achieve reasonably workable accommodations to life. Do they turn into exemplars of mentally healthy, fully self-actualized people? Probably not. Are we? Are you? The point is that some improve their lives, although they still have problems.

In terms of therapy, we still view the clients as active strugglers, trying to make their life work as best they can, trying to bring some order into it, trying to solve problems and get their needs met. We see them as actively thinking and creatively trying things out (albeit sometimes dysfunctionally). We want to join with them rather than work on them. We have particularly found empathic listening to be welcome with such clients. This population can be very active. In addition, they may well need other things, such as skills training (Linehan, 1993) and social interventions (Teusch, 1990) to help them create more livable lives.

Q: What is your stand on medication? What about clients who have biologically based problems, such as schizophrenia, attention deficit disorder, or bipolar affective disorder?

A: Our stand on medication is simple: If medications are available and helpful, why shouldn't clients use them? If a person has a problem with a biological component and can be helped by medication, so much the better. At the same time, psychotherapy could be used to help the person use his or her resources to cope optimally with the problem. However, we are opposed to the current paternalistic attitude that medications are the "treatment of choice" in many instances, such as for depression, and that therapists are therefore supposed to encourage or even order clients to get such medication. People should have freedom of choice in their treatment. Forcing a client to take medication also interferes with the therapist–client relationship.

We view biologically based psychological disorders like we view any other biologically based disorder. A biologically based problem is a problem for the client as active self-healer to struggle with and to live with and to work around. There is a person "there" inside the schizophrenic person trying to make a livable life, struggling with whatever demons are foisted upon him or her by biology. This is not different from a person struggling to make a livable life who has been paralyzed in an automobile accident, or who has multiple sclerosis or any other major disease. We help the proactive, self-righting person cope as best he or she can with his or her biology. People often show incredible resilience in overcoming even severe neurological disorders, as Oliver Sacks has observed (see chapter 3). We work with their potential for resilience.

Q: You have based your argument in part on the dodo bird verdict that all therapies work about the same for different disorders. What if it turns out that some specific treatments really do work better for different disorders?

A: Our argument is in part derived from the dodo bird verdict, but whatever truth our point of view possesses does not rest on it. We think the idea that the client's active self-healing potential is so strong that it overwhelms differences in treatments is one explanation for the dodo bird findings. However, we would hope that by learning more about how clients self-heal, we are able to come up with more specifically helpful things to do. In other words, if we are right, we would hope that eventually we do come up with procedures that contradict the dodo bird verdict. There are probably a few already.

Q: Your model of therapy rests heavily on the idea of dialogue and collaboration. But there are some teenagers who are so out of control that the efforts of parents, teachers, and counselors to dialogue with them have been to no avail. What has seemed to work with some of them is to get tough. The tough-love approach is one example. Another is to send them away to special schools where discipline is strictly enforced. Many kids will "shape up" in such environments. Similar programs have been used with substance abusers. Yet that seems almost completely antithetical to your point of view.

A: That is a complicated topic, and there is no easy answer. First, practically, we believe that if all else has failed, then we have to be open to anything that will work, regardless of philosophical biases. Second, the fact that such programs can work does not contradict the idea that the client is an active self-healer. In fact, even these approaches will work only if ultimately they engage the client. However, it is true that such approaches are based neither on collaborative dialogue nor on trusting clients' wisdom, at least initially.

Some clients are so entrenched in their dysfunctional behavior patterns that they may need the radical challenge of a completely different structured environment to mobilize their self-healing resources. What is common to programs in which individuals go away somewhere and live for several months while they are in the program or in which they are intensively involved in a program on a daily basis is that the individuals are presented with a consistently different environment than they have had to cope with before. In a behavioristic sense, this environment supports a whole new set of behaviors, and clients must adjust to that environment to survive. As they do this, they begin to access more proactive and prosocial parts of themselves. It is interesting, in terms of our point of view, that many teenagers and substance abusers who are helped by these approaches ultimately do feel empowered by them. They feel that they have developed discipline, direction, and goals, not that they have been shaped into anything by an outside force. It is more accurate to say they have been challenged into this.

The issue is really one of setting limits. Effective limit setting is a way of providing healthy challenges to individuals' capacities for taking the initiative to find more proactive ways of coping. Life essentially is a process of coping with limits. A person paralyzed in an automobile accident has had a limit imposed that he or she must cope with. He or she must learn to deal with the limit in a creative and productive way. Good parents set limits for their children while respecting and promoting their initiative and intelligence. Tough-love approaches set tough limits, but they work (when they work) because they are fair and provide a healthy challenge to the teenager.

How to set limits effectively so that they promote and support individuals' natural tendencies to self-right and self-heal, yet get them to move in a proactive direction, is complex. We can only hint at it here. On the basis of research on parental discipline practices (Hoffman, in press; Mussen & Eisenberg, in press), sheer power assertion (i.e., coercion, intimidation, control through fear and punishment) is not effective. Power assertion in the form of setting limits needs to be accompanied by equity and logic. Tough-love procedures work when clear—consequences are clearly specified and applied impartially and fairly, even though they are tough. If you follow the rules, you have certain rights and privileges. If you do not, you do not get those rights and privileges. Paradoxically, these approaches may empower teenagers because they ultimately put responsibility in the hands of the teenager: either get home on time or be locked out, either behave or go to jail where no one will bail you out, either follow the rules of the school or lose your privileges. These rules make very clear that the power ultimately lies in the teenagers' hands as to what happens to them. Thus, there is nothing inherently contradictory between believing in limit setting and believing in individuals' self-healing potential. The issue is more how limits are set than that limits are set and if contingencies are equitable and fair. In some of these programs, at least as reported on television, the setting of limits sometimes has verged on the use of intimidation and coercion. We find this disturbing. Consistent with our view, however, it is interesting that many teens, even in programs such as these latter ones, seem to be able to self-heal and self-right. At the same time, we prefer a more dialogical approach, even with children and addicts, unless setting tough limits with consequences is required as a last resort. W. R. Miller and Rollnick (1991) showed that empathy-based approaches can work with addicts.

Q: You've been critical of the medical model. But I work with clients with schizophrenia who hear voices and suffer from various disabling delusions. I've also worked with people with bipolar affective disorder who, in the manic phase, do self-destructive things such as spend all the family's money buying cars they cannot afford. And then there are people with obsessive–compulsive disorder who are disabled by their rituals, and panic-disordered people who cannot leave their houses. Yet you don't think these things are disorders that need treatment?

A: The medical model consists of two components: its view of psychological problems (as *DSM* disorders) and its view of psychotherapy. We are far more concerned with its impact on psychotherapy practice.

Even if we were to think of psychological problems as disorders, therapy practice is still fundamentally different from medical practice. It is still primarily an educational enterprise and must rest heavily on the client's own investment and involvement. Medications will work whether or not the rationale for them makes sense to the client. Psychotherapy does not work without the active, thoughtful collaboration of the client, mainly because there really is not any "drug" or "treatment" that is operating on the person. The client's own active efforts to understand, the client's own ideas, and the client's own efforts to find and create meaning and coherence in life are really what makes the processes work. Therapists need to join up with these client processes and work in tandem with them. Even when we work with people with obsessive–compulsive disorder, or borderline personality disorder, or schizophrenia, we adopt a fundamentally different relationship to them than we would if we were their physician prescribing medication (or any other kind of treatment) for them.

The idea that a psychological problem is best conceived of as a disorder is an extension of ideas from medicine into psychology. It may or may not be a useful way to conceptualize psychological problems. The disorder idea in medicine assumes that there is something that is disrupting the integrity and functioning of the body. Similarly, to say that someone with a psychological problem has a disorder is to assume that something is disrupting what would otherwise be the person's normal functioning. The goal then becomes to remove the disorder. Many other ways of conceiving of psychological problems have been proposed by behaviorists, family systems theorists, and humanistic psychologists over the years. Calling something a disorder is a way of conceptualizing it. At the present time, the disorder view has become predominant, but primarily because agencies that pay for psychotherapy think in medical-model, *DSM* terms, not because research has proved it to be the superior way. Certain things may well turn out to best be conceptualized as disorders, especially ones that have a biological component. On the other hand, many of the things people bring into therapy do not fit the disorder concept very well, in our opinion.

Q: You keep talking about psychotherapy as helping clients "solve problems." Yet we do not see psychotherapy as problem solving, but rather as helping clients grow, develop, become more authentic, and become more psychologically sound individuals.

A: Most clients come into therapy to "puzzle solve" about problems in their lives. Some therapy theories propose that puzzle solving is not the issue; broader and deeper issues of personal change and growth are. When we talk about problem solving, we conceive of it broadly. It merely means that clients come into therapy to move forward, to achieve something they have not achieved in the past. People struggling with how to integrate early childhood experiences or how to be more themselves are problem solving in a broad sense of the term as much as people trying to figure out how to best discipline their children.

CONCLUSION

In this chapter, we considered a variety of issues related to practice from our perspective. We made the following points:

- There are multiple reasons for resistance. Therapists should try to understand the implicit proactivity in client resistance and look for solutions that respect the client's frame of reference.
- Assessment that focuses on characteristics of the client and the client's life—such as aspects of the client's personality, the stage of change the client is in, or the forces interfering with client self-healing—is more helpful than *DSM* diagnoses to facilitate client self-healing in a collaborative therapeutic relationship.
- Several aspects of the field of psychotherapy interfere with therapists adopting a proactive model of the client as self-healer. First, the therapist is the expert on the client rather than an expert on what kinds of procedures may help clients

mobilize their self-healing potential. Second, a negative attitude toward clients is promoted by some of the field's theoretical constructs. Third, many of the ways we construe therapy disempower the client. Fourth, we are trained to privilege the therapist's frame of reference over the client's frame of reference.

- We considered objections to our viewpoint, such as that some clients have too serious problems to self-heal, some problems include biological components, and some clients do not act like self-healing agents.

IV

CONCLUSION

11

IMPLICATIONS FOR THE PROFESSION
OF CLINICAL PSYCHOLOGY

The idea that the client provides the primary healing force in therapy has implications for psychotherapy integration, research, training, and practice in clinical psychology. In addition, it raises issues such as how one believes in the client as active self-healer and still practices in a system in which one has to follow the medical model? In this chapter, we consider these implications and issues.

IMPLICATIONS FOR THE INTEGRATION OF PSYCHOTHERAPY

The psychotherapy integration movement is based on the idea that each different therapy has something to offer. This has both theoretical and practical implications. At the theory level, this has led to a search for underlying common factors that exist in each approach. It has also led to a search for one ultimate "megatheory" of psychotherapy. At the practice level, different systems have been developed for integrating the procedural contributions of different approaches. We consider each of these areas.

Theoretical Issues: Common Factors and the Search for a Megatheory

Our whole book is based on the idea that the most important common factor in therapy is the client. The client is also the ultimate integrative therapist (H. Arkowitz, personal communication, April 1993; Gold, 1994). Different therapies emphasize fixing different aspects of human functioning. They all can work because the human being is an interconnected whole. Working in one area of a person's functioning can cause ripples affecting other areas. For instance, a client who explores the past in psychoanalysis may also change dysfunctional cognitions, learn to trust feelings, liberate creativity, and engage in self-generated exposure. A client who challenges dysfunctional cognitions may spontaneously develop more acceptance and access to feelings and work through related aspects of past conflicts. All of this may be going on while the client is also being an informal community psychologist or family systems theorist—integrating what he or she is learning in therapy into his or her life space.

Not all clients will explicitly incorporate aspects of all therapies. Yet if the person is a system embedded in larger systems, then changes in one part of the system will often reverberate and change other parts. Each approach will emphasize a different aspect, but each will have the potential to affect other aspects implicitly embedded in the person's life system. It will not be necessary for each therapy to deal with all aspects of the person because, as a whole person, the client will ultimately make whatever changes are needed.

Consider two apparently disparate therapy approaches for panic disorder: cognitive–behavioral therapy and client-centered therapy. Their philosophies and methods are about as different as they could be. Yet there is an interesting convergence in their views of what the client needs to learn to stop having panic attacks. Cognitive–behavioral therapies (e.g., Barlow, 1988) assume that panic is primarily a *fear of fear*: Clients have one attack of panicky symptoms and then become fearful. They either worry that they are going to have another panic attack at an inopportune moment or that they are having a heart attack. They cope with this fear by self-observing in a fearful and vigilant manner. They become highly sensitized to internal cues that might signal the onset of the feared event. What clients need to learn in cognitive–behavioral therapy is that these internal cues are not signals of something dangerous. They do this primarily through exposure and cognitive restructuring of their exaggerated or distorted thoughts.

For client-centered therapy, problems arise from the manner in which the person relates to him- or herself. He or she has learned from childhood experiences with judgmental parents that internal experience is not to be trusted. He or she comes to view his or her own self and experience critically. He or she therefore has developed a proneness to be vigilant toward inner experience, looking for signs of danger in it. Panic attacks would be one manifestation of this more generalized lack of self-trust and self-acceptance. What clients learn in client-centered therapy is a different manner of relating to their experience: one of acceptance, observation, and empathic listening, that is, that their inner experience is not dangerous. They further learn a process-focused way of living (see chapter 7), that is, to explore experience to see what it means rather than jump to premature conclusions about potential outcomes (e.g., having a panic attack or a heart attack). Therapists foster this through creation of a safe, process-focused empathic atmosphere. They carefully listen to the client's exploration of experience, and they support and model an acceptant, noncatastrophizing manner of self-relating. This leads to clients' learning to proactively explore whatever problems they may be having. They gradually approach fears, try behavioral experiments on their own ("Maybe going out to a sporting event is worth taking the chance of having a panic attack—I won't die from it"), and eventually discover that their desire to live a fulfilling life is more important than their fears. They also learn that their experience is not intrinsically dangerous or bad, and stop critically overobserving it.

In cognitive–behavioral therapy for panic disorder, the goal is specific: Learn to stop fearfully overreacting to internal cues, and learn to stop thinking catastrophically about the feared events. In client-centered therapy, the goal is more general: Adopt a different manner of relating to the self. The kinds of changes clients report might be compatible with whatever therapy they were in. Clients in cognitive–behavioral therapy might say they have stopped catastrophizing about specific feared events and have stopped misinterpreting internal experience. Clients in client-centered therapy might say they have "become more themselves."

But clients in cognitive–behavioral therapy might say if asked that they feel they have "become more themselves" as well, and clients in client-centered therapy might say "I'm not sure how it happened, but I just trust myself more now—if my heart starts to pound I don't get so frightened of it." In other words, each may be making some of the learnings and discoveries emphasized by the other approach.

We therefore think of each therapy as a different tool, or set of tools. These different tools may actually have different specific immediate effects. Cognitive therapy may really change dysfunctional cognitions. Psychoanalysis may really produce insights into transference. Experiential therapies may really produce changes in manner of self-relating. But clients take these different changes and use them to change their lives. It might look like all the therapies work about the same, when in fact they really do produce specific effects.

Thus we have an apparent paradox. In chapter 2 we argued that the evidence does not support the idea of differential effects of different therapies. But there we were talking at the level of global outcome. There is little evidence, for instance, that one approach to therapy is differentially more effective with depression than another approach. However, it is possible that different therapies do produce different specific effects, but that clients, who are holistic agents, are able to take the specific effects produced by whatever therapy they are in and use those specific effects to overcome their depression. Thus, therapies could have differentially specific effects at the level of immediate impact but not at the level of global outcome.

If this is true, then the search for one "megatheory" of psychotherapy at the present time may be premature. Different theories emphasize different aspects of the client, and each may provide a different route toward personal development. As such, the unique insights of each needs to be preserved. At some time in the distant future, someone will be able to come up with a theory that both preserves the unique insights of each approach while integrating them together. But until we know more about how different aspects of human functioning are weighted and fit together, it is unlikely that any one theory will be able to present itself as *the* truly integrative one (Bohart, 1992). If there is any one candidate on the horizon, personality theorists have suggested that it will most likely be a systems conception (Emmons, 1993). We do not think an integrated theory is necessarily desirable anyway because different people seem to resonate with different paths toward personal growth (Stiles, Shapiro, & Elliott, 1986).

Practical Issues: Technical Eclecticism

Technical eclecticism is the idea that the therapist will use "whatever works." Studies have found that 30% to 40% of therapists in practice are eclectic (Norcross, 1986). Our experience training graduate students is commensurate with this. Graduate student therapists want help with specific client problems. They may operate from one theoretical bias, but they do not care where they get helpful ideas for what they do.

We argued in chapter 9 that choosing just the right technique at the right time may frequently not be that important. Because clients can creatively use what they learn from techniques, there will be no simple one-to-one relationship between an intervention and its ultimate effects. Arkowitz (1997a) reported using a cognitive self-help book to teach a self-help class on alleviating depression. The participants scored as clinically depressed on various measures. He found that some of the class members seemed to get better even if they did not follow the exercises. This suggests that it was not the specific exercises so much as the more generalized opportunity to confront problems, explore them, and think about them that ultimately led to change, at least for some participants.

On the other hand, clients have different personalities and, we suspect, learning styles, and different approaches may be differentially appealing to them. We agree with writers like Beutler and Clarkin (1990), who did not believe that trying to pick the right procedure for a specific diagnosis is as useful as trying to figure out what approaches and procedures an individual client will be best able to use. Some clients might be more amenable to nondirective approaches, others to more directive approaches. Some might be more attracted to action-oriented behavioral approaches, others to introspective, thoughtful, self-reflective approaches. Some clients might prefer one at one stage in therapy and another at another stage (Gold, 1994; Prochaska, 1995). Gendlin's (1969) original research on experiencing found that only those clients who related to their experience in a self-empathic, open way benefitted from the open-ended dialogical atmosphere of traditional client-centered therapy. He suggested that others might need more action-oriented strategies. Another useful system that tries to differentially match client with approach has been developed by Lazarus (1981). His system is based on assessing areas of client functioning, such as behavior or affect, and matching strategies to area of intervention.

IMPLICATIONS FOR RESEARCH ON PSYCHOTHERAPY

The main research implication of the idea that the client is the major generator of change in therapy is that we need to learn far more about how clients implement change (Arkowitz, 1997b). Our models have been so therapist driven that the bulk of the research is on what therapists do in therapy. We only know a little about how clients actually experience therapy on a moment-to-moment basis. We also know very little about how clients use therapy in their everyday lives. Yet clients routinely report creative leaps from what they have learned in therapy. We gave the case of Margaret in the introductory chapter, a woman diagnosed as a paranoid schizophrenic, who spontaneously developed the idea of helping a coworker who was feeling "paranoid," which led her to generally develop better social relationships. Another client, Scott, complained for weeks about his boss' indifference and lack of supervision and guidance. The therapist well-meaningly suggested talking to the boss about the problem. Scott totally rejected this suggestion. The therapist empathically listened to and came to understand Scott's reasons for not wanting to openly discuss the issue with the boss. Subsequently, Scott found a creative solution: He struck up a conversation with the boss about their mutual interest in art. This led to a positive shift in their relationship.

More knowledge is needed about (a) the contextual factors that contribute to the maintainance of client problems, (b) the contextual factors that inhibit or facilitate self-healing, (c) how clients implement what they learn in therapy, and (d) how clients creatively develop what they learn in therapy. Knowing more about assessing what clients think their problems are, what makes sense to them in terms of their frame of reference, what they prefer as a way of changing, and what their learning styles are may help therapists more effectively help them.

In particular, we know very little about *how* to help clients help themselves. As we have noted, some clients may only need and do better with a therapist who primarily listens; other clients may do better with some kind of structured regimen or protocol. In our experience, this does not vary as a function of diagnosis or problem. We have known clients who can self-heal from depression or trauma with an empathic listening therapist, whereas others wanted and needed a structured learning approach, in which they were given specific guidance. What was the difference? We are not sure, other than the reactance dimension discussed by Beutler et al. (1991). We do not even believe that clients higher in self-efficacy were the ones who did better solving problems on their own in a more nondirective approach. Some of our clients, apparently feeling low in self-efficacy or feeling helpless, have flourished in a relatively nondirective setting, whereas others, apparently higher in self-efficacy, have wanted and preferred more structure. We need much more specific knowledge about which clients, with what characteristics, will differentially learn and flourish better in different types of learning environments, such as the ones we described in chapter 5. These include learning environments that are primarily nondirective, structured but oriented primarily toward creativity and discovery, or structured and oriented primarily toward modification of emotion and behavior and the teaching of skills.

There are two implications of the idea that the client is an active self-healer that go against research trends in the field. First, the *events* approach to psychotherapy research is based on the idea that it is significant events in therapy that cause change (Mahrer, 1988; Rice & Greenberg, 1984). Researchers study events such as the expression of emotion (Mahrer, Lawson, Stalikas, & Schachter, 1990), insight (R. Elliott, 1984), experiencing (Mathieu-Coughlan & Klein, 1984), or the use of procedures like the two-chair technique (Greenberg, 1984), and they attempt to link these events up to therapy outcome. This is certainly valuable and much has been learned. Indeed, it is highly likely that significant events in therapy often do contribute to overall outcome. However, most therapists we know have had clients who show no strong emotion, do not seem to gain insight, do not seem to experience, may not get into challenging their dysfunctional cognitions, or resist doing their behavioral homework assignments, and yet they still change.

Because clients are active self-healers, it is not necessarily the case that it is specific events in therapy that cause change. We can envision an active client who goes to therapy week after week, does not do any of the things therapists think are supposed to make change happen, but who is observing, thinking, and experiencing anyway. He or she synthesizes from hours and hours of therapy what he or she needs to change. There will be no specific events that precipitate change. This is why, we believe, clients often say it is the *climate* in therapy that is helpful more so than specific techniques or procedures (see chapter 2). The lessons they learn may be the lessons they have taught themselves from these hours and hours of therapy, as they experimented and thought in their everyday lives, as well as in therapy. This suggests that it may be factors like the model the therapy situation provides for dealing with problems that may sometimes be most helpful. Even when it is specific events that are helpful, it may be specific events as idiosyncratically perceived and experienced by clients, rather than what "objectively" happened. There is some evidence that what clients remember as significant events bears little resemblance to what therapists or outside observers think are the important events in therapy (R. Elliott & James, 1989; Yalom & Elkin, 1974).

We do not denigrate this research tradition. Much of value has been learned from it. In many cases, significant events in therapy are important. The problem is that this strategy is based on the typical assumption that therapy is what therapists do. If clients are the most important "therapists," then we need to turn our wheels around and study the idiosyncratic pathways to change that clients create, especially the cases in which change is created by breaking the rules of good therapy.

Randomized Controlled Clinical Trials

The idea of the client as the major precipitator of change flies in the face of the currently most popular research strategy, that of the randomized controlled clinical trial. Many, besides ourselves, are critical of this design (Goldfried & Wolfe, 1996; Greenberg, 1991; D. A. Shapiro, 1996; Wolfe, 1994). The randomized controlled clinical trial, as described in its current form by its advocates (e.g., Task Force on Promotion and Dissemination of Psychological Procedures, 1995), is a design in which a manualized treatment is provided for a specific disorder (preferably identified in DSM terms). In addition, outcome is measured in a standardized form, specifically as symptom reduction, and the amount of change is compared across therapy groups and control groups. This design is a thorough-going embodiment of the medical model in psychotherapy. The goal is to treat disorder, and the assumption is that it is the specific treatment that alleviates the disorder. One tries to demonstrate a specific, linear causal relationship between a specific treatment and a specific outcome, just as one tries to demonstrate that a specific medication has a specific effect in medicine. A key assumption is that the "force" of change lies in the independent variable (the treatment) rather than in the dependent variable (the client).

However, if causal force primarily resides in clients and in how they use techniques and procedures, or if causal relationships between therapist interventions and client outcomes are complex and nonlinear (as many believe, e.g., Greenberg, 1991; Stiles & Shapiro, 1989), then this design is a limited one for learning about how people change. Its use may primarily be for global demonstrations of therapeutic effectiveness to outside agencies (Wolfe, 1994).

To force therapies to "empirically validate" themselves using this design (e.g., Task Force on Promotion and Dissemination of Psychological Procedures, 1995) is to force many therapies, especially therapies that more explicitly rely on client self-healing, to try to fit themselves into a research design that distorts rather than illuminates (Bohart, O'Hara, & Leitner, 1998). It reminds us of the sisters in *Cinderella* cutting off parts of their feet to try to fit into the glass slipper. Furthermore, it ipso facto presents a distorted picture of therapy because it demands that therapy look like the medical model. All the complexities about psychotherapy and personal change that do not fit within this model, such as other possible outcomes, or how therapy functions as a complex interactive process, are eliminated by this reductive research model. This research model should not be abandoned, but it should be only one of many for evaluating the helpfulness of psychotherapy.

In summary, if the idea that the client is the major healing force in therapy were taken seriously, we would have less research done in which randomized controlled clinical trials are used to compare one approach to therapy with another for a specific disorder. More research would be done looking at idiosyncratic client pathways to change. Eventually this would recycle into the development of more effective and helpful therapies. Next we look at manualization and the recent move to empirically validated treatments in more detail.

Manualization

At the present time there is much talk, pro and con, about the manualization of psychotherapy. Manualization was originally developed to meet the needs of researchers who wanted to assure standardized practice for purposes of experimental control using the randomized controlled clinical trial methodology. However, it has since been argued that practice itself should be manualized (e.g., Task Force on Promotion and Dissemination of Psychological Procedures, 1995). One might expect that we would be opposed to manuals, and that is partially true. We do not really believe manuals can specify therapy practice with the degree of precision that some researchers think they are achieving by manualizing. At best, even with the most well-spelled-out cognitive–behavioral manuals, manuals provide only a loose framework, a scaffolding if you will, which then must be fleshed out by the active, synthetic efforts of the therapist dealing with particular clients. We also do not believe that it is even meaningful to talk about manualizing an intelligent conversation between two sentient beings.

However, manuals can be useful if they are taken for what they are:

loose guidelines, or generalized platforms for therapeutic operation. Furthermore, it is more meaningful to talk about manualizing *procedures* than it is to talk about manualizing *therapy*. If one is going to use a cognitive–behavioral procedure for panic, one should probably study a manual for its use and apply it accordingly, although one should be on the alert for when a creative deviation from the manual is called for. However, procedures are not therapy. Therapy is the empathic meeting of minds within which procedures are used and that should not be manualized precisely in order that the therapist and client together be able to intelligently converse and engage in creative problem solving when required.

Requiring manualization for research purposes, however, only makes sense if therapy really is akin to a medication that can be applied to a disorder, and where causality can be assessed in a simple, linear causal way. Many have argued that this is really not an appropriate model for the complex, nonlinear, recursive, interactive process that characterizes something which involves dialogue between two intelligent beings.

There is also the question of how meaningful it is to adhere to a manual, and how meaningful manuals really are in capturing the healing processes in therapy. Barlow (1996) argued that there is some evidence that for the relatively straightforward, linear treatment packages used in some cognitive–behavioral treatments, adhering to the manual has been shown to be better than therapist flexibility. However, these approaches lend themselves to manualizability more so than some other approaches and really can be applied in a kind of systematic, linear fashion. It would not be surprising that deviation here might be more dysfunctional than functional. On the other hand, manualization of more complex forms of psychotherapy, such as brief dynamic therapy, does not function in the same way. Strupp and Anderson (1997), Anderson (1997), and Binder (1993) pointed out that important components of treatment simply are unmanualizable. Even in following the manual to the letter, therapists can be differentially effective depending on their own individual sensitivity and creativity, and therapists who mechanistically adhere to the manual do not do as well as those who are more flexible.

An analogy might help. There are innumerable cases in real life in which going "by the book" has been counterproductive. In war there have been many "manuals" written over the years. Equally, there have been many cases in which an innovative general breaks the mold and defeats the army that goes by the book. There are many other examples, such as "treatment plans" for a football game that have to be abandoned in the middle of the first quarter because the game is going in a totally unexpected way, and so on. Even in medicine, anyone who has watched the television series *ER* knows that crisis work cannot be manualized in any traditional sense. One must be able to flexibly and innovatively respond in the moment to unexpected contingencies. In so doing, one may use proceduralized knowledge, but it is also obvious that frequently what to do is not clear. The individual physician's clinical judgment is not only useful but also the only real basis for proceeding.

In working with an intelligent other, whose contributions are the primary reason the process works at all, rigid adherence to a manual would seem to be the antithesis of what is needed. The manual becomes the "driver" of therapy, not the intelligence of the two parties involved. Manuals should be aids that are used flexibly and intelligently, not cookbook recipes. Manuals, ultimately, are useful jumping-off places, good bases to work from under many circumstances, but places to leave and improvise from when necessary. No matter how specific a manual is, actual moment-by-moment behavior in the real world is more specific, detailed, and varied and not totally specifiable by any manual.

Empirically Validated Treatments

Driven by managed care and the enterprise of developing guidelines for therapeutic treatment, there has been an increased interest in developing lists of therapies that have been empirically shown to work for specific disorders, using the criteria of the randomized controlled clinical trial methodology described earlier. Books are beginning to appear with regularity on topics such as "what works for whom" (e.g., Roth & Fonagy, 1996). Most of these books fall within the medical model and follow the assumption that therapy is a business of choosing specific treatments to alleviate specific disorders. A task force of Division 12 of the American Psychological Association has, in this tradition, developed a list of so-called empirically validated treatments (Task Force on Promotion and Dissemination of Psychological Procedures, 1995).

From the standpoint of the client as an active self-healer, this movement is unfortunate. There is nothing wrong with identifying treatments that are helpful for symptom reduction with specific disorders. This can be useful, although the research these conclusions are based on has problems (Seligman, 1995; Wampold, 1997). What is unfortunate about it is that many advocates of this approach wish to equate all therapeutic efficacy with their reductive definition. It has been argued, for instance, that earlier psychotherapy research is out of date because it did not use the twin criteria of manualization and specification of treatment for disorder. This leads to the disenfranchisement of psychotherapies for which there is evidence of effectiveness, but not under the managed-care-driven empirically validated treatments criteria.

For instance, there is considerable evidence for the helpfulness of client-centered therapy (R. Elliott, 1996). Yet client-centered therapy is not included in the empirically validated treatments list, because it is not a treatment for a disorder, it has not been so studied, and most studies were not specifically manualized. But client-centered therapy is not properly conceived of as a treatment for a disorder. The empirically validated treatments criteria make sense only if one thinks about therapy from within the framework of the medical model. If therapy is not a matter of applying a *treatment* to a *disorder*, then neither manualization nor being specific about the disorder being treated makes any sense. If, for instance, therapy is not treatment at all, but rather a consultative relationship between two intelligent beings in which they mutually decide on their course of action (and that course of action may change over time as a product of their ongoing mutual collaboration), then it makes no sense to manualize (except in a very general sense as a statement of principles) or even to say that a specific treatment is being applied to a disorder. In fact, in such a process, there simply is no standardized "independent variable" that is being applied to a dependent variable.

We believe that therapy should be research *based*. However, being research based can mean many things. For instance, Grawe (1997), in his presidential address to the Society for Psychotherapy Research, presented a model for *research-informed* therapeutic practice that is compatible with what we have been arguing for in this book. (In fact, one of Grawe's common factors is client activity and agency.) This model relies on using various evidence-based common factors in therapy, rather than on a treatment-by-disorder framework. As such, therapists who practice from a wide range of perspectives, but who honor Grawe's research-informed principles in so doing, could be said to be practicing in an evidence-based fashion. Similarly, it has been argued that any therapy that is based on providing a good therapeutic relationship and respecting and working with client agency and involvement is research based (Bohart et al., 1998), for reasons we have documented in this book.

We do not object to the procedures themselves that are provided in the list of empirically validated treatments. We actually agree with the recommendations of this task force that clinicians should be familiar with these treatments and be willing to offer them to clients if appropriate. However, we do not believe that it is the prerogative of the clinician to unilaterally select a treatment for a client and then apply it to a client from a list of empirically validated treatments. Instead, we believe the possibility that clients might want to choose their own treatment and work with it in their own way must always be on the forefront of the clinician's mind. Clients should be given the chance to make a choice. They should be told, for instance, if it might seem to matter to them, that panic disorder can be "treated" with an empirically validated symptom-oriented approach, which has been shown to be quite effective in the limited sense of symptom reduction. Or they might prefer a more open-ended discovery-oriented approach, which may have not been specifically "validated" for panic disorder but which has been shown to be helpful in a general sense, and which is more likely to offer the client the opportunity for self-change at a deeper level, a level that some theorists of panic disorder have argued is really of more primary importance (e.g., Wolfe, 1992). Clients should be involved as full co-participants in selecting treatment. Furthermore, even if an empirically validated treatment is selected, it can be applied in a way compatible with our client-as-self-healer metamodel. That means that, once again, clients can be involved as full co-participants, not merely in the form of actively complying with treatment and practicing the interventions, but in the planning and creating sense.

PRACTICE IMPLICATIONS

In this section, we consider some of the implications for professional practice. We first look at the implications for the development of new therapeutic strategies. Then we look at implications for practicing in a world dominated by the medical model. After that, we consider self-help. Finally, we conclude with a discussion of implications for working with involuntary clients.

Implications for the Development of New Therapeutic Strategies

Most of the efforts in development of new therapeutic strategies have been focused on developing new techniques to have a certain effect, or to solve a certain problem, or on new therapeutic approaches. Therapists now have a vast armamentarium of techniques and over 400 different approaches to therapy, with no noticeable quantum leap forward in effectiveness. This is actually not surprising, because the research shows that the two most important variables in effective therapy are client involvement and the therapeutic relationship. The key variables appear to be the ability of therapists to establish a relationship with clients, reach them, and get them to open up and invest their energies in the therapy process. If this is so, then therapists have been devoting their energies in the wrong place. Because these variables seem to be more important than techniques, therapists need to learn more about how to do these things. For the most part, this has been quite neglected, primarily because it is generally seen only as preliminary to the "real" part of therapy—the implementation of the techniques and operations. Yet, not unlike foreplay in sex (sorry—one of us *is* a sex therapist!), without effective preliminaries, what comes later will not work.

Perhaps learning more about how to effectively dialogue with clients will be a start. As therapists, we need to learn more about effective listening and how to train it. We also need to learn more about how to respond in ways that promote and carry forward effective and productive dialogue.

Neimeyer (1996), writing from a constructivist point of view, made one attempt. He identified some of the dialogical things he does that seem to promote intelligent conversations (although he does not call them that). Some of these include (a) accentuating, in which the therapist focuses attention on some important aspect of experience that might otherwise be overlooked; (b) contrasting, in which therapist and client explore a conflict or discrepancy in the client's experience; and (c) weaving, in which the therapist tries to connect strands of related material. It is important to note that these are things that most therapists in particular and good conversationalists in general do intuitively. What is valuable in Neimeyer's work is his identification of them so that we might learn more about them and become more skilled in their use. Becoming more skilled in conversational arts may be one of the major things therapists can do to further their ability to be helpful to clients.

In particular, we view the client's entering into a process-focused state of mind (see chapter 7) as the "gatekeeper" to helpful therapy. If clients are too demoralized, or feel too threatened, they may be so self-critical or defensive that they are unable to enter into the "working" state of mind in which their attention is on the process of learning rather than on the outcome of learning or on self-evaluation. Getting the client "involved" means, among other things, supporting the client if the client is able to enter into this working state of mind, or helping the client get into this state of mind. We discussed ideas for how to do this in chapter 7, but we need to know much more about how to help clients become productively engaged in the learning process that is therapy.

Training

Training implications follow from what we just said about the development of new therapeutic strategies. We need to shift the emphasis in training to dialogical skills and place a greater emphasis on empathy as a way of knowing (rather than as a way of establishing rapport for purposes of intervention). Training needs to help therapists develop more positive images of clients—images that focus on the clients' potential for health (Seligman, 1998) and proactivity, their capacities for positive adjustment even in the face of overwhelming numbers of strikes against them, and metaphors that let therapists see the wisdom in their clients' defensiveness, resistance, and dysfunctional behavior so that therapists can more effectively "join up" with them and create collaboration. Instead of images of therapy as fixing the client, training needs to use images of people working together to solve problems and to create win–win solutions. It would be nice if the images of clients that are taught increased the therapists' chances of liking clients and viewing them as collaborators rather than as adversaries.

The Medical Model

Throughout this book, we have used the medical model as the foil for our point of view. We do believe there are aspects of the medical model that can conflict with therapy practice that takes seriously the idea that clients are the primary source of healing. At the same time, the medical model has been of great benefit to both therapists and clients. In a society that respects medicine as much as American society does, clinical psychology's partnership with the medical model has legitimized psychotherapy and has allowed many clients to get help through health insurance. Furthermore, many clinicians find it useful to conceptualize client problems in *DSM* terms.

At the present time, the medical model seems to have achieved a kind of paradigmatic dominance, which means that in many settings if one wants to practice psychotherapy one is going to have to practice within it. In such contexts, it is the therapist's formal responsibility to choose treatment as the medical expert. The idea that the client and therapist would genuinely collaborate in deciding on a treatment plan would be rejected. In fact, there are now cases in which therapists are being held responsible to require some clients to seek medication, a most noncollaborative attitude. But can therapy be practiced from within a medical-model framework and still honor the idea of the client as an active self-healer? We believe it can. In fact, one of us, doing sex therapy in a urological setting, has regularly worked within the medical model. One can diagnose and "treat" and still honor the client's self-healing potential. It is a matter of how one does it. At the same time, the medical model can pose dangers for working with clients as active self-healers, particularly if one applies it in a paternalistic fashion.

First, one must realize that diagnosis is not inherently evil. It depends on how one uses it. If one views its functions largely as ones of classification, conceptualization, and communication, then diagnosis can be used for its heuristic value of communicating to third-party payers and to other mental health professionals. It can also be helpful for conceptualizing problems and focusing on treatment. If one views a diagnosis as a classification heuristic rather than a fact about the client, the diagnosis will not narrow attention to the client's deficiencies so that one overlooks the idiosyncratic nature of the client's experience and the client's self-healing potentialities. Therapists need to keep their eyes on the client, not on the *DSM* diagnosis. In addition to classification and communication, there are cases in which diagnoses can suggest a therapeutic approach that might be useful (Task Force on Promotion and Dissemination of Psychological Procedures, 1995).

Second, in a medical-model setting, although the therapist is ultimately responsible for the choice of treatment plan, this can still be decided on in a largely collaborative fashion with the client. Many therapists we know do just this. Such freedom may become limited if rigid application of the empirically validated treatments idea holds sway. Otherwise, therapists and clients can pretty much dialogue together and mutually decide on a treatment plan in most cases, as long as the therapist takes final responsibility for it.

Third, even in the medical model, diagnoses and treatment plans change over time when new contingencies arise. Therefore, therapists can continue to work collaboratively with clients. This means that the two together will creatively shape the emerging process of therapy to meet whatever new contingencies arise (just like in war, in football games, in relationships, in politics, or in most other human activities). At the formal level of note taking and writing treatment plans for managed-care agencies, the therapist will need to once again take responsibility for the shifts in treatment plan and provide a rationale, but the actual process can be a creatively collaborative one.

In fact, most good therapists we know of who practice in medical-model settings practice precisely like this. They view the medical-model aspects of diagnosis and treatment as parts of the job environment and work with them rather than against them. Some believe that the medical model aspects are helpful, but some do not. There may be occasional chaffing for some, but mostly these clinicians are able to function comfortably and ethically.

Even those who believe in the medical model, who believe that it is their job to decide for clients what their problems are and what appropriate treatment is, can still practice in a manner mostly compatible with the idea of the client as an active self-healer. The danger comes from the potential in the medical model to encourage and support paternalistic thinking, in which the therapist assumes he or she really does know better for the client. A physician can get away with paternalistic thinking, but a therapist, whose job it is to enlist the active thoughtful collaboration of the client, may well interfere with that goal if he or she treats the client paternalistically. Therapists can be prescriptive and directive if they do it in a collaborative, dialogical fashion, just as good teachers can be prescriptive and directive while teaching calculus, but still rely on the active intelligence of the student and still proceed dialogically.

A major casualty of paternalistic practice within the medical model can be client creativity and resourcefulness. Because the therapist chooses the treatment and applies it, unique and insightful contributions of the client could be overlooked. This may work fine in many cases. Paradoxically, because clients are so resilient, most of them may flourish under paternalistic application of the medical model, as they would under almost any other therapeutic model. But, on occasion, blinding practitioners to the creativity and resourcefulness of their clients will be harmful. This will be especially important when unique solutions are needed. With psychological therapies, in which the issues dealt with are the very issues of how the self relates to oneself, others, and the world, dialogical therapy in which the active intelligence of the client is an essential component would seem to be a must. Next, we consider aspects of the medical model in more detail.

DSM *Diagnosis*

We, along with many others (e.g., Beutler, 1989), do not believe that DSM diagnosis is a prerequisite to the provision of good therapy in many cases. At the same time, responsible diagnosis, especially when problems involve some kind of organic component, can be very important. However, from the standpoint of the client as an active self-healer, there are several problems that could potentially be created by focusing on DSM diagnoses if the therapist gets blinded by them. First, DSM diagnoses focus the therapist on symptom removal. This may be fine in some settings and may meet some clients' needs. However, a focus on symptom removal can blind the therapist to times when it might be better to help clients focus on proactive coping with life circumstances, as well as focus more on health and possibility (Seligman, 1998). The pathology focus that DSM encourages is limiting, because many of the problems people bring to therapy do not really fit the disorder concept. Having to think along pathological lines limits the therapist's ability to help people solve the problems in living that bring many to therapy. Second, believing in client self-healing makes clients' choices of treatment and their own preferred problem-solving strategies much more important than their diagnosis. Third, DSM diagnoses, medical-like in their form, say nothing about clients' experience of their problems, clients' frame of reference, or clients' values, goals, or life projects. Circumstances are not really taken into account either. Good therapists need not be blinded by this, but a DSM framework does not help therapists focus on things that we think are important if the client is an active self-healer.

In regard to this last point, DSM categories are crude, and the labels do not help empathically tune into the client's experience. DSM diagnoses can obscure rather than clarify the nature of problems people are struggling with. Therapy usually is much more specific than DSM diagnoses. Strategic therapists, for instance, might choose vastly different interventions for two depressed clients, depending on the particulars of each client's circumstances. Depression is often a response to life circumstances. Simply diagnosing it and treating it as a disease to be remedied misses the point that the client may need to deal with an important life issue, such as a crisis over personal values. Greening (1996) gave the example of a businessman who, at the peak of his success, became depressed because he did not find his success personally meaningful. Treating his depression as a pathogen to be removed, either psychologically or medically, misses the point that he was dealing with a crisis in values. In fact, in this particular instance, the man tried medication and then chose to forgo it because he preferred to be depressed and explore what that meant.

Treatment Plans

Treatment plans make sense within the medical model but do not necessarily make sense outside of it. They do not make sense for approaches that rely primarily on clients' self-discovery as the modality of change. It is difficult to imagine either Carl Rogers or Sigmund Freud writing and then following treatment plans. Both plans would probably say something like, "Listen! Listen! Listen!"

Treatment plans are neither philosophically "in paradigm" nor "out of paradigm" for us. Because our approach is a metamodel, it can be used either with those who prefer not to use treatment plans or with those who do use them. What is far more important than whether or not a treatment plan is used is whether it is used paternalistically or collaboratively.

Choice of Therapies

One of the problems with the medical model is that philosophically it sets the therapist up as the expert on the client. It then becomes the business of the more knowing expert to choose what is appropriate for the less knowing party, the client. It is precisely this belief, applied in a paternalistic fashion by some therapists, that has led to some of the more notorious abuses in recent years. The prime example is therapists unilaterally deciding, based on their beliefs, that clients have been sexually abused even though clients do not remember any such abuse. The therapist then tells clients they have been abused and that they must recover from and deal with the abuse if they are to be healed. If clients do not want to do this, but instead want to deal with issues they think are important in their own way, they are told they are in denial. The therapist then sets out to "recover" the memories—whether doing so fits the agenda of the client or not.

We do not believe that therapists' making unilateral choices for clients based on empirically validated treatments is much better. At least there are some data that these choices work for the carefully selected subpopulation of clients on which the studies were done. But therapists would still be making unilateral choices for clients based on the therapists' point of view, when clients are active self-healers and their intelligent participation in therapy should be included. Clients should have a choice of therapies, even ones that have not been empirically validated by the limited criteria of the Division 12 Task Force.

We need to recognize that therapies do different things. They are really alternative ways of achieving ultimately similar ends, not unlike different approaches to exercise or entertainment. Just as we would not expect everyone to like the same kind of music or movies, or to exercise in the same way, we should not expect everyone to prefer or be helped by the same kinds of therapy. Different therapies should not be compared with one another. Clients may want the different things the different therapies have to offer. Some clients with depression, for instance, may prefer to view it as an existential crisis and to approach it that way. Others may prefer to view it as a matter of lack of behavioral skills and dysfunctional cognitions and work with it that way. Still others may prefer to view it as having to do with various compromises and strategies of living that one has learned in early childhood.

In a truly liberated profession of therapy, clients would be given a choice of which way they would prefer to approach their problem. They would be given full knowledge of the different paths. We would strive for an educated clientele, and education would be seen as part of our profession. Even if the clients' problems fit a diagnosable *DSM* category, they would still have the right to make an informed choice of what kind of help they are given.

Self-Help

Arkowitz (1997a) pointed out one of the practical applications of the idea of client self-healing. Capitation is coming. Therapy providers will get a fixed amount of money and then be responsible to provide services as needed. This will put a premium on supplying services efficiently. Because many clients seem to be able to help themselves with self-help materials, this may become one way of doing this. Evidence has already suggested that computer-based therapy programs work about as well as seeing live therapists. Self-help procedures can be taught in a classroom format (Arkowitz, 1997a), and self-help or mutual support groups continue to provide comfort and guidance for millions (even for serious "disorders" like borderline personality disorder). It has even been pointed out that we are a nation of self-helpers (Seligman, 1994).

Computers are already changing the nature of therapy. Not only is therapy being provided over the Internet, but virtual reality also promises to provide training programs that, because of their vivid experiential quality, may turn out to be more effective than either in vivo exercises or imagination exercises (Glanz, Durlach, Barnett, & Aviles, 1996).

Types of Self-Help

There are a number of different forms of self-help. The three basic groupings are self-help books, computer-assisted self-help, and self-help groups. We shall not do a survey of self-help in this book. However, we shall make some brief comments. Self-help books can be divided into several categories. First, there are books that primarily seem to function by providing a general philosophical overview, with some general precepts for changing. Books like *Men Are From Mars, Women Are from Venus* (Gray, 1992) provide a general framework for viewing problems. If they help, it is probably by providing readers with an interpretive framework they may be able to use to understand what is happening to them. They also provide generalized prescriptions about what to do differently. Thus, a woman may be able to reassure herself, when confronted by some odd communication by her husband, that he is "from Mars." (We are not joking; we have run into women who do this.) This may permit her to be more allowing and accepting of him, less critical of him or of herself, and thus able to focus on other avenues to find workable solutions with him rather than blaming either him or herself. Whether a given individual can use this or not is probably quite idiosyncratic, and probably depends on where the person is in the change process (see Prochaska et al., 1994). Clients who are motivated and past the contemplation stage will probably be better able to use them. Another factor may be the individual's degree of demoralization and preexisting levels of self-efficacy. Those who already feel somewhat self-efficacious probably will be better able to use such books.

Other books provide specific exercises. Some are discovery-oriented exercises, more along the lines of psychodynamic and humanistic therapies (e.g., Gendlin, 1981; Mahrer, 1989). Such exercises may include exploring family life, feelings, dreams, relationships, and values. The belief is that an increase in self-awareness will promote self-healing. Once again, this is probably true to the extent that the individual (a) takes to such exercises and (b) is able to use them productively to change. We suspect that it is more introspective individuals who may find such exercises particularly useful.

Finally, still other books, primarily developed by cognitive–behaviorists, also provide specific exercises but are more action oriented. They include detailed instructions for specifically overcoming dysfunctional beliefs, changing behavior, setting goals, and so forth. Examples include Burns (1980), Greenberg and Padesky (1995), and Zilbergeld and Lazarus (1987). They focus far less on the explanatory aspect of self-healing, the narrative restorying, or perspective-shift aspects and far more on specific techniques and procedures for changing unwanted behaviors and emotions. Once again, such books will be helpful to the extent that the individual is able to implement what is in the book, use it to provide support for his or her own self-guided discovery-oriented activity, or "buy into" the framework.

Along the lines of self-help books, there are also self-help videotapes and audiotapes. There are different videotape demonstrations of sex skills, for instance, and videotapes designed to help couples learn how to communicate. Many self-help books have been made into audiotapes, or there are audiotapes designed to accompany them. For instance, we use an audiotaped version of Schwartz's (1997) cognitive–behavioral treatment for obsessive–compulsive disorder with appropriate clients. We also use an audiotaped version of Seligman's (1994) *What You Can Change and What You Can't* to provide an overview of the various possibilities for self-improvement.

Overall, we suspect that self-help books (as well as videotapes and audiotapes) provide support for some of the following self-healing functions. First, they can help normalize experience, thus lifting morale and helping overcome demoralization. By so doing, they can help promote more of a mastery-oriented focus on the part of the individual on problem solving rather than on the question of whether "I am good or bad." Second, they can help restory the individual's experience in a way that reduces anxiety, creates coherence, and makes people feel better so they can focus more proactively on moving toward the future. Third, gaining a new perspective on the problem, or having a new interpretive framework, the individual now has a tool for understanding specific situations in a way that helps him or her "get out of his or her own way" so he or she can focus on more proactive solutions. Fourth, the framework may provide direct hints to proactive solutions, and certainly encourage trying new things out. Fifth, discovery-oriented techniques may promote new discoveries and perspective shifts. They may also promote acceptance and letting go, we well as encourage action. Sixth, specific cognitive–behavioral self-help books may provide a framework for the systematic application of naturally occurring self-healing processes, such as challenging dysfunctional cognitions, exposure, behavioral practice, relaxation, and the practice of acceptance and letting go.

Computer-assisted self-help programs are probably helpful in a manner similar to self-help books. One advantage of such programs is that they are more interactive than books.

Self-help, or mutual support (Jacobs & Goodman, 1989), groups are a major source of self-help and serve as many or more individuals as does therapy. Self-help groups come in all shapes and sizes, with various degrees of involvement and assistance provided by professionals. There are self-help groups for serious mental disorders such as schizophrenia, borderline personality disorder, and, of course, addictions. There are self-help groups for eating disorders, anxiety disorders, bereavement, and sufferers from various diseases. Goodman and Jacobs (1994) delineated some of the change processes in self-help groups, and they include many of the processes we have already noted: mutual support and validation of one another's experience, a framework for interpreting experience, concrete guidance, and empathic understanding. As with other forms of self-help, some individuals appear to be helped as much or more by self-help groups as by professionally provided services (e.g., Bright et al., 1997). In other cases, professionally provided services are needed, and in still other cases the two can be combined. Much more research is needed to know who will benefit from what. Self-help groups generally provide analogues of the first three types of learning opportunities of therapy: a supportive working space, an opportunity for co-constructive dialogue, and interpersonal learning.

Self-help groups are now going on-line. Already there are spontaneously occurring self-help groups for a variety of problems on the Internet. For instance, there is an on-line support group for people with problems associated with borderline personality disorder (Sleek, 1997a). Randi Kreger (as quoted in Sleek, 1997a) noted that "[t]he 'netizens' I have met . . . aren't waiting for professionals to come up with the answers. . . . They're sharing coping strategies, exchanging technical information, and offering emotional support to intimate strangers who understand exactly what they're going through" (p. 20).

On-line activities may have enormous potential for providing a kind of self-help therapy. Art's 20-year-old daughter, an online "expert," has wondered if the role-playing that people engage in over the Internet in various game situations could help them develop social skills as well as a greater capacity for perspective taking. Of course, such role-playing could also enhance and reinforce dysfunctional behaviors and attitudes as well. The Internet may have great potential for positive promotion of personal growth, as well as great potential for the promotion of destructive behavior. It is potentially an incredible area for the building of facilitative learning environments.

Lastly, we mention an informal version of another kind of self-help, which is the provision of information by means of talk-show therapists and television shows like *Oprah*. Talk-show therapists, as well as advice columns like *Dear Abby*, provide generalized advice and counseling. As such, what they provide is too nonspecific and not tailored enough to the concrete particulars of an individual's life to really be considered therapy. What they provide will be useful to the degree that the individual receiving the advice is able to creatively, accurately, and persistently implement it or use it to generate his or her own alternatives. Television shows that present endless variations on human problems ("Mothers who have sex with daughters' girl friends" and so on) provide individuals with a host of vicariously experienced situations in which they can think through what they believe is right or wrong and hear others' opinions (including the opinions of professionals who appear on the shows). Watching such shows undoubtedly creates the opportunity for a kind of vicarious dialogue. Observers also get to participate vicariously in the dramas of others' lives, role-play various solutions, and through this, possibly develop their own answers. How often such answers are useful or not is a question for empirical research.

This kind of self-help parallels a related kind of self-help that has been available for centuries: learning and problem-solving through the reading of novels, biographies, the seeing of plays and movies, the hearing of folk tales, and so on. Although we know of no studies of this, informally we know of individuals who have used models from literature to help them solve personal problems. *The Catcher in the Rye's* Holden Caulfield has probably helped countless late adolescents through the transition to early adulthood. We also know of cases in which models have been used destructively. Rock stars or movie stars who commit suicide or model violence probably provide negative models. It is an interesting empirical question as to when such activities are helpful and when they are harmful.

In summary, individuals are motivated to help themselves, and there are many forms of self-help materials available. Future research is needed to specify what is helpful, what is harmful, and to whom.

Using Self-Help With Clients

Because of our belief in clients' self-healing potential, we believe in supporting clients' self-help efforts whenever possible. We are wholly in sympathy with the 1970s community psychology movement of "giving psychology away" (Larson, 1984). We regularly recommend self-help books or tapes to our clients if appropriate. However, we do not consider ourselves experts on self-help materials. We have no formal algorithm for deciding when to offer self-help materials to our clients or how to match up a particular self-help possibility with a particular client at a particular time. One general principle that does seem useful and is supported by research (e.g., Beutler et al., 1991) is that highly reactant clients, clients driven by a desire to maintain their independence and autonomy, seem more likely to actively want and use self-help material in the form of books, tapes, or computer programs. In our experience, they are also unlikely to be interested in self-help groups. Another heuristic we used is the degree of self-directed mastery-oriented behavior (see chapter 7) shown by the client. Clients who are able to adopt a process-focused, mastery-oriented state of mind are more likely, in our experience, to be able to use self-help material on their own outside of therapy.

In any case, the simple test for us is, does the client show an interest in self-help material, and, if offered, do they take advantage of it? Sex therapy is actually a matter of self-help anyway. Even when exercises such as sensate focus are assigned, clients do them in the privacy of their homes. Art regularly suggests they read Zilbergeld's (1992) *The New Male Sexuality* or Barbach's (1975) *For Yourself*. Some clients return to report that the book by itself has helped them and to ask if they could try doing the exercises on their own. Several clients have taken the books and "run with them" and have almost seemed relieved that there was a book that they could use on their own rather than have to work with a therapist. Videos have also sometimes been suggested as a form of self-help for sexual dysfunctions.

With couples in therapy, we have suggested books like Beck's (1988) *Love Is Never Enough*, Wile's (1988) *After the Honeymoon*, Weiner-Davis's (1992) *Divorce Busting*, or Gottman's (1994) *Why Marriages Succeed or Fail*. With other kinds of problems, we have regularly suggested self-help books so that clients can become informed and empowered. With a client with depression, even if we are working primarily from a client-centered stance, we have suggested Burns's (1980) *Feeling Good*, and more recently, with clients struggling with a variety of affective problems (depression, anxiety, or anger), we have recommended Greenberger and Padesky's (1995) *Mind Over Mood*. Generally, we suggest books with the idea that the client read the book and then we and the client will decide what to do with it. The client can informally work with the exercises him- or herself if he or she so wishes, or we can incorporate them into our therapy work if the client so wishes. The decision is made mutually. Many clients have not chosen to formally work with the books in therapy. Rather, they read them, and then informally incorporate their ideas into our ongoing work. We have also suggested Prochaska et al.'s (1994) book *Changing for Good*, which is based on their stages-of-change model that we have previously alluded to in this book, to a number of clients as a kind of general, all-purpose self-help book.

We are also highly open to referring clients to self-help groups if they are interested. Once again, the simple test of whether a client should go to a self-help group is whether or not he or she is interested. However, we are more likely to suggest it to those who need more social support, who we think would profit from gaining the validation and normalization that can come from being with others who share similar problems (e.g., the "I'm not alone" feeling), or those with special problems where group support and group expertise in coping with the problem can make a significant contribution.

Following are two examples of how we have used self-help in therapy. Sam, age 40, came in feeling like he was abnormal because he was having what he saw as a problem gaining erections. He did not immediately gain an erection just because he was naked with a woman. Instead, it took stimulation from his partner. Lately even that wasn't working. He was given Zilbergeld's (1992) *The New Male Sexuality* to read. It was specifically suggested that he read the chapter on the myths about male sexual prowess that can make most men feel inferior. It was also suggested that he do the exercise in which he tried to identify his conditions for good sex. He returned a week later feeling considerably better. He realized that he had been putting an unfair burden on himself to live up to "superstud" images of male sexual performance, and that he and his partner were currently trying to make love under conditions that were not optimal for him. As he began to forgive himself for being the way he was, he was able to ask his partner to practice some of the exercises in the book, and over a period of a few weeks had begun to gain erections once again. He did this mostly on his own with the aid of the book, simply checking in with the therapist to make progress reports.

In another example, Leslie came into therapy feeling depressed and disappointed with her life. She was in her 40s and had only recently gotten married for the first time. However, she was unhappy with her husband. He was not living up to the ideal image of the husband she had always held. Leslie's life, as she told it, had been one disappointment after another. She had been disappointed in love, she was now too old to have a child, she had been fired from jobs, and now, even though she held a job as a nurse, it was not a fulfilling one. Leslie had once been diagnosed as having major depressive disorder and had been hospitalized. On release from the hospital, she had joined a self-help group for recovering mental patients (Low, 1950). This group had helped her learn how to deal with her previous anger and disappointments, but she had not been going recently. In therapy, she decided to rejoin the group. The group, along with the therapist, helped her evaluate her marriage, realize that while imperfect, her husband was a decent man and a basically good partner, and gradually she was able to become more accepting of her life.

Helping Clients Use Their Own Natural Resources

Another implication of the perspective of the client as active self-healer is that therapists should be highly sensitive to and supportive of any and all activities of the client outside of therapy that have a life-promoting and self-healing quality. We are highly sensitive to helping clients use naturally occurring resources in their natural environments. This includes informal self-help groups in the form of people they can talk to, as well as life-promoting activities such as involvement in volunteer activities, church activities, neighborhood organizations, political causes, sports, or religion and prayer. Almost anything can be healing if it is life promoting. Joining the Sierra Club and going hiking was beneficial to one person. Another person began to donate time to food kitchens on Thanksgiving and Christmas. Still others have gotten involved in local theater groups. Several clients have helped themselves through prayer and through their religious commitments.

Prevention

As might be expected, we are strongly in favor of prevention programs. From our point of view, building strong mental health is a much more profitable enterprise than trying to help people when they develop problems. We will not attempt to survey all the myriad efforts at prevention here. This includes the many early childhood prevention programs, communication skills training, parent training, premarital counseling, and so on. It also includes all the uses of cognitive–behavioral programs that are used in health care and pain management to help people cope with stress, deal with pain, cope with disease, and so on. It also includes programs to train optimistic thinking (Seligman, 1990), improve emotional coping (Goleman, 1995), and promote constructive behavior (Stipek & Bohart, in press). Finally, it can include programs such as Pennebaker's (1990) journaling programs, which help prevent disorders in college students.

Working With Involuntary Clients

Working with clients who are in therapy involuntarily is a major challenge. Consider a male client is referred by a court for therapy because he has been convicted of childhood sexual abuse. He denies that he did it even though the evidence is convincing that he did. Is this not a case where the client-as-self-healer model fails? After all, the client is certainly not going to self-heal on his own. He would not even be there if it were up to him. Certainly he is not going to simply be helped by an empathic listener.

However, we believe that actually these clients are the best evidence for our point of view. It is clear that without their active agentic involvement and participation, little is likely to happen. Thinking about these clients is perhaps the best way to get a clear sense of what the client as active self-healer implies. If therapy were really a mechanistic treatment that operated on clients, as it is often portrayed, then simply getting client compliance to participate in the treatment at the point of a court-ordered "gun" should work. After all, even if one is forced to take medication against one's will, it will still have its effects. Thus, if we could essentially coerce participation in therapy, it ought to work. Under threat of going to jail, perhaps we could coerce clients to challenge their dysfunctional cognitions, practice communication skills, talk about their feelings, and so on. Perhaps, facetiously, we could even hold a gun to their heads and make them do the exercises. Do we really think this would work? It ought to if therapy were really a treatment consisting of techniques that operated on dysfunctional behaviors, weak egos, dysfunctional cognitive schemas, and so on. Yet people who work with these populations know that clients can go through the motions with these procedures over and over without the procedure ever really "taking." Why not? It is because these procedures are not treatments, but rather are learning opportunities, and unless clients avail themselves of the learning opportunity they will not learn.

This means that we must involve the clients and convince them that we have something of use to them. We must interest them in what we have to offer so that they are motivated to take advantage of the learning opportunity we have. The problem is that they have no reason to trust us.

Furthermore, we are not really there as their agents alone, but as agents of society. As therapists, we are caught between two systems: the societal system, which we must protect and defend, and the therapist–client system, which usually works best when clients feel we are on their side. But we are not exclusively on their side. We are on their side *and* on the side of society. We cannot pretend to be exclusively on their side. Nonetheless, we can respectfully listen and acknowledge that, ultimately, the power to effect change lies only in their hands. If they do not want to change, we cannot make them. Then we must find a way of engaging them in dialogue. Through that dialogue, it is hoped we can convey that we are on their side as well as the side of society and that we would like to find a win–win solution for all concerned. We convey to them that we are really interested in taking them seriously, and we try to empathically understand their point of view while dialectically trying to get them to consider the opposite point of view.

Recently we attended a "summit" on violence in Long Beach, California. There was much discussion about preventing gang violence. The whole upshot was that all the programs, strategies, and interventions would not help if power were not given to the gang members themselves to institute their own change. One counselor from San Pedro, California, talked about the positive changes that occurred by giving gangs ownership of the problem. Others talked about the true power for change coming from the communities themselves, not from the professional agencies. All the agencies can do is help the communities, but the power lies in the communities and individually, in the gang members.

Yet this is almost completely antithetical to our thinking in psychotherapy under the influence of the medical model. We believe the power lies with us to change people. And courts think we have the power to change people also, even against their will. Yet, especially when we are working with the equivalent of gangs—clients who do not trust or respect us, who see us as outside intruders there to control their lives—it is especially then that we must realize that the true power for change lies within clients. We need to be the kind of people clients can gradually come to trust enough to open up to, and we must ultimately trust *them*, if we are to get anywhere. Otherwise the situation becomes one of trying to use threat, coercion, intimidation, or oppression to solve the problem.

Believing that clients have a natural capacity for self-righting and self-healing does not mean that (a) they will automatically move in the direction of what we see as more effective behavior or (b) they will automatically adopt our agendas. As with a gang, we must find ways of dialoging with them so that they can see that their capacity for self-righting and self-healing is better mobilized in directions other than those they have previously been going in. Think to yourself when a client is resisting, How are *they* experiencing this? Why does it "make sense" from their point of view to be resisting? How are they trying to "self-heal" by resisting? This may help you effectively dialogue with them.

CONCLUSION

There are a number of conclusions on the idea that the client is an active self-healer for the field of psychotherapy and clinical psychology. For psychotherapy integration, it is suggested that each approach to therapy is a different pathway to change, dealing with different aspects of the person's functioning. Different clients take to different approaches. It is unlikely that we will have a unifying theory of psychotherapy until we know far more about how different aspects of human functioning fit together. Technical eclecticism, in terms of matching up different approaches to different client learning styles, personalities, or stages of change, is one potentially fruitful way to proceed.

Implications for research include the following:

- We need to know more about how therapy helps from clients' points of view, including how clients use therapy to make change.
- We also need to know more about which clients prefer which types of learning environments therapy can provide.
- The *events* research paradigm may only partially capture how therapy works because clients are capable of creating change for themselves without engaging in any of the processes that therapists identify as significant for creating change.
- The randomized controlled clinical trial paradigm is not an optimal one for genuinely understanding how therapy works.
- The empirically validated treatments approach to identifying helpful therapies is limited because it is based in the medical model.
- Manualization may make sense for procedures but it does not make sense for therapy as a whole, and the only perspective from which it does make sense is if one thinks about therapy as analogous to a drug that is being applied to a condition.

In terms of implications for practice, we suggest that one can practice under the medical model and still honor the idea of the client as an active self-healer if one thinks about treatment plans and diagnoses as heuristics. However, the medical model and diagnosis can be dangerous if they create a paternalistic "I know better than you" attitude in the therapist. We believe clients ideally would be fully informed about different therapies and fully involved in the choice of what kind of therapy they receive. In terms of generating new techniques, we think that because client involvement seems to be the single most important factor in whether therapy works, generating more and more techniques to fix the client's problems is probably less important than finding better ways of involving the client in the process. This will include, among other things, therapists becoming better "conversational experts." Self-help procedures are particularly useful and cost efficient. It is also very useful to draw on naturally occurring resources in the client's life space, such as his or her religious beliefs, involvement in various life-enhancing activities, or personal support systems. Prevention of problems before they start through enhancing people's skills is important. Finally, working with involuntary clients is one of the biggest challenges faced by any therapist. However, understanding that even involuntary clients are active agents capable of self-healing provides a better basis for approaching them than viewing them as defective because they "resist" treatment.

REFERENCES

Agor, W. H. (Ed.). (1989). *Intuition in organizations.* Newbury Park, CA: Sage.

Albee, G. W. (1982). Preventing psychopathology and promoting human potential. *American Psychologist, 37,* 1043–1050.

American Psychiatric Association. (1994). *Diagnostic and statistical manual of mental disorders* (4th ed.). Washington, DC: Author.

Anderson, T. (1997, August). Therapists' creative capacity for forming positive therapeutic alliances. In L. Leitner (Chair), *Therapist creativity in experiential and constructivist therapies.* Symposium conducted at the 105th Annual Convention of the American Psychological Association, Chicago.

Angus, L. E. (1992). Metaphor and the communication interaction in psychotherapy: A multimethodological approach. In S. G. Toukmanian & D. L. Rennie (Eds.), *Psychotherapy process research: Paradigmatic and narrative approaches* (pp. 187–210). Newbury Park, CA: Sage.

Arkowitz, H. (1997a, April). Clients as cognitive therapists for their own depression. In A. Bohart (Chair), *The client's active role in change: Implications for integration.* Symposium conducted at the Convention of the Society for the Exploration of Psychotherapy Integration, Toronto, Ontario, Canada.

Arkowitz, H. (1997b, December). *Will the "real" therapist please stand up: Understanding the client's active role in the change process.* Paper presented at the meeting of the North American Society for Psychotherapy Research, Tucson, AZ.

Arkowitz, H., & Messer, S. B. (Eds.). (1984). *Psychoanalytic and behavior therapy: Is integration possible?* New York: Plenum.

Bakan, D. (1996). Origination, self-determination, and psychology. *Journal of Humanistic Psychology, 36,* 9–20.

Bandura, A. (1986). *Social foundations of thought and action.* Englewood Cliffs, NJ: Prentice-Hall.

Bandura, A. (1997). *Self-efficacy.* New York: Freeman.

Bankoff, E. A., & Howard, K. I. (1992). The social network of the psychotherapy patient and effective psychotherapeutic process. *Journal of Psychotherapy Integration, 2,* 273–294.

Barbach, L. G. (1975). *For yourself: The fulfillment of female sexuality.* New York: Signet.

Barlow, D. H. (1988). *Anxiety and its disorders.* New York: Guilford Press.

Barlow, D. H. (1994). Psychological interventions in the era of managed competition. *Clinical Psychology: Science and Practice, 1,* 109–122.

Barlow, D. H. (1996). Health care policy, psychotherapy research, and the future of psychotherapy. *American Psychologist, 51,* 1050–1058.

Barlow, D. H., & Craske, M. G. (1989). *Mastery of your anxiety and panic.* New York: Graywind.

Barsalou, L. W. (1985). Ideals, central tendency, and frequency of instantiation, as determinants of graded structure in categories. *Journal of Experimental Psychology: Learning, Memory, and Cognition, 11,* 629–654.

Barsalou, L. W., & Prinz, J. J. (1997). Mundane creativity in perceptual symbol systems. In T. B. Ward, S. M. Smith, & J. Vaid (Eds.), *Creative thought: An investigation of conceptual structures and processes* (pp. 267–308). Washington, DC: American Psychological Association.

Beck, A. T. (1987). Cognitive therapy. In J. K. Zeig (Ed.), *The evolution of psychotherapy* (pp. 149–163). New York: Brunner/Mazel.

Beck, A. T. (1988). *Love is never enough.* New York: Harper & Row.

Beck, A. T., Emery, G., & Greenberg, R. (1985). *Anxiety disorders and phobias: A cognitive perspective.* New York: Basic Books.

Beck, A. T., Rush, A. J., Shaw, B. F., & Emery, G. (1979). *Cognitive therapy of depression.* New York: Guilford Press.

Belenky, M. F., Clinchy, B. M., Goldberger, N. R., & Tarule, J. M. (1986). *Womens ways of knowing: The development of self, voice, and mind.* New York: Basic Books.

Berg, I. K., & Miller, S. D. (1992). *Working with the problem drinker: A solution-focused approach.* New York: Norton.

Berg, J. H. (1987). Responsiveness and self-disclosure. In V. J. Derlega & J. H. Berg (Eds.), *Self-disclosure: Theory, research and therapy* (pp. 101–130). New York: Plenum.

Bergen, R. (1991). *Beliefs about intelligence and achievement-related behaviors.* Unpublished doctoral dissertation, University of Illinois.

Bergin, A. E., & Garfield, S. L. (1994). Overview, trends, and future issues. In A. E. Bergin & S. L. Garfield (Eds.), *Handbook of psychotherapy and behavior change* (4th ed., pp. 821–830). New York: Wiley.

Bergin, A. E., & Lambert, M. J. (1978). The evaluation of therapeutic outcomes. In S. L. Garfield & A. E. Bergin (Eds.), *Handbook of psychotherapy and behavior change* (2nd ed., pp. 139–190). New York: Wiley.

Beutler, L. E. (1989). Differential treatment selection: The role of diagnosis in psychotherapy. *Psychotherapy, 26,* 271–281.

Beutler, L. E. (1995). The germ theory myth and the myth of outcome homogeneity. *Psychotherapy, 32,* 489–494.

Beutler, L. E. (1996, August). *What works with whom: Developing effective treatment plans.* Continuing education workshop presented at the 104th Annual Convention of the American Psychological Association, Toronto, Ontario, Canada.

Beutler, L. E., & Clarkin, J. F. (1990). *Systematic treatment selection.* New York: Brunner/Mazel.

Beutler, L. E., Engle, D., Mohr, D., Daldup, R. J., Berjan, J., Meredith, K., & Merry, W. (1991). Predictors of differential and self-directed psychotherapeutic procedures. *Journal of Consulting and Clinical Psychology, 59,* 333–340.

Binder, J. L. (1993). Observations on the training of therapists in time-limited dynamic psychotherapy. *Psychotherapy, 30,* 592–598.

Bohart, A. (1978, April). *The structure of personal revolutions.* Paper presented at the Western Psychological Association Convention, San Francisco.

Bohart, A. (1980). Toward a cognitive theory of catharsis. *Psychotherapy: Theory, Research, and Practice, 17,* 192–201.

Bohart, A. (1982). Similarities between cognitive and humanistic approaches to psychotherapy. *Cognitive Therapy and Research, 6,* 245–250.

Bohart, A. (1990). A cognitive client-centered perspective on borderline personality disorder. In G. Lietaer, J. Rombauts, & R. Van Balen (Eds.), *Client-centered and experiential psychotherapy in the nineties* (pp. 599–622). Leuven, Belgium: Leuven University Press.

Bohart, A. (1991). Empathy in client-centered therapy: A contrast with psychoanalysis and self psychology. *Journal of Humanistic Psychology, 31,* 34–48.

Bohart, A. (1992). Does psychotherapy integration have any "guts"? Or: Yes, cognitive therapy is integrative, but so what? *Journal of Psychotherapy Integration* (Newsletter), *2,* 154–156.

Bohart, A. (1993). Experiencing: The basis of psychotherapy. *Journal of Psychotherapy Integration, 3,* 51–67.

Bohart, A. (1995a). Mr. Lake. *Journal of Psychotherapy Integration, 5,* 95–106.

Bohart, A. (1995b). The person-centered psychotherapies. In A. S. Gurman & S. B. Messer (Eds.), *Essential psychotherapies* (pp. 85–127). New York: Guilford Press.

Bohart, A., & Associates. (1996). Experiencing, knowing, and change. In R. Hutterer, G. Pawlowsky, P. F. Schmid, & R. Stipsits (Eds.), *Client-centered and experiential psychotherapy: A paradigm in motion* (pp. 190–212). Vienna: Peter Lang.

Bohart, A., & Boyd, G. (1997, December). *Clients' construction of the therapy process: A qualitative analysis.* Paper presented at the meeting of the North American Association of the Society for Psychotherapy Research, Tucson, AZ.

Bohart, A., & Greenberg, L. S. (1997). Empathy and psychotherapy: An introductory overview. In A. Bohart & L. Greenberg (Eds.), *Empathy reconsidered* (pp. 4–31). Washington, DC: American Psychological Association.

Bohart, A., O'Hara, M., & Leitner, L. M. (1998). Empirically violated treatments: Disenfranchisement of humanistic and other psychotherapies. *Psychotherapy Research, 8,* 141–157.

Bohart, A., & Rosenbaum, R. (1995). The dance of empathy: Empathy, diversity, and technical eclecticism. *The Person-Centered Journal, 2,* 5–29.

Bohart, A., & Tallman, K. (1996). The active client: Therapy as self-help. *Journal of Humanistic Psychology, 36,* 7–30.

Breuer, J., & Freud, S. (1955). *Studies on hysteria.* London: Hogarth Press. (Original work published 1895)

Bright, J. I., Baker, K., & Neimeyer, R. A. (1997, December). Professional and paraprofessional group treatments for depression: A comparison of cognitive behavioral and mutual support interventions. In K. Baker (Chair), *The Memphis Depression Project: Professionally and paraprofessionally led mutual support and cognitive behavioral groups for depression*. Symposium conducted at the meeting of the North American Society for Psychotherapy Research, Tucson, AZ.

Brodley, B. T. (1996). Empathic understanding and feelings in client-centered therapy. *The Person-Centered Journal, 3*, 22–30.

Browner, S., Muscatine, R., & Bohart, A. (1993). Untitled presentation. In A. Bohart (Chair), *How All Good Therapy is Experiential*. Symposium conducted at the Society for the Exploration of Psychotherapy Integration Convention, New York.

Bucci, W. (1995). The power of the narrative: A multiple code account. In J. W. Pennebaker (Ed.), *Emotion, disclosure, and health* (pp. 93–124). Washington, DC: American Psychological Association.

Buck, R., & Ginsburg, B. (1997). Communicative genes and the evolution of empathy. In W. Ickes (Ed.), *Empathic accuracy* (pp. 12–43). New York: Guilford Press.

Burns, D. D. (1980). *Feeling good*. New York: William Morrow.

Burns, D. D., & Nolan-Hoeksema, S. (1991). Coping styles, homework compliance, and the effectiveness of cognitive behavioral therapy. *Journal of Consulting and Clinical Psychology, 59*, 305–311.

Burton, M. V., Parker, R. W., & Wollner, J. M. (1991). The psychotherapeutic power of a "chat": A verbal response modes study of a placebo attention control with breast cancer patients. *Psychotherapy Research, 1*, 39–61.

Calahan, D. (1987). *Understanding America's drinking problem*. San Francisco: Jossey-Bass.

Cantor, N., & Zirkel, S. (1990). Personality, cognition, and purposive behavior. In L. Pervin (Ed.), *Handbook of personality* (pp. 135–164). New York: Guilford Press.

Carkhuff, R. R., & Berenson, B. G. (1967). *Beyond counseling and therapy*. New York: Holt, Rinehart & Winston.

Caspar, F. (1997). What goes on in a psychotherapist's mind? *Psychotherapy Research, 7*, 105–126.

Chess, S., & Thomas, A. (1984). *Origins and evolution of behavior disorders*. New York: Brunner/Mazel.

Christensen, A. (1992, April). The challenge of nonprofessional therapies. In M. Jacobs (Chair), *Extending the integrative boundaries: What self-change processes can teach us*. Symposium conducted at the Convention of the Society for the Exploration of Psychotherapy Integration, San Diego, CA.

Christensen, A., & Jacobson, N. S. (1994). Who (or what) can do psychotherapy: The status and challenge of nonprofessional therapies. *Psychological Science, 5*, 8–14.

Clark, H. H. (1991). Words, the world, and their possibilities. In G. R. Lockhead

& J. R. Pomerantz (Eds.), *The perception of structure* (pp. 263–278). Washington, DC: American Psychological Association.

Clark, L. F. (1993). Stress and the cognitive–conversational benefits of social interaction. *Journal of Social and Clinical Psychology, 12,* 25–55.

Cohen, J. (1994). The earth is round (*p* < .05). *American Psychologist, 49,* 997–1003.

Comas-Diaz, L. (1992). The future of psychotherapy with ethnic minorities. *Psychotherapy, 29,* 88–94.

Cooper, J. (1995). Cooperative learning "versus" collaborative learning: Should we care? *Cooperative Learning and College Teaching, 6*(1), 1–2.

Cooper, J. (1996). Research in cooperative learning in the mid-1990s: What the experts say. *Cooperative Learning and College Teaching, 6*(2), 2–3.

Corsini, R. J. (1989). Introduction. In R. J. Corsini & D. Wedding (Eds.), *Current psychotherapies* (4th ed., pp. 1–18). Itasca, IL: Peacock.

Covington, M. V. (1992). *Making the grade: A self-worth perspective on motivation and school reform.* Cambridge, England: Cambridge University Press.

Cowan, P. (1978). *Piaget: With feeling.* New York: Holt, Rinehart & Winston.

Craske, M. G., & Barlow, D. H. (1993). Panic disorder and agoraphobia. In D. H. Barlow (Ed.), *Clinical handbook of psychological disorders* (2nd ed., pp. 1–47). New York: Guilford Press.

Cross, D. G., Sheehan, P. W., & Kahn, J. A. (1980). Alternative advice and counseling psychotherapy. *Journal of Consulting and Clinical Psychology, 48,* 615–625.

Davis-Floyd, R., & Arvidson, P. S. (Eds.). (1997). *Intuition.* New York: Routledge.

De Shazer, S. (1985). *Keys to solution in brief therapy.* New York: Norton.

Diener, C. I., & Dweck, C. S. (1978). An analysis of learned helplessness: Continuous changes in performance, strategy, and achievement cognitions following failure. *Journal of Personality and Social Psychology, 36,* 451–462.

Diener, C. I., & Dweck, C. S. (1980). An analysis of learned helplessness: II. The processing of success. *Journal of Personality and Social Psychology, 39,* 940–952.

Dominowski, R. L., & Dallob, P. (1995). Insight and problem solving. In R. J. Sternberg & J. E. Davidson (Eds.), *The nature of insight* (pp. 33–62). Cambridge, MA: MIT Press.

Dossey, L. (1995). How should alternative therapies be evaluated? An examination of fundamentals. *Alternative Therapies in Health and Medicine, 1*(2), 6–10, 79–85.

Duncan, B. L., Hubble, M. A., & Miller, S. D. (1997). *Psychotherapy with "impossible" cases: The efficient treatment of therapy veterans.* New York: Norton.

Duncan, B. L., Solovey, A. D., & Rusk, G. S. (1992). *Changing the rules: A client-directed approach to therapy.* New York: Guilford Press.

Dweck, C. S. (1975). The role of expectations and attributions in the alleviation of learned helplessness. *Journal of Personality and Social Psychology, 31,* 674–685.

Dweck, C. S. (1991). Self-theories and goals: Their role in motivation, personality, and development. In R. A. Dienstbier (Ed.), *Nebraska symposium on motivation, 1990: Perspectives on motivation* (Vol. 388, pp. 199–235). Lincoln: University of Nebraska Press.

Dweck, C. S., & Bempechat, J. (1983). Children's theories of intelligence. In S. Paris, G. Olsen, & H. Stevenson (Eds.), *Learning and motivation in the classroom* pp. 239–256. Hillsdale, NJ: Erlbaum.

Dweck, C. S., Chiu, C., & Hong, Y. (1995). Implicit theories and the role in judgments and reactions: A world from two perspectives. *Psychological Inquiry, 6*, 322–333.

Dweck, C. S., Hong, Y., & Chiu, C. (1993). Implicit theories: Individual differences in the likelihood and meaning of dispositional inferences. *Personality and Social Psychology Bulletin, 19*, 644–656.

Dweck, C. S., & Leggett, E. L. (1988). A social–cognitive approach to motivation and personality. *Psychological Review, 95*, 256–273.

Dweck, C. S., & Reppucci, N. D. (1973). Learned helplessness and reinforcement responsibility in children. *Journal of Personality and Social Psychology, 25*, 109–116.

Efran, J. S., & Blumberg, M. J. (1994). Emotion and family living: The perspective of structure determinism. In S. M. Johnson & L. S. Greenberg (Eds.), *The heart of the matter* (pp. 172–206). New York: Brunner/Mazel.

Egan, G. (1982). *The skilled helper* (2nd ed.). Monterey, CA: Brooks/Cole.

Eisenberg, N. (1998). Introduction. In N. Eisenberg (Ed.), *Handbook of child psychology: Vol. 3. Social, emotional, and personality development* (pp. 1–24). New York: Wiley.

Elder, G. (1986). Military times and turning points in men's lives. *Developmental Psychology, 22*, 233–245.

Elkin, I. (1994). The NIMH treatment of depression collaborative research program: Where we began and where we are. In A. E. Bergin & S. L. Garfield (Eds.), *Handbook of psychotherapy and behavior change* (4th ed., pp. 114–142). New York: Wiley.

Elliot, E. S., & Dweck, C. S. (1988). Goals: An approach to motivation and achievement. *Journal of Personality and Social Psychology, 54*, 5–12.

Elliott, R. (1984). A discovery-oriented approach to significant change events in psychotherapy: Interpersonal process recall and comprehensive process analysis. In L. S. Greenberg & L. N. Rice (Eds.), *Patterns of change* (pp. 249–286). New York: Guilford Press.

Elliott, R. (1986). Interpersonal process recall as a psychotherapy process research technique. In L. S. Greenberg & W. Pinsof (Eds.), *The psychotherapeutic process* (pp. 503–528). New York: Guilford Press.

Elliott, R. (1996). Are client-centered/experiential therapies effective? A meta-analysis of outcome research. In U. Esser, H. Pbast, & G. W. Speierer (Eds.), *The power of the person-centered approach: New challenges–perspectives–answers* (pp. 125–138). Koln, Germany: GwG Verlag.

Elliott, R., & James, E. (1989). Varieties of client experience in psychotherapy: An analysis of the literature. *Clinical Psychology Review, 9,* 443–467.

Ellis, A., & Whiteley, J. M. (Eds.). (1979). *Theoretical and empirical foundations of rational–emotive therapy.* Monterey, CA: Brooks/Cole.

Emmons, R. A. (1999). *The psychology of ultimate concerns: motivation and spirituality in personality.* New York: Guilford Press.

Epstein, R. (1991). Skinner, creativity, and the problem of spontaneous behavior. *Psychological Science, 2,* 362–370.

Erdley, C. A., & Dweck, C. S. (1993). Children's implicit personality theories as predictors of their social judgments. *Child Development, 64,* 863–878.

Erdley, C. A., Loomis, C., Cain, K., Dumas-Hines, F., & Dweck, C. S. (1997). Relations among children's social goals, implicit personality theories and responses to social failure. *Developmental Psychology, 33,* 263–272.

Feshbach, N. D. (1997). Empathy: The formative years—implications for clinical practice. In A. Bohart & L. S. Greenberg (Eds.), *Empathy reconsidered: New directions in psychotherapy* (pp. 33–62). Washington, DC: American Psychological Association.

Feshbach, S., Weiner, B., & Bohart, A. (1996). *Personality* (4th ed.). New York: Heath.

Fiedler, K., & Semin, G. R. (1988). On the causal information conveyed by different interpersonal verbs: The role of implicit sentence context. *Social Cognition, 6,* 21–39.

Finke, R. A. (1995). Creative insight and preinventive forms. In R. J. Sternberg & J. E. Davidson (Eds.), *The nature of insight* (pp. 255–280). Cambridge, MA: MIT Press.

Fisch, R. (1990). Problem-solving psychotherapy. In J. K. Zeig & W. .M. Munion (Eds.), *What is psychotherapy? Contemporary perspectives* (pp. 269–273). San Francisco: Jossey-Bass.

Fisher, J. (1995). Uniformity myths in eclectic and integrative psychotherapy. *Journal of Psychotherapy Integration, 5,* 41–56.

Flavell, J. H. (1979). Metacognition and cognitive monitoring. A new area of cognitive–developmental inquiry. *American Psychologist, 34,* 906–911.

Foa, E. B., Steketee, G. S., Grayson, J. B., & Doppelt, H. (1983). Treatment of obsessive-compulsives: when do we fail? In E. B. Foa & P. M. G. Emmelkamp (Eds.). *Failures in behavior therapy.* New York: Wiley.

Foa, E. B., & Kozak, M. J. (1991). Emotional processing: Theory, research, and clinical implications for anxiety disorders. In J. D. Safran & L. S. Greenberg (Eds.), *Emotion, psychotherapy, and change* (pp. 21–49). New York: Guilford Press.

Foa, E. B., & Rothbaum, B. O. (1997). *Treating the trauma of rape: Cognitive behavioral therapy for PTSD.* New York: Guilford Press.

Foa, E. B., Molnar, C., & Cashman, L. (1995). Change in rape narratives during exposure therapy for post traumatic stress disorder. *Journal of Traumatic Stress, 8,* 675–690.

Frank, J. D. (1974). Psychotherapy: The restoration of morale. *American Journal of Psychiatry, 131,* 271–274.

Frankl, V. (1963). *Man's search for meaning.* New York: Washington Square Press.

Frazier, P. A. (1991). Self-blame as a mediator of postrape depressive symptoms. *Journal of Social and Clinical Psychology, 10,* 47–57.

Frick, W. (1987). The symbolic growth experience: Paradigm for a humanistic–existential learning theory. *Journal of Humanistic Psychology, 27,* 390–405.

Garfield, S. L. (1994). Research on client variables in psychotherapy. In A. E. Bergin & S. L. Garfield (Eds.), *Handbook of psychotherapy and behavior change* (4th ed., pp. 190–228). New York: Wiley.

Gediman, H. K., & Lieberman, J. S. (1996, March 14). An interview with Dr. Helen K. Gedmian and Dr. Janice S. Lieberman. *Psychotherapy Books News, 30,* 7.

Gendlin, E. T. (1964). A theory of personality change. In P. Worchel & D. Byrne (Eds.), *Personality change.* New York: Wiley.

Gendlin, E. T. (1967). Therapeutic procedures in dealing with schizophrenics. In C. R. Rogers, E. T. Gendlin, D. J. Kiesler, & C. B. Truax (Eds.), *The therapeutic relationship and its impact* (pp. 369–400). Madison: University of Wisconsin Press.

Gendlin, E. T. (1968). The experiential response. In E. Hammer (Ed.), *Use of interpretation in treatment* (pp. 208–227). New York: Grune & Stratton.

Gendlin, E. T. (1969). Focusing. *Psychotherapy: Theory, Research and Practice, 6,* 4–15.

Gendlin, E. T. (1981). *Focusing.* New York: Bantam.

Gendlin, E. T. (1984). The politics of giving therapy away: Listening and focusing. In D. Larson (Ed.), *Teaching psychological skills: Models for giving psychology away.* (pp. 287–305). Monterey, CA: Brooks/Cole.

Gendlin, E. T. (1990). The small steps of the therapy process: How they come and how to help them come. In G. Lietaer, J. Rombauts, & R. Van Balen (Eds.), *Client-centered and experiential psychotherapy in the nineties* (pp. 205–224). Leuven, Belgium: Leuven University Press.

Gendlin, E. T. (1996). *Focusing-oriented psychotherapy.* New York: Guilford Press.

Gibbs, R. W., Jr. (1997). How language reflects the embodied nature of creative cognition. In T. B. Ward, S. M. Smith, & J. Vaid (Eds.), *Creative thought: An investigation of conceptual structures and processes* (pp. 351–374). Washington, DC: American Psychological Association.

Glanz, K., Durlach, N. I., Barnett, R. C., & Aviles, W. A. (1996). Virtual reality (VR) for psychotherapy: From the physical to the social environment. *Psychotherapy, 33,* 464–473.

Glucksberg, S., & Keysar, B. (1990). Understanding metaphorical comparisons: Beyond similarity. *Psychological Review, 97,* 3–18.

Goetz, T. E., & Dweck, C. S. (1980). Learned helplessness in social situations. *Journal of Personality and Social Psychology, 39,* 249–255.

Gold, J. R. (1980). *A retrospective study of the behavior therapy experience.* Unpublished doctoral dissertation, Adelphi University.

Gold, J. R. (1994). When the patient does the integrating: Lessons for theory and practice. *Journal of Psychotherapy Integration, 4,* 133–158.

Gold, J. R. (1996a). *Key concepts in psychotherapy integration.* New York: Plenum.

Gold, J. R. (1996, April b). Untitled presentation. In A. Bohart (Chair), *The client as integrative psychotherapist.* Symposium conducted at the Convention of the Society for the Exploration of Psychotherapy Integration, Berkeley, CA.

Goldfried, M. R. (Ed.) (1982). *Converging themes in psychotherapy.* New York: Springer.

Goldfried, M. R. (1995). *From cognitive–behavior therapy to psychotherapy integration.* New York: Plenum.

Goldfried, M. R. (1997, April). *Cognitive–behavioral theory and technique for psychodynamic/non-behavioral therapists.* Workshop presented at the Convention of the Society for the Exploration of Psychotherapy Integration, Toronto, Ontario, Canada.

Goldfried, M. R., & Padawer, W. (1982). Current status and future directions in psychotherapy. In M. R. Goldfried (Ed.), *Converging themes in psychotherapy* (pp. 3–50). New York: Springer.

Goldfried, M. R., & Wolfe, B. (1996). Psychotherapy practice and research: Repairing a strained alliance. *American Psychologist, 51,* 1007–1017.

Goleman, D. (1995). *Emotional intelligence.* New York: Bantam.

Goodman, G., & Jacobs, M. (1994). The self-help, mutual support group. In A. Fuhriman & G. Burlingame (Eds.), *Handbook of group psychotherapy* (pp. 489–526). New York: Wiley.

Gottman, J. (1994). *Why marriages succeed or fail.* New York: Simon & Schuster.

Gould, R. L. (1978). *Transformations.* New York: Simon & Schuster.

Gould, R. L. (1989). *Therapeutic learning program* [Computer software]. Santa Monica, CA: Interactive Health Systems.

Gould, R. A., & Clum, G. A. (1993). A meta-analysis of self-help treatment approaches. *Clinical Psychology Review, 13,* 169–186.

Grawe, K. (1997). Research-informed psychotherapy. *Psychotherapy Research, 7,* 1–20.

Grawe, K., Caspar, F., & Ambuhl, H. (1990). Differentielle psychotherapieforschung: Vier therapieformen im vergleich [The bernese comparative psychotherapy study]. *Zeitschrift fur Klinische Psychologie, 19,* 287–376.

Gray, J. (1992). *Men are from Mars, women are from Venus.* New York: Harper Collins.

Greenberg, L. S. (1984). A task analysis of intrapersonal conflict resolution. In L. N. Rice & L. S. Greenberg (Eds.), *Patterns of change* (pp. 67–123). New York: Guilford Press.

Greenberg, L. S. (1991). Research on the process of change. *Psychotherapy Research, 1,* 3–16.

Greenberg, L. S., & Elliott, R. (1997). Varieties of empathic responding. In A. Bohart & L. S. Greenberg (Eds.), *Empathy reconsidered: New directions in psychotherapy* (pp. 167–186). Washington, DC: American Psychological Association.

Greenberg, L. S., Elliott, R., & Lietaer, G. (1994). Research on experiential psychotherapies. In A. E. Bergin & S. L. Garfield (Eds.), *Handbook of psychotherapy and behavior change* (4th ed., pp. 509–542). New York: Wiley.

Greenberg, L. S., & Paivio, S. (1997). *Working with emotions in psychotherapy.* New York: Guilford Press.

Greenberg, L. S., Rice, L. N., & Elliott, R. (1993). *Facilitating emotional change: The moment-by-moment process.* New York: Guilford Press.

Greenberg, L. S., & Safran, J. D. (1987). *Emotion in psychotherapy.* New York: Guilford Press.

Greenberg, L. S., & Watson, J. (1998). Experiential therapy of depression: Differential effects of client-centered relationship conditions and process-experiential interventions. *Psychotherapy Research, 8,* 210–224.

Greenberger, D., & Padesky, C. A. (1995). *Mind over mood: A cognitive therapy treatment manual for clients.* New York: Guilford Press.

Greening, T. (1996, August). Can we help Humpty Dumpty, and can he help himself? In A. Bohart (Chair), *How clients create change in psychotherapy: Implications for understanding.* Symposium conducted at the 104th Annual Convention of the American Psychological Association, Toronto, Ontario, Canada.

Grencavage, L. M., & Norcross, J. C. (1990). Where are the commonalities among the therapeutic common factors? *Professional Psychology: Research and Practice, 21,* 372–378.

Guidano, V. F. (1987). *Complexity of the self.* New York: Guilford Press.

Gurin, G., Veroff, J., & Feld, S. (1960). *Americans view their mental health.* New York: Basic Books.

Hammond, D. C., Hepworth, D. H., & Smith, V. G. (1980). *Improving therapeutic communication.* San Francisco: Jossey-Bass.

Harter, S. (1990). Processes underlying adolescent self-concept formation. In R. Montemayor, G. R. Adams, & T. P. Gullotta (Eds.), *From childhood to adolescence: A transitional period?* (pp. 205–239). Newbury Park, CA: Sage.

Harvey, J. H., Orbuch, T. L., Chwalisz, K. D., & Garwood, G. (1991). Coping with sexual assault: The roles of account-making and confiding. *Journal of Traumatic Stress, 4,* 515–531.

Hayes, S. C., Folette, W. C., & Follette, V. M. (1995). Behavior therapy: A contextual approach. In A. S. Gurman & S. B. Messer (Eds.), *Essential psychotherapies: Theory and practice* (pp. 128–181). New York: Guilford Press.

Hayes, S. C., & Gifford, E. V. (1997). The trouble with language: Experiential avoidance, rules, and the nature of verbal events. *Psychological Science, 8,* 170–173.

Heide, F. (1989, April). Untitled presentation. In *Negative outcome in psychotherapy.*

Symposium conducted at the Convention of the Society for the Exploration of Psychotherapy Integration, Berkeley, CA.

Helson, R. (1993). Comparing longitudinal studies of adult development: Toward a paradigm of tension between stability and change. In D. C. Funder, R. D. Park, C. Tomlinson-Keasy, & K. Widaman (Eds.), *Studying lives through time* (pp. 93–120). Washington, DC: American Psychological Association.

Hinsz, V. B., Tindale, R. S., & Vollrath, D. A. (1997). The emerging conceptualization of groups as information processors. *Psychological Bulletin, 121,* 43–64.

Hobfall, S. E. (1989). Conservation of resources: A new attempt at conceptualizing stress. *American Psychologist, 44,* 513–524.

Hoffman, M. (in press). Empathy, justice, and moral internalization. In D. Stipek & A. Bohart (Eds.), *Constructive and destructive behavior.* Washington, DC: American Psychological Association.

Hofstader, D. R. (1979). *Godel, Escher, Bach: An eternal golden braid.* New York: Basic Books.

Hollon, S. D., & Beck, A. T. (1994). Cognitive and cognitive–behavioral therapies. In A. E. Bergin & S. L. Garfield (Eds.), *Handbook of psychotherapy and behavior change* (4th ed., pp. 428–466). New York: Wiley.

Horvath, A. O. (1995). The therapeutic relationship: From transference to alliance. *In Session, 1,* 7–17.

Hoyt, M. F. (1994). *Brief therapy and managed care.* San Francisco: Jossey-Bass.

Humphreys, C., & Bohart, A. (1998, April). *Therapists rated on facilitation of clients' active role in change.* Paper presented at the Western Psychological Association Convention, Albuquerque, NM.

Jacobs, M. (Chair). (1995). *Computer psychotherapy: The direction of the future?* Symposium conducted at the Western Psychological Association Convention, Los Angeles.

Jacobs, M., & Goodman, G. (1989). Psychology and self-help groups: Predictions on a partnership. *American Psychologist, 44,* 536–545.

Jacobson, N. (1995). The overselling of therapy. *Family Therapy Networker, 19,* 40–51.

Jagacinski, C. M., & Nicholls, J. G. (1987). Competence and affect in task involvement and ego involvement: The impact of social comparison information. *Journal of Educational Psychology, 79,* 107–114.

Janis, I. L. (1982). *Groupthink.* Boston: Houghton Mifflin.

Janoff-Bulman, R. (1989). Assumptive worlds and the stress of traumatic events: Applications of the schema construct. *Social Cognition, 7,* 113–138.

Jenkins, A. H. (1995). *Psychology and African-Americans* (2nd ed.). Needham Heights, MA: Allyn & Bacon.

Jenkins, A. H. (1996, August). Enhancing the patient's dialectical abilities in psychotherapy. In A. Bohart (Chair), *How clients create change in psychotherapy: Implications for understanding change.* Symposium conducted at the 104th Annual Convention of the American Psychological Association, Toronto, Ontario, Canada.

Johnson, M. (1987). *The body in the mind.* Chicago: University of Chicago Press.

Johnson, W. R., & Smith, E. W. L. (1997). Gestalt empty-chair dialogue versus systematic desensitization in the treatment of a phobia. *Gestalt Review, 1,* 150–162.

Jordan, J. V. (1997). Relational development through mutual empathy. In A. Bohart & L. S. Greenberg (Eds.), *Empathy reconsidered: New directions in psychotherapy* (pp. 343–352). Washington, DC: American Psychological Association.

Jordan, J. V., Kaplan, A. G., Miller, J. B., Stiver, I. P., & Surrey, J. L. (Eds.). (1991). *Women's growth through connection: Writings from the Stone Center.* New York: Guilford Press.

Kampis, G. (Ed.). (1991). Creative evolution in nature, mind, and society [Special issue]. *World Futures, 32*(2–3), 63–195.

Kanfer, F. H., & Gaelick, L. (1986). Self-management methods. In F. H. Kanfer & A. P. Goldstein (Eds.), *Helping people change* (3rd ed., pp. 283–345). New York: Pergamon.

Kanfer, F. H., & Goldstein, A. P. (1986). *Helping people change* (3rd ed.). New York: Pergamon.

Kegan, R. (1982). *The evolving self.* Cambridge, MA: Harvard University Press.

Kelly, G. (1969). Ontological acceleration. In B. Maher (Ed.), *Clinical psychology and personality: The selected papers of George Kelly* (pp. 7–45). New York: Wiley.

Kleinman, A. (1988). *Rethinking psychiatry: From cultural category to personal experience.* New York: Free Press.

Klerman, G. L., Weissmann, M. M., Rounsaville, B. J., & Chevron, E. S. (1984). *Interpersonal psychotherapy of depression.* New York: Basic Books.

Klopfer, B. (1957). Psychological variables in human cancer. *Journal of Projective Techniques, 21,* 331–340.

Kohlenberg, R. J., & Tsai, M. (1987). Functional analytic psychotherapy. In N. Jacobson (Ed.), *Psychotherapists in clinical practice: Cognitive and behavioral perspectives* (pp. 388–443). New York: Guilford Press.

Kohut, H. (1979). The two analyses of Mr. Z. *International Journal of Psychoanalysis, 60,* 3–27.

Kolb, D. A. (1984). *Experiential learning.* Englewood Cliffs, NJ: Prentice-Hall.

Kopp, R. R. (1995). *Metaphor therapy.* New York: Brunner/Mazel.

Kroll, J. (1988). *The challenge of the borderline patient.* New York: Norton.

Krupnick, J. L., Sotsky, S. M., Simmens, S., Moyher, J., Elkin, I., Watkins, J., & Pilkonis, P. A. (1996). The role of the therapeutic alliance in psychotherapy and pharmacotherapy outcome: Findings in the National Institute of Mental Health Treatment of Depression Collaborative Research Project. *Journal of Consulting and Clinical Psychology, 64,* 532–539.

Kuhn, T. S. (1970). *The structure of scientific revolutions* (2nd ed.). Chicago: University of Chicago Press.

Lakoff, G. (1987). *Women, fire, and dangerous things: What categories reveal about the mind.* Chicago: University of Chicago Press.

Lambert, M. (1992). Psychotherapy outcome research. In J. C. Norcross & M. R. Goldfried (Eds.), *Handbook of psychotherapy integration* (pp. 94–129). New York: Basic Books.

Lambert, M. J., & Bergin, A. E. (1994). The effectiveness of psychotherapy. In A. E. Bergin & S. L. Garfield (Eds.), *Handbook of psychotherapy and behavior change* (4th ed., pp. 143–190). New York: Wiley.

Landrine, H. (1992). Clinical implications of cultural differences: The referential versus indexical self. *Clinical Psychology Review, 12,* 401–415.

Langer, E. J., & Park, K. (1990). Incompetence: A conceptual reconsideration. In R. J. Sternberg & J. Kolligian (Eds.), *Competence considered* (pp. 149–166). New Haven, CT: Yale University Press.

Larson, D. (1984). *Teaching psychological skills: Models for giving psychology away.* Monterey, CA: Brooks/Cole.

Latham, G. P. (1996, August). *Critical issues in goal-setting theory and research: Moving beyond 1990.* Invited address presented at the 104th Annual Convention of the American Psychological Association, Toronto, Ontario, Canada.

Lazarus, A. A. (1981). *The practice of multimodal therapy.* New York: McGraw-Hill.

Leitner, L. M. (1994, July). *Emotions, desires, passions: Critical aspects of personal construct psychotherapy.* Paper presented at the North American Personal Construct Network Conference, Indianapolis, IN.

Leitner, L. M. (1995). Optimal therapeutic distance: A therapist's experience of personal construct psychotherapy. In R. Neimeyer & M. Mahoney (Eds.), *Constructivism in psychotherapy* (pp. 357–370). Washington, DC: American Psychological Association.

Leitner, L. M., Faidley, A. J., & Celentana, M. A. (in press). *Diagnosing human meaning making: An experiential constructivist approach.* In R. Neimeyer & J. Raskin (Eds.), *Disorders of construction.* Washington, DC: American Psychological Association.

Lepper, M. R., Greene, D., & Nisbett, R. E. (1973). Undermining children's intrinsic interest with extrinsic rewards: A test of the "overjustification" hypothesis. *Journal of Personality and Social Psychology, 28,* 129–137.

Lewinsohnn, P., Munoz, R., Youngren, M. A., & Zeiss, A. (1986). *Control your depression.* Englewood Cliffs, NJ: Prentice-Hall.

Linehan, M. M. (1993). *Cognitive–behavioral treatment of borderline personality disorder.* New York: Guilford Press.

Linehan, M. M. (1997). Validation and psychotherapy. In A. Bohart & L. S. Greenberg (Eds.), *Empathy reconsidered: New directions in psychotherapy* (pp. 353–392). Washington, DC: American Psychological Association.

Llewelyn, S. P., Elliott, R., Shapiro, D. A., & Hardy, G. (1988). Client perceptions of significant events in prescriptive and exploratory periods of individual therapy. *British Journal of Clinical Psychology, 27,* 105–114.

Low, A. (1950). *Mental health through will training.* Glencoe, IL: Willet.

Lubart, T. J. (1994). Creativity. In R. J. Sternberg (Ed.), *Thinking and problem solving* (pp. 290–333). New York: Academic Press.

Luborsky, L., McClellan, A. T., Woody, G. E., O'Brien, C. P., & Auerbach, A. (1985). Therapist success and its determinants. *Archives of General Psychiatry, 42,* 602–611.

Luborsky, L., Singer, B., & Luborsky, L. (1975). Comparative studies of psychotherapies: Is it true that "everyone has won and all must have prizes"? *Archives of General Psychiatry, 32,* 995–1008.

Lucius, Y. M., Emley, E., Lee, M., & Bohart, A. (1997, April). *Agent of change in psychotherapy: A qualitative inquiry of the phenomenon.* Paper presented at the Western Psychological Association Convention, Seattle, WA.

MacIsaac, D. S. (1997). Empathy: Heinz Kohut's contribution. In A. Bohart & L. S. Greenberg (Eds.), *Empathy reconsidered: New directions in psychotherapy* (pp. 245–264). Washington, DC: American Psychological Association.

Mahoney, M. J. (1980). Psychotherapy and the structure of personal revolutions. In M. J. Mahoney (Ed.), *Psychotherapy process: Current issues and future directions* (pp. 157–180). New York: Plenum.

Mahoney, M. J. (1991). *Human change processes.* New York: Basic Books.

Mahrer, A. R. (1988). Discovery-oriented psychotherapy research: Rationale, aims, and methods. *American Psychologist, 43,* 694–702.

Mahrer, A. R. (1989). *Dreamwork: In psychotherapy and self-change.* New York: Norton.

Mahrer, A. R. (1996). *The complete guide to experiential psychotherapy.* New York: Wiley.

Mahrer, A. R., Lawson, K. C., Stalikas, A., & Schachter, H. M. (1990). Relationships between strength of feeling, type of therapy, and occurrence of in-session good moments. *Psychotherapy, 27,* 531–541.

Marten, P. A., & Barlow, D. H. (1993). Implications of clinical research for psychotherapy integration in the treatment of the anxiety disorders. *Journal of Psychotherapy Integration, 3,* 297–312.

Martin, J. (1997). Mindfulness: A proposed common factor. *Journal of Psychotherapy Integration, 7*(4), 291–312.

Marziali, E., & Angus, L. (1986, June). *The development of a sequential system for coding therapist interventions and patient responses.* Session presented at the meeting of the Society for Psychotherapy Research, Ulm, Germany.

Masten, A. S., Best, K. M., Garmazy, N. (1990). Resilience and development: Contribution from the study of children who overcome adversity. *Development and Psychopathology, 2,* 425–444.

Mathieu-Coughlan, P., & Klein, M. H. (1984). Experiential psychotherapy: Key events in client-centered interaction. In L. N. Rice & L. S. Greenberg (Eds.), *Patterns of change* (pp. 194–212). New York: Guilford Press.

Matthews, R. S., Cooper, J. L., Davidson, N., & Hawkes, P. (1995). Building bridges between cooperative and collaborative learning. *Cooperative Learning and College Teaching, 6*(1), 2–5.

McAdams, D. P., & de St. Aubin, E. (Eds.). (1998). *Generativity and adult development.* Washington, DC: American Psychological Association.

Meichenbaum, D. (1977). *Cognitive behavior modification: An integrative approach.* New York: Plenum.

Meichenbaum, D., & Goodman, S. (1971). Training impulsive children to talk to themselves: A means of developing self-control. *Journal of Abnormal Psychology, 77,* 115–126.

Meyer, A. E. (Ed.). (1981). The Hamburg Short Psychotherapy Comparison experiment. *Psychotherapy and Psychosomatics, 35,* 81–207.

Miller, S. D., Duncan, B. L., & Hubble, M. A. (1997). *Escape from Babel.* New York: Norton.

Miller, W. R., & Rollnick, S. (1991). *Motivational interviewing: Preparing people to change addictive behavior.* New York: Guilford Press.

Millon, T., Everly, G., & Davis, R. D. (1993). How can knowledge of psychopathology facilitate psychotherapy integration? A view from the personality disorders. *Journal of Psychotherapy Integration, 3,* 331–352.

Muellar, C. M., & Dweck, C. S. (1998). Praise for intelligence can undermine children's motivation and performance. *Journal of Personality and Social Psychology, 75,* 33–52.

Mussen, P., & Eisenberg, N. (in press). Child-rearing and pro-social behavior. In D. Stipek & A. Bohart (Eds.), *Constructive and destructive behavior.* Washington, DC: American Psychological Association.

Neimeyer, R. A. (1996). Process interventions for the constructivist psychotherapist. In H. Rosen & K. T. Kuehlwein (Eds.), *Constructing realities* (pp. 371–412). San Francisco: Jossey-Bass.

Neimeyer, R. A., & Mahoney, M. J. (Eds.). (1995). *Constructivism in psychotherapy.* Washington, DC: American Psychological Association.

Neisser, U. (1988). Five kinds of self-knowledge. *Philosophical psychology, 1,* 35–59.

Newfield, N. A., Kuehl, B. P., Joanning, H. P., & Quinn, W. H. (1991). We can tell you about "psychos" and "shrinks": An ethnography of the family therapy of adolescent drug abuse. In T. C. Todd & M. N. Selekman (Eds.), *Family therapy approaches with adolescent substance abusers* (pp. 277–310). Boston: Allyn & Bacon.

Nicholls, J. G. (1992). Students as educational theorists. In D. H. Schunk & J. L. Meece (Eds.), *Student perceptions in the classroom* (pp. 267–286). Hillsdale, NJ: Erlbaum.

Nickerson, R. S. (1994). The teaching of thinking and problem solving. In R. J.

Sternberg (Ed.), *Thinking and problem solving* (pp. 409–450). New York: Academic Press.

Norcross, J. C. (1986). Eclectic psychotherapy: An introduction and overview. In J. C. Norcross (Ed.), *Handbook of eclectic psychotherapy* (pp. 3–24). New York: Brunner/Mazel.

Norcross, J. C. (1995). Dispelling the dodo bird verdict and the exclusivity myth in psychotherapy. *Psychotherapy, 32*, 500–504.

Norcross, J. C., & Aboyoun, D. C. (1994). Self-change experiences of psychotherapists. In T. M. Brinthaupt & R. P. Lipka (Eds.), *Changing the self* (pp. 253–278). Albany: State University of New York Press.

Norcross, J. C., Glass, C. R., Arnkoff, D. B., Lambert, M. J., Shoham, V., Stiles, W. B., Shapiro, D. A., Barkham, M., & Strupp, H. H. (1993). Research directions for psychotherapy integration: A roundtable. *Journal of Psychotherapy Integration, 3*, 91–132.

Norem, J. K. (1996, August). *Cognitive strategies and the rest of personality.* Invited address presented at the 104th Annual Convention of the American Psychological Association, Toronto, Ontario, Canada.

Oatley, K. (1996, August). *What writers, readers, and psychologists tell us about fiction.* Invited address presented at the 104th Annual Convention of the American Psychological Association, Toronto, Ontario, Canada.

O'Hanlon, W. H., & Weiner-Davis, M. (1989). *In search of solutions: A new direction in psychotherapy.* New York: Norton.

O'Hara, M. M. (1986). Heuristic inquiry as psychotherapy: The client-centered approach. *Person-Centered Review, 1*, 172–184.

O'Hara, M. M. (1997). Relational empathy: Beyond modernist egocentrism to postmodern holistic contextualism. In A. Bohart & L. S. Greenberg (Eds.), *Empathy reconsidered: New directions in psychotherapy* (pp. 295–319). Washington, DC: American Psychological Association.

Omer, H., & Alon, N. (1997). *Constructing therapeutic narratives.* Northvale, NJ: Jason Aronson.

Orlinsky, D. (1989). Researchers' images of psychotherapy: Their origins and influence on research. *Clinical Psychology Review, 9*, 413–442.

Orlinsky, D. E., Grawe, K., & Parks, B. K. (1994). Process and outcome in psychotherapy—noch einmal. In A. E. Bergin & S. L. Garfield (Eds.), *Handbook of psychotherapy and behavior change* (4th ed., pp. 270–376). New York: Wiley.

Orlinsky, D. E., & Howard, K. I. (1980). Gender and psychotherapeutic outcome. In A. M. Brodsky & R. T. Hare-Mustin (Eds.), *Women and psychotherapy* (pp. 3–34). New York: Guilford Press.

Paivio, S., & Nieuwenhuis, J. (1998). *Efficacy of emotionally-focused therapy for adult survivors of child abuse.* Manuscript submitted for publication.

Pennebaker, J. W. (1990). *Opening up: The healing power of confiding in others.* New York: Morrow.

Pennebaker, J. W. (1995). Emotion, disclosure, and health: An overview. In J. W.

Pennebaker (Ed.), *Emotion, disclosure, and health* (pp. 3–10). Washington, DC: American Psychological Association.

Pennebaker, J. W. (1997). Writing about emotional experiences as a therapeutic process. *Psychological Science, 8,* 162–166.

Perkins, D. N. (1995). Insight in minds and genes. In R. J. Sternberg & J. E. Davidson (Eds.), *The nature of insight* (pp. 495–533). Cambridge, MA: MIT Press.

Phillips, J. R. (1984). Influences on personal growth as viewed by former psychotherapy patients. *Dissertation Abstracts International, 44,* 441A.

Pinsof, W. M., Wynne, L. C., & Hambright, A. B. (1996). The outcomes of couple and family therapy: Findings, conclusions, and recommendations. *Psychotherapy, 33,* pp. 321–331.

Polyani, M. (1967). *The tacit dimension.* New York: Anchor.

Prochaska, J. O. (1995). An eclectic and integrative approach: Transtheoretical therapy. In A. Gurman & S. Messer (Eds.), *Essential psychotherapies* (pp. 403–440). New York: Guilford Press.

Prochaska, J. O., & Norcross, J. C. (1982). The future of psychotherapy: A Delphi poll. *Professional Psychology, 13,* 620–627.

Prochaska, J. O., DiClemente, C. C., & Norcross, J. C. (1992). In search of how people change: Applications to addictive behaviors. *American Psychologist, 47,* 1102–1114.

Prochaska, J. O., Norcross, J. C., & DiClemente, C. C. (1994). *Changing for good.* New York: Morrow.

Project MATCH Research Group. (1997). Matching alcoholism treatments to client heterogeneity: Project MATCH posttreatment drinking outcomes. *Journal of Studies on Alcohol, 58,* 7–29.

Rennie, D. L. (1990). Toward a representation of the client's experience of the psychotherapy hour. In G. Lietaer, J. Rombauts, & R. Van Balen (Eds.), *Client-centered and experiential therapy in the nineties* (pp. 155–172). Leuven, Belgium: Leuven University Press.

Rennie, D. L. (1994a). Clients' deference in psychotherapy. *Journal of Counseling Psychology, 41,* 427–437.

Rennie, D. L. (1994b). Storytelling in psychotherapy: The client's subjective experience. *Psychotherapy, 31,* 234–243.

Rennie, D. L. (1997, April). Aspects of the client's control of the therapeutic process. In A. Bohart (Chair), *The client's active role in change: Implications for integration.* Symposium conducted at the Convention of the Society for the Exploration of Psychotherapy Integration, Toronto, Ontario, Canada.

Rice, L. N., & Greenberg, L. S. (Eds.). (1984). *Patterns of change: Intensive analysis of psychotherapy process.* New York: Guilford Press.

Rice, L. N., & Kerr, G. P. (1986). Measures of client and therapist vocal quality. In L. S. Greenberg & W. M. Pinsof (Eds.), *The psychotherapeutic process: A research handbook* (pp. 73–106). New York: Guilford Press.

Rice, L. N., & Saperia, E. P. (1984). Task analysis of the resolution of problematic reactions. In L. N. Rice & L. S. Greenberg (Eds.), *Patterns of change* (pp. 29–66). New York: Guilford Press.

Rieber, R. W., & Carton, A. S. (Eds.). (1987). *The collected works of L. S. Vygotsky*. New York: Plenum Publishing.

Robbins, L. (1979). Addict careers. In R. Dupont, A. Goldstein, & J. O'Donnell (Eds.), *Handbook on drug abuse*. Rockville, MD: National Institute on Drug Abuse.

Roberts, A. H., Kewman, D. G., Mercier, L., & Hovell, M. F. (1993). The power of nonspecific effects in healing: Implications for psychosocial and biological treatments. *Clinical Psychology Review, 13*, 375–391.

Roberts, M. (1997). *The man who listens to horses*. New York: Random House.

Robinson, L. A., Berman, J. S., & Neimeyer, R. A. (1990). Psychotherapy for treatment of depression: A comprehensive review of controlled outcome research. *Psychological Bulletin, 108*, 30–49.

Rogers, C. R. (1957). The necessary and sufficient conditions of therapeutic personality change. *Journal of Consulting Psychology, 21*, 95–103.

Rogers, C. R. (1961). *On becoming a person*. Boston: Houghton Mifflin.

Rogers, C. R. (1986). Reflection of feelings. *Person-Centered Review, 2*, 11–13.

Rosenbaum, R. (1994). Single-session therapies: Intrinsic integration? *Journal of Psychotherapy Integration, 4*, 229–252.

Rosenbaum, R. (1996). Form, formlessness, and formulation. *Journal of Psychotherapy Integration, 6*, 107–118.

Rosenbaum, R., Hoyt, M. F., & Talmon, M. (1990). The challenge of single-session therapies: Creating pivotal moments. In R. A. Wells & V. J. Gianetti (Eds.), *Handbook of the brief psychotherapies* (pp. 165–189). New York: Plenum.

Rossi, E. L. (1993). *The psychobiology of mind–body healing*. New York: W. W. Norton.

Roth, A., & Fonagy, P. (1996). *What works for whom?* New York: Guilford Press.

Rowe, C. E., & MacIsaac, D. S. (1991). *Empathic attunement*. Northvale, NJ: Jason Aronson.

Ryan, V. L., & Gizynski, M. N. (1971). Behavior therapy in retrospect. Patients' feelings about their behavior therapies. *Journal of Consulting and Clinical Psychology, 37*, 1–9.

Rychlak, J. F. (1994). *Logical learning theory*. Lincoln: University of Nebraska Press.

Sachse, R. (1992). Differential effects of processing proposals and content references on the explication process of clients with different starting conditions. *Psychotherapy Research, 2*, 235–251.

Safran, J. D., & Segal, Z. V. (1990). *Interpersonal process in cognitive therapy*. New York: Basic Books.

Schafer, R. (1992). *Retelling a life*. New York: Basic Books.

Schegloff, E. A. (1991). Conversation analysis and socially shared cognition. In

L. B. Resnick, J. M. Levine, & S. D. Teasley (Eds.), *Perspectives on socially shared cognition* (pp. 150–171). Washington, DC: American Psychological Association.

Schleier, C. (1998, February). Medicine: Dr. Oliver Sacks treats the brain by understanding the heart. *Biography*, pp. 78–82.

Schooler, J. W., Fallshore, M., & Fiore, S. M. (1995). Epilogue: Putting insight into perspective. In R. J. Sternberg & J. E. Davidson (Eds.), *The nature of insight* (pp. 559–587). Cambridge, MA: MIT Press.

Schwartz, J. M. (1997). *Brain lock: Free yourself from obsessive–compulsive behavior* [Audiocassette]. New York: HarperCollins.

Schwitzgabel, R. (1961). *Streetcorner research: An experimental approach to the juvenile delinquent.* Cambridge, MA: Harvard University Press.

Scogin, F., Bynum, J., Stephens, G., & Calhoon, S. (1990). Efficacy of self-administered treatment programs: Meta-analytic review. *Professional Psychology: Research and Practice, 21,* 42–47.

Sechrest, L. B. (1996, August). What inferences can be drawn from the *Consumer Reports* Survey, design issues. In L. Bickman & M. S. Salzer (Cochairs), Consumer Reports *Mental Health Survey results—practice and policy implications.* Symposium conducted at the 104th Annual Convention of the American Psychological Association, Toronto, Ontario, Canada.

Segal, D. L., & Murray, E. J. (1994). Emotional processing in cognitive therapy and vocal expression of feeling. *Journal of Social and Clinical Psychology, 13,* 189–206.

Seifert, C. M., Meyer, D. E., Davidson, N., Patalano, A. L., & Yaniv, I. (1995). Demystification of cognitive insight: Opportunistic assimilation and the prepared-mind perspective. In R. J. Sternberg & J. E. Davidson (Eds.), *The nature of insight* (pp. 65–124). Cambridge, MA: MIT Press.

Seligman, M. E. P. (1990). *Learned optimism.* New York: Knopf.

Seligman, M. E. P. (1994). *What you can change and what you can't: The complete guide to self-improvement.* New York: Simon & Schuster.

Seligman, M. E. P. (1995). The effectiveness of psychotherapy: The *Consumer Reports* Survey. *American Psychologist, 50,* 965–974.

Seligman, M. E. P. (1998, April). Positive social science. *APA Monitor, 29*(4), p. 2.

Seligman, M. E., Maier, S. F., & Geer, J. H. (1968). Alleviation of learned helplessness in the dog. *Journal of Abnormal Psychology, 73,* 256–272.

Selmi, P. M., Klein, M. H., Greist, J. H., Sorrell, S. P., & Erdman, H. P. (1990). Computer-administered cognitive–behavioral therapy for depression. *American Journal of Psychiatry, 147,* 51–56.

Sfard, A. (1998). On two metaphors for learning and the dangers of choosing just one. *Educational Researcher, 27,* 4–13.

Shapiro, D. A. (1996). "Validated" treatments and evidence-based psychological services. *Clinical Psychology: Science and Practice, 3,* 256–259.

Shapiro, F. (1995). *Eye movement desensitization and reprocessing*. New York: Guilford Press.

Shlien, J. F. (1997). Empathy in psychotherapy: A vital mechanism? Yes. Therapist's conceit? All too often. By itself enough? No. In A. Bohart & L. S. Greenberg (Eds.), *Empathy reconsidered: New directions in psychotherapy* (pp. 63–80). Washington, DC: American Psychological Association.

Shostrom, E. L. (1986). *Three approaches to psychotherapy III* [Transcript]. Corona Del Mar, CA: Psychological & Educational Films.

Sleek, S. (1997a, July) Online network provides forum for patients. *APA Monitor, 28*(7), 20.

Sleek, S. (1997b, July). Treating people who live life on the borderline. *APA Monitor, 28*(7), 20–21.

Sloane, R. B., Staples, F. R., Cristol, A. H., Yorkston, N. J., & Whipple, K. (1975). *Psychotherapy versus behavior therapy*. Cambridge, MA: Harvard University Press.

Smith, M. L., Glass, G. V., & Miller, T. I. (1980). *The benefits of psychotherapy*. Baltimore: Johns Hopkins University Press.

Stamps, D. (1997, February). Communities of practice: Learning is social, training is irrelevant. *Training: The Human Side of Business, 34*(2), 35–40.

Stein, D. M., & Lambert, M. J. (1995). Graduate training in psychotherapy: Are therapy outcomes enhanced? *Journal of Consulting and Clinical Psychology, 63*, 182–196.

Stern, D. N. (1985). *The interpersonal world of the infant*. New York: Basic Books.

Sternberg, R. J., & Davidson, J. E. (Eds.). (1995). *The nature of insight*. Cambridge, MA: MIT Press.

Stiles, W. B. (1995). Disclosure as a speech act: Is it psychotherapeutic to disclose? In J. W. Pennebaker (Ed.), *Emotion, disclosure, and health* (pp. 71–92). Washington, DC: American Psychological Association.

Stiles, W. B., & Shapiro, D. A. (1989). Abuse of the drug metaphor in psychotherapy process-outcome research. *Clinical Psychology Review, 9*, 521–544.

Stiles, W. B., Shapiro, D. A., & Elliott, R. (1986). Are all psychotherapies equivalent? *American Psychologist, 41*, 165–180.

Stipek, D., & Bohart, A. (Eds.). (in press). *Constructive and destructive behavior*. Washington, DC: American Psychological Association.

Stolorow, R., Brandchaft, B., & Atwood, G. (1987). *Psychoanalytic treatment: An intersubjective approach*. Hillsdale, NJ: Analytic Press.

Strupp, H. H., & Anderson, T. (1997). On the limitations of therapy manuals. *Clinical Psychology: Research and Practice, 4*, 76–82.

Strupp, H. H., & Hadley, S. W. (1979). Specific versus nonspecific factors in psychotherapy: A controlled study of outcome. *Archives of General Psychiatry, 36*, 1125–1136.

Stubbs, J. P., & Bozarth, J. D. (1994). The dodo bird revisited: A qualitative study of psychotherapy efficacy research. *Applied and Preventive Psychology, 3,* 109–120.

Svartberg, M., & Stiles, T. C. (1991). Comparative effects of short-term psychodynamic psychotherapy: A meta-analysis. *Journal of Consulting and Clinical Psychology, 59,* 704–714.

Szasz, T. (1998). The healing word: Its past, present and future. *Journal of Humanistic Psychology, 38*(2), 8–20.

Tallman, K. (1996). *The state of mind theory: Goal orientation concepts applied to clinical psychology.* Unpublished master's thesis, California State University Dominguez Hills.

Tallman, K., & Bohart, A. (1999). The client as common factor: Clients as self-healers. In M. A. Hubble, B. L. Duncan, & S. Miller (Eds.), *The heart and soul of change: The role of common factors in psychotherapy, medicine, and human services* (pp. 91–131). Washington, DC: American Psychological Association.

Tallman, K., Robinson, E., Kay, D., Harvey, S., & Bohart, A. (1994, August). *Experiential and non-experiential Rogerian therapy: An analogue study.* Paper presented at the 102nd Annual Convention of the American Psychological Association, Los Angeles.

Tangney, J. (in press). The role of guilt and shame in constructive and destructive behavior. In D. Stipek & A. Bohart (Eds.), *Constructive and destructive behavior.* Washington, DC: American Psychological Association.

Task Force on Promotion and Dissemination of Psychological Procedures, Division of Clinical Psychology of the American Psychological Association. (1995). Training and dissemination of empirically-validated psychological treatments: Report and recommendations. *The Clinical Psychologist, 48,* 3–23.

Task Force on Psychological Intervention Guidelines. (1995). *Template for developing guidelines: Interventions for mental disorders and psychosocial aspects of physical disorders.* Washington, DC: American Psychological Association.

Taylor, S. E., Pham, L. B., Rivkin, I. D., & Armor, D. A. (1998). Harnessing the imagination: Mental simulation, self-regulation, and coping. *American Psychologist, 53,* 429–439.

Tedeschi, J. T., & Felson, R. B. (1994). *Violence, aggression, and coercive actions.* Washington, DC: American Psychological Association.

Teusch, L. (1990). Positive effects and limitations of client-centered therapy with schizophrenic patients. In G. Lietaer, J. Rombauts, & R. Van Balen (Eds.), *Client-centered therapy in the nineties* (pp. 637–644). Leuven, Belgium: Leuven University Press.

Todd, J., & Bohart, A. (1994). *Foundations of clinical and counseling psychology* (2nd ed.). New York: HarperCollins.

Triandis, H. C. (1989). The self and social behavior in differing cultural context. *Psychological Review, 96,* 506–520.

Triandis, H. C. (1996). The psychological measurement of cultural syndromes. *American Psychologist, 51,* 407–415.

Truax, C. B. (1996). Reinforcement and nonreinforcement in Rogerian psychotherapy. *Journal of Abnormal Psychology, 22,* 225–229.

Utman, C. H. (1997). Performance effects of motivational state: A meta-analysis. *Personality and Social Psychology Review, 1,* 170–182.

Vaillant, G. E. (1993). *The wisdom of the ego.* Cambridge, MA: Harvard University Press.

Van Balen, R. (1990). The therapeutic relationshiip according to Carl Rogers: Only a climate? A dialogue? Or both? In G. Lietaer, J. Rombauts, & R. Van Balen (Eds.), *Client-centered and experiential psychotherapy in the nineties* (pp. 65–86). Leuven, Belgium: Leuven University Press.

Vanaerschot, G. (1997). Empathic resonance as a source of experience-enhancing interventions. In A. Bohart & L. S. Greenberg (Eds.), *Empathy reconsidered: New directions in psychotherapy* (pp. 141–166).

VandenBos, G. R. (Ed.). (1996, October). Outcome assessment of psychotherapy [Special issue]. *American Psychologist, 51,* 1005–1089.

Wachtel, P. (1977). *Psychoanalysis and behavior therapy: Toward an integration.* New York: Basic Books.

Wachtel, P. (1993). *Therapeutic communication.* New York: Guilford Press.

Wampold, B. E. (1997). Methodological problems in identifying efficacious psychotherapies. *Psychotherapy Research, 7,* 21–44.

Wampold, B. E., Mondin, G. W., Moody, M., Stich, F., Benson, K., & Ahn, H. (1997). A meta-analysis of outcome studies comparing bona fide psychotherapies: Empirically, "all must have prizes." *Psychological Bulletin, 122,* 203–216.

Ward, T. B., Finke, R. A., & Smith, S. M. (1995). *Creativity and the mind.* New York: Plenum.

Washburn, M. (1988). *The ego and the dynamic ground.* Albany: State University of New York Press.

Watson, D. L., & Tharp, R. G. (1989). *Self-directed behavior: Self-modification for personal adjustment* (5th ed.). Pacific Grove, CA: Brooks/Cole.

Watson, J. C., & Greenberg, L. S. (1996). Emotion and cognition in experiential therapy: A dialectical constructivist perspective. In H. Rosen & K. Kuehlwein (Eds.), *Constructing realities* (pp. 253–276). San Francisco: Jossey-Bass.

Watson, J. C., & Rennie, D. L. (1994). Qualitative analysis of clients' subjective experience of significant moments during the exploration of problematic reactions. *Journal of Counseling Psychology, 41,* 500–509.

Watzlawick, P. (1987). "If you desire to see, learn how to act." In J. K. Zeig (Ed.), *The evolution of psychotherapy* (pp. 91–100). New York: Brunner/Mazel.

Watzlawick, P., Weakland, J. H., & Fisch, R. (1974). *Change: Principles of problem formation and problem resolution.* New York: Norton.

Wegner, D. M., & Lane, J. D. (1995). From secrecy to psychopathology. In J. W. Pennebaker (Ed.), *Emotion, disclosure, and health* (pp. 25–46). Washington, DC: American Psychological Association.

Weil, A. (1995). *Health and healing.* New York: Houghton Mifflin.

Weil, M. M., & Rosen, L. D. (1997). *Technostress*. New York: Wiley.

Weiner, B. (1986). *An attributional theory of motivation and emotion*. New York: Springer-Verlag.

Weiner-Davis, M. (1992). *Divorce busting: A revolutionary and rapid program for staying together*. New York: Simon & Schuster.

Weiss, J., Sampson, H., & the Mount Zion Psychotherapy Research Group. (1986). *The psychoanalytic process: Theory, clinical observations, and empirical research.* New York: Guilford Press.

Werner, E., & Smith, R. (1982). *Vulnerable but invincible: A longitudinal study of resilient children and youth*. New York: McGraw-Hill.

Wexler, D. A. (1974). A cognitive theory of experiencing, self-actualization, and therapeutic process. In D. A. Wexler & L. N. Rice (Eds.), *Innovations in client-centered therapy* (pp. 49–116). New York: Wiley.

White, R. W. (1959). Motivation reconsidered: The concept of competence. *Psychological Review, 66*, 297–333.

White, R. W. (1965). The experience of efficacy in schizophrenia. *Psychiatry: Journal for the Study of Interpersonal Processes, 28*, 199–211.

Wickramasekera, I. (1998). Secrets kept from the mind, but not the body and behavior. *The Independent Practitioner, 18*, 38–42.

Widom, C. S. (1989). Does violence beget violence? A critical examination of the literature. *Psychological Bulletin, 106*, 3–28.

Wile, D. B. (1981). *Couples therapy*. New York: Wiley.

Wile, D. B. (1984). Kohut, Kernberg, and accusatory interpretations. *Psychotherapy: Theory, Research, Practice, and Training, 21*, 353–364.

Wile, D. (1988). *After the honeymoon: How conflict can improve your relationship*. New York: Wiley.

Wolfe, B. E. (1992). Self-experiencing and the integrative treatment of the anxiety disorders. *Journal of Psychotherapy Integration, 2*, 29–44.

Wolfe, B. E. (1994). Adapting psychotherapy outcome research to clinical reality. *Journal of Psychotherapy Integration, 4*, 160–170.

Wolpe, J. (1990). *Analysis of a social neurosis: Treatment possibilities* [Videotape No. C289-CPV17]. Phoenix, AZ: Milton H. Erickson Foundation.

Wylie, M. S. (1994, March/April). Endangered species. *Family Therapy Networker*, pp. 20–33.

Yalom, I. D., & Elkin, G. (1974). *Every day gets a little closer: A twice-told therapy*. New York: Harper Books.

Yaryura-Tobias, J. A., & Neziroglu, F. (1997). *Biobehavioral treatment of obsessive–compulsive spectrum disorders*. New York: Norton.

Zajonc, R. B. (1965). Social facilitation. *Science, 149*, 269–274.

Zilbergeld, B. (1992). *The new male sexuality*. New York: Bantam.

Zilbergeld, B., & Lazarus, A. A. (1987). *Mind power*. New York: Ballantine.

Zimring, F. (1990). Cognitive processes as a cause of psychotherapeutic change: Self-initiated processes. In G. Lietaer, J. Rombauts, & R. Van Balen (Eds.), *Client-centered and experiential psychotherapy in the nineties* (pp. 361–380). Leuven, Belgium: Leuven University Press.

AUTHOR INDEX

Eisenberg, N., 64, 271
Elder, G., 76
Elkin, G., 283
Elkin, I., 27, 42
Elliott, R., 27, 29, 46, 48, 115, 116, 218,
　　238, 262, 280, 282, 283, 286
Ellis, A., 194, 209
Emery, G., 32, 75
Emmons, R. A., 186, 280
Erdley, C. A., 173
Everly, G., 10

Fallshore, M., 206
Feld, S., 38
Felson, R. B., 37
Feshbach, N. D., 238
Feshbach, S., 68
Finke, R. A., 54, 214
Fiore, S. M., 206
Fisch, R., 65
Fisher, J., 28
Flavell, J. H., 181
Foa, E. B., 12, 120, 121, 124, 220, 251
Follette, V. M., 134
Follette, W. C., 134
Fonagy, P., 286
Frankl, V., 58
Frazier, P. A., 71
Freud, S., 74

Gaelick, L., 159, 160
Garmazy, N., 58
Garwood, G., 43
Gendlin, E. T., 65, 75, 115, 120, 203,
　　207, 209, 295
Gibbs, R. W., Jr., 206
Ginsburg, B., 207, 249
Glanz, K., 294
Glass, G. V., 27
Glucksberg, S., 54, 59, 210
Gold, J., 50, 149
Gold, J. R., 14, 211, 278, 281
Goldberger, N. R., 239
Goldfried, M. R., 14, 16, 22, 107, 133,
　　140, 283
Goldstein, A. P., 159, 193
Goleman, D., 301
Goodman, G., 43, 296

Goodman, S., 196
Gottman, J., 299
Gould, R. L., 34
Grawe, K., 27
Gray, J., 295
Greenberg, L. S., 32, 115, 116, 120, 121,
　　133, 143, 207, 220, 238, 251,
　　262, 268, 282, 283
Greenberg, R., 75
Greenberger, D., 295, 299
Grencavage, L. M., 135
Guidano, V. F., 58, 63
Gurin, G., 38

Harter, S., 63
Harvey, J. H., 43, 115
Harvey, S., 48
Hawkes, P., 53
Hayes, S. C., 134, 155, 157
Helson, R., 62
Hinsz, V. B., 237
Hobfall, S. E., 89
Hoffman, M., 271
Hollon, S. D., 251
Hong, Y., 174
Horvath, A. O., 35, 112
Hovell, M. F., 41
Howard, K. I., 34, 38
Hoyt, M. F., 22, 145, 251
Hubble, M. A., 14, 37
Humphreys, C., 110–111

Jacobs, M., 34, 43, 296
Jagacinski, C. M., 187
James, E., 283
Jenkins, A. H., 149, 208
Joanning, H. P., 49
Johnson, M., 206
Johnson, W. R., 251
Jordan, J. V., 128, 146

Kahn, J. A., 38
Kampis, G., 63
Kanfer, F. H., 159, 160, 193
Kaplan, A. G., 146
Kay, D., 48
Kegan, R., 58

Wile, D. B., 75, 98, 241, 247, 299
Wolfe, B. E., 22, 283, 284, 288
Woody, G. E., 33–34
Wylie, M. S., 7, 114

Yalom, I. D., 283
Yaryura-Tobias, J. A., 37
Yorkston, N. J., 27

Youngren, M. A., 160

Zajonc, R. B., 109
Zeiss, A., 160
Zilbergeld, B., 45, 160, 203, 212, 295, 298, 299
Zimring, F., 197
Zirkel, S., 45

SUBJECT INDEX

Case histories (*continued*)
trusting intuition, 76–77
Catharsis, emotional, 120–121
seen as harmful, 114–115
Change. *See also* helplessness; mastery behavior
ability for, 187–188
belief in, 173–174
in circumstances, 76
client theories of, 94–95, 245–246
contextual, 38–39
degree of, 62
and experiencing, 206–208
nature of, 59–62, 94–95, 262
strategies for, 40
Change process, 119–126, 134–136
Chess, S., 39
quoted, 37
Chiu, C., 174–175
Christensen, A., 33
Christianity, and agency, 98–99
Clark, L. F., 116
quoted, 122–123, 126
Clarkin, J. F., 280
Class issues, 266–267
Client. *See also* collaboration; involvement, client's; motivation, client's; problem solving; resistance; self-healing; therapist-client relationship
active, xi, 15
as agent, 97–99, 102, 228, 283–284, 286, 301–303
and choice of "treatment," 287–288
as common factor, 277–280
as co-therapist, xii, 224–225
creativity of, xi–xii
deceptive, 264
difficult, 167–200, 227
as equal, 243
evaluation of therapy, 50–52
as expert, xiv–xv, 16
"good," 199
as integrative therapist, 278
involuntary, 301–303
passive, 15, 267–268
proactive potential of, 99, 103
as problem solver, xii–xiv, 3–4, 17–18, 57, 102, 199, 234
role of, 9, 14–15
seen as self-deceptive or immature, 95–98
as self-expert, 145

as self-healer, 95–104, 116–119, 250, 281–283
severely disturbed, 268–269
signs of helplessness, 176–177
use of term, 9
Client-as-self-healer model. *See* self-healing model
Clinchy, B. M., 239
Clinical trials, randomized controlled, 283–284
Closure, premature, 228, 233
Clum, G. A., 34
Cognitive psychology, human agency in, 53–54
Collaboration, 235–238, 250–257. *See also* therapist-client relationship
with active self-healing client, 140–142
frame of reference for, 238–249
and medical model, 290–291
obstacles to, 263–266
therapy process as, 223–227
types of, 139–142
Comas-Diaz, L., 257
Common factors, 134–135, 277–280
Communication. *See* collaboration; dialogue; empathic listening; self-disclosure; therapist-client relationship
Community psychology movement, 17, 298
Compliance, 6, 140–141
Computers
and self-help, 297
and therapy, 34, 294
Concentration, maintaining, 178–180
Concepts
and experiencing, 205–206
use of, 210–211
Conflict, 226–227
Confrontation, 248
Consumer Reports study (1995), 27, 51–52
Contingency management, 76
Conversation, intelligent, 225–227, 254, 289
Conversational responsiveness, 126
Cooperation, importance of, 226
Coping, 66–67
Corsini, Raymond, 201
Co-thinking, therapist's, 125
Craske, M. G., 160

Creativity, 59, 75, 153
  and client thinking, 213–214
  lack of, 89
  nurturing, 70, 124, 131–132, 141,
    228–229
  in psychological problems, 67
Crisis, and need for therapy, 89
Critical function, restoring, 121

Danger, perception of, 154
Davidson, N., 213–214
Defensiveness, 68–69, 103, 190, 192
Defensive pessimism, 265–266
Depression, 77–80, 116–119, 292–293
Desensitization, systematic, 132–133,
    159, 193–194, 212
de St. Aubin, E., 39
Determinism, reciprocal, 158
Diagnosis, 6, 10, 17, 189, 262, 290. *See*
    also medical model
DSM, 292–293
Diagnostic and Statistical Manual of Mental
    Disorders (4th ed.), 9–10, 92,
    262
  diagnosis and, 292–293
Diagnostic systems, 262
Dialectics, 63, 212–213
Dialogue
  co-constructive, 16, 18–19, 129
  and dialectical thinking, 213
  relationship as, 236
  therapist-client, 224–225, 288–289
  in two-chair procedure, 131–132
DiClemente, C. C., quoted, 40
Diener, C. I., 168, 177, 186–187
Difference, among clients, 103–104,
    234–235
Disclosure. *See* self-disclosure
Discovery, 144, 206
Dis-identify, 75
Dodo bird verdict, 26–33, 36, 52, 270
  implications of, 27–28
  objections to, 28–31
"Doing something different," 74
DSM-IV. *See Diagnostic and Statistical*
    Manual of Mental Disorders
Dumas-Hines, F., 174
Duncan, B. L., 3–4, 143–145, 223, 240,
    245
Dweck, C. S., 57, 168–175, 177, 182,
    186–188

Eclecticism, technical, 280–281
Ecological wisdom, 66, 239–241
Ecology, of problem, 240–241
Education, human agency in, 53
Effort dilemma, 187–188
Efran, J. S., 74
  quoted, 135
Elder, G., 38
Elliot, E. S., 171–172
Elliott, R., 29–30, 32, 49–51
Ellis, A., 107, 111, 130, 187, 194–195
EMDR, 147, 207, 220
Emley, E., 51
Emotion, and experiencing, 205, 207–
    208
Emotional reprocessing, 120–121
Empathic attunement, 246
Empathic listening, 142, 147, 234
  case histories, 116–119
  in collaborative therapy process, 250
  importance of, 110, 115–119, 231–
    232, 253, 261
  meaning of, 242–243
  objections to, 113–115, 123
  and severely disturbed client, 269
Empathic reflecting, 124–126
Empathic responding, 197, 232
Empathic understanding, 243–246
Empathic vantage point, 239–242
Empathy, 235–236, 238–239, 265, 289
Entity-incremental distinction, 170–176
Environment
  for creativity, 214
  inhibiting, 92
  safe, 227
  therapeutic, 112–119, 128
Epstein, R., quoted, 59
Erdley, C. A., 174–175
Erdman, H. P., 34
Erickson, Milton, 107, 145
Errors
  cognitive, 209
  as information, 170
  in therapy, 185
Evaluation. *See also* approval; assessment;
    diagnosis
  concerns about, 178–181
  in life, 182–183
  necessary, 190
Expectations for success, client's, 45
Experience, acknowledging, 119–120

Experiencing, 15, 120–121, 202–208.
    See also TEB cycle
  emotional, 125
  and thinking, 209–210, 214–215
Experimentation, behavioral, 215–216
Expert validation, desire for, 91–92
Exploration, 184–185, 191, 232–234
Exploring, 102–103, 144. *See also* TEB
    cycle
Exposure, 74, 79, 120–121, 161
Extinction, 140, 161
Eye movement desensitization and re-
    processing (EMDR), 147, 207,
    220

Failure, in therapy, 185. *See also* helpless-
    ness
Faith and hope, role in medical model,
    7–8, 12
Feedback. *See also* dialogue
  client, 232–233
  corrective, 233
Feelings, trusted, 76. *See also* intuition
Fiedler, K., 174
"Finding other paths," 79
Fine-tuning. *See* change; tinkering
Fisch, R., 13
Foa, E. B., 32, 121, 124, 161
  quoted, 12
Focus, client's, 178–183, 189. *See also*
    lens analogy; outcome focus; pro-
    cess focus
Focusing procedure, Gendlin's, 207
Folk methods, use of, 235, 257
Frame of reference
  collaborative, 238–249
  therapist's, 265
Frank, Jerome, 45
Free association, 192–193
Freud, Sigmund, 13
Frick, W., 53
Functioning, levels of, 63

Gaelick, L., quoted, 160
Gang violence, 302
Garfield, S. L., 44–45
  quoted, 27–28, 31, 45–46
Garmazy, N., quoted, 39
Gate-keeper concept, 173–174

Geer, J. H., 168
Gendlin, E. T., 99, 125, 143, 152–153,
    207, 239, 281
Generativity, client's, 39, 141, 162, 228–
    230
"Getting outside of oneself," 76
Gifford, E. V., quoted, 54
Gizynski, M. N., 51
Goal characteristics, 191
Goal evaluation, 72
Goal orientation, 167–177, 183–191
Goals, 45
  and helplessness/mastery behaviors,
    172–173
  in life, 182–183
  of therapy, 225
Goetz, T. C., 174
Gold, J. R., 50–51, 97, 254
Goldberger, N. R., 239
Goldfried, M. R., 11–12, 135, 140, 159
Goodman, G., 296
Gould, R. A., 34
Graded task assignments, 195
Grawe, K., 135–136, 287
  quoted, 14
Greenberg, L. S., 27, 29–30, 32, 131,
    143, 262
Greenberger, D., 157
Greene, D., 188
Greening, T., 292–293
Greist, J. H., 34
Grencavage, L. M., 135
Group, two-person, 236–238
Group think, 237
Guilt, 71
Gullibility, of therapist, 248

Hadley, S. W., 33
Hambright, A. B., 30
Hammond, D. C., quoted, 114
Hardy, G., 50–51
Harvey, J. H., 43, 123–124
Harvey, S., 48–49
Hayes, S. C., quoted, 54
Heide, F., 256–257
Helping others, 79–80
Helplessness, 88–89, 168–177
  clues to, 176–177
  and outcome focus, 178–182
  and self-esteem, 186–187
Helpless pattern, 168–172

Hepworth, D. H., quoted, 114
Hofstader, D. R., 152
Hong, Y., 174
Hubble, M. A., 3–4, 143–145
Human agency, 52–53
Human being, as self-righting organism, 58–59
Human body
  bodily felt shifts, 220–221
  and experiencing, 206
Humphreys, C., 122

Imagination, and experiencing, 207
"Impossible cases," 144–145
Impulsiveness, 71–72
Incremental-entity distinction, 170–176
Individualism, 92
Information, lack of, 91
Information-processing model, 155
Inner logic, of client's perspective, 241
Insight, 218–220
Intake interviews, 189
Integration of therapy approaches by client, 50
Intelligence, entity vs. incremental, 170–171
Interpretation, 141
Intervention, 13, 115, 265
  empathic, 255–257
  and state-of-mind model, 198–199
  therapist-client relationship as, 235–236, 246
Intuition
  therapist's, 249
  trusting, 76–77, 81–82
Involvement, client's
  empathic reflecting and, 124–125
  importance of, xiii, 43–44, 109–110, 136, 264, 289, 303–304
  and involuntary client, 301–303
  and passive client, 267–268

Jacobs, M., 296
Jacobson, N., 33
James, E., 50
Janis, I. L., 237
Janoff-Bulman, R., 71
Jenkins, A. H., 39, 212
Joanning, H. P., 49–50

Jordan, J. V., 120
Journaling, 43, 120, 122–123
Judgment
  moralistic, 98
  suspension of, 192–193

Kanfer, F. H., quoted, 160
Kay, D., 48–49
Kelly, G., 66
Klein, M. H., 34
Klopfer, B., 41–42
Knowing, separate and connected, 247
Kohut, H., 149, 253
Kozak, M. J., 161
Kreger, Randi
  quoted, 297
  "Walking on Eggshells" (with Mason), 10
Kuehl, B. P., 49–50
Kuhn, T. S., 59–60

Lakoff, George, 205–206
Lambert, M., 28, 33, 36
Lane, J. D., 119
Latham, G. P., 191
Lazarus, A. A., 212
Learning
  kinds of, 59–62
  therapist's support for, 230–231
Lee, M., 51
Leggett, E. L., 57, 168–169, 172–173
Lens analogy, 180–181
Lepper, M. R., 188
Lewin, Kurt, 65
Lietaer, G., 29–30
Life space, concept of, 65–67
Limit setting, 271
Linehan, M. M., 239–240, 242
Listening. See empathic listening
Literature, and self-help, 298
Llewelyn, S. P., 50–51
"Looking for other paths," 72
Loomis, C., 174
Lubart, T. J., 214
Luborsky, L., 27
Lucius, Y. M., 51

Mahrer, A. R., 143
Maier, S. F., 168

and therapy approach, 261–262
Perspective, therapist's, 246–249, 263–266
Perspective shift, 80–81, 217–218. *See also* insight
Pessimism, 88–89, 265–266
Phillips, J. R., 50
Philosophy of life, teaching, 130
Physician, 5
  and patient self-disclosure, 126–127
Physician-patient relationship, 7
Piaget, Jean, 105–106
Pinsof, W. M., 30
Placebo, active, 42
Placebo effect, 41–42
Positive focus, 231
Posttraumatic stress, 81, 220
Power, client's, 225
Practicing, 61
Praise. *See* approval
Prevention programs, 300–301
Prinz, J. J., quoted, 206
Proactive potential, client's, 99, 103
Proactivity, and resistance, 260
Problem, psychological, 59. *See also* diagnosis; problem solving; self-healing model
  biologically based, 269–270
  client theories of, 244–245
  creation of, 67
  ecology of, 240–241
  nature of, 6, 9–10, 17–18
  origins of, 65–69
  redefining, 253
Problem solving, 273. *See also* client; mastery behavior; TEB cycle
  case history, 254–255
  creative, 72–73
  dialectics of, 63
  empathic, 254–255
  and empathic listening, 119–126
  logic and, 93–94
  "logic of steps" in, 152
  model for, 91
Procedures. *See also* therapy techniques
  choice of, 251–252, 280–281
  decision to stay with or change, 253–254
  ineffective, 253
  manualizing, 285
Process diagnosis, 262
Process focus, 178, 180, 182–191, 289

and behavioral therapy, 193–194
and cognitive therapy, 194–196
and humanistic therapy, 196–198
and psychodynamic therapy, 192–193
and reinforcement, 188–190
Prochaska, J. O., 37, 40–41, 69, 95, 135, 262
  quoted, 40
Project MATCH, 27
Pseudomastery pattern, 173, 186
Psychoanalysis, Freudian, 148–149, 152
Psychology. *See* cognitive psychology; community psychology movement; psychotherapy; therapy approaches
Psychosis, 82–83
Psychotherapy, 5, 34–35. *See also* self-healing model; therapy; therapy approaches
  client evaluations of, 50–52
  and medical model, 8–14
  as treatment, 286–288
Psychotherapy integration movement, 277–281
Puzzle solving, 59–60

Quinn, W. H., 49–50

Reactions, problematic, 214–215
Reflecting, 197
Reflection of feeling, 238
Reflexivity, 46
Reframing, 75–76
Reinforcement, potential problems with, 188–190
Relationship. *See* physician-patient relationship; therapist-client relationship
"Relationship, to be in," 236
Relaxation, 132–133, 193
Rennie, D. L., 46–48, 122, 214, 237
  quoted, 46–47, 215
Reporting, in medical model, 5–6
Reppucci, N. D., 168
Representation, 121–123
Research
  events approach, 282–283
  and procedure choice, 251–252
  and self-healing model, 281–288

Skill building, 73, 79, 133–134, 159,
      193–194
   generative, 216
Sloane, R. B., 51
Smith, M. L., 28
Smith, V. G., quoted, 114
Social learning theory, 158
Social rejection, 174
Social skills, 174
Social support, and self-healing, 38
Social support networks, 89–90
Society for Psychotherapy Research, 287
Society for the Exploration of Psycho-
      therapy Integration, 97
Solovey, A. D., 240
Solutions. See problem solving
Sorrell, S. P., 34
Space, lack of, 91
Spontaneous recovery, 36–37
Stamps, D., quoted, 53
State of mind, 178. See also outcome fo-
      cus; process focus
   as common factor, 191–198
   switching, 182–183
State-of-mind model, 182–184, 198
   implications for therapy, 183–191
Stein, D. M., 33
Stephens, G., 34
Stiles, T. C., 33
Stiles, W. B., 90, 126
   quoted, 119
Stolorow, R., 98
Strategies, for self-healing. See self-
      healing
Strategies, therapeutic, and state-of-mind
      model, 188–191
Stress reduction, and creativity, 213–214
Structured exercises, 130–133, 141, 156,
      212, 229, 295
Strupp, H. H., 9, 13, 33, 110–111, 285
Stuck point, 145, 230
Svartberg, M., 33
Szasz, T., 13

"Talking with others," 73–74, 79
Tallman, K., 48–49
Tangney, J., 71
Tarule, J. M., 239
TEB cycle, 202–204
   products of, 216–221
Teenagers, self-healing and, 270–272
Television, and self-help, 297

Test anxiety, 181
Tharp, R. G., 160
Therapeutic distance, optimal, 236
Therapist
   as attentive listener, 103
   attitudes of, xiv, 16, 19
   client-centered, 108
   and client involvement, 109–110
   client's "creation" of, 112
   as companion, 108, 143
   dealing with resistance, 261
   as empathic listener and responder,
      124–126
   experiential, 115
   as expert, 16, 97, 99, 233, 235, 237,
      264, 291, 293
   as good teacher, xv, 107–108, 129–
      134, 140–141, 156, 254
   as guide, 108, 141
   gullibility of, 248
   as healer, 113–115
   implementation of self-healing princi-
      ples, 227–235
   intuition of, 249
   as liberator, 141
   in medical model, 5
   as member of creative team, 141
   models of, 108
   and moralistic judgment, 98
   negative attitude toward client, 264–
      266
   objectivity of, 248–249
   operating principles of, 235–249
   as participant consultant, 16
   perspective of, 246–249, 263–266
   role of, 9, 15–17, 20
   skills of, 289
   strategic, 22
   talk-show, 297
   training of, 33–34, 289
Therapist-client relationship, 235–236.
      See also collaboration
   and dodo bird verdict, 32
   function of, 19–20
   and implementation of self-healing
      principles, 227–235
   in medical model, 11–12
   role of, 113–114
   as safe workspace, 112
   as tool for client self-healing, 35–36

ABOUT THE AUTHORS

Arthur C. Bohart, PhD, professor of psychology at California State University, Dominguez Hills. He is professionally active in both the Society for the Exploration of Psychotherapy Integration and the Humanistic Psychology Division of the American Psychological Association. He has published articles on psychotherapy integration, experiencing in psychotherapy, empathy, constructivism, couples therapy, and the role of the client as self-healer. He is the coeditor of *Empathy Reconsidered: New Directions in Psychotherapy* (with Leslie S. Greenberg) and of two textbooks: *Foundations of Clinical and Counseling Psychology* (with Judith Todd) and *Personality* (with Seymour Feshbach and Bernard Weiner).

Karen Tallman has a master's degree in clinical psychology and in educational measurement and statistics and has published articles in clinical and social psychology. She is completing a PhD in educational psychology and technology at the University of Southern California, with an emphasis on motivational research. Her interests include enhancing expert performance and supporting the efforts of novices. Tallman's current research focuses on the development of a measure to predict adaptability to change and performance in business and educational settings. She also evaluates educational programs.